JUDAISM in COLD WAR AMERICA 1945-1990

edited
with introductions by
Jacob Neusner
UNIVERSITY OF SOUTH FLORIDA

A Garland Series

Contents of Series

Volume 1
The Challenge of America: Can Judaism Survive in Freedom?

Volume 2
In the Aftermath of the Holocaust

Volume 3
Israel and Zion in American Judaism: The Zionist Fulfillment

Volume 4
Judaism and Christianity: The New Relationship

Volume 5
The Religious Renewal of Jewry

Volume 6
The Reformation of Reform Judaism

Volume 7
Conserving Conservative Judaism: Reconstructionist Judaism

Volume 8
The Alteration of Orthodoxy

Volume 9
The Academy and Traditions of Jewish Learning

Volume 10
The Rabbinate in America: Reshaping an Ancient Calling

VOLUME 5

The Religious Renewal of Jewry

edited with introduction by
Jacob Neusner

Garland Publishing, Inc.
New York and London 1993

Introduction copyright © 1993 by Jacob Neusner
All rights reserved

Library of Congress Cataloging-in-Publication Data

The Religious renewal of Jewry / edited by Jacob Neusner.
    p.   cm. — (Judaism in Cold War America, 1945–1990 ; v. 5)
  ISBN 0–8153–0080–8
  1. Judaism—United States—History—20th century. 2. Jews—United States—Identity. 3. Jews—United States—Cultural assimilation. 4. Secularism—United States. I. Neusner, Jacob, 1932–   . II. Series.
BM205.R44 1993
296'.0973'0904—dc20   92–34799
                                                                                      CIP

Printed on acid-free, 250-year-life paper
Manufactured in the United States of America

Contents

Volume Introduction vii

Judaism in the Post-Christian Era
Eliezer Berkovits 2

The National Religious Institutions of American Jewry
Amitai Etzioni 14

The Role of the Synagogue in the American Jewish Community
Abraham J. Feldman 26

The A-Theological Judaism of the American Community
Norman E. Frimer 36

The Ordination of Women
Robert Gordis 47

Those Entitled to Be Jews
Ben Halpern 55

Religious Trends in American Jewry
Will Herberg 61

The Integration of the Jew in Contemporary America
Will Herberg 73

The American Jew and His Religion
Arthur Hertzberg 83

The Nation and the Individual
Abraham Joshua Heschel 106

A Love-Letter to My Congregation
Manuel Laderman 124

"Who Hast Not Made Me a Man": The Movement for Equal Rights for Women in American Jewry
Anne Lapidus Lerner 131

Jews By Choice: Their Impact on the Contemporary American Jewish Community
Egon Mayer 167

An Experience of Prayer
Jacob Neusner 182

Judaism in the Secular Age
Jacob Neusner 185

Synagogue and Center: The Symposium in Retrospect
Jacob Neusner 208

The Passing of Jewish Secularism in the United States
Herbert Parzen 227

Power in a Midwestern Jewish Community
Kenneth D. Roseman 239

The Intellectual and Contemporary Jewish Life
Richard L. Rubenstein 266

Is the Synagogue Becoming a Church, the Rabbi a Priest? Religious and Secular Aspects of Jewish Community
Henry Siegman 273

The Sociology of the American Synagogue
Marshall Sklare 285

Sacred Survival: American Jewry's Civil Religion
Jonathan S. Woocher 295

My "Commentary" Problem—and Ours
Michael Wyschogrod 308

Acknowledgements 323

Introduction

The third generation of Jews in America adopted religion as its medium for ethnic identification. It served as a legitimation of an ethnic affiliation. So the Torah stood not so much for a covenant with God and the account of who Israel is and what it must do, but rather stood as an emblem for a group. In classical Judaism (including its contemporary expressions), the holy life—the things one did to conform to the will of God, or, in secular terms, the behavior patterns imposed by the Judaic tradition—was (and is) personal and participative. Every man, woman, and child had a myriad of deeds to perform as a Jew. No one was exempt from following the holy way of living. Everyone was expected to share in it equally. One did not speak of how others should keep the Sabbath. One kept the Sabbath, along with everyone else in the community. People said their own prayers, advanced their own education in the tradition, and did their own good deeds. Prayer, study and the practice of good deeds were personal and universal. To be a Jew meant to do a hundred *mitzvot* (holy actions) every day. But that is not how the third generation wanted things. They wanted to be Jewish, when they wanted, and not Jewish, when they wanted, and to choose whatever they wanted. This redefinition of the limits and dimensions of being Jewish, rejecting the sense of obligation and commitment that had characterized Jews in earlier generations and other countries, was a response to the free choice made available to all Americans by the character of the free society of the USA.

The result, for American Jews, was to reverse the canard of another age: "Be a Jew at home and a human being when you go forth," meaning, keep your Judaism in the closet. In Cold War America, the pattern was the opposite. The home was neutral, but to be Jewish involved behavior in politics and in public, thus, "be an undifferentiated American at home, and a Jew when you go forth." In consequence, in modern America, to be a Jew primarily means to join an organization, but not personally to effect its purposes. The individual is lost in the collectivity. Joining means paying dues, providing sufficient funds so that other people may be hired to carry out the purposes of the organization. The "joining" is the opposite of what is meant, for it is impersonal and does not bring people together, but verifies their separateness. The relationship of one person to the next is reduced to the payment of money. It is passive, for one does not actually do much, if anything at all. Universally condemned by the preachers, "checkbook Judaism" is everywhere the norm.

Consequently, the primary mode of being Jewish and living the "holy life" has moved from the narrow circle of home, family, and small group to the great arena of public affairs and large institutions. The formation of large organizations, characteristic of modern life, tends to obliterate the effective role of the individual. In the Judaic situation, however, even the synagogue, with its substantial budget and massive membership, its professional leadership and surrogate religiosity, follows this pattern. If to be a Jew now means to take an active part in the "Jewish Community," then the holy life means paying one's part of the budget of the organizations that call themselves the community. By contrast, Jews in other countries identify being Jewish with either synagogue membership (at home, in Johannesburg or Sydney or London) or with becoming an Israeli (by emigrating to the State of Israel or by focusing one's Jewish life mainly upon Israeli matters), or both. In general, both modes of being Jewish involve personal participation, not simply money-giving.

People join organizations because they have been convinced, primarily because of the patterns established, or already imposed, by others, that this is what "Judaism" expects of them. The result is the concentration of power in the hands of the few who actually determine what organizations do. These few are not democratically elected, but generally come out of an oligarchy of wealthy and influential men (only a few women are included). But even these men do not actually effect the work of the community. They raise the funds and allocate them, but local funds are in fact spent by the professional bureaucrats trained to do whatever the organizations do. In general, their work is to keep the organization alive and prosperous.

What has all this to do with "being Jewish"? Should we not have started an account of religious renewal with an account of what "the Jews believe" or what "Judaism teaches"? Indeed we should, if what Jews believed and what classical Judaism taught decisively shaped the contemporary realities that define what, in everyday life, it means to be a Jew. Since we ask what it means to be a Jew in America, the first thing we want to know is: What do people do because they are Jewish? And the answer is: They join organizations and give money. In this respect, what makes a person Jewish in American society primarily depends on which organization he or she joins and to what worthy cause he or she gives money.

That the "holy way" should have become the "culture of organizations" tells us that modernity has overtaken the Jews. What characterizes group life in modern times is the development of specialists for various tasks, the organization of society for the accomplishment of tasks once performed individually and in an amateur way, the growth of professionalism, the reliance upon large institutions. What modern humanity gains in greater efficiency and higher levels of competence cannot be given up because of nostalgia for a way of life few now living in a traditional society would want to preserve. But as everyone recognizes, the cost of "progress" is impersonality and depersonalization. The real question is not whether to return to a more primitive way of living, but how to regain the humanity, personality, individual self-respect, and self-reliance necessarily lost in the new way.

The underlying problem that faces American Jews is understanding what the ambiguous adjective "Jewish" is supposed to mean when the noun "Judaism" has been abandoned. To be sure, for some Israelis and American Jews, to be a Jew is to be a citizen of the State of Israel—but that definition hardly serves when Israeli Moslems and Christians are taken into account. If one ignores the exceptions, the rule is still wanting. If to be a Jew is to be—or to dream of being—an Israeli, then the Israeli who chooses to settle in a foreign country ceases to be a Jew when he gives up Israeli citizenship. If all Jews are on the road to Zion, then those who either do not get there or, once there, choose another way are to be abandoned. That makes Jewishness dependent upon rather worldly issues: This one cannot make his living in Tel Aviv, that one does not like the climate of Affula, the other is frustrated by the bureaucracy of Jerusalem. Are they then supposed to give up their share in the "God of Israel"?

American Jews half a century ago would not have claimed "religious" as an appropriate adjective for their community. Today they insist upon it. The moralists' criticism of religion will always render what is meant by "true religion" ever more remote, so we need not be detained by carping questions. But can there be religion with so minimal a quotient of supernatural experience, theological conviction, and evocative ritual, including prayer, as is revealed in American Judaism? If one draws the dividing line between belief in a supernatural God and atheism, then much of American Jewry, also much of American Judaism, may stand on the far side of that line. If the dividing line is, in the words of Kristor Stendahl, "between the closed mind and spiritual sensibility and imagination," then American Jews and American Judaism may stand within the frontier of the religious, the sacred.

Let us begin with the substitution of organizations and group activity for a holy way of life lived by each individual. What the Jews have done in their revision of the holy way is to conform to, and in their own way to embody, the American talent at actually accomplishing things. Americans organize. They do so not to keep themselves busy, but to accomplish efficiently and with an economy of effort a great many commendable goals. They hire "professionals" to do well what most individuals cannot do at all: heal the sick, care for the needy, tend to the distressed at home and far away. In modern society people do not keep guns in their homes for self-protection. They have police. Nations do not rely upon the uncertain response of well-meaning volunteers.

They form armies. The things American Jews seek to accomplish through their vast organizational life derive from their tradition: They want to educate the young and old, to contribute to the building of the ancient land, to see to it that prayers are said and holidays observed. Now hiring a religious virtuoso may seem less commendable than saying one's own prayers, but it is merely an extension of the specialization people take for granted elsewhere.

In archaic times people believed that salvation depended upon keeping to the holy way, so each person kept to it, made himself sufficiently expert to know how to carry out the law. In other religious communities today, this same viewpoint persists. Catholics and Protestants take for granted that they should go to church to pray. Jews regard communal prayer as less important, though Judaism has not changed its position on this matter. They tend to observe the religious way of life in diminishing measure, as the generations of American Jews pass on, from third to fourth to fifth. Today few believe that supernatural salvation inheres in prayers, dietary taboos, and Sabbath observance. It is therefore curious that the Jews nonetheless want to preserve the old salvific forms and symbols, as they certainly do. Few pray. Fewer still believe in prayer. It is astonishing that the synagogues persist in focusing their collective life upon liturgical functions. Perhaps the best analogy is to a museum, in which old art is preserved and displayed, though people do not paint that way anymore, may not even comprehend what the painter did, the technical obstacles he overcame. The synagogue is a living museum and preserves the liturgical and ritual life of the old tradition. Why should Jews choose this way, when earlier in their American experience they seemed to move in a different direction? Is it nostalgia for a remembered, but unavailable experience of the sacred? Is the religious self-definition they have adopted merely an accommodation to American expectations? Or do they hope the archaic and the supernatural may continue to speak to them?

The figure of the rabbi calls forth the same wonderment. Why call oneself "rabbi" at all, if one (man or woman) is not a saint, a scholar, a judge? Given the ultimate mark of secularization—the complaint that rabbis no longer reach high places in the Jewish community—should we not ask, "What is still sacred in the rabbi and his or her learning, calling, leadership?" The answer would be, nothing whatsoever, were it not for people's relationships to rabbis, their fantastic expectations of them. Rabbis, unsure of their role, at once self-isolated and complaining about their loneliness—whatever they are, they are rabbis. They know it. The people know it. They look to rabbis as holy men or women. No nostalgia here: The rabbi is a completely American adaptation of the ancient rabbinic role. But American society never imposed the peculiar, mainly secular definition of "Jewish clergyman" upon the modern rabbi. For two hundred years American Jewry had no rabbis at all. Leadership lay with uneducated men, businessmen mainly. And the rabbis they now have are not merely Judaic versions of Protestant ministers or Roman Catholic priests, but uniquely Judaic as well as exceptionally American. The remembrance of rabbis of past times—of the saints, scholars, and holy men of Europe—hardly persists into the fourth generation and beyond. The rabbi, profane and secular, is the only holy man or woman they shall ever know. So onto him or her they fix their natural, human fantasies about men and women set apart by and for God.

The holy people, "Israel," of times past has become "the American Jewish community," uncertain what is Jewish about itself, still more unsure of what "Jewish" ought to mean. Surely the lingering crisis of self-definition, characteristic of modern men and women in many situations, marks the Jew as utterly modern and secular. Add to this the second component of the holy people's self-understanding: concern for what the Gentiles think of Jews, readiness to admit this negative opinion into the Jewish assessment of the Jews. This submission to universal opinions and values hardly characterizes a holy people, set apart from all others. Frail and uncomfortable, hating those "Jewish traits" in themselves that set Jews apart from everyone else, and wanting to be Jewish but not too much, not so much that they cannot also be undifferentiated Americans—this is the holy people that traversed thirty-five centuries of human history, proud, tenacious, alone? Can they claim their collectivity to be holy, separate and apart? Surely in the passage from the sacred to the secular, the holy people has disintegrated, become a random group of discrete, scarcely similar individuals. Yet while that may seem to be so, the one point Jews affirm is that they shall be Jews. This they have in common.

The very vigor of their activity together and the commonalities of a quite discrete folk suggest that the group, once a people, is still a people. The secular separateness of the Jews, their inner awareness of being a group, their outward view of themselves as in some ways apart from others—this separateness is probably all modern man can hope for socially to approximate "the holy." The archaic "holy people" has passed from the scene. In its place stands something different in all respects but the most important: its manifest and correct claim to continue as Jews, a different, separate group, and the claim that this difference is destiny. The relationship between secular Zionism and sacred messianism, modern nation building and the myth of the return to Zion at the end of time, is complex. It seems clear that the pattern recurs, perhaps most vividly, in the modern and secular modulation of the myth of the holy land.

Let us address the matter of doctrine, "Torah," in the mythic language of Judaism. The grandchildren of Jews who would not have understood what theologians do not only write theology, but correctly claim it to be Judaic. The third generation produced religious intellectuals. This is the decisive evidence that something new has been created out of something old. Contemporary American Judaism, for all its distance from the classic forms of the past, its unbelief and secularity, constitutes a fundamentally new and autonomous development, not merely the last stages in the demise of something decadent. American Judaism calls forth, in the task of formulating a systematic account of its faith, the talents of philosophical sophistication and religious conviction, able to speak in the name, even in the words, of the classic tradition, but in a language alien to that tradition. To be sure, the Jews' response to Judaic theology thus far is routine and inconsequential. The best books reach a tiny audience, the worst only a slightly larger one. The finest theological journals are read chiefly by those who write for them, or aspire to. So the theological movement must stand by itself, as evidence of the modernity and secularity of the theologians, on the one side, but of their participation in the traditional sacred values and in the archaic texts, on the other.

American Judaism constitutes something more than the lingering end of old ways and myths. It is the effort of modern men and women to make use of these ways and myths to form a religious way of living appropriate to an unreligious time and community. Spiritual sensibility and, even more, the remnants of the archaic imagination are the sources for the unarticulated, but evident decision of American Jews to reconstruct out of the remnants of an evocative, but incongruous heritage the materials of a humanly viable, meaningful community of life. To have attempted the reconstitution of traditional villages in the metropolis and of archaic ways of seeing the world in the center of modernity would have been to deny the human value and pertinence of the tradition itself. But few even wanted to try. In the end the effort would have had no meaning. The Jews had the courage to insist that their life together must have more than ordinary meaning. In American Judaism they embarked upon the uncertain quest to find, if necessary to invent, this meaning. Despite their failures, the grotesque form they have imposed upon the old tradition, this uncommon, courageous effort seems to me to testify to whatever is good and enduring in modernity. But whether good or not, abiding or ephemeral, all that modern men and women have, and all that they shall ever have, is the mature hope to persist in this quest.

If American Judaism produced one fundamental and unique change in the historic religion, it is in regularization and normalization of the religious rights of women. In the last half-century Jewish women passed from an abnormal to a normal status in Reform, Reconstructionist, and Conservative Judaisms. Women were first ordained as rabbis by Reform Judaism. Synagogues of all three Judaisms accorded to women full equality in religious rites, and in the management and administration of synagogues. The importance of these events, commencing in the earliest 1970s, was to grant American Judaism access to sources of vitality, intelligence, religious sensibility, and spirituality that had formerly been cut off. In the religious renewal of the third generation, the advent of a specifically Judaic feminism thus marks the single most important event, and—it now is clear—one that is emblematic and enduring for American Judaism.

The Religious Renewal of Jewry

Judaism in the Post-Christian Era

ELIEZER BERKOVITS

THERE WAS A PHASE IN WORLD HISTORY THAT may be called the Christian era. It designates that period in which Christianity, including Christian civilization and culture—all that goes under the name of the West—was the dominant and dominating force. We suggest that this phase is now at an end. We propose that Judaism ought to take adequate cognizance of this important change in the world situation and develop its attitude and its religious policies accordingly.

The Christian era did not start with the birth of Jesus. It dates from the first half of the fourth century, commencing when Constantine the Great established Christianity as the state religion of the Roman Empire. The characteristic mark of the era was militancy. This was inherent in its beginnings: Christianity did not capture the Roman Empire by the power of a religious idea but by the sword of the emperor. As soon as Christianity was established, Judaism was declared an odious heretic sect, and its propagation was forbidden under the penalty of death. All other religions were completely oppressed and actually exterminated. Christianity's conquering march all over Europe began. It was a conquest in the true sense of the word: Europe was Christianized by the power of the imperial sword. The Saxons, the Franks, many of the aboriginal tribes, were placed before the choice: baptism or death. Uncounted numbers chose death. *Cuius regio cuius religio,* the principle by which faith was determined in the religious wars that tore Europe apart after the Reformation, was also the principle by which, from the earliest days of the established church, Christianity was spread across the face of the earth. Even the vast missionary activities in Asia and Africa were possible only because the Western colonizing powers which opened up these new lands were Christian. The preachers of the gospel marched in the wake of the swift and terrible sword of Constantine.

This era has come to an end in our days, before our own eyes. It has reached its conclusion because the sword of Constantine has been passed on to numerous other hands. The Soviets are holding it mightily in their grip; Red China has taken possession of it; the dark millions of Africa are acquiring it; hundreds of millions of Moslems, Buddhists and Hindus have learned to wield it. Christianity is no longer the decisive power or influence. From now on, world history

---

ELIEZER BERKOVITS *is the chairman of the department of Jewish philosophy at Hebrew Theological College in Skokie, Ill.*

will be determined by the interplay of many forces, many cultures and civilizations, most of them non-Christian, some of them anti-Christian.

II

THIS CHANGE IN THE WORLD SITUATION carries with it weighty consequences for Christianity, which the Church, especially the Roman Church, has not been slow to appreciate. *Nolens volens* the age of Christian militancy is over; "baptism or death" is gone forever. The reason, as we noted, is that now so many non-Christians, too, have acquired the sword of Constantine. They can wield it no less effectively than the Christian powers did in the past; they are in the majority, and now they, in turn, have the power to be intolerant, to oppress and persecute no less crushingly than did Christianity through the long and dark centuries of the Christian era.

The new revolutionary distribution of the balance of power in the *ecumene* is ultimately responsible for the new Christian ecumenism. An interesting illustration of this was provided by the discussion on human freedom which took place at the Vatican Council. It would seem that, notwithstanding the arguments in the Council about the theological niceties of the final formula, the Church now affirms the principle of freedom of religious worship and human conscience. Following the discussion, we could not help thinking of the old adage about the mills of God which, though they grind slowly, grind exceedingly fine. We recalled that the freedoms of religion and conscience existed in the Roman Empire at the beginning of the rule of Constantine the Great. In fact, they were affirmed anew in Constantine's own Edict of Tolerance. But that was before he converted to Christianity. When Christianity became the state religion of the empire tolerance was abolished, freedom of religion proscribed, and freedom of conscience eradicated. This state of affairs continued through the dark centuries that followed in the form of oppression, persecution, auto-da-fés, religious wars and massacres. But now things are changing. After sixteen centuries of Christianity regnant in the world, the Church is ready to champion ideals which were realized by mankind in the heathen Roman Empire, not to speak of Judaism or the secularisms of the last four centuries. What has brought about this *volte-face* of the Church? Nothing but the fact that Christianity is no longer supreme in the world. When the Church leaders speak of freedom of religion, they mean first of all freedom for Christians to adhere to their faith in Communist lands. When they affirm freedom of conscience, they mean primarily freedom for the Church to propagate Christianity in Asia and Africa among Moslems, Buddhists, Hindus, and among the followers of all kinds of tribal cults. Christianity is now on the side

76 : *Judaism*

of tolerance because this is the post-Christian age of world history, because in this post-Christian era the old policies of intolerance are no longer viable. Any policy of Christian intolerance would be self-defeating, for it would justify intolerance on the part of the non-Christian powers, civilizations and religions. It would ultimately boomerang onto the heads of hundreds of millions of Christians the world over. Ecumenism or no ecumenism, tolerance and a measure of official friendliness toward other religions and philosophies of life have today become matters of practical politics for the Church and for Christianity.

III

WHAT SHOULD BE THE JEWISH ATTITUDE, facing Christianity in the post-Christian era of world history?

We must, above all, understand history—that this is, in fact, the post-Christian era. We must understand the significance and the implications of this revolutionary change. From now on Christianity will have to rely for its propagation, as any decent religion should, on the methods of persuasion. All the friendlier statements about Jews and Judaism made in this new age by the Church and Christianity must be comprehended in the light of the change imposed by external historic developments upon Christianity. This certainly applies to the Vatican Council's schema on the Jews. It was forced on the Church by the new historic constellation. There are, of course, many Christians who feel ashamed of the abominable crimes committed by Christendom against Judaism and the Jewish people. However, the uncharitable haggling in the Council about the final version of the schema in itself proved that the sense of shame in some Christian consciences alone would never have sufficed to produce even that extremely guarded and political declaration.

An understanding of the implications of the new situation itself ought to help those Jews who are in contact with Church authorities and Christian leaders. Often they represent Judaism and the Jewish people without a mandate. At least let them speak with courage, self-assurance and with all the dignity to which sixteen centuries of Jewish martyrdom in Christian lands obligates them. For the first time since the early days of the fourth century there may be a confrontation between Judaism and Christianity in freedom. Let it, indeed, take place in freedom!

Confrontation in freedom means that the scope of the confrontation must not be reduced to the provincial dimensions of Jewish-Christian understanding in the United States. Its significance must not be falsified for cheap considerations of public relations. Jewish-Christian confrontation in freedom is confrontation in the world-historic context of Israel's own Messianic history. In this new type of encounter with Christianity our generation must stand for all the generations that ever lived and suffered in Christian lands. It must stand for all the innumerable generations that never beheld the light of day because those who were destined to be their progenitors perished before their time under the bloody yoke of Christian oppression. We must face Christianity as the children of the *am olam*, the eternal people, viewing historic developments *sub specie aeternitatis*. I have never sensed so acutely that we are indeed the *am olam* as in these days when we are able to survey the Christian performance from the beginning of the Christian era to its end. We have been there all the time; we alone know what it has meant.

It is our responsibility to sum up the meaning of that era, unimpressed by Christian claims, guided exclusively by our own experience. In terms of the Jewish experience in the lands of Christendom, the final result of that age is bankruptcy—the moral bankruptcy of Christian civilization and the spiritual bankruptcy of Christian religion. After nineteen centuries of Christianity, the extermination of six million Jews, among them one-and-a-half million children, carried out in cold blood in the very heart of Christian Europe, encouraged by the criminal silence of virtually all Christendom, including that of an infallible Holy Father in Rome, was the natural culmination of this bankruptcy. A straight line leads from the first act of oppression against the Jews and Judaism in the fourth century to the holocaust in the twentieth. In order to pacify the Christian conscience it is said that the Nazis were not Christians. But they were all the children of Christians. They were the fruit of nineteen centuries of Christianity—the logical fruit of violence and militancy, oppression and intolerance, hatred and persecution, which dominated European history for the sixteen centuries since Constantine the Great. Without the contempt and the hatred for the Jew planted by Christianity in the hearts of the multitude of its followers, Nazism's crime against the Jewish people could never have even been conceived, much less executed. What was started at the Council of Nicea was duly completed in the concentration camps and the crematoria. This has been a moral and spiritual collapse the like of which the world has never witnessed before for contemptibility and inhumanity. Judged in the light of our own experience and under the aspects of the Messianic history of the *am olam*, we are confronting a morally and spiritually bankrupt civilization and religion. This knowledge should determine our attitude. In its light ought we define our position in relationship to the various issues which have arisen in the wake of this new Jewish-Christian encounter in freedom.

IV

THE SCHEMA ON THE JEWS HAS NOW been officially promulgated by the Vatican Council. It has thought fit to declare solemnly before all the world that the Jews are not to be considered a people accursed by God; the Jews are not collectively guilty for the death of Jesus. We cannot help wondering whether in the opinion of the leaders of the Church these are still the Middle Ages or almost the Middle Ages. For many centuries it was they who have been doing the persecuting, they who perpetuated abominable acts of inhumanity against the Jewish people, but now they condescend to tell the world that we are perhaps not guilty nor to be considered accursed by God.

Underneath such lack of sensitivity to historic truth still lingers the barbarous concept that the fact that someone is persecuted and made to suffer by others is proof that something is wrong with him. For many centuries Christian clerics, theologians and historians have maintained that the fact that Jews had lost their homeland, were scattered over the face of the earth, everywhere persecuted and held in contempt, was in itself proof that they were an accursed people, punished for the crime of having killed Jesus. In 1947 this thesis could still be found in history books written for the enlightenment of Christian youth (see *The Foot of Pride*, Malcolm Hay, p. 22).

If it ever occurred to an isolated Christian that the "proof" was perhaps not altogether convincing, since it was man and not God who imposed all this suffering on the Jew, he could easily calm his conscience with the Christian logic of the Church Father, St. John Chrysostom, who showed that it was really God after all who was punishing the Jews. For, he argued, could man do all this to the Jews "unless it had been God's will?" By the same logic, not so long ago in Christian lands they would light the faggots under the poor creatures accused of witchcraft or cast them into deep water. If they burned or drowned, they were guilty of the crime of which they were accused. The Vatican Council's declaration about the Jews reveals how deeply rooted the logic of Chrysostom still is in the Christian psyche. Given the premises of Chrysostom's logic, it might seem Christian charity to declare that these Jews, though they suffered and were persecuted, are nevertheless not to be considered a people accursed by God.

This is, indeed, progress. A non-Christian, however, is not impressed. To such noble Christian sentiments he might prefer the teaching of the heathen Socrates who maintained that it was better to suffer than to inflict suffering, nobler to be martyred than to inflict martyrdom. Followers of Socrates will be inclined to say that those who make others suffer are more likely to be a people accursed by God than those who are made to suffer by them. In this respect Jews are much closer to the heathen Socratic tradition than to the Christian. Many centuries ago their Pharisaic teachers interpreted for them the words of *Ecclesiastes*, "God seeketh that which is pursued," to mean: "The wicked pursues the righteous—God seeketh the pursued; the righteous pursues the righteous—God seeketh the pursued; the righteous pursues the righteous —God seeketh the pursued; the wicked pursues the wicked—God seeketh the pursued; and even when the righteous pursues the wicked, God seeketh the pursued" (*Vayikra Raba*, 27:5, and *Tanhuma, Emor*, 9). Always God seeks the pursued. To be told after sixteen centuries of oppression and persecution in Christian lands by those responsible for these acts of inhumanity that the Jews are not a people accursed by God is an offense not so much to Jews as to God.

At one point, when it seemed that the Vatican Council was about to exonerate the Jewish people completely of the guilt of deicide, there were some precipitate Reform rabbis who felt that the Jews ought to reciprocate such a noble gesture by acknowledging Jesus as a prophet. It would seem to us that if there were to be any reciprocating Jewish acknowledgment, it should be commensurate with the Christian pronouncement. It might be said, for example, that the appropriate reciprocating gesture on the part of Jewry could be a solemn declaration that the man who endured the crucifixion is not to be regarded as accursed by God. Of course, Jews will never issue such a declaration, because they have never believed in Chrysostom's type of reasoning. Nor do they suffer from the illusion that they personally and humanly represent God on earth. They are, therefore, in no position to dispense God's curse or His blessing. They deem it more respectful toward God to leave such dispensations to Him.

V

MANY CHRISTIAN AND JEWS ARE THESE DAYS advocating the idea of a Jewish-Christian dialogue. The schema on the Jews recommends such "fraternal dialogues," in order to foster "a mutual knowledge and respect." We ought to analyze this from several approaches—emotional, philosophical, theological, and practical.

We feel that, emotionally, we are not as yet ready to enter into a fraternal dialogue with a church, a religion, that has been responsible for so much suffering, and which is ultimately responsible for the murder of our fathers and mothers, brothers and sisters in the present generation. There are, of course, Jews who are only too eager to undertake such a dialogue. They are either Jews without memories or Jews for whom Judaism is exclusively a matter of public relations, or confused or spineless Jews unable to appreciate the meaning of confrontation in full freedom. For Jewry as a whole an honest fraternal dialogue with Christianity is at this state emotionally impossible. The majority of the Jewish people still mourn in a very personal sense. In a hundred years, perhaps, depending on Christian deeds toward Jews, we may be emotionally ready for the dialogue.

On the level of philosophical thought, contact and interchange of ideas are certainly to be desired. Jews are familiar with Barth and Tillich, Maritain and Gabriel, no less than with Sartre or Radhakrishman. This, however, is not a specific Jewish-Christian dialogue. It is the dialogue in the intellectual realm which Judaism has carried on with all cultures and religions at all times. There is no more reason or need for a Jewish-Christian dialogue than for a Jewish-Moslem, Jewish-Hindu, Jewish-existentialist, or Jewish-atheist dialogue. The realm of thought is universal.

As to a dialogue in the purely theological sense, nothing could be more fruitful and pointless. Judaism is Judaism because it rejects Christianity, and Christianity is Christianity because it rejects Judaism. What is usually referred to as the Judeo-Christian tradition exists only in Christian or secularist fantasy. As far as Jews are concerned, Judaism is fully sufficient. There is nothing in Christianity for them. Whatever in Christian teaching is acceptable to them is borrowed from Judaism. Jews do not have to turn to the New Testament for the "two laws"; Jesus was quoting them from the Hebrew Bible. And whatever is not Jewish in Christianity is not acceptable to the Jew.

There are many who believe that Jews and Christians have at least the "Old Testament" in common. This is a serious misunderstanding. The Jews have no "Old Testament." The very fact that for the Christians it is the "Old Testament" indicates that it is not identical with the Hebrew Bible. This is not a matter of mere semantics. The "Old Testament" asks for a New Testament; the Hebrew Bible is complete within itself. The Christian interpretation of Biblical Judaism is not the Judaism of the Hebrew Bible. The Christian, reading his "Old Testament," discerns history and teaching which are essentially different from what is contained in the Jewish Bible: from the Christian point of view Biblical Judaism, as found in the "Old Testament," is altogether *preparatio evangelica*—a preparation for the divine epiphany as the Christian finds it in the New Testament. From the Jewish point of view, the very essence of Biblical Judaism and the very core of Biblical teaching about God rule out such divine self-revelation. From the Jewish point of view, the "Old Testament" is the Gentile's misinterpretation of the very gist of the message of the Hebrew Bible. When Christians use the term "Judeo-Christian," "Judeo" means something fundamentally different from what is Jewish for the Jew. Nor does Judaism have a common spiritual patrimony with Christianity in the Patriarchs and the Prophets: in Jewish understanding, the God of Abraham is not the triune deity of Christianity.

There is a noteworthy contradiction as regards this matter of the "fraternal dialogue" in the pronouncements of the Vatican Council. On the one hand, the Council encourages dialogues with other religions; on the other, it also affirms that the Roman Catholic Church is the only repository of all true religion. What then is the purpose of the dialogue for the Church? There is nothing that Christianity may gain by it. The schema on non-Christians concedes that other religions may contain some rays of divine light in their beliefs and teaching. Yet, it is to be understood that all these rays of light are comprehended in greater purity and perfection in the Church. How then is dialogue possible? One does not enter into a dialogue in honesty when one is convinced from the beginning that one is in possession of all the truth and one's partner in the dialogue is in error. This is not dialogical encounter. It can have only one purpose—to spread the good tiding to the unfortunate ones who have not yet seen one's own light.

VI

THIS, WE HAVE SEEN, IS THE POST-CHRISTIAN ERA. In former times Jews were commanded to appear before popes, bishops, and kings in order to defend their beliefs in religious disputations. These popes, bishops, and most Christian kings were also the judges. In these disputations the Jews could never be sure whether to win or lose was better for them. It also used to be customary to impose on Jewish communities the indignity of compelling them to admit missionary preachers into the synagogues to listen to their sermons and boorish insults. These channels of "communication" with the Jewish people are no longer open. They are now to be replaced by "fraternal dialogue."

But there is no reason why Jews should be interested. Judaism does not have the ambition to save mankind, because it never maintained that mankind was lost without it. Judaism is the only possible way of life for Jews. Only Jews are lost without it. As to non-Jews, Judaism maintains that "the righteous of all the peoples have a share in the world-to-come." Judaism is free from missionary zeal. In turn, there is no reason on earth why it should make itself accessible to "fraternal dialogue" with a religion which, by its very premises, declares others to be in error and thus, from the outset, destroys the basis of a true dialogical situation.

But might not a Jewish-Christian dialogue have some beneficial, practical effects? Would it not further inter-religious understanding? The strange reality, however, is that whereas among Christians it is the clerics, theologians, and the more committed and knowledgeable Christians who propagate the idea of inter-religious understanding, the Jewish enthusiasts include the less committed Jews, the public-relations experts, the secularists. From such a dialogue, that in its very premises lacks intellectual honesty and emotional sincerity, it would be most unwise to expect any genuine deepening of inter-religious understanding. The greater the hopes one places in such a "dialogue," the greater the disappointments which must follow.

However, independently of all considerations of inter-religious politics, we reject the idea of inter-religious understanding on ethical grounds.

First of all, it represents a distortion of historic truth; it is a falsification of the true nature of the Judeo-Christian tragedy. It suggests a measure of mutuality in the responsibility for that tragedy; as if there had been friction and conflict because we did not know each other well enough; as if there had been struggle between Jews and Christians because they were not familiar with each other's noble religious traditions and beliefs. This is not the case. There were no conflicts or wars. There was only unilateral oppression and persecution. We reject the idea of inter-religious understanding as immoral because it is an attempt to whitewash a criminal past.

Further, the idea of inter-religious understanding is ethically objectionable because it makes respect for the other man dependent on whether I am able to appreciate his religion or his theology. In the official summary of the Vatican Council's schema on non-Christians we read that "the Council wants to foster and recommend a mutual knowledge and respect which is the fruit, above all, of Biblical and theological studies as well as of fraternal dialogues." We find the suggestion that mutual knowledge and respect among people should be the fruit of Biblical and theological studies, as well as of inter-religious dialogue, repugnant. It implies that if I am able to appreciate another man's religious beliefs I ought to respect and love him; if not, my contempt for him is understandable and justifiable. This is still conceived in the old questionable tradition of religious persecution. It is not a matter of whether Christianity acknowledges fragmentary truths in Judaism. All we want of Christians is that they keep their hands off us and our children! Human beings ought to treat each other with respect and hold each other dear independently of theological dialogues, Biblical studies, and independently of what they believe about each other's religion. I am free to reject any religion as humbug if that is what I think of it; but I am duty-bound to respect the dignity of every human being no matter what I may think of his religion. It is not inter-religious understanding that mankind needs but inter-*human* understanding—an understanding based on our common humanity and wholly independent of any need for common religious beliefs and theological principles.

VII

THERE ARE SOME WHO BELIEVE THAT, in an age such as ours, when religion is being assailed on all sides by secularism, materialism, and atheism, Judaism and Christianity ought to form a common religious front in defense of religious values and ideals.

It will be found that the policy of a common front may be laid down as a general principle only in areas of inter-human endeavor and not in the specifically inter-religious realm. A common front is useful and necessary in the struggle for freedom of conscience and worship, for peace and social justice; our interests are identical in these fields of human striving. In the post-Christian era, however, these goals of freedom, peace, and social justice have universal validity. It would be extremely foolish to seek their realization by means of a narrowly Jewish-Christian religious front. On the other hand, in the specifically religious realm, a common interest cannot be predicated as a general principle. There, Jewish and Christian interest may occasionally coincide in certain specific situations; in others, it may not. Under a condition of freedom, each group ought to decide on its course of action in accordance with its own insight and understanding.

The confrontation between religion and secularism occurs first in the intellectual realm, in the heart and mind of the believer himself. Here Judaism must maintain its complete independence. In the intellectual confrontation with secularism Judaism must not become a mere adjunct to Protestant or Roman Catholic theology. Any close association with Christian thought is ultimately bound to cause confusion within Jewish thinking. It may cripple our ability to articulate the relevance of the specific Jewish position in our times. It would also be detrimental to Judaism's effectiveness: because of its fewer dogmas, Judaism is intellectually in a far better position to develop a philosophy or theology which can meet the intellectual onslaught of secularism. This is not easy, but it will be easier without the burden of a common religious front.

Even in the field of ethics and of the application of ethical principles to actual social or international conditions, one must be cautious about any joint Jewish-Christian endeavor. In many parts of Asia and Africa, Christianity has been compromised because of the close connection between colonial conquest and missionary activities. Closer to home, in the light of the Christian performance in the past and because of the practical requirements of Christian politics in the post-Christian era, it is not always easy to determine what is humanitarian-ethical deed and what is Christian propaganda. An example to ponder is Pope Paul VI's peace mission to the United Nations. The speech on behalf of world peace was a fine oration. It came, of course, rather late in history. In earlier periods, a pope's stand on universal peace and

84 : *Judaism*

brotherhood could have stopped wars, expulsions, and massacres. Unfortunately, when it could have been most effective—in the Christian era—the papacy was unaware of its universal mission for peace. Today, peace is a popular slogan. What was once placed by Isaiah before the conscience of mankind as an ideal has now become an inescapable demand of practical world politics. Today the bomb itself is the most convincing argument for peace. "Make peace or perish" is its unmistakable message. In the final reckoning, when in a situation of world crisis the issue of war or peace in this atomic age will be decided, the pontifical plea will count for very little.

* * *

It would seem then that, on the whole, we have to go our own way. We have to work hard to make Judaism a significant philosophy of life in the intellectual climate of our age. We have to prove it to be a significant form of living which takes due cognizance of the moral predicaments of our days. We must equip it with the ability to articulate the truth of God in relationship to the vital issues of present-day human existence. If, as we develop our own position in the intellectual, ethical, theological, and religious realms of twentieth-century human endeavor, we find other religions working beside us, all the better. If not, we shall not be concerned, An awe-inspiring task lies ahead of us. Hard work, challenging and exacting, is to be done on the interpretation of Judaism and its implementation in this new era. We have every reason to continue with faith and confidence in our path. This is one of those rare turning points in history when we feel the breath of eternity about us. Having survived miraculously, the world historic mystery of Israel has been deepened ever more by Israel's return to the land of its origins, in accordance with the faith of the dark centuries of homelessness.

No one can foretell what this new era holds in store for mankind. Bue we are here at the threshold of the new age. We who were there when the Christians era began; we in whose martyrdom Christianity suffered its worst moral debacle; we in whose blood the Christian era found its end—we are here as this new era opens. And we shall be here when this new era reaches its close—we, the *edim,* God's own witnesses, the *am olam,* the eternal witness of history.

THE NATIONAL RELIGIOUS INSTITUTIONS OF AMERICAN JEWRY

AMITAI ETZIONI

THE AMERICAN JEWISH COMMUNITY is often analyzed by distinguishing the theological or social or economic differences of the groups that go to make it up. But the religious institutions of this community have been examined less frequently. Investigators have usually assumed that Jewish religious life is more or less "congregational" and that control of it rests in the hands of local leaders. Over the last eighty years, however, each of the three branches of Judaism has developed—as have the Baptists and even the Congregationalists—a rather extensive national structure of institutions. It is a commonplace to note that strongly hierarchic religions can control and affect the religious life of their members in many ways; and though Jewish institutions are very far indeed from being neatly ordered parts of one hierarchic structure, yet the institutions do exist, and it is worth examining them to understand the ways in which they affect the religious life of their members.

Superficially, the organizational makeup of the Reform, Conservative, and Orthodox movements are quite similar. Each has a so-called lay organization of congregations; each has a professional association of rabbis; and each has a rabbinical school which serves as a spiritual and, to some degree, organizational

---

Dr. Etzioni is a graduate (1954) of the Hebrew University, Jerusalem. He obtained his Master's degree there in 1956 and his doctorate at the University of California at Berkeley in 1958. He is presently Associate Professor of Sociology at Columbia and a research associate in the university's Institute of War and Peace.

center of the movement. But the influence exerted by these institutions varies quite considerably within each of the three groups.

In the examination of the influence of these institutions on Jewish religious life, an inquiry which deserves many volumes, we choose to focus on one central issue: the degree to which the national institutions support more traditional as against more innovative forms of religious expression and ritual. Following the Jewish tradition, we see in the continuous observance of the various Jewish rites a central indicator of the degree to which each movement is "traditional," whatever its theology may be.

Rabbis and laity often use the term "right" to refer to what we call here traditional, and "left" to what we refer to as innovative. But since "left" and "right" are used also to designate differences in theology, and since a person who is, let us say, "left" in ritual might be "right" in theology, these terms seem to add more confusion than clarity and hence will be avoided. We will characterize groups as more or less traditional, or innovating, keeping "traditionalistic" to refer to the most traditional groups. Of course, there are in all three movements individuals whose religious behavior varies a great deal; our concern here is with the effects national Jewish institutions have on general trends toward traditionalism or religious innovation. Hence we will necessarily have to make generalizations, not doing full justice to the special position of Rabbi X in movement Y, or even to this or that group of three to six congregations which follow a course different from the rest of their movement.

OF ALL the national religious Jewish institutions, the Conservative institutions are the most elaborate and most centralized; their effect is somewhat similar to the effect that is often attributed to a hierarchical religion: the institutions support the traditional elements of the religious movement, countering the secular pressures of the laity; they generate a traditional "party line"; they tend to support the rabbi in conflicts with the congregations when the issue is one of tradition versus change. Conservative institutions are succeeding increasingly in their endeavor to make the rabbi the movement's representative; he is encouraged if he successfully supports its traditions and is himself supported if —while serving the cause prudently and wisely—he clashes with the laity. Of course even religious organizations are not composed of saints: personal loyalties, sympathies, and cliques play a role. But since, as we shall see, the "higher ups" tend to be more traditional in their position toward religious behavior than those lower down the scale, and since they have a personal commitment to the success of their view, these personal ties and cliques often lend support to the policy which they favor.

The Conservative institutional framework has three tiers: at the top is a charismatic leader who also serves as the organizational head, Rabbi Louis Finkelstein, the chancellor of the Jewish Theological Seminary; the second level consists of the faculty of the Seminary; and the third, of two national organizations, the professional association of Conservative Rabbis (the Rabbinical Assembly) and the lay organization of the congregations (the United Synagogue of America). Formally, these three organizations—the Seminary, the Assembly, and the United Synagogue—are autonomous, equal in standing and rights. But formal relationships have a way of adjusting themselves to the needs of particular situations. In practice, it is clear that the Seminary is the dominant institution of the Conservative movement.

Rabbis, board members, and worshippers in Conservative synagogues are quick to tell you, with an admiration that is mixed with a trace of annoyance, that the Seminary is actually Orthodox. Members of the Rabbinical Assembly point out that to all intents and purposes the service in the Seminary is Orthodox (while there is no *mechizah*, men and women are not seated together); that the Seminary chapel uses an Orthodox and not the Conservative prayerbook; and that the rabbi of the chapel and the pattern of his service are both Orthodox. Finally, while there are "all kinds" of faculty in the Seminary (even the head of the "innovative" Reconstructionists), the majority, and in controlling authority, are quite Orthodox in their personal religious life. This generally traditional orientation of the Seminary affects the outlook and activities of the other two organizations and so comes to color the quality of the entire Conservative movement in various ways.

The first of these is through the personal influence of its leader, which goes much beyond the boundaries of the Seminary. Secondly, the Seminary has a monopoly on the training of Conservative rabbis; as a highly effective educational institution, it often succeeds in instilling its spirit into its graduates. Moreover the leaders of both the Rabbinical Assembly and the United Synagogue are also Seminary graduates and hence have the usual indebtedness and respect students feel for their masters. But not less important than these factors and more frequently overlooked is the "institutional" influence the Seminary wields over the other Conservative organizations. The fact that the headquarters of both the Assembly and the United Synagogue are in the buildings of the Seminary (which is not the case with either the Reform or the Orthodox movements) illustrates this informal subordination.

This is not to imply that the Rabbinical Assembly is without influence in "higher circles" or never "talks back to authority." There is constant grumbling among the Assembly's membership, the rabbis, about what some of them consider excessive control from above. A young rabbi, who examined the minutes of the national meetings of the Assembly, found that at every single meeting of the Assembly this complaint was expressed in one covert way or another, frequently in the argument over some "verdict" laid down by the Seminary authorities in matters of Jewish rites. But never did the grumbling amount to more than a decision to appoint a committee to study the relationships between the Assembly and the Seminary. Rabbis are even reluctant to mention, much less to use, the big club they hold over the Seminary: the fact that they head the local drive for funds by which the activities of the whole movement are financed. The money goes to the Seminary, which then grants a small part of it to the Assembly. Thus the informal subordination of the Rabbinical Assembly is even better illustrated in its subdued grumbling than in its overt acceptance of the Seminary leadership and guidance.

Of the Rabbinical Assembly and the United Synagogue the former is the more powerful. It is, in fact, the most powerful professional association of rabbis in America; many of its members fondly refer to it as "our labor union," for in addition to enforcing an ethical code, the association maintains a welfare program for its members and, to some degree, also controls the allocation of pulpits among them. Congregations are free to choose any rabbi who fulfils their special needs, but they are expected to do so through a placement commission. The commission is composed of representatives from the Seminary, the Assembly, and the United Synagogue, and is situated in the Seminary. If the slate of available rabbis it provides is rejected, another one is supplied; but each slate is accompanied by efforts to convince the congregational representatives of the necessity of retaining rabbis the commission believes are both suitable for the congregation and within the movement's tradition. These efforts often result in sending the congregation a somewhat more traditional rabbi than the congregation would have itself selected. The single most important member of the commission is the executive director of the Rabbinical Assembly—currently Rabbi Wolfe Kelman, a graduate of the Seminary who works in close cooperation with it.

The Assembly's influence lies in the control it can exert over its own members, the rabbis: the majority of Conservative rabbis will not accept invitations from congregations without the approval of the placement commission. For rabbis who are in great demand, getting approval is mainly a matter of good form; they know it is very likely to be granted. Asking for it is in conformity with the rules and habits of their association. For young or less popular rabbis the gaining of approval is more significant. To move from one congregation to another without such approval—and rabbis often move from five to eight times in the course of their careers—means that a rabbi loses the commission's support for his next move.

IT IS TRUE, of course, that at present there is a general scarcity of rabbis, and among the Conservatives in particular (this is documented in a fine study of the "rabbinical labor force" by Eli Ginzberg). Thus, practically every rabbi, with or without the Assembly's or the commision's support, can find a pulpit, at worse a small pulpit in the South, or become a chaplain in the armed forces, in a prison, or in county hospitals. But rabbis, like ministers and other professionals, prefer to serve large congregations in big cities close to centers of Jewish and cultural life. Appointments to these pulpits, to the degree that the Assembly controls them, provide the informal sanctions and rewards which help the Assembly to enforce its "line" and discipline. This is not to imply that all the "plum" pulpits are controlled by the commission. The older, larger, richer congregations of the bigger cities tend to be independent in spirit and to carry considerable weight in the movement. Hence, when they want to get a certain rabbi, let us say a rabbi who would build some national reputation for himself by writing articles in Jewish magazines and delivering speeches at national conventions, they are likely to get him. Moreover, the rabbi who builds up such a reputation, by virtue of it, gains considerable independence of the various sanctions and controls. Still, the majority of the rabbis, and it seems an ever increasing number, "play it safe" by getting at least the approval—if not the assignment—of the Assembly; and many congregations, it seems in growing numbers, go through the placement commission, hence the Seminary and the Assembly, in their search for a rabbi.

Like many associations which control attractive positions, the Rabbinical Assembly is a rather exclusive organization. Only graduates of the Seminary, advocates of the proper mixture of tradition and innovation, are assured automatic membership. Though quite a few graduates of the rabbinical school of Yeshiva University (Orthodox) serve Conservative congregations, only a limited number of them have been accepted by the Assembly. Non-Seminary graduates are now requested to take some courses in the Seminary before applying for membership, and when they are interviewed about their religious positions they cannot appear too Orthodox (they are embarrassed if they wear a head-cover during the interview), nor too un-Orthodox (recently a rabbi was rejected because he said that his wife shopped on Saturday). In general, however, to be accepted they must hew closer to the line of the Seminary than even the average Conservative rabbi.

The Assembly has a code which its members are required to follow, a code supported by such formal sanctions as suspension of placement privilege and even expulsion. Two items of the code read as follows: "Members of the Rabbinical Assembly may negotiate only through the offices of the placement commission." "At no time will a member of the Rabbinical Assembly submit his name, or even indirectly cause his name to be submitted, as a candidate without the prior approval of the commission." Some additional ten items spell out the other "don'ts" which are intended to strengthen its influence over the rabbis, the pulpits, and, through both, over the religious tendencies of the movement.

THE UNITED SYNAGOGUE OF AMERICA is the weaker sister of the Assembly, and the second arm of the Seminary. It is, presumably, an organization of the congregations. More accurately, however, it is an organization *for* the congregations that was founded by the Seminary and is run by a rabbi according to rules and standards formulated under the active leadership of the Seminary faculty. In part its function is to increase lay cooperation in maintaining the proper religious orientation. (A congregation was recently suspended for not following the ruling against Bingo in the synagogue; and another was not accepted as a member because its members' children write in its school on Saturday.)

The relatively weak position of the congregational organization is reflected in its "Standards for Synagogue Practice" —the code to direct lay leaders. Considerably influenced by the "employees," the rabbis, and their representatives in the Seminary court, these "standards" explicitly recognize the superior authority of the rabbis in all "spiritual" matters— and there seem to be no others. The first article of the "Standards," which were adopted in 1957, reads: "The United Synagogue of America recognizes the Committee of Jewish Law and Standards of the Rabbinical Assembly of America as its authority on Jewish Law." (As we shall see, the parallel article in the constitution of the Reform congregations stresses the autonomy of these congregations.) The second reads: "Each congregation shall look to its rabbi, by virtue of his election as spiritual leader of the congregation, as its authority on all matters of Jewish law and practice . . ." One function of this item, it has been suggested to the author by a leading authority in the field, is to assure the rabbi that whatever he decides to do about Halachah in his own congregation shall not be questioned by the Rabbinical Assembly or the Seminary. In other words, it assures each rabbi that he will not be censured for siding with the laity in such matters as organs, mixed seating, and driving to the synagogue on the Sabbath. At the same time this item, strongly supported by the Assembly and actually formulated by one of its leaders when the Standards were drawn up, defends the rabbi who wishes to adhere to the line he internalized while a student at the Seminary, within the limits local circumstances and prudence allow, against undue pressure of the laity, the congregation. Whatever power and impact the laity might have in real life, it is one indicator of the power of the movement that the whole Standards do not contain a single word about the authority of the laity or its representatives.

In short, then, of the three Conservative institutions, the most powerful is the Seminary. Through its head, its former students, and its control of certain key positions in the Rabbinical Assembly and the United Synagogue of America, it manages to exert a rather constant "traditional" pressure upon the Conservative movement.

But this pattern is not typical of Jewish religious organizations in America. In the Reform movement the institutions of rabbis, laity, and school are less centralized; and the movement in general concerns itself somewhat less with the struggle of tradition and innovation and considerably more with a commitment to "social action" and a struggle over Zionism.

UNLIKE the Conservative movement, one building does not house all three Reform organizations: the Hebrew Union College—Jewish Institute of Religion (its rabbinical school, otherwise known as the College); the Central Conference of American Rabbis (otherwise known as the Conference); and the Union of American Hebrew Congregations (its organization of congregations, otherwise known as the Union). Moreover, the Reform movement not only does not consider its rabbinical school its central authority but operates under the dual authority of the rabbinical and the lay institutions. The stronger of these two, again unlike the Conservative movement, is the lay one.

Historically, the Conservative Seminary developed long before the Conservative movement. It served as the basis of the Conservative expansion that came with the Americanizing of the East European Jews at the turn of the century, and it has always been the single source of Conservative rabbis. But the Reform College is the result of a recent merger of two schools (the Hebrew Union College of Cincinnati and the Jewish Institute of Religion in New York), and until this merger rabbis could receive their training in either institution. Reform lacks, in other words, the centralizing strength of a common training place of all its spiritual leaders and hence a source of common tradition. (It remains to be seen whether the recent merger will change this.)

Partly as a result of this lack and also in part because the College is not led by as strong a personality as heads the Seminary, and because the organization of congregations (the Union) has separate headquarters, the staff members of the Union, though many of them are rabbis, are more inclined to give their allegiance to the Union's "line" and to its leader, Rabbi Maurice Eisendrath, than to the rabbinical association or to the College. The fact that the president of the Union, the many heads of its divisions, and many members of its commissions and committees are rabbis, does not mean that the Union is strongly affected by the Conference (the Reform rabbinical association) the way the Conservative United Synagogue is affected by the Rabbinical Assembly, or that the Union is not predominantly "lay" in outlook and line. Because of the rapid turnover of the leadership in the Conference, and the continued leadership and stability of career in the Union, because of the considerable lay interests of the Reform rabbis in general (human rather than narrowly religious matters, and some other factors too complicated to be pursued here), the Union—staffed with rabbis as it may be—is still an organization of the laity, responsive to its positions and needs, not an organization *for* the congregations by rabbis. Yet the Union's influence in itself is comparatively small, in part because of its constitution and due to the formal structure of its constitution whose preamble reads:

Nothing contained in this Constitution or the By-Laws shall be construed so as to interfere in any manner whatsoever with the mode of worship, the school, the freedom of expression and opinion, or any of the other congregational activities of the constituent congregations of the Union.

This clearly limits the Union's ability to control the congregations.

Article VIII is now under criticism by the Union leadership precisely because it obstructs the development of a guide for the congregations. Without taking any position regarding an innovation-tradition issue, Rabbi Eisendrath, speaking for the Union, has made a strong appeal for the guide:

> Hats on, hats off: rabbis robed, rabbis unrobed; *avec* Atorah, *sans* Atorah; one day Rosh Ha-Shana and two days likewise; Ashkenazic pronunciation and Sephardi likewise; kosher kitchens in Reform social halls—all this and ham and bacon too . . . some may call this the "free development of the religious idea" and bless it with the sacrosanct shibboleth of "autonomy, autonomy, autonomy" — but with a candor borrowed from and a courage inspired by [Isaac Mayer] Wise, I too call it "anarchy, and utter chaos."

Any such guide would require a change in Article VIII so as to increase the role of the national organization in the local organization's life.

Despite the absence of a central authority in the Reform movement, there is an influential source of traditional or neo-traditional tendencies in the local congregations and their leaders. There is, in fact, a long tradition among some Reform congregations to be more "right" than the Reform national organizations.[1] The rightist tendency of these congregations is reflected in their inducing rabbis to re-introduce such "rituals" as Bar Mitzvah and the observance of the second day of Rosh Ha-Shanah (in some cases under the explicit threat to go Conservative "otherwise") and their attempt to return to more traditional American Jewish patterns, such as having the main service on Friday, using Hebrew instead of English, and so on.

The Reform movement has about six hundred congregations, of which half have been established since World War II. Since these newer congregations are in many cases more to the "right" than the older ones, strictly speaking there are only fifty to one hundred that can properly be called classical Reform, extreme "innovators," over against new Reform, or neo-traditionals. (That the new laity seems to be "on the side of history," that is, the general trend to the right, may be one of the deeper reasons why the Union, the lay organization of congregations, has gained in influence since World War II, that is, since the beginning of the general religious revival).

All the Reform *institutions,* however, present a middle-of-the-road religious position; moreover, in matters of tradition *vs.* innovation they play a less active role than the Conservative Seminary does. The Reform institutions exert their full influence and leadership on questions of social action and Zionism.

Social action has continued to be one of the most important issues of Reform from its very first days. ("The heart of religion concerns itself with man's relation to man," Rabbi Eisendrath has recently said.) The Reform leadership has only recently opened a bureau in Washington from which it could support political legislation concerning desegregation, anti-discrimination, and fair employment. Some of the more powerful older congregations objected violently. They argued that a Jew who joins a synagogue does not give it a mandate to represent him politically; that action should be taken by individuals or single congregations but not by the movement as such. (Others suggest that these congregations—which include many of America's richest Jews—are politically conservative and their real objection is to the strong liberal bent of some of the

---

[1] Nathan Glazer suggested that the development of the Conservative movement can be traced to a protest of rightist Reform members against the leftist leadership concentrated around the College in the 1880's.

Reform rabbis and leaders.) Despite such objection, Union leadership wields its influence and guidance on questions of social action with the full support of the rabbinical association—and the institutional leadership will probably put through a strong social action program such as, by now, is traditional in the Reform movement. In the other two movements, social action stirs relatively little interest, among other reasons because it is felt to be "Reform business."

Zionism is another major issue in the Reform movement. Rabbis, board members, and other leaders all talk with considerable pride of Reform's internal struggles concerning the American Council for Judaism, an anti-Zionist organization that drew most of its members from the Reform. "They cannot get any more anti-Zionist rabbis," a major Reform leader said. "All they can do is check that the rabbi we send them is not an adherent Zionist who will talk about Israel all the time." To Conservatives and to the Modern Orthodox, on the other hand, Zionism is not such a central issue; both movements take a practically unanimous (and basically positive) position. Thus, in summary, the Reform leadership is less centralized than the Conservative leadership and somewhat less active in regard to the religious issues of "right" and "left," exerting its influences more clearly on the secular issues of social action and Zionism.

THE ORTHODOX MOVEMENT is again quite different from the other two. Most importantly, it is no longer growing. Both the Conservative and the Reform membership have tripled in the last fifteen years, and each is hard pressed to find enough rabbis to staff their congregations, the number of which have doubled during that time. But the Orthodox have difficulty holding both congregations and rabbis: less than a third of the rabbinical graduates of Yeshiva University hold pulpits; many of those who do not, become businessmen or scientists (there is an association of Orthodox scientists, many of whom have graduated from the Yeshiva rabbinical school); and some become teachers or take other non-pulpit—though acceptably "Jewish"—positions.[2] Even a number of those who become rabbis, however, eventually end up serving Conservative congregations—out of conviction or because of economic pressures.

The framework of the Orthodox organization is also very different. In the first place, it offers almost no centralization at all. There are four main rabbinical organizations (many rabbis are "free lancers"); many more Yeshivot, all of which train rabbis; and no one central organization of congregations. Finally, there is no central authority that regulates these institutions and associations.

Modern Orthodoxy (which represents the more innovating part of Orthodox Jewry) offers the most centralized elements of the Orthodox movement and resembles somewhat the Conservative organization. Yeshiva University serves as its spiritual and organizational center. The majority of the members of its rabbinical association (the Rabbinical Council) and most of the association's leaders are graduates of Yeshiva and work in close contact with its masters. The Union of Jewish Congregations of America, however, Modern Orthodoxy's parallel to the United Synagogue, is less

---

[2] It should be noted that many of the students at the rabbinical school of Yeshiva University never intended to become practicing rabbis in the first place, like their predecessors in European Yeshivot.

tied to this spiritual center than its Conservative counterpart and draws rabbis and leadership from sources other than Yeshiva. The most striking difference between this segment of the Orthodox movement and the Conservative movement lies in the degree of control their respective rabbinical associations can impose. A Modern Orthodox rabbi can readily attain a gratifying pulpit without the support or consent of his rabbinical association or the Yeshivot. Because of the strong tendency to leave the pulpit for non-rabbinical positions, few sanctions can be applied. Hence, whatever "line" the Yeshiva supports, it brings to that "line" much less influence than do its counterparts in Conservative or even in Reform Judaism.[3]

To what effect, then, is the limited institutional power of the Modern Orthodox movement used? Yeshiva University, like the Seminary, is more traditional than the rabbis, and the rabbis that it produces are more traditional than their congregations. It is a commonplace among the Modern Orthodox rabbis that most of them cannot eat in the homes of the presidents of their congregations, or even of the more devoted members, because the latter do not observe *Kashruth* to a degree their rabbis consider satisfactory.

While the Yeshiva, like the Seminary, serves to counter lay pressures, there is a crucial difference in that, while the Seminary is instrumental in moving the Conservatives to the right, the Yeshiva — because of its limited power — cannot block the leftist trend of Modern Orthodoxy; it can only slow it down.

The emphasis which the leaders of Modern Orthodoxy, the Yeshiva heads and faculty, place upon Day Schools reflects both the weaknesses of the movement and the tenor of its efforts. To an increasing extent, Hebrew Day Schools have become the core of the "conservation" and restoration activities of Modern Orthodoxy. Parents are often thought of as lost—a desert generation—but with the Day School Modern Orthodoxy attempts to save the children. The Orthodox movement has learned that children who go to the Day Schools not only tend to accept and maintain the Orthodox tradition but sometimes bring their parents back to that tradition as well. (The parents first participate in the children's services, then develop their own Orthodox *shul*.) The head of a central Yeshiva pointed out that he assesses his graduates first of all according to their ability to run Day Schools. This emphasis upon the younger generation would seem to be a perfectly understandable reaction of a movement under strong leftist pressures, a movement, moreover, doing less well than either of its two counterparts.

ONE MEASURE of the institutional differences I have been discussing is the role of the rabbi in each of the movements. Rabbis constitute, so to speak, the middle rang of the contemporary Jewish religious community, standing somewhere between the national superstructure and the congregations and their members. J. Carlin and S. Medlovitz have shown, in their outstanding study, "The American Rabbi: A Religious Specialist Responds to Loss of Au-

---

[3] To some degree, Modern Orthodoxy, again unlike the Conservative movement, also contains a separation of spiritual and administrative leadership under the respective guidance of Rabbi J. B. Soloveitchik, a professor at Yeshiva University, and Dr. Samuel Belkin, its president.

thority,"[4] that the trend among all these movements is toward the "Protestantization" of the rabbi. Sometimes deliberately, sometimes unwittingly, contemporary rabbis tend to emulate the Protestant minister. The traditional Jewish conception of the rabbi is in decline; the stress today is not upon the roles of judge, scholar, or teacher of one's "generation," but those of preacher, congregational organizer, and administrator. This much can be said in common for all American rabbis (short of those belonging to the right Orthodox); even so, there are enormous differences among the three movements in the degree to which the traditional elements have been lost.

The Modern Orthodox rabbi, "by definition," is the least affected; yet because of the movement's constant "leftward" trend, he too is under pressure to "adjust." Moreover, since the movement has few sanctions over its rabbis, since many leave the rabbinate, and some choose to serve Conservative congregations, it can hardly offset such adjustment under pressure from below.

The modern rabbi tends the sick, counsels the mentally ill, directs those who need relief, and above all—he preaches. The quality of the sermon has become a major criterion by which congregations elect rabbis and by which promotion is gained to more important pulpits and to national reputation. (This is less true of the Conservative but more true of the Reform rabbi; Reform rabbis on the average spend about two days a week working on their sermons, considering this their major single chore.)

Because of the different institutional arrangements, both Reform and Conservative rabbis are under different kinds of pressures. Each of them must be a super-administrator in order to run efficiently the various activities, institutions, and associations which make up most modern congregations; in addition, each must direct, or at least participate in, a large number of "social" activities that have little or no religious meaning. The strains that these requirements impose on the rabbis are sometimes exaggerated—the new generation of rabbis in particular is much more aware of these problems and much more able to deal with them. Nevertheless, most of the graduates of the College, the Seminary, and the Yeshiva tend to identify with their teachers and masters. Many, at least for a few years, hope to be religious scholars, or "intellectuals" (quite a few try to remain affiliated with their educational institutions in order to realize these aspirations). Rabbinical education as often as not rather deliberately prepares its students for the pulpit as it was or ought to be and so increases the crisis that ensues upon graduating and getting out into the congregational world.

ONE SHOULD NOT be too hasty in pointing out the undesirable effects of such training. Congregations pressure the rabbi toward the direction of social administration; the educational institutions train him in the opposite direction, toward scholarship and spiritual aspirations—with the result that between these diametrically opposed approaches a rabbi often has to compromise. Of course, if the gap is too large a compromise cannot be reached; if the strain on the rabbi is too great he may even leave the rabbinate. (Training that is too far removed from "reality" supplies one reason why about two-thirds of the

---

[4] Published in *The Jews,* edited by Marshall Sklare. The following comments are based in part on this study.

graduates of Yeshiva University's rabbinical school do not hold pulpits.)

Yet once the rabbi is "out there" in the congregation, despite the official policy of the Conservative and the Reform bodies that he is the final authority on Jewish law, the institutional leaders are more inclined to help him reach a "proper" compromise with the congregations, that is, in line with the movement's tradition as interpreted by its leadership and institutions—though the need to reduce conflicts between the rabbi and the congregation is also taken into account. But even in the centralized Conservative movement, the support—which concerns not only questions of tradition versus innovation but those of "intellectual" rabbis versus administrative and "social" ones—is far weaker than that given by any church-like religion.

An analysis of the role of the rabbi suggests the same general conclusion which emerges from the analysis of the interplay among the various institutions which constitute the national framework of the three movements: the general trend is toward a *more* traditional (or neo-traditional) pattern of Jewish religious life, but *not* toward a traditionalistic one. The Reform movement, with the exception of a hard core of "Classical Reform" congregations, seems to be moving in the more traditional direction; the Conservatives *in toto* are becoming still more traditional. Modern Orthodoxy, on the other hand, tends to accept some of the innovative patterns introduced by the other two movements, with only a small segment sticking to a militant, traditionalistic line.

The role the national institutions of the three movements plays in this trend toward a more traditional Jewish life varies from movement to movement. In the Reform the major driving force seems to be at the moment a grass root movement, led by the young new Reform congregations. Among the Orthodox, where the institutional structure is the weakest, the grass-root movement is in the less traditionalistic direction. The institutional structure is playing a limited anchorage role, attempting to reduce the drift in the innovative direction. It is among the Conservatives that the institutional structure exerts itself most, in leading the movement, despite some congregational resistance, in the more traditional, and in my book hence more Jewish, direction.

THE ROLE OF THE SYNAGOGUE IN THE AMERICAN JEWISH COMMUNITY

Rabbi Abraham J. Feldman

Mr. Chairman, were it not for the fact that I still feel the wheels of my auto and the road seems to be still extending ahead of me, I would take you to task for suggesting that I have any lingering desire that is causing a sense of frustration to find other presidencies to hold. I don't know what Israel Goldstein's experience was when he was president of the Synagogue Council, but may I suggest to you that after one has had two years of this presidency, and they were the kind of years that I have had, that is the presidency to finish all presidencies. I have had all I want. I never asked for what I got....

As I came into this hotel and I hadn't quite finished signing my name on the register someone rushed over and said, "Thank God you are here. Dr. Goldstein has just begun to speak. You better come right in. You will take care of the registering later. You should hear Dr. Goldstein because there are going to be some conflicting points of view." Well, I just listened to my good friend Israel and I think the sound of our disagreement will fade away into a קול דממה דקה. There are disagreements, yes; but they are not so profound and they are not world shaking nor even community shaking.

Before I go on, may I say to the Rabbinical Assembly that I appreciate more than I can tell you the courtesy of your invitation, and that I welcome the opportunity to meet with you. While I am aware, that I am here primarily because for one month more I hold the presidency of the Synagogue Council of America, and you are not unaware of my relationship to the Central Conference of American Rabbis, I know you will understand that it is as an individual that I speak, that I am not deputized to represent here today either the Synagogue Council of America or the Central Conference of American Rabbis.

What I say is a personal judgment and a personal conviction. All the more am I flattered by and grateful for your welcoming me into your midst, and the compliment you paid me of wanting to hear what I think about this subject under discussion.

Now, in stating my views I shall not attempt to document my conclusions. I am deliberately avoiding all such pretensions. Ours has been a long, long history and our literature reveals so many diverse facets and diverse judgments that each of us can find in our history and in our literature abundant "quotes" to defend his views, however one differs from another. Besides, being what I am, I may be suspected, with good reason, of not deeming myself necessarily bound by the patterns of the past or being committed to defend older views.

I know the saying of the sages אין ישראל נגאלין עד שיעשו כולם אגודה אחת — but I have also learned in the years of my experience, and mine is now one of the longer ministries in American Jewry, that "Jewish unity," so-called, might be had at too costly a price. The price of "Jewish unity," whatever that may mean, might be a regimentation of practices. It might be formal conformity, without essential conviction. It could be a form of liberalism which borders on hypocrisy, a sort of watered down liberalism which says: because I am a liberal I can afford to go along with the stricter constructionist, and because I am a מקיל I can go along with the מחמיר. The price might also be, and I have seen it happen, an ultimate indifference to Jewish life, a type of cynicism which says: Let the hierarchy — that is, the philanthropic "ba'ale batim" and the professional executives, the people who Jewishly qualify primarily for the עליות שטומע, but who have recently been encouraged to wag their tongues on the "principle" of ווער עס האט די "מאה" זאגט די דעה, let these handle the affairs of the Jewish community. They will have their own way anyhow.... The price of so-called unity might be also the surrender, the wiping away of all honest differences in the interpretation of the מהות of the Jewish heritage. Instead of having the wholesome aliveness of אלו ואלו, they would establish an authoritarian dogmatic אלו only!

Is "Jewish unity" then a case of mere wishfulness, only a myth as to desirability, possibility and probability? The answer would of course depend upon the definition of the phrase. Now, of course, if I attempted to do that I would go into the area which Dr. Goldstein discussed so well. But I am limiting myself, as I was requested to, to the specific theme, "The Role of the Synagogue in the American Jewish Community." And I limit myself also in this matter of community, to the consideration of the role of the synagogue in the local community. Rabbi Goldstein covered the national scene, and while I do not altogether agree with him, I think our disagreement is largely a matter of semantics.

What do we mean by "The Synagogue" when we speak of The Role of the Synagogue in American Jewish Life?

There are two possible understandings. One is that concept of the synagogue as the overall spiritual experience and heritage of our people. It is that of an institution without organization, without walls, (as the Sabbath is an institution), which has been over the centuries the home of the Jewish spirit, at once a symbol and a concept, but never, never a delimited organism. In this sense we speak, and we all do, I am sure, of the Synagogue *generic*, which is a synonym for the Jewish religion. The other is the concept of the Synagogue as an organization, a building, a building which a particular social unit, a congregation, owns, controls and administers, and sometimes "Synagogue" becomes the synonym for a congregation.

When we speak, as all of us do, of "the centrality of the synagogue," or when we speak, as we are attempting to do in this twilight hour, of the role of the synagogue in the American Jewish community, it happens that some of those who speak, whether affirmatively or negatively, confuse these two concepts, these two understandings of the word "synagogue" and use them interchangeably, and that is confusing indeed.

There are those who think of the influence of and the control by a congregation, something which in the American Jewish life, as Rabbi Goldstein has suggested, is completely impossible, and is undesirable even if it were possible. I mean the notion that any particular congregation could be the controlling element and force of a total Jewish community. With rare exceptions — and this in the smaller communities — in every one of our communities, outside of those that I except, there are *several* Jewish congregations and synagogues and they differ in their interpretations of Judaism, they differ in their Jewish definitions, they differ in their religious practices. Under the impact of the American democratic ideal, and under the impact of the necessities of Jewish life in America, the several congre-

[192]

gations, or the several synagogues in any one community, however they differ, exist, each of them, as of right and not on sufferance. The sustaining members of these synagogues proceed to create the joint agencies for Jewish community action. But in the sphere of their religious life they go each their own way, and then combine for joint action on the level of their total community.

Now, with all deference, I suggest, gentlemen, that if anyone connected with any particular congregation or synagogue in a community gets it into his head that he, be he Rabbi or a member of the congregation, that he should by virtue of his identification with a particular synagogue, give direction to other Jewish agencies, direction which he insists must be presumed to be authoritative because he presumes to speak in the name of his particular synagogue, then I must say to you that that individual should have his head examined for fallacious reasoning, and his soul examined for his unmitigated חוצפה. I include the Rabbis and the "ba'ale batim" together. So far as we Rabbis are concerned, we ought to have the humility to recognize and to acknowledge that our training for the rabbinate does not automatically make us experts in social organization, in the technique of case work, in the mechanics of campaigns; that by reason of our training we are not unchallengable authorities in hospital administration or welfare services, or any of the other multiple services of our Jewish community. Our ordination does not qualify us for ecclesiastical suzerainty or for any other type of dominance or domineering in the Jewish community.

But having said that, which I think needs to be said and should be said *by a Rabbi*, let me hasten to assert what is a profound conviction with me, that in the larger sense of the word "Synagogue," the synagogue as the symbol of the Jewish spiritual, ethical, moral idealism, must be and can be the central influence in Jewish community living. And from *it*, as the symbol of the totality of Jewish religious content, the challenges and the motivations are derived for community action and community organization. Let this synagogue, in this broader sense in which I speak of it — I am not speaking of *my* קלויז or *your* שטיבל — disappear, and Jewish life would disappear and those institutions about which we are agonized today would not have to be in existence at all. The point I am trying to make is this: That we who are *primarily* not just the servants of the synagogue but the sons of the synagogue, we *and* our fellow Jews who are affirmatively religious, though we may express our religion in different ways, we must in the process of active participation in community living be concerned with spiritual values and the spiritual attitudes in Jewish life. We must be the monitors of Jewishness, not only admonishing, not only reproving, but encouraging and counseling in the paths of duty, to be walked in with a sensibility to the historic and the enduring ideals of the synagogue, ideals and standards which all of us cherish and acknowledge!

In my own attitude to Jewish community life — and I know this will shock some here because I have discussed this matter with some of the individuals here — I recognize no secularism in Jewish community life! As a son of the synagogue and its servant, I recognize that in the specialization of the functions of life which now is the mode of life which we know and which we cannot change if we would, we have specialists in every area of Jewish life. And I suggest to you, gentlemen, that because one is a specialist in Center work and another is a specialist in Family work, Family Welfare or Case Work, and yet another is a specialist in administration of the Home for the Aged, or the hospital, or the foster home program, he is not by reason of working in these organizations outside the scope, the influence, the periphery of the synagogue. He, too, is doing the Lord's work. He is doing the synagogue's work. And I turn to him again and again, I turn to him as an expert in an area of life in which I cannot have expertness, and refer to him the tasks in which he has greater competency than I have. He is not my hateful competitor! He is my welcome co-worker in the life of the Jewish community.

To assure this relationship, and there are some of my colleagues from my own community here who know the truth of what I am saying, we in our community have always insisted, and I think we have successfully persuaded those who serve the Jewish community through agencies other than the individual synagogues, that the teachers in the synagogue, the professionals of the synagogue, if you will, are to serve on every governing board of every Jewish institution in our community. There was a time when this was resisted but there is no resistance now.

In passing, let me not forget to suggest, first, that the administrators and the directors of community institutions, with perhaps some exceptions in metropolitan centers, are usually synagogue people. They are no less *of* the synagogue than we Rabbis are. And let us remember, in the second place, that since, when we define our Judaism, we pride ourselves on having no ecclesiasticism, of having no sacerdotalism, no hierarchy, we Rabbis are also laymen, (to use this word that has been borrowed from the church). Even our so-called laity, without any restriction, are part of the same גוי קדוש of which we are a part. We can't have it both ways, gentlemen. We can't denounce sacerdotalism, and we can't boast of the absence of hierarchy, and then ask for ourselves the status of, what used to be called in the church, "ecclesiastical commissioners," in Jewish life.

Please understand. I am not making a blanket defense of the vulgarity and the arrogance and the impudence of some recognizable Jews in the Jewish community. I am only suggesting the need of recognizing that when we are thinking of the role of the synagogue in American Jewish life, or when we insist upon the centrality of the synagogue, that *we* must not equate these with the role of the Rabbi in the Jewish community or the centrality of the Rabbi in the life of the community.

It was something of this concept that I think was implicit in the organization of the Synagogue Council of America some 30 years ago. It was intended that the Council would represent *the Synagogue*, not the individual synagogues, not the individual congregations, each — one of several in a community. It combined the rabbinate and the other people of the synagogue. It recognized the existence of differences and protected all against the dominance by any. It sought unity without uniformity, cooperation without regimentation. It found the areas of religious life which we of the synagogue hold and cherish together. And in relation to the non-Jewish world, it presented a united front of synagogue-oriented Jewry. Today, when the government of the United States wants to contact the Synagogue, it does not have to choose between the Orthodox group, the Conservative and the Reform groups. And when our Christian neighbors want to communicate with religious Jewry, they likewise do not need to make the choice on their own as to which particular group they should seek out. The Synagogue Council is the united front and is the representative agency of religious American Jewry. Within the Synagogue Council, it is possible to have unity without uniformity, without paying an unwarranted price for such unity.

[195]

The recent storms were occasioned by, first, some pathological exponents of ghettoism; second, by a group of very naive, self-segregated למדנים, (the authors of the pathetic איסור); and, third, by several Yiddish journalists, devoid of integrity and utterly lacking in scruples. These are people who said, (and I am quoting now exactly what was told me), "We would rather have Jews un-synagogued than to urge any Jews to become affiliated with a Conservative or a Reform synagogue."

I say, this recent storm has largely blown over and the *responsible* leaders of Orthodoxy deserve credit for the fact that the Jewish community today is not completely splintered. I say, likewise, that the responsible leaders of the Conservative movement and of the Reform movement are to be credited with a remarkable restraint, and with a mature wisdom in publicly ignoring the incidents which these mischievous individuals deliberately fabricated. And I say to you, from my knowledge of what went on and what still is going on, that this restraint on our part helped mightily in preventing a חילול השם which would have done incalculable damage to the total American Jewish community.

Thank God this storm is largely over, and I think that the Synagogue Council today is stronger, is better known certainly, and more favorably known, than it has ever been before, and together, with a greater eagerness, we are seeking to expand the areas of unity as sons of the synagogue. We have many such areas.

First, there was the thought back of the idea that was announced two years ago, that there is a contagion in loyalty, there is an infectiousness in devotion which can benefit all. I have lived long enough to know that when we have a weak Orthodoxy in a community, it does not do the Reform group or the Conservative group any good. I have seen it when any one group is not functioning as it should, that it is not having a wholesome effect and influence on the others. But when every one of our groups is functioning at its utmost, each doing a devoted and dedicated and envisioned job, one group stimulates the other and the whole Jewish community is the better and the stronger and the happier because of it. That was the idea back of the "Back to Synagogue" effort, that we would go out together and make an impact upon the Jewish community, to get all who are un-synagogued into the synagogues of their choices. I believe that there is a blessing in this kind of contagion.

Secondly, I think that through this joint effort and this unity without uniformity, it is possible for us to introduce more of קדושה into all of Jewish life, by really being able to have the synagogue influence Jewish philanthropy and Jewish institutions and Jewish organizations functioning in the Jewish community. But we cannot do it individually if we, the religious leaders, are quarreling among ourselves all the time.

Then there is the area of כלפי חוץ. In dealing with the world outside of the Jewish community, it has become obvious that no one group of the three or four that we have can make שבת for itself. We have to present a united front. The country, the world demand it of us. They want to speak to the total Jewish religious community, to *the* Synagogue, and not to the individual Rabbis and congregations.

Then, again, as Rabbis and congregations, we have problems which are not dissimilar. They may be professional problems or in the area of techniques and it is possible to coordinate, to meet all of those, to discuss them and bring them together, and find the areas in which we can be mutually helpful.

Take the area of publications, for instance. We need popular tracts on Judaism. Those of you who were in the chaplaincy know the tragedy of that. How נעבאכדיק we feel — seeing those boxes with all of the literature that is made available for the Christian soldiers and the paucity of what we have there, only now and then, for our own. We need more of the kind of literature which can speak with the voice of the synagogue and authoritatively.

Again, there is a need for and much help to be derived from having regional conferences of all of the various configurations of the synagogue.

Then the General Assembly, which your own member and former president, Rabbi Max Davidson, organized so magnificently this year. Those of you who were at Columbia University, I am sure will agree that we had there at the General Assembly discussions in areas of controversy but we had every point of view represented, and we had also a splendid example of the possibility of unity with דרך ארץ.

Then there are research projects that could be undertaken in various areas of Jewish life, the spiritual and the religious, if you will.

[197]

And there is the ברכה of שבת אחים גם יחד. Over these many years, those who had been consistently delegated to the Synagogue Council have found cooperation and brotherliness and togetherness, the blessing of comradeship across differences, despite differences, with a sense of mutuality and reverence and decent respect, one for the other.

It is in these and a few other areas where, through the Synagogue Council, an impact can be made upon the total Jewish community. The role of religious groups in the American Jewish community can be enhanced incalculably if the Rabbis, as individuals, are truly חברים and behave as such, if the congregations on the local level do not stoop to market-like competition, if *we* do not try to act as ecclesiastics or attempt to wield power but, rather, act as teachers and guides of Jews who can never be regimented. And also, in relation to the Synagogue Council, if we delegate, you in the Rabbinical Assembly and we in the C. C. A. R., if we delegate our ablest men to represent us in the Synagogue Council, and support it with some generosity and allow it to meet its opposite numbers in church life of whom Rabbi Goldstein spoke, on the level of parity, parity in capacity and parity in facilities and tools with which to work, if the Rabbinical Assembly of America and the Central Conference of American Rabbis, and our congregational Unions, all groups would designate their best people and expect their delegates to attend meetings, and hold them accountable for what is going on; if we provide these patterns of behavior, I think, we may not usher in the ימות המשיח but, at least, we shall begin to have a better coordinated and a more friendly life in the organized American Jewish community.

THE A-THEOLOGICAL JUDAISM OF THE AMERICAN COMMUNITY

NORMAN E. FRIMER

I

JEWISH THINKERS have for several decades now struggled to set forth a theology of American Judaism. For, quantitatively, this Jewish community is the largest ever to have been established in any single country outside the Holy Land. Qualitatively too, it has the resources to rival modern Israel—or at least to coexist with it—as a major center of the Jewish spirit. What has been sorely lacking was a formulation of Judaism which, while viewing American Jewry as an integral link in the chain of Jewish history, simultaneously spelled out in contemporary terms the uniqueness of the American experience and the direction of its Jewish search for purpose and destiny. Such a blueprint could harness the rich abundance of our intellectual and spiritual potential, channelling its power towards an unlimited horizon of cultural efflorescence.

These efforts have failed in the past, state their critics, because they had misjudged the American mood. With the demolition of the idols and ideologies of the Thirties, and the stark exposure of man's capacity in depth for evil, the American Jewish intellectual was filled with despair. He saw and built his philosophy of life on a scaffolding of man's greed and pride and his capacity for sin and corruption.

With such negativism, however, American Jewry would have little truck; this was entirely alien to its historical rootage in an optimistic attitude to life. Faith in man's capacity both to discern and to implement the good was the very warp and woof of the Jewish *anschauung*. Only such a world-view could capture the American Jews' allegiance. In fact, upon its base he began to build a concrete program of positive action. Vigorous community planning, which characterized the post-World War II era, dynamic organizing, building and contributing gave body and vitality to the traditional emphasis on the Good Deed. In the challenging choice between the conviction of man's sinfulness and his active worth, American Jewry gave its unhesitating and overwhelming vote to the latter.

Now, from this very decisive affirmation of the efficacy of the deed has come the hope for a renewal of theological commitment. For the constant increase in Jewish activity, so goes the claim, is bound to generate its own distinct desire for a rationale of Jewish living. And

---

Dr. Frimer serves as Metropolitan Regional Director of the B'nai Brith Hillel Foundation at Brooklyn College. He is the author of several pamphlets, among them "Judaism and Ethics" (B'nai Brith Youth Organization) and "Maimonides for Our Day" (Hebrew Theological College, Chicago).

from this search for meaning will surely emerge a "theology of *mitzvah*," a religious philosophy of doing and believing which will unify and make purposeful the patterns of contemporary Jewish experience. One such exponent is bold enough to hope that these "seekers" might give earnest consideration to the theology of Covenant which, in his words, "seeks to explore and understand the implications of defining theology as a covenant relationship, and specifically to make manifest the nature and meaning of Jewish Covenant with God." Such an interpretation, moreover, in which inner conviction of relationship is bodied forth by the whole personality in the doing, squares most appropriately with the activistic and positive orientation of the American climate, while at the same time providing an enriching continuity with the spirit of the ancient Tradition.

This thesis frankly evoked mixed reactions. As a statement on the great spiritual and intellectual promise of the Jewish community it commands respect and possibly endorsement. As an empirical evaluation of the status quo, it arouses many misgivings. Contemporary Jewish history can be read quite differently!

The almost unanimous consensus of recent studies on the personal and group life of our coreligionists, by such reliable observers of the contemporary scene as Glazer, Herberg, Sklare and others, seems to point up the one unequivocal fact that the motivations currently operative among American Jews are hardly, if at all, rooted in any philosophical let alone theological choices. The identification of Jews today as a "religious" community is no more than an effective "accommodation" to the general institutional pattern of the American way of life. Thereby, American citizens—believers or atheists—are automatically pigeon-holed as members of one of the three religious sub-cultures. In actuality however, what prevails among American Jews is only a new self-acceptance as part of a "social" group and a healthy, affirmative urge for its survival. It is this elemental sentiment which has fostered the program of establishing and supporting the many forms and institutions considered requisite and normal for such status and continuity. But both the program and any subsequent quest for its rationale are being conducted by and large within a sociological frame of reference. The superimposition upon this largely social process of any halo of philosophical or theological decision, conditioned or deliberate, seems at present to be a judgment unwarranted by the data on hand.

IN FACT, THE ESSENCE of the behavioral and thought patterns of American Jewry fits most appropriately into the general climate of America as a whole. The very ethos of this land is still a-theological. It is basically activist and pragmatic, with an overtone of distrust for doctrine or ideology. Inwardness and speculation have rarely been advanced as primary American virtues. The frontiers were conquered and pushed back by doing. There was little time or opportunity, except for the clergy, for metaphysical theorizing. In so many ways that spirit of the frontier is still with us.

More important for our consideration is the fact that it was a productive and successful way of living. What greater proof do we need than the higher and higher standards of comfort ever given to any citizenry in the history of human affairs. And this was only the beginning. That there were innumerable human problems to cope with, did not faze many. They would be faced boldly and confidently, with the unshakable conviction that they could and would be solved in the American way by doing and more doing—by greater production, bigger machines and more ingenious gadgets. This optimism of modern man has been summed up pithily by the great scholar Gilbert Murray, in his classical work, *Five Stages of Greek Religion*. He writes:

> On us the power of the material world has through our very mastery of it and the dependence which results from the mastery, both inwardly and outwardly increased its hold. Capta ferum victorem cepit! We have taken possession of it and now we cannot move without it.

As a consequence, Professor Murray concludes,

> apart from certain religious movements, the enlightened modern reformer if confronted with some ordinary complex of misery and wickedness instinctively proposes to cure it by higher wages, better food, more comfort and leisure; to make people comfortable and trust to their becoming good.

The axiom of *wie es sich christelt, so juedelt es sich* is again applicable. The great disillusionment confronting American Jewry as it saw its great ideals smashed and trod underfoot was sensed by such sensitive thinkers as the Heschels, the Herbergs and the Fackenheims. But they stood alone. In the mass, this spiritual void was not seen as an affliction whose healing must be sought in a renewal of man's soul. The prescription was typically activistic not contemplative. There was so much to do! The ubiquitous flow to the suburbs, the population shift from one part of the country to another called for the establishment of new communities. These, moreover, needed the transplantation and creation of institutional forms and structures, especially in response to peer-group pressure and status. Thus, being active, holding office, carrying communal responsibility, serving one's fellowman and working for a worthwhile cause —these were their own excuse for being. In this way organizational activity and movement were quickly and easily transposed into the key of philosophical direction.

Of course, the deeper cultural and spiritual ills besetting the Jewish community had not been drastically alleviated. Bigger budgets and bigger building could not speak to the human heart. Nor could the gnawing pain of the inner man be eliminated merely by refusing to ackowledge his existence. But there was greater identification with Jewish life and greater activity in association with its institutions. Jewishness began to take the place of Judaism. A psychological, sociological and historical rationale became the successor to a sacred theology. And the life of good deeds the shadowy reflection of the life of the *mitzvah*. (The difference between these two sets of ideas is unequivocally clear. The former is secular in origin and man-centered in purpose; the latter is religious in origin and God-centered in purpose—though man is the inescapable beneficiary.) At the risk of being inappropriately facetious, one must point out that, the similarity in form or function notwithstanding, Jewishness is no more Judaism, a rationale no more theology, and a good deed no more a *mitzvah* than a trumpet is a *shofar*. The term *mitzvah*, unless used merely as a loose figure of speech, must certainly invoke a *m'tzaveh*, the divine Commander. Without this religious direction an act, as Professor Heschel has emphasized, may be crowned as good but not as sacred or holy.

If these findings are correct and the "religious" life of the American and Jewish communities are largely *pro forma*, can one genuinely expect a renewal of theological interest, let alone an acceptance of Covenant? The very categories indispensable to such a relationship—Living God, Commandment (even as *Gesetz*), its converse Sin, and the like—seem utterly absent from the active thought patterns in the American community. A few statistical citations from Will Herberg's "must" book, *Protestant, Catholic and Jew,* prove most edifying. One is, for example, a little surprised to discover that most Americans, over 95% of them, do believe in God. A majority of them also regard religion as exceedingly important. But more surprising is the datum that more than half of the same respondents admitted that in such vital areas of decision as business or politics "their religious beliefs had no real effect on their ideas or conduct." In another test, about 80% of those questioned were of the opinion that even under divine scrutiny, their lives would stand up fairly well. Over 50% in fact insisted that "they were . . . following the rule of loving one's neighbor as oneself all the way." Obviously, there is not the actualization in life of the role of the Living God nor even an acknowledgment in this self-image of a sense of guilt or a reflected unworthiness. It is as if Frank Gibney's *The Operators,* which, to quote a review in the New York *Times,* exposes a society that "protects the corruption it professes to condemn and secretly applauds the by-passing of fesses to embrace"—it is as if this book the moral and ethical precepts it pro- were a documentary on another planet.

II

THE SOURCE of this pallid religion as well as this naive and self-righteous appraisal might well be sought in the events of recent history. The emphasis on the tragic and the absurd in the human predicament and the consequent readmission of God into human affairs did not come to the fore in Western thought until about the end of World War I—and then only in Europe. The theme gained momentum during the deceptive lull preceding the whirlwind of World War II and then exploded into a universal language of the continental literati soon thereafter.

Americans, on the other hand, participated but slightly in this agonizing spiritual odyssey and intellectual "new look." They had little call to do so. America had not known the desolation of war or the cynicism of deceit and betrayal. Her sacrifices had been major in blood, sweat, tears and taxes. But her rich soil remained unravished and her wheat plains and forests unscorched. Disease and hunger had not stalked her borders nor had her cities suffered the hellish torment of buzzbombs and blitzkriegs. Even the specter of death had touched her sons and daughters only at a distance. In addition, America had recovered with remarkable resilience from the staggering blows of Depression and war. Despite the Himalayan problems, even of conversion of both men and machines to peace-time pursuits, the United States emerged after World War II as the most powerful and prosperous nation in the world. (Only most recently has the Soviet Union been regarded as a threatening competitor.) On the whole, therefore, our lot has been a good one. Fortune seemed to have smiled continuously upon us. It began to seem reasonable to assume that all this was probably part of our destiny or our rightful desert. In any event, whatever the rationalization, such favorable conditions are seldom father to existential concerns.

A normal share of such self-esteem and pride could similarly be anticipated among our own Jewish people. We were shaken up for a while in the Thirties by the swelling "wave of the future" which, in an unholy alliance of the forces of reaction and bigotry, threatened to engulf us. The wave, however, soon brooke on the dikes of patriotism, unity and freedom. Except for the expected ebb and flow of the forces of hatemongering, these enemies of the different have not really grown to any eminent stature since. Moreover, the Jewish community participated fully in the struggle against totalitarianism of all shades and with the rest of the citizenry felt it rightfully and deservedly shared in the fruits of victory, namely America's enhanced status, affluence and influence throughout the world as the moral and political spokesman of democracy. American Jewry too, by associated glory, could now emerge as a voice and as a power to be reckoned with around the negotiation table of international Jewish affairs.

True, hardly a Jewish family had escaped the ravages of the Hitlerian holocaust. But its sharp edges had been blunted by time and space. At the beginning the early rumors, whispers, even reports were hardly given credence even by Jews. More than one responsible leader dismissed them as so many "atrocity" stories. Discrimination, pogroms, even interment—these were "old hat" and were bound to evaporate. But slave labor, gas chambers, lamp shades and soap —these were incredibly beyond the grasp of the human mind. Man's bestiality could never descend to such vile depths! In addition, a vast ocean separated us from tragedy and evil, so that for most of us the impact was second and third hand. Most important, when the demoniac ugliness of the Nazi horror was fully unveiled American Jewry was in a providential position to react with an unprecedented outpouring of heart and hand. Heroic efforts were exerted to salvage the shattered and tattered remnants of the catastrophe. Similarly, the courageous actions of American Jewish leadership were a major contribution to the very establishment and sustenance of the State of Israel.

THE OVERWHELMING SUCCESS of these undertakings served to dull any possible feelings of unfulfilled obligation or guilt. Everything conceivable had been done as soon as the task became starkly clear. Moreover, the job was well done and had instilled the American Jew with a greater self-assurance of both identity and purpose. He was now an equal partner in the family of the Jewish people. He had demonstrated an exciting maturity, as if he had risen to responsibility overnight in order to meet the crisis. His home-grown leadership too had exhibited talents of wisdom, astuteness and dedication. And throughout the land there was a buzzing and a booming—organizationally. Jewish life did seem creative and meaningful. American Judaism would help carry on the chain of tradition.

But there is one more piece of data: Jews had just witnessed the most serious challenge to its ancient faith in a God of justice and mercy in all of its history. A third of their brothers and sisters had been wiped out. Yet throughout this bloodbath not only had the world stood silently by the blood of its brothers,

A-THEOLOGICAL JUDAISM OF THE AMERICAN COMMUNITY 149

even more challenging—God had been silent. Nevertheless, the seismograph of American Jewry's spiritual and intellectual equilibrium registered no earth-shaking trauma. Few stormed the gates of heaven in Abrahamitic protest: "Shall the Judge of the whole earth not do justice?" (Gen. 18:26). Few lamented in the tortured accents of a Jeremiah: "Why hast Thou smitten us, and there is no healing for us? We looked for peace, but no good came; And for a time of healing, and behold terror" (Jer. 4:18). Despite the times that "tried men's souls," no epic was inspired to immortalize the agony of a people, nor any gripping penitential prayers to lend tongue to its grief. Was it that the tragedy was too great to be encompassed even by the creative human heart? Or had we searched our souls for ultimate answers, only to find them wanting?

Perhaps the more authentic answer should be that we were no longer posing ultimate questions. We were seeking our solutions to human tragedy, no matter what its proportions, within the frame of social forces definable by man's own relative understanding. For that reason we have striven not for a new theology but for a new and sober rationale. The former, as a quest after ultimate wisdom might, as in the past, at least have had the saving merit of transmuting suffering into an ennobling, purging experience, spurring the Jew on to continued spiritual and intellectual creativity. The latter, despite—or perhaps because of—its earth-chained sobriety, has not seemed to have any similar quickening effect.

The conviction therefore grows that American Jewry did not refuse to accept the theological formulations of the past because they were built on systems of thought alien to the Jew. One is moved to conclude that they were not at all rejected; they didn't even get an open hearing. American Jews were tone-deaf to any theological thesis. This immunity, moreover, found support not alone, as said, in the world of facts pervading the American Jewish way of life, but also in the world of letters from which the American Jew drew his intellectual and spiritual sustenance.

III

A CURSORY SAMPLING of a representative Jewish literature of recent times reveals a plethora of pertinent discussion on such lively issues as Anti-Semitism, Jewish Education, Judaism and Democracy, Jewish Contributions, The Family, The Synagogue and the like. Less often, but frequently enough, there are moving messages built around Jewish alienation and acculturation, the wide-spread neglect of Jewish observance and the diminishing centrality of ethical or moral values. Whatever their content, however, one rarely heard the unequivocal echoes, in either tone or terminology, of the ancient tradition whose language was forthrightly religious and uncompromisingly God-oriented. For the Prophet and Sage, murder was sinful, exploitation a transgression and immorality an abomination because not man's but God's authority had been defied. For them, *chet* was no mere etymological derivative of the verb "to miss the mark." It was a reality, a breach in the dialogue of the divine-human encounter.

In the contemporary process of transvaluation, however, a new rationale had been born. Personal growth and fulfilment, creative survival, historical identity, ritual as "forgotten language," universal values, national mission—these were the new idioms in its vocabulary, new both in form and content. Well therefore might it be said that the vanquished had submerged the victorious. For while secular organizations were obviously giving way to religious institutions, secular thought was still reigning supreme.

In fact, it even penetrated the holy of holies and compelled any residue of classical Jewish thought to fall into line. Man continued to be depicted in American Judaism as the shining crown of creation, about whom Scripture itself testified, "And God made man in His own image" (Gen. 1:27), and "Thou hast had him little less than the angels" (Ps. 8:6). But the duplicity and frailty that have also made up his nature were skipped over quickly. Slight heed was paid to kindred texts which added more somber hues to this divine masterpiece, such as, "For the inclination of man's heart is evil from his very youth" (Gen. 8:21), or "Cause us to rejoice even as many days as those wherein thou hast afflicted us, the years wherein we have seen unhappiness" (Ps. 90:15). Little regard too was given to the striking lesson regarding human nature obviously implicit in the repeated contraposition in the Biblical text of God's eternal demand and man's perennial default, especially when describing some of the most crucial moments in history. Thus for example, the first act in the high drama of Creation closes with a scene of treachery and fratricide. The hosannahs of Exodus are soon lost in the bitter murmurs of ungrateful dissension and failure of nerve. Even the *tremens tremendum* of Revelation quickly evaporates under the heat of the lustful and intoxicating dance round the Golden Calf. But this significant phenomenon was underplayed.

Repeated reference was made to the Talmudic dictum that man was a "partner to the Holy One, blessed Be He, in the acts of Creation." What was omitted was the fact that the Sages would have been the first to insist simultaneously that his was only a junior partnership. Moreover they would have considered it a blasphemy to offer God the vice-presidency. Yet in the idea of Messianism, God's role was almost totally eliminated. That which had classically been a cosmic mystery in whose denouement man's role was at best only synergic, was transformed by our contemporary spiritual spokesmen into a reformistic socio-economic process, a historical myth of progress whose evolutionary fulfilment was inevitably and entirely in the hands of man. Moreover, the apocalyptic features of the "end of days" had been almost entirely blacked out. The prophet Amos' Day of the Lord (8:9), Zephaniah's Day of Wrath (1:15, 16), Malachi's Day of Judgment (3:19), or Ezekiel's final showdown with Gog in the land of Magog (Ch. 28 ff), were seldom allowed to dull the glorious dream of ultimate vindication.

THE CONCEPT of Exile too, so central to classical Jewish thought, was denuded. More significant than its partial distortion into purely a socio-political state of physical uprootedness, more serious than the subtle substitution of the word Diaspora, with all its secular implications, was the almost total elimination of its religious connotation as utter alienation from the Source of all sanctity. The easy, optimistic faith in the forgiving God threw into the shadows the stern, prophetic reality of *Hestar Panim,* of a God withdrawn in deliberate Self-Concealment. *"Il me pardonerra,"* insisted the modern Heines, *"c'est son métier."*

It is true that Judaism has historically been *mitzvah*-centered. Nevertheless *mitzvah* always implied *averah* as well. Classically, in fact, the Scriptural prohibitions of "Thou shalt not" exceeded in number the mandates of "Thou shalt." But more significant is the observation that since Talmudic times there has been an inescapable stress on at least the basic ruling principles of religious faith. Because of the challenges from without, to believe became crucial for the Jew. Moreover, in order to safeguard the integrity of these principles, there was built into the very fabric of Jewish theology the saving balance of dialectical tension. Man had both a *yetzer tov* and a *yetzer ra*. Evil passions were second nature to man, yet with God's grace he could conquer and discipline them and even convert the stumbling block into a stepping stone towards greater nobility and piety. God was both the God of justice and of mercy. He destroyed the wicked utterly yet waited patiently for their repentance until the very day of their death. Israel had been "driven from His Father's table," yet the covenantal relationship was irrevocable.

American Judaism on the other hand has not only deemphasized the theological but also upset this delicate balance. The net result has been a distorted image—even for the believer. First it insisted that doing, for whatever the reason, was more important than believing. Then it excised the realistic though harsh emphases in Jewish belief on the tragic as well as the sanguine, on the paradoxical as well as the rational. As a result, American Judaism became smooth, sober, shallow and uninspiring.

Might it be pointed out parenthetically that nowhere is this charge more painfully documented than in the High Holyday service. Despite the "full houses," no responsible religious leader will gainsay the lack of any intensive or profound personal involvement on the part of those who attend. The congregants are by and large observers not participants, auditors not worshippers. Many proposals have been offered to remedy this prayerless situation. The introduction of more ritual and symbolism, of more responsive reading, of more community singing, the curtailment of the service, a greater intellectual emphasis through study or discussion, more interpretation of prayers—are only some of the suggestions, made in all seriousness. Yet the prescriptions seem of little avail. It could not be otherwise. The illness is religious in origin, yet the cure proffered is technical. The essence of the High Holyday theme is self-examination, an acknowledgment of man's individual and Israel's collective guilt before God and their common need for divine forgiveness. With the absence of any clear faith in a "personal" God to whom men are ultimately accountable, without an unequivocal commitment to the reality of sin and the salvational need for atonement—how gripping or dialogic can such a service be, religiously?

IV

AMERICAN JEWRY desperately needs religious conviction. A Covenant-theology would furnish a sense of rootage in the past, a sense of destiny about the future and a sense of creative urgency regarding the present. Revelation, even as Buberian Covenant, without the content of a binding law, would still be a giant's leap forward and serve as a bridge of communion between man and God. How much more commanding would be an acceptance of Revelation as Rosenzweig saw it, as the covenant of eternal law betwen the Eternal God and His eternal people. In this way, American Jewry would gain the minimal requirements indispensable to a viable and directionful community, namely, a common set of high beliefs and practices, a common sense of memory and destiny. Around these could be rallied the loyalties of a people, whose whole history bespeaks purpose and mission.

For the moment, however, such a desideratum seems wishful thinking. As stated previously, the very conditions precedent are missing, especially the most fundamental, a faith—not just in more faith, nor even in God, but in the Living God of Israel. But such faith is not manufactured syntheticaly. It is cultivated and grows organically, and as yet the soil is arid and unyielding. Years of arduous soil-breaking are required before such a spiritual harvest can even be expected.

The best proof for such a prognosis can be adduced from the religious climate pervading the campuses of this land. The Jewish college students are the pace-setters of our tomorrow. Yet most of them, except for the minority who are already committed to some "oxy" or "ism" are not prepared to affirm honestly a faith in a "personal" God who is not alone the Creator and God of Nature but the Redeemer and God of History. They are even less open to the Biblical claim central to a Covenant-theology that at Sinai there occurred the most religiously radical and intellectually scandalous event in all of human history, that at the 'Sinaitic stand" there was a sanctifying moment of supreme meeting between man and God, Israel and the Ever-Present.

That there has been a remarkable and unprecedented resurgence among all youth of a genuine interest in religion and religious experience is beyond contradiction. High Holyday services are well attended and discussion on religious topics is excitingly pursued as peace and politics were in previous generations. Countless more young people are actually reading and examining basic Judaic sources. The world and thought of a Buber, a Rosenzweig, a Heschel, a Herberg and even the more mystical Rav Kuk are becoming increasingly familiar to both the undergraduate, graduate and faculty members of the academic family. But interest is not commitment and study is not faith. A vast intellectual and spiritual chasm separates the two.

There is every reason to believe that, well-bruited revivals not-withstanding, the adult picture is currently not much different. Despite the upsurge in identification and affiliation, religious loyalty and practices are still probably "a mile wide and less than an inch thick." How does one therefore generate a desire for crisis-theology if, except among the rare Cohens, Fackenheims and Herbergs, there is neither an express need for theology nor an acknowledgment of any spiritual crisis? "Religion as usual —only more so" seems the popular slogan of the day.

V

THE ONE SOURCE of hope seems, paradoxically, to stem from the very sterility of the soil. Perhaps it may generate its own power of fructification. The very speed of our What-Makes-Sammy-Run society, and the by-products of ennui and anomie of the affluent society, are beginning to irritate those penultimate "religious" questions which psychologically seem to precede the ultimate ones. Robert Hutchins, in his stimuating book *Conflict in Education*, affirmed that people have already begun to do this very thing. They ask pointedly "whether a longer life is necessarily a good thing, if that life is aimless, whether improvement in the material conditions of existence can solve the fundamental problems of existence, whether . . . science and technology can give us the wisdom to use the power they have brought us for the benefit rather than the destruction of mankind." Such challenges directed into spiritual channels might hopefully bring to realization at least the first part of the prophecy:

> Behold the days come, saith the Lord,
>   That I will send a famine in the land,
> Not a famine of bread, nor a thirst of water,
> But of hearing the words of the Lord. (Amos 8:11)

The true dynamic must, however, be generated from within. An intellectual revolution must be created in the very psyche of American Jewry. Its pride in its total self-sufficiency may be a refreshing and reassuring contrast to the grovelling posture of yesteryear. Its overweaning excesses are spiritually disastrous. For, as the Talmud points out, there can then be no *lebensraum* for Divinity. Moreover, the contemporary imbalance in theological perspective too needs to be corrected. Not only man's conviction that he is fully competent to recognize and achieve the good must be underscored. He must also be reminded of the existential fact that he possesses a rare genius for destruction, that the "imp of perversity" is most clever in concealing from him the strength of his own evil motivations, even disguising the evil intent in the pure garb of the good deed. For only in both do we have the whole of man.

The religious implications of these life-facts should also be clearly drawn. Man, Judaism claims, cannot be morally or spiritually autarchic. He cannot, entirely on his own powers, know and do the right. He does need divine guidance in all things. Evil can be thwarted only by conforming both the act and its intent to the demand of the Divine will, which in turn blesses them with His divine favor. Admittedly this is most difficult of apprehension, let alone of achievement. Yet there seems to be no other alternative road.

In such a revolution, Jewish education too must undergo a radical examination in both the area of goals and content. It is after all one of society's most significant and most effective laboratories of citizenship training and social change. In yesterday's "religious milieu," where religious truths were held to be self-evident, there may have been little need to teach them. They could be absorbed almost osmotically through the very pores of one's daily Jewish experience. Today, however, they are strange and even "foreign" and must with deliberate effort be made familiar and kindred to the total Jewish heritage. But as presently constituted, the Jewish schools, in their primary stress, are Jewish "vocational" institutions, putting their major concentration on the transmission of basic facts and necessary skills. An average graduate, at the end of his academic peregrinations, will at best possess a substantial backlog of technical "know-how" for his formal participation in institutional life and even a fundamental command of original texts. All too meager, however, will be his theological understanding which, even in limited and elementary measure, can by its profound insight regarding God, Man and the Universe provide substance, direction and purpose to his total life.

THESE VAST religious changes will not, however, come overnight. Even if they did it might not be healthy. For Judaism has historically looked with deep qualms upon the phenomena of conversions or revivalism in the mass. Affirmative faith in the Living God, as both belief and reliance, is so uniquely individualistic. Its authentic attainment comes only after years of trial and experience. For no man knows the source of its being, or even the nature of its transmission, so that its elixir might be distilled and shared bountifully with others. Yet its constancy and universality bears witness to its essentiality for the children of men.

American Jewry, however, now stands only with the child, Abraham, who, as the Midrash depicts, first had to strive throughout the long cycle of the day and night before he was prepared to acknowledge the living reality of the One God. Much time may no doubt have to elapse before, like Abraham the mature man, it will hear and accept the divine call, "And be ye a blessing." Even thereafter, the road to the foot of Sinai is long and demanding.

Whether history can be telescoped and the spiritual odyssey of a people speeded up is certainly speculative. For a community like a person seems to move at its own inexorable pace. Nevertheless, a strong faith and a determined confidence in American Jewry's potential for greatness must characterize the patient vigil for the day of decision. Until then, the remnant of the "committed community," whose members in a free process of self-selection stand as sentinels of the Tradition, shall no doubt continue, as in the past, to carry the responsibility for Jewish continuity and creativity.

The Ordination of Women

ROBERT GORDIS

The issue of the ordination of women for the rabbinate, which has stirred a furor in American Jewry, has dimensions that go far beyond narrow religious concerns. The swirling controversy that has raged around the question makes it clear that there are far-reaching social and cultural implications, as well as deeply ingrained psychological attitudes, both on the conscious and the unconscious level.

Nevertheless, for those who value the Jewish religious tradition and grant it authority in their lives — and essentially it is only for them that the issue is significant — the broader social, ethical, and cultural aspects of the ordination of women enter into the picture only *after* the religious element has been dealt with.

Opponents of women's ordination have continued to proclaim that "the Halakhah is opposed to the ordination of women." Relying on the reiteration of the formula, they have rarely stooped to presenting evidence. Instead they have nurtured the implication that the material is too recondite and complicated for examination by generally intelligent laymen. They have insisted that it can be fathomed only by a handful of Halakhic experts, and whoever disagrees with their conclusions is, by definition, not a Halakhic expert!

This tactic is one more striking illustration of a phenomenon characteristic of contemporary Jewish life — the existence of a cultural, social, and ethical lag 20 or 30 years behind society at large. Thus, precisely at a time when the doctrine of papal infallibility has encountered increasing opposition in Roman Catholic circles, the idea of rabbinic infallibility has become an increasingly popular doctrine in the Jewish religious community: "The law is thus and so because we say so." The old Talmudic principle *neitei sepher veneheze*, "Let us take the book and see,"[1] is largely ignored. Instead, there are pronouncements *ex cathedra* handed down in the name of an august authority who rarely deigns to disclose the basis for his judgment. In the past, the Talmud encouraged students and colleagues to disagree with their master so that the truth might emerge. Today, those who have had the temerity to question these august judgments are not being refuted but are attacked as lacking in respect for the Torah and in deference for its only true expositors.

The sincerity of those opposed to rabbinic ordination for women is not being questioned — only their right to arrogate to themselves the sole authority to decide the issue by fiat rather than by presentation of evidence. Actually, when the contention "The ordination of women is forbidden by the Halakhah" is examined in the light of the evidence, it becomes clear that the absolute judgments pronounced on the subject bear an uncanny resemblance to the Emperor's "new clothes" in Hans Christian Andersen's tale.

A preliminary observation is in order: rabbis today bear the oldest honorific designation in continuous use in human history. The title "rabbi" is far older than any honorary degree or academic distinction in vogue today.

At the same time, the rabbinate represents virtually a new calling, since the functions designated by this ancient title have undergone a far-reaching transformation. The term "rabbi" is an old label on a bottle of new wine. Elsewhere I have attempted to trace the five principal stages in the rabbinate from Talmudic times to the present, and the end of the development of the office is not yet in sight.[2] The modern rabbi, for good or for ill, and perhaps for good *and* for ill, is a *novum* in Jewish experience. It is therefore not at all astonishing that the subject of the ordination of women is not discussed in traditional sources, because past generations never contemplated the possibility. To offer an extreme analogy, nowhere do we encounter a discussion whether Martians are obligated to put on *Tefillin* or are required to observe the Noahide laws.

In the absence of any direct testimony on the subject, opponents of the ordination of women have had recourse to various rabbinic passages from which they have sought to draw inferences of their own, a procedure that is entirely legitimate. We need, however, to examine these passages in detail and discover whether in fact they have any bearing upon the issue. It is not without significance that, during the relatively brief history that the question has been actively discussed, many of the passages that were originally advanced with great assurance have now been tacitly abandoned and new texts offered instead.

ROBERT GORDIS, *editor of* Judaism, *is Professor of Bible and Rapaport Professor in the Philosophies of Religion at the Jewish Theological Seminary.*

Some arguments against ordination are homiletic rather than Halakhic in character. Thus one rabbinic scholar cited the Mishnah, "*Hakol šōḥatin ûsěḥitátán kěšērah ḥûṣ meḥērēš šōteh veqátán*," "Everyone is eligible to slaughter an animal, except a deaf mute, an insane person, or a minor."[3] This passage, it was argued, proves that the Rabbis permitted a woman to be a *shoḥet* but not a rabbi. The contention scarcely requires refutation.

One congregational rabbi in a letter to an Anglo-Jewish weekly declared, "The Halakhah is opposed to women's ordination," and then cited a Talmudic reference, *Sotah* 20a. While the uninformed reader might imagine that the text bears upon the subject under discussion, it actually deals with the biblical law regarding the ordeal undergone by a woman accused by her husband of adultery (Numbers, chapter 5).

In this connection, the Talmud quotes two diametrically opposed opinions of Mishnaic teachers: "On the basis of what has been said above, Ben Azzai says, 'A man is required to teach Torah to his daughter (so that if she should ever have occasion to undergo the ordeal of the accused wife, she would know that any merit she possesses would create a suspension of punishment for her).' Rabbi Eliezer says, 'Whoever teaches his daughter the Torah is teaching her obscenity (because from the Torah she would learn how to circumvent the law and hide her immorality).'"

Evidently, the writer of the letter wishes to infer from Rabbi Eliezer's statement that since it is forbidden to teach Torah to a girl, she obviously cannot be ordained as a rabbi. Even this view, however, is the opinion of only one sage and is contradicted in the very same passage by the view of another. What is more, Rabbi Eliezer was one of the most conservative and strong-willed of the scholars, who held highly individual views. Time and again, the vast majority of his colleagues did not hesitate to overrule his judgment, as in the famous case of the "Stove of Achnai" in *Baba Metzia* 59b. So, too, while virtually all his colleagues interpreted the famous phrase "an eye for an eye" in Exodus 21:24 to mean that monetary compensation is to be given for an injury, Rabbi Eliezer took the biblical phrase literally.[4]

Undoubtedly, in the Middle Ages, the restrictive opinion of Rabbi Eliezer regarding the education of women was adopted by some later authorities. However, I would be interested to learn whether the American rabbi would operate on the theory that the teaching of Torah to women is prohibited in the case of his own daughters and whether he forbids girls to be enrolled in his Hebrew school.

It may be added that the Talmud nowhere condemns Rabbi Hananya ben Teradyon for giving his daughter Beruriah an intensive education in the Written and the Oral Torah. On the contrary, as the wife of Rabbi Meir, her opinions are cited with respect and sometimes even prevail over the views of her male colleagues.[5]

Another proof-text has been found in Maimonides' Code, *Mishneh Torah*, where he repeats the substance of a Tannaitic midrash. Among the biblical laws regarding the qualifications of a king, the provision is included: "You may indeed set as king over you him whom the Lord your God will choose. One from among your brethren you shall set as king over you; you may not put a foreigner over you who is not your brother."[6] The *Sifre* comments: "A king, not a queen,"[7] a statement which Maimonides rephrases: "Only males may serve as monarchs."[8]

In view of an aggadic statement comparing rabbis to kings,[9] Maimonides' judgment that women cannot be kings is now used to declare them ineligible to serve as rabbis!

It is difficult to believe that this aggadic passage is being seriously offered for deciding the Halakhah. But if it is being advanced seriously, it may be pointed out that the Pharisees, who were the predecessors of the Tannaim in the fashioning of traditional Judaism, had no difficulty in accepting Shelom-Zion (Salome Alexandria), the widow of King Alexander Jannaeus, as legitimate queen during the Second Temple (76-67 BCE). Indeed, they praised her friendly relations with Simeon ben Shetah and her adherence to Pharisaic norms.[10] Similarly, in the first century of the Common Era, when the royal house of Adiabene adopted Judaism, Queen Helene is praised for her piety and philanthropy, and no word of censure is raised against her rule, though, to be sure, she may have sat on the throne with her husband King Monobaz.[11]

The argument is raised that the laws of *niddah* (the separation which the Halakhah enjoins for the period before, during, and after menstruation), would effectively preclude a woman's officiating as a rabbi. It may be granted that this consideration would be effective in a right-wing community of Hasidim, where all regulations of *niddah* are punctiliously observed and where women in general have no social contact with men outside their immediate families. Exclusive of these enclaves, there is scant evidence that the social segregation of women during their menstrual periods is observed, even in Orthodox circles.

I worship in an Orthodox synagogue that is militant in its adherence to Orthodox interpretation of Halakhah and is attended by very large numbers of women. After a decade, I have yet to encounter one instance where a woman refrained from shaking hands with a man who extended his hand in greeting. Moreover, many, if not most, of these women, young and old, are gainfully employed or attend college or are active in the public sector. I doubt whether even those who observe the regulations regarding the *mikveh* adhere to the other traditional prohibitions in their daily lives. I am not discussing the rationale of the laws of *niddah*;[12] I am simply noting the fact that in Conservative (and most Orthodox) practice these bans on social intercourse play no part. On the other hand, if a woman rabbi wished to observe these prohibitions, she would be as free to do so in the rabbinate as in any other calling.

We now turn to what is generally recognized as the strongest Halakhic argument against the ordination of women — the contention that the traditional Halakhah exempted women from the obligation (*ḥiyyubh*) of prayer. This exemption in turn is buttressed by the Talmudic principle that "women are free from commandments that must traditionally be performed at specific times" (*mitzvot aseh šehazman gerama*).

Before examining the implications that are being drawn from this rule, it should be noted that the principle was far from universally applied. Always there were exceptions. Time-bound obligations, such as the kindling of Sabbath and festival lights, hearing the *shofar* on Rosh Hashanah, and the blessing of the *lulav* (four species) on Sukkot were held to be obligatory for women. So, too, rabbinic law commanded women as well as men to hear the reading of the *megillah* on Purim, "since they, too, were involved in that miracle of salvation."[13] It is therefore a reasonable conclusion that the principle that women were excused from the obligation to observe *mitzvot* having a specific time-frame is a generalization from a few specific instances and not a universally binding rule.[14] In other words, the Gemara, as is often the case, observing a series of concrete statements of the Mishnah on different subjects, seeks to evolve an underlying principle to cover them all. The generalization, incidentally, may or may not have been in the minds of the authors of the various passages in the Mishnah.

In our case, the rule is clearly *descriptive* and not *prescriptive*, as the many exceptions make clear.[15] The application of this rule to women's prayer is, therefore, a rationalization after the fact rather than a reason for its enactment. Apologetics aside, the retention of this rule is an expression of the inferior status of women and of their segregation from public life.[16]

Nor is this all. The exemption of women from the obligation (*mitzvah*) of prayer was justified on the ground that the manifold tasks devolving upon them as homemakers made it impossible for them to observe prayer and other time-bound obligations at the specified hour. The contention may have had a measure of validity in the past, when a woman's household duties were onerous and unlimited; it clearly has little justification today. In this age of labor-saving devices, a woman who is a homemaker, even if she takes care of a family, has at least as much free time available as her husband, who is a worker, a businessman, or a professional engaged in his occupation all day long. As for the woman who is gainfully employed outside the home, she is in exactly the same position as her male counterpart.

The American historian James Harvey Robinson once said that every event in history has a good reason and a real reason. In the case of the *mitzvah* of prayer for women and their exclusion from the *minyan*, the truth is that the real reason is not good and the good reason is not real.

Let us grant that the Talmudic principle cited above was originally established by the Sages out of a sense of genuine compassion for women, whose working day coincided with all their waking hours, with virtually no leisure at all. It would be ironic to invoke this principle, which the Sages established out of consideration for women in the past, to serve as a basis for discrimination against them in the present. However, even if all these considerations are brushed aside and the principle maintained that "women are exempt from the obligation of prayer," its bearing upon on the ordination of women as rabbis is tenuous in the extreme. The major functions of the modern rabbi — preaching, teaching, conducting funeral services, serving as *mesadder kiddushin* ("officiant" at marriage ceremonies), personal counselling, and adult education — are none of them prohibited by extant rabbinic sources.

The speciousness of the argument becomes clear when it is recalled that it is the cantor and not the rabbi who is the *shaliaḥ ṣibbur* (the messenger of the congregation). The rabbi may read some prayers in English or supplement the service, but the function of leading the congregation in prayer is essentially that of the cantor or laymen.

One may also question the logic of the contention that one who is not *obligated* to pray cannot fulfill the function for one who is. Obviously, a woman is not *forbidden* to pray, and if we were to accept the principle that a pray-er can exempt the non-pray-er, there would be no logical ground for denying this to the woman. When a fire breaks out in a building, the fireman is obligated by his occupation to rush in and save the life of a child. The general citizen has no such obligation, but he is not *prohibited* from leaping into the building and saving the child. *Meʿikkara dedina pirkhah*, "the original assumption is dubious."

The doctrine that the *shaliaḥ ṣibbur* must be a person obligated to pray is subject to challenge from another direction as well. According to the Halakhah, the *shaliaḥ ṣibbur* conducting a service is fulfilling the obligations for the worshippers who cannot pray for themselves. The provision stems from a time, before the invention of printing, when prayerbooks were scarce, so that many Jews could not pray on their own. So, too, the law had in mind pious and observant Jews who, because of the pressures of their work, were unable to read their prayers at the proper time. Today the situation is totally different. Prayerbooks are available everywhere. The majority of Jews who do not engage in prayer are not prevented by preoccupation but by indifference. To deprive a community of the service of a woman rabbi for these anachronistic reasons certainly argues a strange scale of values.

Another objection, more germane to our theme, has also been raised. Since according to rabbinic law, women are ineligible to serve as witnesses, a woman rabbi would be incapable of signing as an *edh* on a *ketubbah*. It is true that the Halakhah today excludes women as witnesses and places them on a par with minors and deaf-mutes with regard to testifying before a religious court.[17] The issue needs further analysis.

For many, if not for most people today, the principle of the exclusion of women as witnesses is morally questionable. In a society where women were sheltered and had little experience or contact with the world at large, there might perhaps have been some basis for regarding their testimony as inexpert and therefore inadmissible. To defend such a principle today is, for most people, morally repugnant and sexist. To bring the Halakhah in this respect into conformity with our ethical standards constitutes part of the unfinished business of contemporary Judaism. That the Halakhah in the past reflected the inferior status of women in a society where they played no role in general society is understandable; for modern Halakhah to perpetuate this status in a society where women participate in all areas of life is unconscionable. It is noteworthy that even in Israel, where right-wing religious authorities have a virtual monopoly in many areas of Israeli life, the exclusion of women as witnesses in the secular courts has not been proposed.

But even before the age-old doctrine of the inadmissibility of women as witnesses is modified, there is a striking precedent in Halakhah for making an exception for a woman rabbi acting as a witness at a wedding. The precedent is particularly impressive, because it occurs in an area dealing with the sanctity of the person and the inviolability of the marriage bond. If a woman's husband disappears, she is left an *agunah*, a chained wife, doomed to perpetual widowhood. The Rabbis of the Mishnah sought every conceivable method for ameliorating her tragic status. They went so far as to rule that if the woman herself had evidence that her husband had died, her unsubstantiated testimony to that effect was accepted.[18]

This ruling set aside no less than three *fundamentals in rabbinic jurisprudence*: the first, already referred to above, that a woman was ineligible as a witness; the second requirement, going back to the Bible, that two witnesses are required to establish valid testimony;[19] and the third, the rabbinic principle *adam karobh ʾetzel ʿatzmo*, "Each person is close to himself," and therefore his testimony on an issue in which he himself is involved is invalid.[20] Thus, it is clear that the Rabbis did not hesitate to modify basic legal procedures in the case of a putative *eshet ʿish* (a married woman), which represented an issue of the utmost gravity. Nevertheless, when considerations of humanity were at stake, the Rabbis were prepared to suspend the three fundamental principles out of a sense of compassion.[21] We should do no less in the interests of justice.

Strictly speaking, the entire issue of the ineligibility of women as witnesses is irrelevant to their ordination as rabbis. *There is no necessity for the rabbi, male or female, to serve as a witness at a wedding.* The rabbi's role is that of a *mesadder kiddushin*, the arranger of the marriage ceremony. Two other witnesses can be, and often are, co-opted for the *ketubbah*.

At this point the Halakhists who are opponents of the ordination of women become "sociological" and ask us to consider the position of a small community in which the rabbi is the only religious functionary. If the rabbi were a woman, she might be called upon to act as the *ḥazzan* (cantor). In the case of a marriage ceremony, she might need to serve as a witness for the *ketubbah*, especially because of the paucity of religiously observant witnesses.

The response, however, might be put as follows: The Rabbis of the Talmud *šaqedu ʿal taqqanat benot yisra'el*, "were diligent for the welfare of the daughters of Israel."[22] Surely in such special cases, where the happiness and welfare of a bride and groom are involved and they wish to be married "according to the Law of Moses and Israel," the entire thrust of the Halakhah and its underlying spirit suggest the approach to be adopted where no other proper witness is available: it is entirely appropriate that a woman, both religiously knowledgeable and observant, be recognized as a legitimate witness in special instances such as these, as happened with the Mishnaic ruling with regard to the testimony of an *agunah*.

In conclusion, it is clear that these objections, while ostensibly based on the Halakhah, are indirect at best and far-fetched at worst. In the face of major problems confronting the survival of Judaism, the role of women in contemporary society and the ethical issues involved, no Halakhic objections of substance have been adduced. *The truth is that the Halakhah neither sanctions nor forbids the ordination of women – it never contemplated the possibility.*

In the absence of clear-cut Halakhic sources against the ordination of women, opponents of the idea have advanced another argument — it is a matter of *minhag*, custom, and, as the popular saying has it, "a custom supersedes a law."[23] It is undeniable that custom plays a very important role in Jewish religious practice and is enshrined in Jewish literature; many customs are highly appealing because of the piety and ethical sensitivity they express or their colorful folk-character. It is, however, a far cry from this observation to the conclusion that *minhag qua minhag* is sacrosanct and not subject to analysis and critique. The customs, local and general, to be found in Jewish communities have different points of origin, serve diverse functions, and vary widely in their value and significance. Thus, authorities as eminent as Rabbi Solomon ibn Adret and Nahmanides opposed the practice of *kapparot* on the eve of Yom Kippur,[24] and Rabbi Joseph Karo, the author of the *Shulhan*

Arukh, called it a *minhag šetut*, a custom of folly, stupid custom.[25] In the history of Judaism, countless customs have arisen, flourished, and disappeared. To set up the *minhag* as the final arbiter is to violate the inner spirit of a religion that has produced the Talmud as a monument to rational discussion, the establishment of consensus, and the practice of justice and equity.

A study and analysis of the Halakhah throughout its history discloses two basic characteristics, which varied in importance in different periods but were never totally lacking: (a) a responsiveness to emerging religious and ethical insights; and (b) an awareness of new social, economic, political, and cultural conditions.[26] It is clear that these factors, far from being extra-Halakhic or anti-Halakhic, constitute an integral element in the Halakhic process. We have examined the passages in traditional Halakhic sources allegedly opposed to the ordination of women and have found that they neither favor nor oppose the idea. We are, therefore, not stepping outside the parameters of Halakhah in presenting the case for the admission of women to the rabbinate against the background of conditions prevalent in contemporary society in general and in the Jewish community in particular.

As the oldest living tradition in the Western world, Judaism began as a male-centered and male-dominated society, as was every other civilization up to and including our own age. It was, therefore, entirely natural — and requires neither apology nor apologetics — that women, though honored and loved, occupied a subordinate position in Jewish society. Their inferior status with regard to marriage, divorce, the levirate, inheritance, and many other aspects of life is clear and undeniable, and has been documented time and again.

Male domination was so all-pervasive that it often was unconscious. One instance will suffice. The Talmudic dicta *qol* (and *śeʿar*) *beiša ʿerwah*,[27] "A woman's voice (and hair) is sexually seductive," have their analogues in other cultures. The judgment was undoubtedly true in a society where a woman was sequestered and had no contact with any male outside her immediate family. Yet there is no corresponding statement, "A man's voice (and hair) is sexually seductive (to a woman)." But if the first statement is true, so is the second. The various regulations governing *ṣeniyut*, modesty, apply in overwhelming measure to the behavior of women.[28] Yet the virtue is surely as applicable to males as to females!

The greatness of traditional Judaism lies in the fact that, originating in the ancient world, which was overwhelmingly male-dominated, the Halakhah was able to register so much progress during Mishnaic, Talmudic, Geonic, and even medieval times toward reducing the prerogatives of the male and increasing the rights of the female. Since the law always codifies the positions attained by society at an earlier period, it is no wonder that the process of conferring full equality upon women has not been completed. This is true in secular law and not merely in the Halakhah.

Nevertheless, the progress of women toward equality has been phenomenal. In our day, women have achieved positions certainly more advanced than the law codes would indicate. Each change in the status of women has inevitably brought not merely new opportunities but also new problems in its wake. That there are changes that should not be greeted with enthusiasm may be true, but it is beside the point — the overall process of women's liberation is irreversible. It may be hindered; it cannot be halted.

Except in ultra-rightist religious groups, few women in Western society would accept *Kinder, Kirche und Küche*, "children, church, and kitchen," as representing the boundaries of their world. Since the beginning of the century, women have greatly expanded their occupational roles. In the past, the only occupations open to them outside the home were as domestic servants and governesses or, a little higher in the social scale, as nurses and school teachers. Early in this century, women came into offices as clerical workers against strong opposition, and they literally fought their way into law and medicine. The battle for women's suffrage is still vividly recalled both in the United States and abroad. These women set a process in motion that now includes such formerly unlikely fields as the army, navy, trucking, contact sports, politics, and public administration — the trajectory is not yet spent.

It is undeniable that the entrance of women into independent careers has placed new strains on relations between husbands and wives, parents and children, and on the institution of the family as a whole. When both husband and wife pursue independent careers, there is no longer a full-time homemaker available, so both partners must shoulder additional duties after completing their day at the office. This is, of course, a permanent and universal problem.

More serious difficulties may also arise. The new interests and broader social contacts of the wife bring her new stimuli and new opportunities. They may also bring in their wake new temptations and relationships that may threaten the marriage bond. If either partner is offered a better job in a new community, the unity of the household is threatened: the "long-distance marriage" with weekends together is hardly a recipe for long-term happiness. On the other hand, if one or the other partner forgoes the new opportunity, the decision is bound to be painful. Obviously, some *modus vivendi* must be achieved in each individual case, but there is a price to pay.

Nevertheless, no one seriously suggests reversing the trend — as if that were possible — by expelling women from the labor market. Instead, the path of wisdom is to seek to cope with the new conditions, to overcome the problems, and to utilize the gains for the general welfare. In life, the solution of a problem offers not total ease and peace of mind, but rather the opportunity to face new problems and register new advances.

The ordination of women represents such a step in the movement for equal rights, the consequences of which will need to be faced in due course.

When women enter the rabbinate, it will surely appear strange and even uncomfortable at the beginning, but not as strange as it would have been in 1880 or 1780, when there was no public role for women in Judaism and little more in general society. In the world of our great-grandfathers, the role of women was governed by the rabbinic interpretation of the passage in Psalms: *kol kebudah bat melekh penimah*. The verse was taken to mean, "All the glory of a king's daughter lies within [the home]."[29] To have ordained women as rabbis in an earlier age would have been obviously counter-productive, since women had only a private role in society. Hence the appearance of a woman on a pulpit would have been a sensation that would have disrupted the traditional values of communal prayer and the study of Torah.

Today the situation is radically different. Undoubtedly, there will be a process of adjustment, painful at times, and the success of the process will vary with individuals and groups. In this connection, it should be kept in mind that the issue is not that women *must* be ordained and congregations *must* accept women rabbis, but that women may be ordained and congregations should be free to accept or reject them as their rabbis.

Nor is this an artificial issue. It has been reported that of the 240 students presently enrolled in the Reform and Reconstructionist seminaries in the United States, 25 percent, or 60, are women. It is also known that many of these 60 female rabbinical students are Conservative both in theory and in practice, loyal to Jewish tradition, observing the Torah and the *mitzvot*. By excluding them from rabbinical training at the Seminary we are driving some of the most potentially valuable human resources available to us out of the movement. This impoverishment of our potential spiritual leadership is a great loss not only for Conservative Judaism, but for Judaism as a whole. For I profoundly believe, with all due recognition of the virtues and achievements of our sister movements, that it is Conservative Judaism that holds the key to a vital and meaningful Judaism in the modern day.

T he accession of women to the rabbinate will be particularly valuable in view of the shortage of dedicated and knowledgeable personnel in Jewish life. The rapid tempo of geographical and occupational mobility among American Jews has led to the decentralization of Jewish communities and the breakup of the large concentration of Jewish population into hundreds of smaller communities. Many, if not most of them, are totally bereft of competent Jewish leadership, and their survival is gravely imperiled.

In addition, there is an unmistakable movement in American Judaism today to overcome the impersonalization and mass character of our larger congregations. Many are mammoth institutions with memberships running into hundreds, even thousands, in which the individual, already stripped of much of his sense of personal worth in society at large, seeks in vain to recover a sense of identity. Differing widely in orientation, background, and interests, *minyanim*, *shtiblach*, and *havurot* have proliferated. They are united by this quest for a "do-it-yourself" Judaism with a large measure of personal participation and a warm feeling of community.

This evidence of renewed interest in Judaism deserves the enthusiasm with which it has been greeted. Yet the fact remains that the creation of small, independent groups completely unrelated to existing synagogues and therefore competitive with them is not the total solution to the problem of the survival of Judaism. The destruction of large synagogues and synagogue-centers would represent a substantial loss of the energies in the building of these institutions by dedicated men and women over many years.

Nor is this all. The creation and maintenance of well-staffed, properly graded, adequately housed Jewish schools, both on the elementary and the high school levels, requires substantial financial resources beyond the power of a *minyan*. Adequate adolescent and adult education programs also require substantial memberships and considerable funding. Attractive social and cultural programs for singles are a crying necessity today. Badly needed centers for personal counselling, particularly under religious auspices, would also be virtually impossible, if, for example, a congregation of 1,000 families were to be dissolved and in its stead 20 independent groups of 50 families apiece were to emerge.

The solution, I believe, is to be sought in the retention and the restructuring of the synagogue so that it will serve as the base for all these activities and as the source and center for smaller "special interest" groups, such as *havurot*. All too often, the high hopes reposed in these groups have not been realized, primarily because they need properly trained personnel to work with them. Women rabbis would help fill the need for a far larger number of rabbis on congregational staffs than is now available. If the recent experience, admittedly brief, of some Christian churches is any indication, many ordained women rabbis will gravitate to the fields of childhood, youth, and adult education and personal counselling.

The past half century has witnessed the opening up for rabbis of many non-congregational positions in such fields as academics, communal organizations, and professional counselling. As a result, the number of Conservative congregations has continued to increase. An expansion in the number of available rabbinical students and graduates would, therefore, help meet the current needs of American Judaism — we can use all the help we can get.

The needs of the Jewish community constitute only one element in the picture. The other includes the broad ethical dimension. To continue to exclude women from this area of service when they are admitted to virtually all others will surely alienate many ethically sensitive men and women, particularly among our youth, and drive potentially creative members of the Jewish community out of Jewish life. Judaism has always prided itself on being in the vanguard of ethical progress, whether it be in the areas of personal rights, universal education, political freedom, social justice, or international peace.

Today the Jewish community is acutely conscious of the threat to its survival posed by the defection and alienation of many of its youth, often the most creative and sensitive members. The agonizingly difficult task of winning their loyalty and commitment to Judaism would become far more difficult if the ordination of women were to be denied. They would regard it as a sign of the petrifaction of Judaism, a betrayal of its pretensions to ethical significance. The youth might well be reinforced in their estrangement from their spiritual roots if Conservative Judaism, which carries the mantle of a living Jewish tradition, were to deny equality to women at a time when there is both a deep desire to serve and a crying need for the service — that there is no substantive objection from the area of Halakhah would aggravate the situation.

What possible considerations are there against the ordination of women? It is noteworthy that it is no longer being argued that women are intellectually inferior and therefore incapable of pursuing the course of study. Our experience with women students at the Seminary demonstrates their intellectual capacities.

Nor can it be maintained that the admission of women to the Rabbinical School would be a frivolous expression of sensationalism, or, as some have elegantly expressed it, a "gimmick." I know several women who are enrolled as rabbinical students or have been graduated and are serving as rabbis. They are serious people who know full well what difficulties lie ahead. Undoubtedly, many women who undertake such a course of study may fall away, in view of the obstacles they will encounter. It will require determination, dedication, and courage of a high order for a woman to go through the course of study and then run the gauntlet of prejudice and discrimination still rife in the community at large. The ordination of women will need to be accompanied by a campaign of education for the laity.

Another contention that has been advanced against the ordination of women runs as follows: "Each sex has its specific role. The roles of men and women are separate but equal. We do not want women to act like men." The first contention is partially true, but misleading; the second completely untrue. Advocates of the ordination of women are not asking that women act like men, only that they act as rabbis. There is nothing specifically masculine involved in teaching, preaching, counselling, or engaging in any other aspect of the rabbinate. If Deborah and Huldah could take their place among Israel's prophets, women can take their place among Israel's rabbis.

As for the threadbare doctrine of "separate but equal," one would imagine that two decades and more after the historic Supreme Court decision of 1954, it would be clear to all that "separate but equal" means "separate and unequal." That is the nub of the question.

In sum, both on ethical and on pragmatic grounds, taking into account the crying needs of Jewish life and the call for equal opportunity to serve on the part of Jewish women, we must conclude that their ordination is highly desirable, indeed a necessary element in any program designed to advance the health of Judaism and strengthen the survival of the Jewish community.

One may hope that when passions cool and calm consideration of the issues prevails, those who have been doubtful on the issue or opposed to it, like those who favor it, will recognize that the goal to which all energies must be directed is *lehagdil Torah ulha²adir*, "to magnify the Torah and make it glorious." ■

Notes

1. B. Sanh. 6b.
2. Cf. "The Rabbinate — Its History, Functions and Future," reprinted as Chap. 16 in R. Gordis *Understanding Conservative Judaism* (New York, 1978).
3. B. Hullin 1:1.
4. B. Baba Kamma 84a.
5. Tos. Kelim, Baba Metzia 1:6.
6. Deut. 23:20,21.
7. Sifre, Shofetim, sec. 157/ Cf. alia, B. Ber. 49, "Rab said, 'The covenant, Torah and royal rule . . . do not apply to women.'"
8. Mishneh Torah, Hilkhot Shofetim, V, 1-5.
9. B. Gittin 62a.
10. B. Betzah 48a; Midrash Berešit Rabba 91:3.

11. See B. Baba Batra 11a; P. Pe ah 1:1. 15b; Tos. Peah 4:18 and Josephus *Antiquities* 21:17.
12. A sophisticated argument for the laws on *niddah* on mystical-philosophic grounds is offered by Rachel Adler, *Tumah and Taharah, End and Beginnings*, with an appendix, comment, and response in Elizabeth Koltun, ed., *Jewish Women* (New York: 1976), 63-71.
13. B. Meg. 4a.
14. That the generalization is not a hard-and-fast rule becomes even clearer from a careful examination of the sources. Of eight time-bound *mitzvot* from which women are ultimately exempted, only three are based on incontrovertible Talmudic law: *sukkah, lulav*, and *shofar* (B. Suk. 38a; B. Kid. 33b), while there is substantial debate on two others, ṣiṣit and *Tefillin* (B. Erub. 96b; B. Kid. 35a; Men. 43a). On the

omer, there is no Talmudic exemption; on the *Shema*, the Babylonian Talmud exempts women (*Ber.* 20a, b), but the Palestinian Talmud implies the existence of dissenting opinions (see *Ber.* 25b). Nevertheless, Maimonides lists all of them among time-bound positive commandments from which women are exempt (*Sepher Hamitzvot*, end of "Affirmative Precepts"). Out of 60 positive commandments listed by him as incumbent on the individual, women are exempt from 14: eight affirmative precepts limited by time; *Shema*, *Tefillin* (head and arm), *sisit*, the counting of the *Omer*, living in a *sukkah*, taking the *lulav*, hearing the *shofar*; and six are not limited by time. These include the study of Torah and the commandment to procreate children.

On the other hand, there are more affirmative precepts equally linked to time from which women are *not* exempt, listed in the Talmud: *Kiddush* (B. *Berakhot* 20a), fasting (B. *Sukkah* 29a), *matzah* (*Kidd.* 34a), rejoicing on festivals (*ibid.*), *haqhēl*, "assembling once in seven years" (see Deut. 31:12, *ibid.*), sacrificing and eating the Paschal lamb (*B. Pesahim* 91b).

Finally, there are four affirmative precepts of rabbinic origin limited in time that are obligatory for women: lighting Hanukkah lights (*Shabbat* 23a), reading *Megillat Esther* (*Meg.* 4a), drinking the four cups of wine (*Pes.* 108a), and reciting *Hallel* on Pesah night (B. *Suk.* 38a).

15. This judgment coincides with that of Rabbi Saul J. Berman, "The Status of Women in Halakhic Judaism," *Tradition*, Fall, 1973, who writes, "So the Mishnah is descriptive of *some* of the laws regulating the status of women, but is inaccurate as a general description and is certainly not a useful prediction principle."

16. Rabbi Berman (*ibid.*) argues that only the motive for keeping women out of the public sphere explains their ineligibility to serve as witnesses and their exclusion from many *mitzvot*. But this motive incorporates a conception of the inferiority of women not applied to their male counterparts.

17. See Rambam, *Edut* 9:1, 2, who bases the disqualification of women on the Bible's use of the masculine in referring to witnesses (*Sifre Deut.* 190; *M. Rosh Hashanah* 1:8; *B. Shevuot* 30a). However, this argument is rejected by Joseph Karo "since the Torah always uses the masculine" (*Keseph Mishneh* on *Yad Edut* 9:2). Nonetheless the Rambam's view has prevailed in practice.

18. *Yebamot* 16:7, where the stricter opinions of Rabbi Eliezer and Rabbi Joshua, who insist on two witnesses and of Rabbi Akiba who does not wish to accept the woman's testimony, are overridden by the majority of the Sages. Cf. *M. Yeb.* 15:8; *B. Yeb.* 13b, 114b, N. 6.

19. Deut. 19:15.

20. *B. Sanh.* 10a.

21. It is noteworthy that Barukh Halevi Epstein, *Torah Temimah, Devarim*, 126a, col. 2, declares that the ineligibility of women as witnesses "*lav kelal gamur hu*," "is not a fixed principle" and proceeds to give instances where their testimony is accepted. For the Responsa literature, see *Encyclopedia Judaica*, vol. 16, 586.

22. *B. Kethubbot* 10a and parallels.

23. *P. Yeb.* 12:1; *P. Baba Metzia* 7:1, *Sopherim*, chap. 14.

24. Adret opposed it because of its similarity to the Azazel rites on Yom Kippur (Lev. 16:5-22) and he called it a "heathen superstition" (*darkhei ha'emori*, Responsa, Part 1, no. 395).

25. *Shulhan Arukh, Orah Hayyim* sec. 605. His language was later toned down to read, "It is best to avoid the custom." The Rama, however, declares that it has been practiced "in these lands" (i.e., the Polish-German communities) and therefore defends its retention. See J.Z. Lauterbach's study of the rite in his *Rabbinic Essays* (Cincinnati, 1915), 354-76.

26. The evidence in all areas of Jewish law is presented in R. Gordis, "A Dynamic Halakhah: Principles and Procedures" (*Judaism*, Vol. 28, No. 3, Summer, 1979, pp. 263-282). A symposium by 17 scholars representing every school of thought in contemporary Judaism, and a "Reply to the Responses" by the author of the original article, appears in the Winter, 1980 issue of *Judaism*, under the title "Jewish Law: Eighteen Perspectives."

27. *T. Ber.* 25a; *Kid.* 70a.

28. See L.M. Epstein, *Sex Laws and Customs in Judaism* (New York, 1948), 25-66.

29. Ps. 45:14. See *B. Gittin* 12a and Rashi *ad loc.*

Those Entitled To Be Jews

BEN HALPERN

PROFESSOR SHAYE COHEN'S PAPER IS PROPERLY impartial, or methodologically unconcerned, about the controversy that has arisen over the "recent decision of the Reform and Reconstructionist rabbinate to adopt a patrilineal principle for determining the Jewish status of children born of an intermarriage." I doubt whether most of the papers contributed to the present symposium will confine themselves to purely historical criticism of Cohen's hypothesis (that the matrilineal principle was taken up from Roman legal practice by rabbis in the period of the Mishnah). Prof. Cohen argues that intellectual influences and a technical interest in problems of purity and mixtures, rather than the social needs of that ancient time, explain the rabbis' departure from biblical patriliny. Today, the issue clearly arises out of considerations of social need, and, I dare say, most contributors will approach it in terms of their respective general positions on Jewish and social issues.

As a secular Zionist and an occasionally practicing historian, I have no difficulty whatever in accepting the idea that the rabbinical jurists responded to contemporaneous influences and interests in their interpretation of legal texts. I assume without question that jurists and legal scholars who discuss the matter today will do the same — whether or not they are prepared to admit it. My own interests and preconceptions lead me to deal with the current rather than the historical issue, and to approach it on its most general, broadest base.

The decision to recognize children of Jewish fathers as entitled to a place in the community by descent, without further qualification, obviously responds to the new situation of an American Jewry whose sons are intermarrying with non-Jews at a substantial rate. It seeks to ease the way for many marginal men, having options and incentives to become either Jew or Gentile, to choose their Jewish identity without undergoing special tests and procedures. It clearly reflects the sense of many in the community that, in the face of so many factors tending to sap its strength and reduce its numbers, traditional rules that make it harder to be a Jew should be revised.

This is only the latest of numerous demands for adjustment that modern conditions have made upon the Jewish tradition. One should mention, in this connection, the explicit recognition of the legitimacy of civil marriage which Napoleon exacted of his Jewish subjects nearly two centuries ago. The Sanhedrin that he convoked may have stipulated the

BEN HALPERN *is professor emeritus, Brandeis University.*

need for a supplementary religious ceremony, for internal purposes, but this did not obviate the possible halakhic complications invited by increasingly prevalent civil marriage. There are certainly a fair number of Jews in all Western countries whose parents, or recent ancestors, were united in civil marriage under rules different from rabbinic practice, and who might be judged "illegitimate" — *mamzerim* — if their antecedents were carefully examined by the Israeli rabbinic courts today. For many years, such problems were tacitly evaded simply by having no occasion (or generally accepted tribunal) to raise an issue about them. We have remained a united community for many decades — at least, in our public aspect — simply by taking at his word whoever identifies himself as a Jew — barring, of course, cases where there is clear evidence of fraudulent intent.

Another historic occasion that raised the issue anew, in an aggravated form, was the enactment of compulsory jurisdiction of the rabbinic courts over the personal status of Jews in Israel. There was now, within the authoritative political structure of Israel, a tribunal committed to apply to all Jews within its jurisdiction traditional rules for permissible marital relations. Until then, observant traditional Jews may have had to guard themselves by discreet inquiry against illegitimate marriages — of *kohanim* with divorcees, or legitimate Jews with *mamzerim* (though it may have been far more common to check whether a pious Jew could safely eat in another Jew's house); now there were officials duty-bound to check such matters, according to set procedures and regulations. The unity of the Jewish people, so far as it depended on uniform rules of permissible marriage, could no longer be maintained by avoiding public division over such cases, but became subject to publicity and proclamation.

Yet, at first, another set of rules, for the application of Israel's Law of Return, limited the impact of rabbinical jurisdiction. Here one could benefit from the provisions of the law (governing the rights of Jews to immigrate and be naturalized) upon submitting a good-faith declaration that he/she was a Jew. But political ambitions, exploiting political opportunities, have killed that chance of preserving unity through benign neglect, and subjected the issue of "Who is a Jew?," on the broadest scale, to injurious attention.

The earlier principle of the Law of the Return, accepting a good-faith self-identification as sufficient evidence of being a Jew, expresses the secular national consciousness that arose in Eastern Europe over a hundred years ago. Its criterion for entitlement to be recognized as a Jew, part of the Jewish community, is that one knowingly shares the Jewish fate. Secular Jews, like others, also have their criterion for being a *good* Jew: not simply sharing, but taking the Jewish fate as a personal commitment, and cultivating the historical consciousness that gives it meaning. One is entitled to be recognized as a Jew, from the secular standpoint, without being a good Jew. Neither Orthodoxy nor Orthopraxy nor any other form of positive religious commitment is necessary, as we all know, to make one share in the Jewish fate. To impose such additional requirements — or, for that matter, to make an adequate level of national, historical self-consciousness such a requirement — would be incompatible with the secular nationalist conscience. It is one thing to choose leaders on grounds of their special qualifications; it is quite another to make acceptance into the community depend on them, or use them to block some groups, or unfairly privilege others, in regard to rights and duties that should be equally open to all.

It is obvious where such a principle would necessarily place a secular nationalist in the controversies between the rival religious positions on matters recently in dispute. What would be most desirable would be the institution of civil marriage in Israel. That would remove the compulsion on Jews (and Muslims, and members of other recognized sects) to submit to an authority that they may not inwardly accept, and allow them the option voluntarily to pair off, as they do now, according to the domestic way of life that they are wont to follow. Such a set-up, familiar to American and other Western Jewries, would itself eliminate the difficulties that Conservative and Reform rabbis and laymen encounter in Israel, and it might enable them to arrive freely at some *rapprochement* with Israeli traditions as well. But if this way out is not under discussion, then, certainly, the official recognition that Liberal and Conservative Judaism seek in Israel ought to be supported. It would make a public institution, to be sure, out of religious differences that ought to enjoy the right of private association; it would turn nuanced shadings into sharp-edged divisions. But it would also remove invidious discrimination among Jews and eliminate harmful coercion — and this consideration far outweighs the other.

Much the same arguments apply to the proposal to validate patrilineal descent, and not only inheritance through one's mother, as a title to be recognized as a Jew. A secular nationalist must certainly sympathize with the motives that, one assumes, underpin the decision to adopt this reform. It is possible, of course, that what lies behind it, for some advocates, is fear of the religious vacuum, or the positive religious alternatives that might absorb such persons if the synagogue failed to remove questions of their Jewish legitimacy. More likely, it is not fear of such alternatives but simply the loss to the Jewish community if the synagogue fails to integrate them that is the effective motive. This is a consideration that must count with any concerned Jew.

The proposed reform has its obvious drawbacks — what one might call the side-effects of the therapy. Like any institutional innovation in a previously ill-defined situation, it turns blurry compromises into clearly opposed positions, tacit understandings into vocal disputes. The history of Zionism, too, repeatedly saw pragmatic agreements with non-Zionists turn into ideological conflict with anti-Zionists when the nationalists put forward new principles in explicit, rather than implied, forms. A new religious thesis is particularly prone to provoke sharp, ideologically rigid counter-statements. Nothing has the intrinsic capacity more openly to divide the Jewish community, formally identified as a religious brotherhood, than an attempt to define the bounds of membership in it in sectarian terms.

Nevertheless, the risks that are undoubtedly being incurrred should not be too alarming. Although we figure as a religious community — a single religious community — in the mind of America-at-large, our religious association is socially, not politically, institutionalized. Whatever conflict and division the new measure adopted by the Reform and Reconstructionist rabbis may engender, it occurs in a community already pluralistic in its cultic structure: not a single Synagogue, but some three or four separate denominations. If we are a single community, nevertheless, this fact inheres in our awareness of a common fate, shared with Jews everywhere, and more specially among all American Jews, in their several denominations and other forms of association and interdependence. What counts is our unity on this basis, and whether the reform undermines it.

It is certainly possible that the provocation of this bold departure from halakhah will, indeed, add to the pressures already straining our communal organization. American Jews, not to speak of Israeli and other Jews, are increasingly divided in their stand on social and political issues — the very matters in which a common fate has allowed us to work together effectively in spite of doctrinal and ritual differences. Those differences, however, have produced, in some cases, splits within the Jewish "polity," the communal organization that represents and acts for the Jews in their relations with others: nineteenth century Germany and Hungary and twentieth century Palestine under the British mandate saw the emergence of separatist Orthodox communities, unwilling to join other Jews in a common association for the protection of common interests. Tendencies to take the same route, which have been noticeable lately in American Jewry, may well be strengthened by the dispute over patrilineal Jewishness.

In spite of such strains, American Jewry will, no doubt, preserve a manageable unity in matters of common interest. The differences among us (which are occasionally exploited by interested non-Jews on particular issues) have far less impact on others than on ourselves. Their definition of "who is a Jew" is usually more liberal and generous than ours — and it is a far from negligible factor in determining the Jewish fate, and who is subject to it. Moreover, in a country where both religious and ethnic organization are private matters, requiring no special public-law sanction, there is not the same pressure for a clean separation. One can avoid offensive association (in some private spheres) with Jews held illegitimate while working with them (in other spheres) where they effectively share the Jewish fate — and the need to apply a consistent principle to the two cases is not pressing, as they do not come under a single, publicly proclaimed law.

There is another probable effect of the reform that, again, seems to reinforce an already observable American Jewish trend. This is the propensity to seek a position for Jews in American life approaching that of the Quakers or Presbyterians, if not the Episcopalians. Members of those denominations are distinguishable from other Americans less by a distinct communal history (though this was once true of the Quakers) than by their distinct, generally recognized status. Not far beneath the surface of the American Jewish public presence, there is the latent wish to have the same sort of acceptance. What makes this difficult is the too stubborn resistance of Jewish history.

The long chronicle of the efforts of modern Jews to suppress, or sublimate, our history of Exile is an old story, not necessary to repeat. Since the Holocaust, and the subsequent campaign to eliminate anti-Semitism from Christian ritual in the name of ecumenical reconciliation, it has taken a form that hopes to smooth over the sharp edges of Judeo-Christian difference. It is hard to estimate to what extent the recognition of patrilineal descent will affect the lives of intermarried couples and their children, but, conceivably, it might help blur their perception of the special, distinctive features of the Jewish fate.

A common historical explanation of the adoption of the matrilineal principle in Judaism (one not accepted by Prof. Cohen) holds that it was instituted by Ezra on the generally accepted psycho-sociological assumption that mothers, and not fathers, impart family values to their children. Even if the history is rejected, the social psychology of this theory would still command fairly general belief. Certainly today, in spite of the tendency for the nuclear family to be isolated, it is the mother's kin rather than her husband's who are likely to form the wider intimate environment of her children. One effect of any intermarriage is likely to be a blurring of the sense of a distinctive Jewish historical fate; and when it is the father alone who is Jewish, this effect is apt to be reinforced.

As previously noted, the specific added impact of legitimizing patrilineal descent, over and above that of intermarriage itself, or even simple acculturation, is very hard to measure. It would not be surprising to find that it is a very minor incremental effect, as the number of persons involved may turn out to be small. Small or large, it adds to the problem that Liberal Judaism already has of bringing home to American Jews a profounder, more informed sense of their identification with the Jewish fate and history. Yet, whatever the difficulties it may entail, the reform is one that a secular Jewish loyalist can only welcome. It signalizes an openness to all who choose to be Jews, and to all the forms in which their Jewishness authentically finds expression, which we must applaud.

RELIGIOUS TRENDS IN AMERICAN JEWRY

WILL HERBERG

THE PAST twenty years have witnessed a remarkable change in the religious situation of the Jews in America. Trends that had prevailed since the earlier days of immigration and that seemed to be part of the very "nature" of American Jewry have been reversed, and new tendencies have emerged that are shaping the American Jewish community in ways undreamed of a generation ago. There can be no doubt that we have entered a significantly new period in the history of American Jewry. It is the purpose of this paper to examine the new situation in its major aspects and to assess the significance of the new trends for Jewish life in America.

I

The outstanding fact defining the new situation is the reversal of the two major trends that characterized the pattern of American Jewish life well through the 1920's—the trend toward the dissolution of Jewishness and the trend toward the abandonment of the Jewish religious tradition and of all religious concern whatsoever. Assimilation and secularism marked the pattern of American Jewish life from the beginning of the great immigration at the end of the last century, although for decades these tendencies, particularly the former, were masked by the continuous influx of new immigrants. When large-scale immigration came to an end during the first world war, the logic of the underlying social and cultural pattern became evident: American Jews were abandoning their Jewishness and losing all interest in their religious heritage. There were not wanting those who were already sounding the knell of American Jewry and confidently relegating the synagogue, along with the church, to the limbo of obsolescent institutions.

The situation is obviously very different today. The trend toward dissolution and secularism, so marked through the twenties, has been halted, even reversed. Among all sections of American Jewry, but particularly among the younger generation, there is a movement of "return". "Return" to what? It is hard to say exactly: return to a new sense of Jewishness, return to the synagogue, return to personal religious concern. These various aspects are often fused and compounded in the movement of "return"; yet they sometimes also exhibit a certain tension, which shows that the un-

---

This paper was presented at the opening session of the 25th Annual Conference of the Yivo in New York City. Mr. HERBERG's writings include essays in *Judaism* and *Commentary* and a volume, *Judaism and Modern Man: An Interpretation of Jewish Religion*.

derlying forces and motives are not of one piece but reflect different facets of the experience of the American Jew in mid-twentieth century America.

The return to Jewishness, to self-affirmation as a Jew and to self-identification with Jewry, is perhaps the most obvious sign of the times. The young people in the colleges—who, let us remember, make up the next generation of American Jews—as well as those out of school who are setting up homes for themselves, recognize and affirm their Jewishness in a way that would have seemed unbelievable some thirty years ago, and to a greater or less degree this is also true of other sections of American Jewry. In a manner that is difficult to define but which can hardly be denied, the events of the thirties and forties—the upsurge of anti-Semitism in Europe on the one hand and the struggle for the establishment of a "Jewish state" in Palestine, on the other—served to heighten the sense of Jewish identification and self-affirmation among American Jews, as among Jews everywhere. This underlying factor of contemporary history cannot be denied; its influence has been wide and pervasive. But it is well to recognize that in the United States at least, it has fallen in with a significant sociological trend, which has not yet been sufficiently studied or appreciated. This trend is signalized by the emergence of the "third generation" of American Jewry. The first generation, the immigrant generation, came with their Jewishness as part of their immigrant heritage; it was embedded in their life and culture. The younger members of that generation, and of the next, revolted against this heritage, and in the process of establishing their independence and adjusting themselves to their new environment, they strove to cast off their Jewishness as part of the immigrant baggage they were so eager to abandon. They were intent—quite naturally and properly intent—upon becoming Americans, and to become Americans they had to cease to be foreigners, which to them only too often meant to cease to be Jews. The third generation is in a very different position; it is secure in its Americanness and does not have an immigrant burden which it is anxious to throw off. It can therefore face the problem of its Jewishness in a new and creative manner, free from many of the anxieties and compulsions that afflicted the earlier generations. How it is coping with the problems of its Jewishness we are only just beginning to discern in vague outline.

But here a question arises that leads us to the heart of the matter. This phenomenon of the "third generation" is common to all of the many immigrant groups that came to these shores in the past century and that have entered into the making of the American people. But in every other case, the emergence of the "third generation"—I refer here to the sociological category; in some cases, it may actually be a fourth or a fifth generation—in every other case, I say, the emergence of the "third generation" has meant the dissolution of the ethnic-immigrant group from which it came and its absorption into the developing mainstream of American life; that is precisely how the American people and American culture have come into being. With the Jews it has been different. The first and second generations of Jews in America repeated the common immigrant pattern: immigrant foreignness followed by an anxious effort to get rid of that foreignness and become American. But the "third generation" of American Jews, instead of somehow finally getting rid of their separateness and dissolving completely into the general community, which is what all other "third generations" have done or are doing, the "third generation" of American Jews are actually returning to Jewishness. How are we to account for this strange anomaly which distinguishes Jews from all other immigrant groups that have gone into the making of America?

We can account for this anomaly only by recognizing that American Jewry cannot be understood if it is taken to be merely one of the many ethnic groups that left the old world for the new in the course of the great migrations of the past century. The Jews who came to America did of course constitute an immigrant group, but their Jewishness was apparently something that transcended their immigrant character in a way that was not true of the merely ethnic or national character of the other immigrant groups. Their Jewishness was apparently something very different from the kind of ethnic or cultural foreignness that tends to disappear with the emergence of the third generation. Had it not been something very different, we would not now be witnessing a return of the "third generation" to Jewishness.

The fact of the matter seems to be that just when the immigrant-cultural basis of American Jewish existence was beginning to disappear with the emergence of a thoroughly American "third generation", American Jewry was becoming transformed into what sociologists call a "religious community". The religious community has, in fact, become the primary context of social location in contemporary American life. When an American asks of a new family in town, "What does he do?" he means the occupation or profession of the head of the family; when he asks, "What are they?" he means to what religious community do they belong—Protestant, Catholic, or Jewish. A century ago, the question, "What are they?" would have been answered in terms of immigrant-ethnic origin, and today it is still answered in some such terms for Negroes as well as for Americans of Oriental or recent Latin American origin. But increasingly, the great mass of Americans understand themselves and their place in American society in terms of the religious community with which they are identified. And "religious community" in this usage refers not so much to the particular denomination, of which there are scores in this country, but to the three great divisions, Catholics, Protestants, and Jews. America is the land of the "triple melting pot", for it is within these three religious communities that the process of ethnic and cultural integration so characteristic of American life takes place.

We can restate all this by saying that while the unity of American life is indeed a unity in multiplicity, the pluralism that this implies is of a very special kind. America recognizes no permanent national or cultural minorities; what Europe knows under this head are in this country regarded as "foreign language" or "foreign culture" groups, whose separateness is merely temporary, the consequence of recent immigration, destined to be overcome with increasing integration into American life. America does indeed know and acknowledge the separateness of so-called minority "races", but such separateness has always involved some degree of segregation and consequent relegation to an inferior status in the social hierarchy. The only kind of separateness or diversity that America recognizes as permanent and yet also as involving no status of inferiority is the diversity or separateness of religious communities. In short, while America knows no national or cultural minorities except as temporary, transitional phenomena, it does know a free variety and plurality of religions, and it is as a member of a religious group that the great mass of Americans understand the status of the Jew in this country and that the American Jew understands himself. This is particularly true of the younger generation of Jews. When they are moved to affirm their Jewishness, and they must do so if only to identify themselves to themselves and to others, they can conceive of no way of doing so except in religious terms. The many substitutes for Jewish religious identification, which were open to earlier generations, are no longer viable to them. It is simply a fact that the average American Jew—I mean the Jew who is acculturated to America—if he thinks of himself as a Jew at all, tends almost automatically to think of himself as belonging to a religious community, even if he himself does not have personal faith. In the Vilna of the 1920's, it was possible for a militantly anti-religious Jewish doctor to assert himself as a Jew by sending his children to a secular Yiddish school, and for a time this pattern was familiar among Jewish immigrants in this country. For some time, too, one could "be a Jew" simply by being a Zionist or by identifying oneself with some Jewish philanthropic cause. All this is becoming increasingly untenable. Today, if the American Jew is to regard himself as a Jew, and if he is to be so regarded by his non-Jewish neighbors and friends, some religious association, however vague, is necessary. The only way in which the Jew can integrate himself into American society is in terms of a religious community.

That is one reason why the "return" to Jewishness of which I have spoken has also meant a return to the synagogue. It is beyond dispute that synagogue construction, synagogue membership, and even synagogue attendance are growing at an unprecedented rate in this country. This is part of a larger movement characterizing the entire American people today, for the growth of religious bodies and the increase in religious affiliation on the part of the American people is one of the most striking facts about the present situation in the United States. In 1900, 36 percent of the American people were reported as religiously affiliated; by 1930, the figure had risen to 47 percent; and by 1950, to 57 percent. In the quarter of a century from 1926 to 1950, the population of the United States rose 28.6 percent; church membership, however, jumped nearly 60 percent. There are no comparable figures applying specifically to the Jews, but all evidence goes to show that the movement of American Jews into the synagogue in recent years has been at least as sweeping and as vigorous as the movement of Americans generally into the church. Many of the older people, who had once broken away and had never thought of the possibility of returning, are back again, but it is primarily the trend of the younger generation that is decisive. For them, the "return" to Jewishness which we are witnessing is in great measure a return to the synagogue, for not only is the synagogue the one enduring and representative Jewish institution; not only is it the unique embodiment through the ages of Jewish spirituality: it is also the characteristically American vehicle of

Jewish self-identification. When a young Jewish couple in New York get married and move out to Westchester or Long Island, the first thing they do is to join the synagogue; quite naturally—for how else are they to express and signalize their Jewishness? The revival of the synagogue in the past fifteen years would have stunned the social prognosticators of a generation ago, who saw in it a culturally moribund institution as well as a remnant of immigrant foreignness. It has turned out to be neither: it has become a thoroughly American institution whose growth is reflecting the current "return" to religion in America.

It is worth noting that the movement back to religion has involved a considerable number of old-line secularist Jews. Indeed, militant secularism in the sense of anti-religion is almost entirely gone; today's secularists are no longer so sure they possess the key to the riddle of the universe, nor are they so certain that religion is the source of all evil and the primary obstacle to man's advancement. Even in Jewish labor circles, once the stronghold of radical anti-religion, there is taking place a notable change of heart, reflecting not only the spirit of the times, but also the new status of labor in the American Jewish community. In all sections of American Jewry, there are those who, without seriously modifying their own religious indifference, have come to adopt what may be called a pro-religious attitude because they recognize that religion possesses a strong "survivalist" potential. I recall the words of a distinguished Jewish scholar of pronounced secularist views: "Jewish religion [he maintained] has proved itself the most stormproof aspect of Jewish life. It is the only force that can preserve the Jews as a group, in America at least". Such people are often ready to associate themselves with the synagogue, give their children a "Jewish education", perhaps even adopt certain of the traditional ritual observances in the home, without thereby implying any religious commitment. With some, as with the scholar I have mentioned, this attitude is a conscious and well-articulated ideology; for the most part, however, it is little more than a vague sentiment, though surely an influential one. In either case, it finds a strong appeal in Reconstructionism, with its combination of a secularist humanistic philosophy in matters of belief and an emphasis on external forms for the sake of "survival" in matters of observance.

But this rather sophisticated pro-religionism without religion is by no means characteristic of all those who are today turning to the synagogue. On the contrary, by and large, those who are "returning" feel themselves sincerely religious, though they are not oblivious to the utility of the synagogue and its educational institutions in keeping their children Jewish. Their religion, however, is generally very far, at least in content, from the faith embodied in Jewish religious tradition. In fact, it often consists of little more than "belief in God", a high regard for Jewish moral teachings, and a feeling that attending synagogue occasionally, giving one's children a "Jewish education", and some ritual observances are necessary for Jewishness. An increasing proportion of younger Jews, it is true, especially those in the colleges, are beginning to look for something more authentically religious and more authentically Jewish; about them I will have something to say in a little while. But by and large, the religion of the average American Jew is as I have described it, a "liberal Judaism" not very far removed from the "liberal Protestantism" of the church around the corner. This is about equally true of the American Orthodox and Conservative groups as of the Reform group, despite important secondary differences among them. Nothing is perhaps more American than this kind of religion, sincere but without content.

And yet one should not leave it on this note. The superficiality of religious content may not be a fair measure of the depth and reality of the religious concern. It is the concern that is crucial, for it is the concern that opens the heart to God. And I think it can be said that for all the shallowness that characterizes so much of contemporary American Judaism, the concern is there to an increasing degree, particularly among the younger generation of American Jews.

Let me, before carrying the argument off in another direction, summarize what I have so far said about the present religious situation in American Jewry. Largely in response to basic influences affecting the entire body of the American people, American Jewry is returning to a renewed sense of its Jewishness, to a renewed affiliation with the synagogue, and to a renewed awareness of religion. This is a reversal of trend of really historical significance. Within this general movement, there is under way another movement, if movement it can be called—a new and growing concern with religion as personal faith and commitment. In such matters, it is difficult to supply "objective" documentation, but I feel that I can with some confidence draw upon my own experience as well as upon the conclusions of other observers. During the past seven years, I have lectured at scores of colleges and universities in all parts of the country, usually in interdepartmental programs that have brought me in touch with either the entire academic community or else a sizable section of it. In the course of these campus programs, I must have had discussions with thousands of Jewish students, in classes, seminars, and lectures, as well as in personal conferences and bull sessions. And, of course, these days, discussions, no matter how they begin, always end up with religion. I think I can say without qualification that interest in, and concern with, religion as manifested by the present student generation, Jewish and non-Jewish alike, is something really extraordinary, and is constantly growing. I have no hesitation whatever in confirming the testimony of Professor Stuart Hughes of Harvard, who states with some surprise: "The avant-garde [of students] is becoming old-fashioned; religion is now the latest thing" (*Saturday Review*, March 3, 1951). It is to this "avant-garde" that we now turn.

II

The new concern with religion as personal faith is much harder to define or describe than the larger movement of return to the synagogue of which it is part; it is, however, just as real, and in the last analysis may prove to be even more important. In varying degrees, this new concern is to be found among all sections of American Jewry, but, as I have just indicated, it is most pronounced and perhaps most vital among the younger people, particularly those in the colleges, for it is the younger people who are most open to new influences and most accessible to rapid shifts in the intellectual and spiritual climate. Within the framework of the social and ideological reorientation of American Jewish life I have described, there is undoubtedly taking place among many of the "returning" generation a real, though by no means clearly defined, shift in fundamental outlook, a change of "mind" and "heart" that sometimes means a radical restructuring of existence. Unsympathetic observers may sometimes find it difficult to detect the conventional marks of religion in this new spirituality, but that does not change the fact that it is truly and profoundly religious, perhaps closer to the enduring tradition of faith than the "liberalized", "modernized", denatured versions of religion that have conventional standing. It is in a basic sense a reflection of the new world that has suddenly emerged in the course of the past generation, a world of total insecurity, a world in which the easy hopes and reliances of earlier decades seem grotesquely unreal and in which some deeper foundation of existence must be found if life is to be liveable at all. Professor H. Richard Niebuhr of Yale has well indicated the nature, as well as some of the deeper sources, of the new spirituality in a study of what he calls "Our Conservative Youth" (*Seventy-Five*, anniversary publication of the *Yale Daily News*, 1953, p. 90).

> Present-day youth [he writes] has to rest its large-scale security on deeper foundations, and this is probably the source of its religious interest.. Some of it is finding no greater security than what an Epicurean philosophy of life affords; but much of it is getting down to the bedrock and finding a foundation on which life can rest unmoved, if not unshaken, in stormy times. There is a venturesomeness in this quest, but it is a hidden thing...

The best of American Jewish youth is also engaged in this quest, but because it is a "hidden thing" it is often overlooked by the outsider. Yet it is of decisive importance, for it is that which gives the "returning" generation its characteristic outlook and temper.

How shall we define this outlook and temper? It is difficult to give any clear account of it because it varies so widely in its personal expression, and in the nature of the case, it can have no official formulation. But I think the following characterization is fairly borne out by the facts, at least as I have come upon them in recent years.

It seems to me that the first, and perhaps basic, aspect of the outlook of the "returning" generation is a thirst for the "metaphysical" that marks it off distinctly from its immediate predecessors. There is wide dissatisfaction with the naturalistic and humanistic philosophies that only yesterday were the mark of the "modern" mind; there is a demand for something deeper, for a philosophy that takes account of the full dimensions of human existence. There is a new feeling for depth and a new sense of realism. The old-fashioned "liberalism" that saw only the surface of things and was therefore totally unprepared for Hitler or Stalin seems quite unintelligible to many of the younger generation, who can hardly fail to be aware of the spiritual "underworld" lurking in the depths. The "returning" generation is hard-boiled and worldly-wise; yet for all its realism, perhaps precisely because of that realism, it reveals an inwardness that stands in striking contrast to the busy activism of the college generations of the thirties and early forties. For this reason, some observers have accused it of apathy, inertia, and unconcern with the issues of the day, but this indictment, though in part perhaps well-founded, overlooks the possibility that the apparent inertia on the surface may, as Richard Niebuhr suggests, hide a venturesomeness and activity in essence much more serious than the externalism of other times. The turn to inwardness reflects a deep need for personal appropriation, and it often expresses itself in a marked distrust of conventional standards and beliefs, in an almost biological allergy to the pat, prefabricated catchwords that are so frequently made to do service as answers to the problems of life. To some people, this attitude may seem to verge on utter skepticism and disbelief, but in this attitude there is also a readiness to listen, an openness to the new, that makes this generation (in Ludwig Lewisohn's words) so "accessible to good". There is above all a genuine desire to recapture, or perhaps better, to recreate for oneself, the substance of Jewishness. As a consequence, there results that surprising interest in, and regard for, tradition that distinguishes this otherwise skeptical generation. "A generation without creeds and Scriptures", notes H. Richard Niebuhr, "has none to reject, but looks with respect on historic affirmations and revelations, orients itself towards them, and seeks to understand their meaning and power... Youth is seeking, fumblingly often, to reclaim the ancestral ground on which previous generations were nurtured, but which they abandoned".

I am well aware that this description is too schematic to be accurate; it applies fully only to the most advanced of the "returning" generation, and even to them only in a general way. And yet it has its truth, and that truth seems to me important. For it is a fact that the generation now in college or recently out of it are beginning to think and feel and be concerned religiously in a way that is startlingly new, yet also everlastingly old. The newness is obvious, often too obvious; but the other side should be emphasized as well. For it is a paradox, yet also a truism, that the thoroughly American, modern "returning" generation often feels itself closer spiritually to its grandparents than to its parents. More than once, I've heard a young man or woman on some college campus tell me in a puzzled way, "You know, I'm really beginning to understand my grandfather; I'm beginning to understand how he feels about things, especially about religion". And I shall never forget the dedication which a young man from New York in a select New England college inscribed on his honor thesis: "To my grandfather, who had the courage to bear witness to the living God in a new world". Here again, but in a much deeper sense, the "third generation" is returning to the first.

This new concern with Jewishness and Jewish faith leads the "returning generation to the synagogue, and the statistics of institutional affiliation and membership bear witness to this "return". They enter the synagogue with eager anticipation, especially if it is for the first time; what they find there is often such as to disconcert and dishearten them in their search for a deeper understanding of their Jewish existence.

I do not want to be unfair to the present-day American synagogue. Under pressure of its environment, it is called upon to perform a thousand and one tasks of which the old-time synagogue knew nothing, and it does most of them well; but in the one task of providing a significant and creative environment for the "returning" generation, it is failing most deplorably. It may plausibly be argued that the expectations of the younger people are perverse and unrealistic and that no synagogue can afford to be diverted from its more important purposes in order to meet them. But it remains a fact that only too frequently the first contact with the synagogue since childhood on the part of these "returning" young men and women is a deeply disillusioning experience which many of them never really get over. Whether they are married couples making their first uncertain venture in synagogue affiliation, or students coming home with vague anticipations, their disappointment is often quite profound. This may come as a shock to many who see people attend services and take their part in various synagogue activities, but one should not be misled by surface appearances. Of course, the "returning" young people, or at least most of them, sooner or later get accustomed to the routine of synagogue life, and some of them even get to like it, but the initial ardency is quenched, the eager anticipation repressed, and whatever remains of the original venture in faith is largely dissociated from the synagogue and its activities and driven to assume what are often questionable forms.

What is wrong with the contemporary synagogue from the point of view of the "returning" generation? To put the whole case in a nutshell, it is the essential secularism, the externalism, and the ingrained mediocrity of the contemporary synagogue, Orthodox, Conservative, and Reform alike, that render it so inadequate in meeting the needs of those who come to it with high, though often vague and ill-defined anticipations. What is the religion to be found in the present-day American synagogue? The religion of the present-day American synagogue is not one but many. It may be a religion of "Jewish values", and that means either ethical culture plus social service or an idealized version of ritual observance. Or it may be a religion of Jewish scholarship, in which acquaintance with texts becomes the vehicle of Jewish identification. It may be a religion of Zionist nationalism or a religion of Jewish folk-culture; a religion of "religious experience", cultivating inspiration and uplift, or a religion of nostalgic sentimentality, feeding on "quaint" little Hasidic tales. Or it may be all of these combined in varying measure. But whichever or whatever it may be, it is equally remote from the kind of faith the "returning" generation is seeking, a faith that will yield some glimpse of the meaning of life in its ultimate terms and some way of living on the level of really significant existence. In a poignant statement published nearly three years ago (*Congress Weekly*, April 9, 1951), Leslie Fiedler expressed the plight of the "returning" Jewish intellectual confronted with the realities of contemporary synagogue Judaism.

> In the Orthodox shuls [Mr. Fiedler wrote], the hasidic fire, the old unity of devotion, are moribund beneath an emphasis on kashrut and the endless pilpul, long since turned into a substitute for any moving faith. In the Reform temples, the glib young rabbi, with his tags from Freud, his sociological jargon, speaks his conviction that God is a "cosmological blur". Like the more debased Protestant churches, the temples have tended to substitute "social service" for religion... These conditions do not prevail universally, of course, but in general, American Judaism has made everything its center but God: amateur psychoanalysis, collecting money

for the Jewish Appeal, hating all Germans, worshiping force, bowing down before a revived nineteenth century nationalism...

What Mr. Fiedler expresses here so vigorously, many young men and women have tried to communicate to me, stumblingly and inarticulately, perhaps, but with quite as much urgency. The language and ideas of the present-day American synagogue strike the intelligent young people of the "returning" generation as something strangely obsolete and utterly remote from the real problems of life. The spiritual atmosphere of the present-day American synagogue proves even more perplexing. I recall a medical student, with a deep religious concern, who had some interesting things to say about the liturgy and form of service of the synagogue he occasionally attended. He found it all very unsatisfactory, primarily because it was not (as he thought it should be) an act of corporate worship in which all are involved, but rather a religious performance put on by the rabbi and hazan and "appreciated" or "enjoyed" by the congregation as audience. Besides, he found that the rabbi "talked too much"; and in fact, the rabbi was always talking, introducing this and explaining that, turning the entire service into a sort of inspirational adult education program. As a result, this young man, and some other young people I know, have more than once decided that they would go to some old-style Orthodox synagogue where, as they put it, "there is less talking and more praying". But of course, in most cases, that won't work either; the cultural barriers are too great, not to speak of their inadequate knowledge of the Hebrew liturgy. So there seems to be no direction in which they can turn to find the "religious substance" they are seeking.

This "religious substance" is but rarely to be found in the present-day American synagogue; the present-day American synagogue is basically an extravert institution, caught up in an endless round of institutional externalities. It is this externalism that the young people who come in search of faith find it hard to take. Perhaps, as I have suggested, the present generation is reacting excessively against the mindless activism of their predecessors. Perhaps; but the fact remains that the present generation is distinctly organization-shy; it is suspicious of "movements" and cannot work up any real enthusiasm for busy programs and bustling activities. But the present-day American synagogue is almost always a big institution that lives by programs and projects and campaigns, and the present-day American rabbi is eminently organization-conscious. The young man or woman who comes to the synagogue with grandiose, perhaps overly romantic notions of a House of Prayer and a House of Study actually finds a big community center in which the synagogue is almost lost. The shock is sometimes one that leaves a deep and lasting imprint.

There is something in the cultural atmosphere of the present-day American synagogue that has a depressing effect on many of the "returning" generation. I have in mind a certain commonplaceness of thought and sentiment, a certain self-satisfied mediocrity, a certain slackness of spiritual tone and stodginess of feeling that cannot but embarrass young people who come to the synagogue with the passion of faith or with the hope of finding it. What they have heard and read, what they have come to feel, has led them to believe that authentic religion may be anything in the world, but it cannot be dull or mediocre. The very stirrings that brought them to the point of "return" render them particularly sensitive, perhaps unduly so, to the dull, philistine atmosphere that so often pervades the synagogue and renders suspect every sign of intellectual or spiritual ferment. The rabbi, especially if he is a younger man, may attempt to resist the wave of mediocrity, but he too is usually engulfed in it along with the others.

What happens to the "returning" generation when it comes to the synagogue and finds it as I have described? It is hard to say exactly because the development is still too new to draw conclusions. But by and large I should say that however disappointed in their expectations, most of them settle down to a kind of passive synagogue connection, which they feel necessary to satisfy their own need for "belonging" as well as to provide their children with a "Jewish education". As time goes on, many of them, altogether too many unfortunately, become routinized and fall in with the conventional mediocrity of the environment, though generally something of the old longing still remains. At the other extreme are those who never become reconciled, whose disillusionment leads to conscious alienation from the synagogue, even to a certain aversion to it. But it is not a total alienation, for it does not lead to active hostility, least of all to anti-religion. What it leads to is a kind of resentfuly private "inner religion" which on occasion takes on extravagant forms, uncontrolled as it is by the regulative forces of tradition and community experience. It is not a healthy development, but sometimes it is perhaps the only way out.

There are, of course, mitigating influences. In the first place, the description I have given of the present-day American synagogue, if taken literally, is altogether too sweeping. There are synagogues in which sensitive young people can find themselves at home and even be moved to an interest in institutional affairs. There are rabbis—I know some of them myself—who show a real understanding of, and sympathy with, the "returning" generation and are able to speak to them in their own terms. There is the widely influential Hillel organization on the campuses, which has shown a remarkable sensitivity to the religious needs and capacities of the Jewish student. And there are the growing intellectual resources at the disposal of the serious-minded American Jew. The writings of Martin Buber are now widely available, and something of Franz Rosenzweig has recently become accessible. There is also the new religious thinking in America, the writings of A. J. Heschel, Emil Fackenheim, and others, as well as a growing accumulation of translations of basic texts. And the writings of outstanding Christian thinkers of the post-"liberal" school—the two Niebuhrs, Tillich, Kierkegaard—can prove useful in developing an intellectual armature of faith. In any case, the "returning" young Jew need not feel alone even when he can find no real place for himself in the synagogue he has joined. Of course, he will be rebuked for succumbing to "mysticism" and "existentialism", the current bogeymen of the philistines. But he need not mind that, for he can see himself part of a new spiritual movement with wide perspectives, corresponding to the deeper realities of human existence and the real needs of the time. In this conviction, he can keep alive the stirrings of faith and thought, the new sense of his Jewishness, that brought him to the point of "return".

There is indeed, I seem to feel, a new type of Jew emerging in America, a Jew to whom the beliefs and traditions of Judaism are not merely inherited routine, but something new, personal, and exciting. To this type of Jew —and he is represented very considerably in the "returning" generation—the old shibboleths and institutional loyalties, the old catchwords and platitudes, have little meaning. He is looking for something deeper and more basic. What he is looking for, I am convinced, can be found in the authentic tradition of Jewish faith. There is only one question: Is the present-day American synagogue in the position to communicate that tradition to him in a way that he can understand and appropriate? Can the present-day American synagogue provide him with a spiritual home adequate to his needs and, in a measure at least, to his expectations? These questions cannot be answered with any assurance at the present time, but upon the answer will depend a good deal of the future of Judaism in America.

III

There is always something rash and presumptuous in speaking about the "religious situation". The religious situation is indeed, in one sense, a part of the total social and cultural situation, and therefore subject to human scrutiny and analysis. But in another sense, it is something that transcends the social and cultural framework in which it is embedded and takes on a dimension that relates it to the divine-human encounter to which it refers. Analysis, forecasts, and programs become dubious, if not altogether irrelevant, for man's faith in response to God's call is not something that can be charted or reduced to plan. When we deal with the religious situation, we are brought up short before the final mystery in a way that is even more immediate than in the ordinary affairs of life. In the end, we know so little, and hope and trust for so much. What I have said about contemporary religious trends in American Jewry must be taken in this spirit and within these limitations. New forces are at work among American Jews, revealing new possibilities of religious life and thought. But we must not fall into the delusion that we have these forces at our disposal and these developments under our control. They remain hidden in the unfathomable reaches of divine providence and human action. We discern, or think we discern, what is happening, but it is not in what we discern that our confidence can be placed. It is rather in the knowledge that God has his purpose with the world and that shall prevail, and in the conviction that in the fulfilment of that purpose, Jewry, including American Jewry, has its part to play. Just what that part is, or will turn out to be in our time, we do not know, but we do know that we have a function to fulfil, in this time as in any other. In this assurance, we can face the present without illusions and the future without fear or misgiving. In this assurance, too, we may permit ourselves to see in the contemporary religious situation signs of promise opening new perspectives of Jewish faith and Jewish existence in America.

THE INTEGRATION OF THE JEW IN CONTEMPORARY AMERICA

WILL HERBERG

THROUGHOUT the long history of the diaspora, the integration of the Jew into his environment has in major part been conditioned by the forms and structures, by the necessities and pressures, of the larger society in which he has found himself. The patterns of Jewish life, individual and corporate, that have emerged have always been closely related to the social and cultural configurations of the non-Jewish community in which they were embedded. So it was in post-exilic Babylonia, and again the "Babylonia" of the Talmud; so it was in Alexandria and the Hellentistic world generally; so it was in medieval Christendom and Islam; so it was in the East European ghetto community of yesterday; and so again it is in contemporary America. It is, of course, possible in each of these cases, and others that might be mentioned, to discover continuities and to trace the operation of perennial "Jewish" factors in a way transcending the particularities of culture and history, but no understanding of Jewish life is possible in terms of such "Jewish" factors alone; the non-Jewish environment has always exerted a significant, though often indirect and hard-to-discern, influence upon the forms and structures of Jewish existence and upon the interpretation of that existence which itself becomes part of existence.

All this is pre-eminently true of present-day America. It is almost self-evident that the forms and structures of Jewish existence in America today, and the specific kind of integration that is characteristic of American Jewry, are defined primarily by the compelling exigencies of the American environment, which have fundamentally recast the conditions of Jewish community life almost within the span of a single generation. It is the purpose of this paper to call attention to some of the main features of the new form of Jewish integration in mid-twentieth century America, and to explore some of the more important implications for contemporary Jewish life. Nothing more than broad generalizations in outline are intended, but it is hoped that these generalizations will be seen to bear some relation to the concrete realities of Jewish life and will help to illumine them for our understanding.

I

The basic fact that constitutes the context of contemporary Jewish integration is the transformation of America in the course of the past generation from a *Protestant* country into a *three-religion* country. It is necessary to

---

Will Herberg is Graduate Professor of Judaic Studies and Social Philosophy at Drew University. This paper was presented at the Second Annual General Assembly of the Synagogue Council of America.

examine somewhat more closely the nature of this transformation and its concomitant circumstances.

Writing just about thirty years ago, Andre Siegfried described Protestantism as America's "national religion," and he was largely right, despite the ban on religious establishment in the Constitution. Normally, to be born an American meant to be a Protestant; this was the religious identification that in the American mind quite naturally went along with being an American. Non-Protestants felt the force of this conviction almost as strongly as did the Protestants; the Catholic and the Jew experienced their non-Protestant religion as a problem, perhaps even as an obstacle, to their becoming full-fledged Americans; it was the mark of their foreignness. (This was true despite the much esteemed colonial heritage of both Jews and Catholics, since it was not the "old American" elements in these two groups that influenced American attitudes, but the newer immigrant masses.) In the familiar Troeltschean sense, Protestantism constituted America's "established church."

This is no longer the case. Today, to be born an American is no longer taken to mean that one is necessarily a Protestant; Protestantism is no longer the obvious and "natural" religious identification of the American. Today, the evidence seems to indicate, America has become a three-religion country: the normal religious implication of being an American today is that one is either a Protestant, a Catholic, or a Jew. These three are felt, by and large, to be three alternative forms of being religious in the American way; they are the three "religions of democracy," the "three great faiths" of America. Today, unlike fifty years ago, not only Protestants, but increasingly Catholics and Jews as well, feel themselves to be Americans not apart from, or in spite of, their religion, but in and through it, because of it. If America today possesses a "church" in the Troeltschean sense — that is, a form of religious belonging which is felt to be involved in one's belonging to the national community — it is the tripartite religious system of Protestant-Catholic-Jew.

This transformation of America from a Protestant into a three-religion country has come about not as the result of any marked increase in Catholics or Jews — the Protestant-Catholic ratio has remained pretty well the same for the past half century, and the proportion of Jews in the general population has probably been declining. It has come about as an accompaniment of the shift in the pattern of identification in twentieth century America. "When asked the simple question, 'What are you?' " Gordon W. Allport has noted, "only ten percent of four-year-olds answer in terms of racial, ethnic, or religious membership, whereas 75 percent of nine-year-olds do so." "Race" in America today means color, white *vs.* non-white, and racial stigmatization has introduced an element of caste-like stratification into American life. For white Americans, ethnicity and religion have been the major forms of self-identification and social location in American society, and with the fading away of ethnic identifications that has been taking place in the course of the past four decades, since the cessation of large-scale immigration, religion has emerged as a major factor in establishing the "kind" of American one is. In effect, America has been transformed in little more than a single generation from a land of immigrants, where ethnic identification was normal and prevalent, even for the native-born children and grandchildren of immigrants, even for Americans of "old American" stock ("Yankees"), into a tripartite society where identification is increasingly in terms of religious belonging. The change in the meaning of the word "intermarriage" (among whites) — once it meant *ethnic* intermarriage ("Abie's Irish Rose"); today, almost everywhere, it means *religious* intermarriage — vividly reveals how the religious community is replacing the ethnic group as a primary form of self-identification and belonging in contemporary America.

Thus has concrete historical reality given the lie to the best prophecies and prognostications of earlier generations. For what has emerged in contemporary America is neither the "cultural pluralism" nor the "melting pot" of which we once heard so much, and still hear on occasion something here and there. "Cultural pluralism" in the old familiar sense — that is, the perpetuation of ethnic-cultural distinctiveness from generation to generation — was never a real possibility in America, and has been completely refuted by what has happened in the course of the past three or four decades. But neither has the "melting pot" theory been vindicated. Not one vast undifferentiated melting pot operates in present-day American life, but a much more complicated system of three "population pools," religiously defined — the so-called "triple melting pot," Protestant, Catholic, and Jewish. The three religious communities referred to in this designation by no means constitute three distinct cultures, to be contrasted with general American culture, as was the case with the older ethnic group; they are at most variants of a common American culture emerging amidst a complex interplay of regional, ethnic, social, religious, and intellectual factors. This is the reality of American life, a reality that would seem to be best expressed in the phrase "three-religion country."

Two words of caution are necessary. In the first place, all that I have said I would claim to be true only by and large. It seems to me to be most true of the new suburban society that is burgeoning out all around us, least true of the rural areas of the country, and measurably true, sometimes more, sometimes less, of the older cities. Other exceptions and qualifications could and should be made; yet I feel that the suggestions I have ventured are significantly true for America as a whole. The other point of caution is perhaps more important. It would be a great error to believe that with the fading out of the older ethnic identifications, ethnicity has ceased to play a part in American social, cultural and religious life. Ethnicity still remains a potent force, which we cannot afford to overlook; but it has been fused with religion into a unique type of ethno-religious structure very different from the combination of religion and ethnicity that was characteristic of the immigrant. Whereas, for the immigrant, religion was regularly an aspect of his ethnicity, was indeed the religious side of his ethnic culture, for the contemporary third generation, ethnic symbols and traditions are taken up, redefined, and expressed through the religious community. For the immigrant, in other words, religion was included in his ethnic identification; for his typically American grandson or granddaughter, on the other hand, the ethnic elements of their heritage, which they are beginning to view so nostalgically, are included in their religious identification. A basic change, and one that has far-reaching implications for contemporary American life, above all for contemporary American Jewish life.

II

It is in terms of this reality that the American Jew must achieve his integration and work out his destiny in contemporary America. For the American Jew, the transformation of America into a three-religion country has meant a status and a security quite without precedent in the millennia of diaspora history. It has meant that, on one level at least, his Americanness and his Jewishness have ceased to be in conflict — perhaps even to be in tension.

Contemporary American Jewry, particularly the rising third generation, has shown an extraordinary facility for adapting itself to the newer religio-social style of American life. In fact, the celebrated three-generation pattern which Marcus Lee Hansen described in connection with Scandinavian Lutherans in the midwest two decades ago is perhaps nowhere so classically, and yet so uniquely, exemplified as among American Jews of the East European immigration. The "return" of the Jewish third generation to its "heritage" defined in religious terms is abundantly evidenced on almost every campus and in almost every suburban community where Jews are to be found. Practically without exception, Americans Jews of the third generation understand their Jewishness as religious belonging, in fact, as a variety of American religious belonging: to be a Jew means to "belong" to the Jewish religion, just as being a Protestant means to belong to the Protestant religion, and being a Catholic means to belong to the Catholic religion. Among older segments of American Jewry, earlier secular definitions of Jewishness in so-called "national" or "cultural" terms are still to be found, though decreasingly, since even the older generations are beginning to feel the influence of third generation attitudes. For the third generation, which like most of America today tends to see American diversity in religious terms, these once familiar secular definitions of Jewishness are quite unacceptable, in fact hardly intelligible. Their Jewishness, or Judaism, is to them their way of fitting into the American tripartite scheme, their way of taking their place in America as Americans.

So, increasingly, is Protestantism for the American Protestant, and even Catholicism for the American Catholic. Yet in the case of the American Jew there is a difference, a difference that enters very significantly into the developing picture of contemporary Jewish community life. With other immigrants, the emergence of the third generation has regularly meant the approaching dissolution of the ethnic group, which the first generation formed and with which the second generation was perforce identified. True, the third generation, in search of a "heritage," is eager to retrieve — "remember," in Marcus Hansen's brilliant phrase — what the second generation was so often eager to "forget" and abandon. But practically all that the third generation of Italians or Poles, for example, can, as Americans, "remember" is the religion of the grandfather; ethnicity in any other sense can hardly come into consideration here, at least directly. And so the emergence of the third generation among Poles or Italians in America has regularly meant the disappearance of "Italianness" or "Polishness," or rather its dissolution into the religious (that is, the Catholic) community. With the Jews, however, it has been otherwise. The first and second generations of Jews in America repeated the common immigrant pattern: immigrant foreignness followed by an anxious effort to overcome that foreignness and become American. But the third generation of American Jews, instead of somehow finally getting rid of their Jewishness, as the Poles were getting rid of their Polishness, and the Italians were getting rid of their Italianness, have actually begun to *reassert* their Jewish identification and to *return* to their Jewishness. For Jewishness has from the beginning been an ambiguous term, with religious as well as ethnic connotations. What the third generation Jew is doing is shifting his understanding of Jewishness from the ethnic to the religious, which makes it possible for him not only to retain but even to reinforce his Jewish identity — something that his Italian or Polish counterpart could never do with his Italian or Polish identity, since that is irretrievably ethnic. In other words, among Jews no less than among other immigrants, the advancing dissolution of the old ethnic group has been accompanied by the returning identification of the third generation with the religious community, but among the Jews alone this religious community bears the same name as the old ethnic group and is practically coterminous with it. The young Jew for whom the old immigrant-ethnic group has lost all meaning, because he is, and intends to remain, an American and not a foreigner, can nevertheless still think of himself as a Jew because to him being a Jew now means identification with the Jewish *religious* community. The dual meaning of Jewishness, reflecting the complex multidimensionality of Jewish existence, has made the "return" movement of the third generation into a source of renewed strength and vigor for the American Jewish community.

All this defines the new form of the Jewish community that is emerging in the suburbs, in the smaller towns where Jews are to be found, and increasingly even in the large cities. It is a community that understands its Jewishness primarily in religious terms, and sees itself as a third to the Protestant and Catholic communities in the tripartite structure of the "three great faiths." It is a community in which ethnic traditions and ethnic reminiscences play a recognized rôle as symbols of "heritage," but in which these ethnic elements are embedded in a religious matrix, as a kind of "enrichment" of community life. It is a community that is both American and Jewish in a very different way from the way that was characteristic of American Jewry up to our time.

The primary fact about Jewish life in this country today is that for the first time since the mass immigration of the nineteenth century began, the Jew is a full-fledged American, and occupies his place in American society as such. To be a Jew is today one of the three recognized ways of being an

American. The thoroughgoing integration of the Jew into American society has been made possible by this fact.

This same fundamental fact may be seen in another and even broader perspective. By and large, being a Jew in America today does not stand in opposition to one's being an American; on the contrary, being a Jew is precisely the way in which the American Jew is an American, just as being a Protestant or being a Catholic is the way his non-Jewish neighbors and friends are Americans. This is something new in the whole history of the diaspora. I do not think it is too much to say that American Jewry is now achieving a form of integration radically different from anything that is to be found in the thousands of years of Jewish experience. We are only just beginning to catch some inkling of the full implications of the essentially new conditions of Jewish life in contemporary America.

I do not want to suggest that because the integration of the American Jew is that of an "American of the Jewish kind" — which seems to me a not inaccurate way of putting it — that conflict and tension between Jew and non-Jew in our society are at an end. Anti-Semitism runs deeper than any merely sociological analysis can penetrate, and even on the sociological level the new tripartite structure of American society would seem to make almost as much for the exacerbation as for the alleviation of intergroup tensions, at least in this period. Anti-Jewish manifestations are, for the moment at any rate, at a very low ebb, but Protestant-Catholic antagonisms seem to be growing sharper. One thing certainly can be said: group conflict in America is taking a new form in which even those who are attacked or slandered are, nevertheless, implicitly acknowledged to be Americans. The taint of foreignness has been largely removed, and with it one of the most vicious sources of embitterment of group relations in this country.

Nor is the new Americanness of the American Jew really called into question by his bond of interest with the State of Israel. Americans are of many and diverse origins, and they have often retained an attachment, largely sentimental, to the "old country," with which American Jewry's relation to Palestine is rather incongruously assimilated. On the other side, this interest of American Jews in the State of Israel is not to be interpreted in classical Zionist terms. American Jews, by and large, simply do not understand what is meant when they are told that they are in Galut; they feel at home in America, and cannot envisage the possibility of any other home. No more than the tiniest proportion of American Jews evince the slightest intention of resettling in Palestine, and this is today true of all generations alike. The way American Jews understand their Jewishness, a "full Jewish life," to use the familiar phrase, is not only possible in America; it would seem even to require the American scheme of things, particularly American democracy, for its achievement. With all his pro-Zionism — which, let it be noted, is not exactly equivalent to Zionism — the American Jew is most thoroughly American in his orientation, in his hopes and aspirations, and in his understanding of his future. He is America-centered at least as much as his Protestant or Catholic fellow-American. This is part of the meaning of his new pattern of integration.

It would take us too far afield to attempt to describe even briefly the new American Jewish community emerging under the sign of third-generation integration. It is increasingly middle class, increasingly suburban, ethnically and culturally more homogeneous than ever. In all this it is characteristically American. American too is the new role of the synagogue in American Jewish life.

The new form of integration I have described, where the Jew takes his place as an American side by side with Protestant and Catholic as an equal citizen of a three-religion country, means that no form of Jewish activity or pattern of Jewish life can be really understood or approved unless it is somehow related to religion. Secular Jewish institutions, so characteristic of the second generation, are rapidly declining; in the suburbs indeed, where the new forms of integration appear most clearly, purely secular Jewish institutions are virtually unknown. In the suburbs again, and in the smaller towns as well, the Synagogue is recognized by Jew and non-Jew alike as the center of Jewish community life; and even in the big-city Jewish settlements, where the older forms and customs are most deeply entrenched, the synagogue is coming to play a more important and central part in Jewish life than it has played since the earliest immigrant days. But, of course, it is a different synagogue. It is no longer a refuge for the recent immigrant from the bewildering strangeness of the new world; it is the most American of American institutions — in fact, the institutional vehicle of the American Jew's identification not merely as a Jew, but also as an American.

The new religion-centredness and synagogue-centredness of contemporary Jewish life follows from the new forms of Jewish identification and integration we have described. This shift, still in its initial stages, is clearly of major significance. Perceptive observers of secularist, non-religious background have been among the first to note and document it. I call attention to a very thoughtful article by C. Bezalel Sherman, which appeared five years ago in the first issue of the quarterly journal *Judaism*. It is significantly entitled "Secularism in a Religious Framework," and makes the point that under the new conditions of American life, even the secularist Jew who wants to remain a Jew can do so only by helping to build up and finding his place within a religious community, for only as a religious community can American Jewry survive. "It is a fact," the article concludes, "that without affiliation to a shul or a temple countless Jewish individuals would remain without concrete identification with the Jewish collectivity." This statement would have seemed utterly preposterous to the "modern-minded" Jew of a generation or two ago; yet today it must appear a mere commonplace to the younger modern set in the suburbs, who join synagogues and send their children to temple schools at a rate unprecedented in American Jewish history. So quickly do fashions in modernity change, and so drastically have the conditions of Jewish life been transformed in one generation.

III

The integration that American Jewry is now achieving under the influence of a stabilized third generation is an integration of adjustment in terms of religious belonging in which Jews have come to constitute one of the "three great faiths" of the American way. Through this form of integration, which has only recently become available on a large scale and with a fair show of permanence, the American Jew has ceased to be an "outsider" and has become a recognized part of America. The frictions, discriminations and difficulties of Jewish existence have by no means been eliminated, but they are diminishing, and what is even more important, they are beginning to impress the American mind as unfair and unjustifiable, since (within the limits of class stratification) the Jews are coming to be more and more "our kind of people," entitled to be treated like the Americans they are. It is hardly to be disputed that American Jews today are achieving an integration into American society more intimate, more genuinely free and equal, than ever before in Jewish history, and it is an integration that is being achieved not at the expense, but rather through the consolidation, of the Jewish community. It is a situation that holds much promise for American Jewry.

But it is a situation that is by no means unambiguous. The very character of the integration creates serious problems on various levels. I want to make two points in particular.

1. The integration of the Jew into American society today is integration through belonging to one of the three religious communities of the American way. But though religion is required as a vehicle of identification and belonging, it is only too often a religion without content, without true personal involvement, without faith or commitment. For purposes of identification and belonging, a contentless religion, a religion of mere externals, can prove more useful than a religion with an inner content of faith, since personal faith may well find expressions that appear from an external institutional standpoint to be unsocial, individualistic, and disturbing. We are confronted today with the strange paradox of more religiousness and less religion: indeed, we are confronted with the possibility that with the rapid spread of religiousness among American Jews in the form of religious identification and synagogue membership, the very meaning of religion in its authentic sense may be lost for increasing numbers. There is great danger, as one Jewish leader recently put it, that our synagogue cards may hide from us the basically secularistic character of our religion. This is a danger that confronts Protestant and Catholic in America as well as Jew, but the Jew perhaps most of all, since the need for religion as an instrument of identification and belonging is today felt most acutely by the Jew. In every assessment of the religious situation, and in every program of religious revival, the ambiguity of contemporary American religiousness must be taken into account.

2. The integration of the Jew into American society today is an integration of thoroughgoing adjustment to the American Way of Life. In one sense,

this is all to the good, for on its own level the American Way of Life contains very much that is admirable for a democratic mass society. But no matter how admirable the social order, an adjustment that strives to be total and without reservation harbors a real danger for the historical vocation of the Jew, and for his sense of "chosenness" in which this vocation is reflected. A Judaism that is not permeated with a sense of the Jew's distinctiveness and essential unadjustedness is both spurious and unviable. The authentic Jew lives on two levels: as a responsible member of the historical community of which he is part, and as a "son of the covenant," a member of the transhistorical community of faith with which his destiny is inextricably linked. The authentic Jew is *in* this world, but never quite *of* it, never fully conformed or adjusted to the world in which he lives. He preserves a sense of transcendence and lives in a state of tension. It is out of this tension of unadjustedness that the dynamic of Jewish existence is engendered, for it is this tension that, humanly speaking, endows the Jew with the ferment of spiritual creativity and the power to fulfil his historical vocation of "giving the world no rest so long as the world has not God" (Jacques Maritain). There is real danger that out of too great an eagerness to be fully integrated into his environment, the American Jew may come to forfeit his essential unadjustedness as a Jew. It is by no means certain how far the Jew can rid himself of this unadjustedness of his, but the very attempt may well prove disastrous to Jewish life. Here too the situation is ambiguous and full of dangerous possibilities.

These ambiguities and perils, real though they are, should not obscure the fact that the kind of integration which the Jew is achieving in present-day America holds out genuine opportunities for creative Jewish life along new and unexplored lines. The challenge to American Jewry is a great and fateful one; particularly fateful is the challenge to Jewish religious leadership, for the problem confronting American Jewry today is perhaps more than ever a religious problem demanding a religious answer.

V

The American Jew and His Religion

ARTHUR HERTZBERG

THE evidence continues to mount in support of the fact that about three-fifths of all the Jews in America today, in 1964, are affiliated with a synagogue.[1] In close to two decades since the end of World War II, we have witnessed the greatest single synagogue-building boom in the whole of Jewish history in the Diaspora. This has taken place in the very same years during which the American Jewish community has been giving hundreds of millions of dollars towards strengthening the new state of Israel. The attendance of the Jewish young upon some form of Jewish education at some time during their early years has now reached the figure of over eighty percent.[2] It is unusual for a thirteen-year-old nowadays not to be Bar Mitzvah.

Atheism is no longer a recognizable force in the American Jewish community, though it was quite prevalent in the immigrant radical movements fifty years ago. The central institutions of the major religious denominations have flourished in recent years as never before. Among the Orthodox, the Yeshiva University has been transformed from the small struggling school of the 1930's to a major center of Jewish and secular learning. The Jewish

[101

Theological Seminary, the central institution of Conservative Judaism, and its allied bodies have at least tripled in size in the last generation. More recently, the influence of Conservative Judaism has been spreading to countries overseas and even to Israel. Reform Judaism has benefited comparably: in the growing strength of its synagogue body, the Union of American Hebrew Congregations; in increases in staff and facilities at its rabbinical seminary, which now has major centers both in Cincinnati and New York; and in its spread, too, to other countries.

In this generation Jewish learning has been increasingly naturalized in many American universities, as a necessary and normal part of the scene, by the creation of chairs of Jewish studies. Though these academic posts are usually officially secular in nature, most of their incumbents have had rabbinic training, and it is tacitly assumed that their work is meant to contribute to a strengthening of the Jewish spirit at these various schools.

This brief sketch of the current scene evokes the image of a religious community which is mindful of and responsible to its Jewish heritage and clearly committed to continuing Judaism in its various contemporary forms. There is, however, a negative side to the picture. Jews do belong to synagogues at least to the degree to which Protestants and Catholics by birth identify with their churches, but it is notorious that, except for the High Holidays, synagogue attendance is radically lower than church attendance.[3] Various studies that have been made in recent years all point to the same conclusion: half of the enrolled Christians, with variations among the persuasions, go to church regularly on Sunday; no more than one, or at most two, in ten of Jews who belong to a synagogue, are there regularly at the Sabbath services.

Nowadays almost all of the Jewish young are attending college. What we are discovering about the religious views and observances of this generation is therefore of great importance. Various studies agree that almost all Catholic college students and most Protestants believe in God; a substantial number among the Jewish students classify themselves as atheists. Attendance at High Holiday worship on campus, in the years when college begins too early for the students to be at home with their parents, is known to be quite spotty. A growing number, perhaps a third, of the students at the most intellectual schools have been declaring themselves as not at all opposed to intermarriage; these views are indeed reflected in a rate of marrying out that now approaches fifteen percent.⁴

The estate of Jewish observance in the American Jewish community must be added to the negative phenomena. To be sure, everyone observes Hanukkah, but the same "everyone" knows that this is a form of dealing with the problem of Christmas. Obedience to the dietary laws, which are mandatory among both the Orthodox and the Conservative, has declined disastrously. A study of the most committed element of the Conservative laity, the members of the boards of congregations, has demonstrated that even in such circles no more than one in three keep completely *kosher* homes. American Orthodoxy is substantially more obedient in this area, but even among this element one-third does not observe *kashrut*. Notoriously, only a small minority of American Jews, mostly to be found among the Orthodox, observe the Sabbath in their personal behavior.⁵

Thus, there is the image of growing numbers, economic prosperity of the religious institutions, and increasing power of the denominational central bodies. Indeed, in relative terms this generation has witnessed the shift of influence within the American Jewish community from the secular organizations which dominated the scene in the 1930's to the religious bodies which, on every level, are increasingly holding the foreground in the 1960's. On the other hand, religion is ultimately not institutions and structures, or even success in adapting to a changing scene. It is faith, and the personal conduct which flows from it. In that deepest dimension Jewish religion in America is failing amidst its great pragmatic successes.

THE COLONIAL EXPERIENCE

This lack of faith is, however, not a new phenomenon; it is a recurrent pattern of Judaism in America from its very beginning. The Jews have been present on this continent for more than three centuries, and upon arrival in New Amsterdam in 1654, Jewish worship was immediately instituted. It has, therefore, been said that there is a continuity to American Jewish history, and to the history of Judaism in America that reaches back to these origins. This notion, as I shall try to demonstrate, is not true. The history of Judaism in America is the story of several fresh beginnings, after earlier thrusts and impulses created by earlier waves of immigration had worn themselves out. The earlier settlers disappeared either by marrying the newer arrivals or through assimilation and intermarriage. The newer immigrants inherited the institutions of the older community, wherever they did not create their own, thus giving the semblance of continuity, but not its reality. The continuing theme of Jewish religious experience in America has been the same: the creation of institutions in accord with the strength and the devotion of immigrants and their children, followed by their attenuation as these agencies are inherited or neglected by grandchildren and great-grandchildren.

Not all of the Jewish immigrants who arrived in America in colonial times were of Spanish-Portuguese origin; it is probable that half of the less than 3,000 Jews who were in America in the Revolutionary period were Ashkenazim.[6] Nonetheless, the Sephardi tradition was transplanted by the earliest founders of the first Jewish communities, and it dominated the American Jewish scene completely until the first quarter of the nineteenth century. All of the six Jewish congregations which existed in 1790 (New York, Newport, Savannah, Philadelphia, Charleston, and Richmond) were Sephardi. That tradition shared with the Ashkenazi the idea that every individual Jew in a community was subject to the discipline of a central body ruled by the Parnassim, i.e., the oligarchy of rich Jews. It goes without saying that all these early synagogues and communities were Orthodox.[7]

Each of the colonial communities tried to regulate the religious behavior of its individual members. One vital ingredient had changed however. From the beginning, Judaism in America was voluntaristic. In Europe governmental power usually enforced at least some of the decrees of the Jewish elders, because the Jewish community as such existed as a legal entity. In America this was not true. Individuals could therefore choose to behave in personalist terms, and excommunication or disapproval by fellow Jews was far less threatening. Beneath the surface of the Orthodoxy of the organized communities, individuals were drifting away; the congregations could only react by imposing sanctions. So, the mother congregation of the Sephardim in America, Shearith Israel in New York, warned transgressors in 1757:

> Whoever . . . continues to act contrary to our Holy Law by breaking any of the principles commanded will not be deem'd a member of our Congregation, have none of the *Mitzvote* of the Sinagoge Conferred on him and when dead will not be buried according to the manner of our brethren.[8]

But there were transgressors beyond the control of this synagogue or any of the others. Even within the settled communities, intermarriage was a rising threat, which westward migration could only increase. In the eighteenth century and the early years of the nineteenth, the Jews in America, like the Catholics, were a small, respectable but exotic minority. Precisely like the Catholics, the earliest elements were drifting away into the life of the majority in the second and third generation. At least fifteen percent of the marriages contracted by Jews in America before 1840 were intermarriages. It is, for example, very revealing that only two American born clergymen, Gershom Mendes Seixas (during the Revolutionary War), and his nephew Isaac Seixas, ever served at Shearith Israel. After 1839, every one of the Sephardim to occupy that pulpit was born and trained abroad; the present American-born incumbent is an Ashkenazi of East European extraction.[9]

CURRENTS OF REFORM

At the beginning of the nineteenth century, the force of immigration from Central and even Eastern Europe was beginning to be felt on the American Jewish scene. These newer immigrants were coming in greater numbers, first as refugees from the Napoleonic Wars and later under pressure of political and economic changes in Germany. They soon began to organize their own synagogues. The first was Rodeph Sholom in Philadelphia, which was founded in 1802; the second was B'nai Jeshurun in New York, organized in 1825. American Jewish historians have remarked with approbation that these events, especially the second, met no real resistance from older Sephardi communities.[10] It is perhaps likely that the absence of resistance betokened a lessening of assurance in the older circles.

The wave of immigration after 1800 was in itself a mélange of people who came from various Central European countries, from Alsace to Posen, and it even included some Polish Jews. These differing elements were able to communicate with each other in what was then the *lingua franca* of this world, Yiddish. Their economic experience, unlike that of the earlier Sephardim, was not in international trade but in petty shopkeeping and trading. The ongoing American thrust to the West, beyond the Alleghenies, swept up quite a number of the newcomers to the budding towns in the Ohio Valley. There they kept many of the earliest stores and, using these as a base, they peddled in the hinterlands. In places like Cincinnati, Cleveland, and Louisville—indeed everywhere beyond the eastern seaboard—the first congregations to appear were all founded by this newer Ashkenazi immigration. On the frontier the influence of Europe counted for much less than in the seacoast cities of the earlier settlement. Even more than the Sephardim, who brought a few religious functionaries with them, these communities were entirely founded by laymen, and generally not learned ones. The facilities for Jewish observance often did not exist until a congregation was several decades old. The exigencies of life on the frontier, rather than theological change, thus created a predisposition towards religious reform which was soon to affect most of the new synagogues created by the Central European immigration.[11]

Between 1789 and 1882 American Jewish numbers grew from less than 3,000 to 250,000. In one crucial decade, from 1860 to 1870, the number of synagogues in America rose from 77 to 189.[12] This "boom" represented the thrust of the immigrants and of their children, who were raised in American homes within which the languages and memories of Europe were still strong. On the other hand, Jewish religious education throughout this period was of very low estate. This was the period in which education as a whole was being taken out of the hands of the religious bodies and made into a public concern of the state. At the end of the eighteenth century, the Sephardim in New York had been conducting their own schools for the young, in which instruction in English and in Hebrew was combined. In the second half of the nineteenth century these schools yielded to the public school. As a form of acculturation, Jewish instruction, regardless of the point of view of the individual synagogue, became largely an affair of Sunday morning, and it remained so in most places until the turn of the century, after the crucial battles out of which the several American Jewish denominations crystallized.[13] Catechisms were, however, not Hebrew, and certainly not the Talmud. Education more than ideology prejudged, within the nineteenth-century American Jewish community, the proposition that the American born were generally to be less loyal to the heritage than their parents, and that whatever loyalties they would have would be more sentiment than knowledge.

The centrifugal forces were many, and such a milieu was particularly hospitable to the influence of strong individuals. In American economic and social history as a whole this was the period of the making of large fortunes by strong-willed buccaneers. Untrammeled by a set structure, they could survive and flourish by the strength of their wills. Mid-nineteenth century American Jewish history can only be understood in a comparable manner. In actual expression, regardless of the radical nature of its theory, Reform Judaism in its cradle in Germany had been forced to be relatively conservative, for the arena within which the battle for change had to be fought was a legally organized Jewish community in which the State was the decisive power. So, some of Abraham Geiger's reforms failed to be allowed because the government was convinced by his enemies that his religious reforming masked a fervor for political revolution.[14] In America Isaac Mayer Wise, the greatest single figure in Reform Judaism, lost the battle from 1846 to 1850 to convert his first congregation in Albany to his views,[15] but he succeeded in Cincinnati. The same pattern occurred in other places, though often it was the pressure of the laity that created reforms, and not the leadership of the rabbi. Indeed, the very first attempt at religious reform in America had occurred earlier in Charleston, South Carolina, in 1824, when a group of laymen had seceded from the Sephardi congregation Beth Elohim in order to create a more dignified service accompanied by organ music. This soon disappeared, but it was a harbinger of the process of assimilation which was weakening the whole of the earliest Jewish population in America. Isaac

Harby, the moving spirit of this group had written, revealingly, in 1826, that not all who agreed with the founders had joined: "The Jews born in Carolina are mostly of our way of thinking on the subject of worship and act from a tender regard for the opinions and feelings of their parents in not joining the society."[16]

The European elements who were coming to the United States in the middle of the nineteenth century were venturesome and revolutionary. By the very fact that they emigrated, these people betokened their greater readiness to try the new, whatever it might be. Religious reform was, therefore, more likely to occur among these more revolutionary people, in the looser circumstances of American life. Nonetheless, the Jewish patterns from which they were emigrating all contained either the immediate reality or the very recent memory of a *kehillah,* i.e., of a centrally organized Jewish community, not only on the local and regional levels but even, in some places, as a legally recognized national body. The battle for Reform in Germany had begun not in the desire to create a separate party but in the hope of carrying the entire community, as it existed officially, into such modernity. The dream of Jewish rabbinic leadership in America in the middle years of the nineteenth century, regardless of shade of persuasion, tended to this image. The rabbis battled each other not for party advantage but for dominance in the total community. Isaac Mayer Wise hoped that a new liturgy which he edited would eventually be accepted by a rabbinic synod as the American way for all synagogues. He failed. In the same hope he founded a rabbinical seminary in Cincinnati in 1871, the Hebrew Union College. It did not remain a non-partisan school, however, because the more traditional elements soon left it. His synagogue body, the Union of American Hebrew Congregations, founded in 1873, was formed with the same dream, and it too could not hold on to those elements which were outraged by the ritual aberrations of the majority.[17]

Throughout the nineteenth century, since many were pressing for religious reform, a more conservative counter-theme was also present. More tradition-minded elements had also come over in the nineteenth-century immigration. Their leader in this period was Isaac Leeser, a German Jew by birth who served in the middle of the century as the minister of the Sephardi synagogue in Philadelphia. His consistent objective was the creation of an indigenous, American community on the lines of a modern traditionalism. Leeser was willing to cooperate with men of other shades of opinion, including Isaac Mayer Wise, but never to the degree of countenancing major reforms. Under Leeser's influence, the first seminary for the training of rabbis to be created in America, Maimonides College, was founded in 1867 and it lasted until 1873; but after his death religious Conservatism became an unorganized force, which had to find itself and create its tools under the pressure of its recoil from Reform. The men who could not find a place in the new Reform structure included a wide diversity of origins and opinion. They ran the gamut from Sabato Morais, an Orthodox Jew and a Sephardi from Italy, to Hungarian Jews of quite liberal persuasion such as Aaron Wise in New York and Benjamin Szold in Baltimore. In these circles the recoil from Reform represented attachment to the Sabbath, dietary laws, and, above all, to Hebrew as the language of prayer.[18] On the intellectual plane, this was a confrontation between rationalism and a historical romanticism. In human terms, it represented an argument about how far one needed to go from the Orthodoxy of the ghetto in order to be acceptably modern. Under the leadership of Morais, these circles created a rabbinic seminary of their own in 1887, the Jewish Theological Seminary of America.

EAST EUROPEAN INFLUENCES

By this time, East European Jewish immigration, which had been growing in America since the Civil War, had reached flood tide after the Russian pogroms of 1881. The newest wave of immigration was Orthodox; so, at least in inclination, were the earlier representatives of more traditional opinion. Nonetheless, the two streams did not really combine. Their crucial encounter occurred in the years before and after the turn of the century. It is in the understanding of what happened in American Jewish life in the twenty years between 1887 and 1906 that we can find the key to the most recent period of American Jewish history.

By the end of the nineteenth century, the German-Jewish immigration had reached its second generation. Economically, it had participated in the great flowering of America that had occurred after the Civil War. Its most cherished self-image was that it had become indigenous to the American scene. Reform had swept the religious board, so that in 1881 only eight of some two hundred major synagogues were still Orthodox.[19] Obviously these Orthodox synagogue members could not be approached through Reform, for they lacked both the language and the manners.[20] The bridge between the existing Jewish community led by German Jews of Reform persuasion and the new immigrant masses was the traditionalist element among the older settlers. The great historical role played by Cyrus Adler was that he, more than any other single individual, was the instrument through which the circle headed by Jacob Schiff created a network of institutions for the Americanization of the East European Jews.

Adler had grown up in Philadelphia, in the group which had known Isaac Leeser; he was a disciple of Morais. Personally, he was Orthodox in behavior, and he was in especial contact with the traditionalists among the European Jewish scholars. He had taught in the original Jewish Theological Seminary, and he became the key person in creating the conditions for reorganizing it in 1902 and for calling Solomon Schechter to be its president. The reconstituted institution had on its board a group of laymen, headed by Jacob Schiff and Louis Marshall, who were not traditionalists but who regarded this venture as necessary for the East European Jewish masses who were coming to America.

This venture began, like many an earlier one in the history of the American Jewish religion, with the dream of being not a part but of ultimately becoming the entire community. There is evidence that it was presumed on all sides that Reform might remain a separate group, the religion of the older settlers, but it was hoped that all the rest would enroll under the banner of westernized traditionalism.[21] This failed in the first decade of the present century. The lay and academic coalition which refounded the Seminary could not agree, and the supposed clientele of the institutions found it too remote in the early years. The division among the founders came to a head in 1906 in a famous battle between Schechter and Schiff over Zionism. The lay and academic leaders of the Seminary fought each other openly in the columns of the newspapers, for

Schechter announced his adherence to Zionism and Schiff found such a notion to be abhorrent.[22]

Schechter was, of course, more authentically in touch with the sentiment of the people who would be attracted to the kind of Jewish spirituality which he and his faculty represented. But none of the intellectual leaders of this group, not even Schechter, could succeed in defining a non-fundamentalist theology of Judaism that was convincingly traditionalist. Their piety was related to the depth of their reverence for the past and to their sense of involvement in the living body of the international Jewish community. A Jewish high church, like the contemporary anti-Zionism of the rabbis of the various West European countries, simply did not speak for the sentiment of the new American Jewish masses. In stance and emotion the founders of this traditionalism in America belonged together with those of their contemporaries who were the makers of the renaissance of secular Hebrew letters in Russia and with the young pioneers who were then going out to Palestine. Had Schechter taken any other position, the school that he headed would have undoubtedly shriveled, for lack of students and faculty.

On the other hand, by the turn of the century, the flood of immigration from Russia and the lands nearby had brought with it a greater cross-section of that Jewish community. Rabbis and scholars of the East European kind had begun to make their appearance. In the various "East Sides" of the largest cities there were sufficient numbers of very new arrivals to create synagogues that reproduced unchanged the customs of the old world. The Yiddish press had begun earlier, in the 1880's, and some sections of it acted as a rallying point for the East European Orthodox sentiment. After 1881, the numerical changes in the numbers of Jewish synagogues in America were startling. In the census of 1880, 270 congregations of all sizes, the overwhelming majority of Reform persuasion, were to be found; by 1890 there were already 533 synagogues in America, and almost all of the new ones were created by the most recent immigrants.[23]

THE EMPHASIS ON TRADITION

Especially outside of New York City, the new arrivals felt the pressure of the then existing American Jewish establishment, which was overwhelmingly Reform. Men like H. Pereira Mendes, i.e., the most Orthodox elements in the relatively small circle of Americanized traditionalists, participated and even took the lead in trying to organize central bodies for Orthodox Judaism in America, in which they and the newer immigrants would belong together. The Union of Orthodox Jewish Congregations was founded under Mendes' presidency in 1898, and most of those who issued the original call for its creation were associated with the Jewish Theological Seminary of America. Nonetheless, this body was soon taken over by Yiddish-speaking recent immigrants, who regarded the Seminary as much too religiously liberal. The East European rabbis, who were fresh from the great *yeshivoth* of Lithuania, Russia and Poland, could not really imagine themselves as belonging together with Western, Seminary-educated rabbis whose lives were not entirely devoted to talmudic learning. These rabbis organized their own body in 1902, the Union of Orthodox Rabbis of America and Canada (the Agudath ha-Rabbanim). Those who belonged to this body were keenly aware that in their own persons they would have increasing difficulty in communicating with the American born young, who were beginning to appear in the families in their charge. Very early, they began to labor for the creation of *yeshivoth* in America of the old type, to produce not only learned laymen but also rabbis who would be as pious and as learned in the Talmud as their fathers, but who would also possess sufficient American education to be able to lead in the new land. The first kernels of the two existing major Orthodox institutions of rabbinic learning in America, the Yeshiva University in New York and the Hebrew Theological College in Chicago, appeared in the 1890's; despite many vicissitudes in the early years, they persisted. In 1915 two struggling *yeshivoth* in New York were combined, under the presidency of Dr. Bernard Revel, into the Rabbi Isaac Elchanan Theological Seminary, out of which has grown the present Yeshiva University, the largest Jewish academic institution in America. As the years have gone by, these schools have not remained alone, for, in every decade since its beginning, Orthodoxy in America has produced its *yeshivoth*. The tendency has indeed been for newer Orthodox groups arriving in America to produce institutions that are even more traditionalist than the older ones.

Two other problems confronted the leadership of Yiddish-speaking American Orthodoxy at its very beginnings. One was the setting of standards for Jewish observance, especially in the area of *kashrut*. This has been a consistent concern not only of the rabbinate but especially of the Union of Orthodox Jewish Congregations, which is today the major single agency in the field of *kashrut* supervision. Variations in degree of strictness even among the Orthodox and, more important, the failure to create real centralization in its organized ranks, have stood in the way of producing complete order in this field. Great Orthodox energies have gone into the field of Jewish education, and it is here that this community has scored its most notable successes. The movement for Jewish parochial education was initiated by these elements, often against violent opposition from their more religiously liberal, Americanized predecessors. The schools that now exist, with perhaps 50,000 students enrolled, are overwhelmingly to this day under Orthodox auspices, even though the Conservatives have entered this field within the last decade.

Within a generation, the East European Orthodox impulse produced its own version of Americanization. This was the notion that it was possible to participate fully in the life of America and yet to live in obedience to every prescription of the law. A second generation began to appear which was at once religiously separatistic and yet willing to cooperate with other bodies on a plane of equality. In 1922 the Young Israel Movement, which had begun in 1912 under the influence of younger leaders of Conservative Judaism, was taken away from them by Orthodox Jews, in the name of a completely Orthodox program and outlook. On the other hand, during this same decade comparable Orthodox elements were willing to join, as the Yiddish speaking Agudath ha-Rabbanim was not, in the formation of the Synagogue Council of America, which is the umbrella organization for all three of the religious denominations. Separatism and cooperation have, indeed, been the twin poles around which the career of Orthodoxy in America has revolved in organizational terms.

The post-1882 immigration not only changed the face of Orthodox Judaism in America; it has radically remade the other two movements. On the surface, the issue has been Zionism, but that has only been the symbol of a deeper movement. The great current represented by the children of the new immigrants can be characterized by three desires: the wish to upgrade themselves socially, either by joining congregations created by older waves of immigration or by establishing their own in an Americanized image; the need to affirm an unideological, often not even overtly religious commitment to the Jewish way; and the desire to continue strong emotions which bound them to the Jewish communities overseas, from which their parents had sprung. The travail of World War I, the continuing difficulties of the inter-war period, and the climactic horror of the Nazi years could only reinforce these feelings. These Jews were glad to be in America and deeply sensitive to what was going on outside this land of freedom. Except as a thin coating at the top, the descendants of the older Jewish community were evaporating from the Conservative congregations and even from those of Reform. The dramatic changes that have taken place in both groups in the last half century have been due not to a change of heart but to a change of population.

Until the death of Cyrus Adler in 1940, Conservative Judaism was headed at the top by a German Jew with Sephardi connections who was a non-Zionist, but in that period the largest single influence was probably that of Mordecai M. Kaplan. His Reconstructionism was religiously radical, almost a form of humanism, but it was unshakably committed to Zionism. Kaplan was the leader of many Jewish intellectuals who were the children of the most recent immigrants, regardless of their religious persuasion. The influence of this thinking was spreading in the 1930's among younger elements of Reform Judaism as well. In 1919, the Central Conference of American Rabbis, the organization of the Reform rabbinate, was still opposed to Zionism. Within two decades, by 1937, this body had moved to an official neutrality that was, in effect, a pro-Zionist position. The makers of the change were in largest numbers rabbis and their congregants who had come to Reform Judaism in recent decades from East European backgrounds. Those who soon organized the American Council for Judaism in opposition to this change quite validly claimed that they spoke for the authentic earlier Reform tradition. They were what remained in the organized Jewish community of the families of the immigrants of the nineteenth century, but the institutions created by their ancestors had been taken away from them.

Religious Diversity and Coordination

In organizational terms, each of the three major groups within American Judaism today possesses well-developed, comparable structures. The earliest to be created were, as we have seen, those of Reform Judaism. It is probable that there are today about a million Jews affiliated with Reform congregations. There are 650 congregations identified with the Union of American Hebrew Congregations. More than 850 rabbis belong to the Central Conference of American Rabbis. From social action to education there is well developed programming at the two national headquarters of Reform in New York and Cincinnati. The Conservatives started later in the creation of their institutions. Their synagogue body was not organized until 1913, but the United Synagogue of America today numbers almost 800 congregations within its ranks. The enrolled strength of the Conservative movement is well over one million; moreover, because this is the middle-of-the-road group, the unaffiliated tend to look to it rather than to the other two as their own. All the recent studies of religious preference, as separate from formal affiliation, show almost unvaryingly that about half the Jews in America regard themselves as Conservative. The Rabbinical Assembly of America, the organization of Conservative rabbis, has a membership approaching 800. The Union of Orthodox Jewish Congregations claims all those synagogues which are not formally identified with the other two groups, some 2,500. Certainly nowhere near that number pay dues to that body. In all its varieties, from English-speaking liberal Orthodoxy to the most recent Yiddish-speaking Hasidic enclaves, Orthodoxy in America today commands the allegiance of perhaps one million Jews. In the Orthodox rabbinate, the Rabbinical Council of America numbers 800; the Agudath ha-Rabbanim perhaps 600; and there are many who are not affiliated with either body. To this day, despite some notable successes of the other two groups in producing their own religious leaders, the Orthodox remain the major suppliers of rabbis for all the divisions of American Jewry, since this group produces all of its own clergy and at least a substantial minority of those who serve the other two groups.[24]

The leadership of the major denominations, and of the various schools within them, have labored for decades to define theological differences among them. This has been particularly marked on the theological left, in the efforts of the Reconstructionists, and in the continuing ferment among the Orthodox, especially as they have battled against the inroads within their group of such Conservative practices as mixed seating. In theory, all the Orthdox groups agree on the revealed nature of all of Jewish law; for the Reform group the moral doctrine of Judaism is divine and its ritual law is man made; the Conservatives see Judaism as the working out in both areas of a divine revelation that is incarnate in a slowly changing and adjusting human history; the Reconstructionists view Judaism as the evolving civilization created by the Jewish people in the light of its highest conscience. But assent cannot be produced in each group for even these minimal definitions. What really marks the various bodies in the mind of the Jewish community is their differences in ritual practice. The Reform, in their overwhelming majority, disregard dietary laws; the Orthodox are committed formally to obey every jot and tittle of them. Even the leaders of Conservative Judaism are, in practice, usually sufficiently liberal about *kashrut* to permit themselves to dine out on food that is not in and of itself *trefah,* regardless of the dishes on which it is prepared. All but the Reform wear hats at divine service, and that custom is slowly returning to some Reform congregations. Only the Orthodox separate the sexes in the synagogue, but the practice is bit by bit becoming less prevalent in English-speaking Orthodox congregations. We are, in reality, on the religious scene confronted by a continuum, at least in native-born circles, in which the ritual variations shade from one group into the other. Each of the groups still has a distinctive character, based on the nature of the majority of its congregations, but the dissimilarities have clearly lessened. Predictions are dangerous but it is not unlikely that in fifty years the three denominational groups will continue to exist; this will, however, represent more the momentum of their separate organizational strengths than any sharpening of theological and ritual differences.

That American Jewish religion is in many senses a continuum is evident, in part, in the freedom with which many people change denominational allegiance as they move. Their choice is very often the nearest synagogue rather than the one that is denominationally the same as the synagogue they just left. This phenomenon is more evident still in the role of the rabbi in the American Jewish religious community. It is substantially the same in all three groups. Not even among the Orthodox, except for a few renowned authorities in the field of talmudic law, is the rabbi today much occupied with rendering decisions on Jewish practice. He is everywhere a preacher, chief executive officer of a congregation, pastor, and moving spirit in the synagogue's educational program. With some variations of emphasis, denominations expect their rabbis to be communal leaders in Jewish affairs and representative figures in the general community. Jewish scholarship, in either its classic or modern forms, is rather low on the list of what congregations demand from their clergy. There are, indeed, a few notable scholars in the practicing rabbinate in America today, but their learning is more a matter of personal predilection than of communal demand. In short, the rabbi in America today is a cross between a pastor or parish priest and the leader of an ethnic group. The East European Ashkenazi tradition produced, at its very end, two images of a proper spiritual leader: either that of the Lithuanian tradition— profound learning—or that of the Hasidic tradition—holiness. The American rabbi today is rich in eloquence, organizational talent, and practical achievement; the American scene has evoked neither intellectual endeavor nor transcendant piety, but it has not done so in American Christianity either. The most Jewish figure on the American scene, the rabbi, is thus in many senses the most American.[25]

In 1926, after the structure of the three denominations was well developed, an initial attempt at co-operation was made in the creation of the Synagogue Council of America, the central body within which both the lay and the rabbinic organizations of all the groups sit together. For certain purposes, especially in the area of official representation before the general community, this co-operation has continued to work. It is nonetheless true that each of the major groups has by and large tried to behave, whenever possible, as if it were the total Jewish religious community. The real effort of organized Jewish religion in America continues to revolve around each individual synagogue and the denomination to which it belongs. There is a sense of belonging to *Klal Yisrael*, the entire Jewish community, but that feeling encompasses all Jews, regardless of their religion or lack of it. There is little sense of special relationship of the religionists with each other.

TRENDS AND PORTENTS

Several factors have operated to strengthen the institutions of American Judaism in the last quarter of a century. To deal first with the obvious ones, the travail of Jewry the world over recalled many American Jews to their moorings. In America as a whole, religious identification has increasingly become respectable, the "American thing to do," especially in the middle classes. As the mass of Jewry moved from its original economic station in the working class and in petty trade to economic affluence, it has conformed to the mores of the majority of that class by becoming "religious." The creation of the state of Israel has certainly served to raise the public dignity of Jewish identity, and that has expressed itself among some, in contemporary American terms, through joining the synagogue.

There was, in addition, perhaps a more fundamental factor: as before in the history of the American Jewish community, the second generation of the immigrants came to maturity by building a religious life in the image of its Jewish memories, tempered by the immediate reality of the America of its day. This had happened in the half century around 1800, through the agency of the small group then present in the country. Indeed, not only synagogues but both proto-Zionism, in the incident of Mordecai Manuel Noah's abortive attempt to found a Jewish territory near Buffalo, and proto-Reform, in Charleston in 1824, had occurred very early. The heyday of American Reform was in the last decades of the nineteenth century and the early years of the twentieth, when the human material which created the imposing synagogues built in that time was overwhelmingly first and second generation.

It can fairly be said that until the recent revival of Reform as one form of the Judaism of the descendants of East European immigrants, almost no Reform congregations, perhaps not even a single one, were founded in America by German Jews of the third generation. The second generation of East Europeans to some degree moved into Reform. Many more expressed themselves religiously by building new cathedral synagogues in the 1920's, during the brief years of prosperity which preceded the crash of 1929. Most of these institutions began as decorous, and therefore, "American," Orthodox congregations, with English sermons, and many were Conservative within two decades. It is not too much to say that the *Minhag America* of the East European second generation was Conservative Judaism, not necessarily always as part of the organized instruments of that group, but as an influence affecting the other two.

The third and fourth generations of previous waves of Jewish immigration were, at most, heirs and not builders or creators. We are now approaching the same point in the career of the last great wave. To be sure, American Jewry has been refreshed since the end of World War II by the arrival of some tens of thousands of deeply Orthodox Jews, those remnants of East European Jewry who survived Hitler. In places like Williamsburg in Brooklyn and a few other enclaves, some of these people, especially the Hasidim, have reproduced their old life. These newest immigrants have exerted a certain influence among older Orthodox elements, and it has been a revitalizing one. It is nonetheless true that the overwhelming majority of American Jews are not recent arrivals. Whatever may be the destiny of the newest Orthodox impulse, the future of the American Jewish community rests in the grandchildren and the great-grandchildren of older settlers. The mass of numbers and the strength of their institutions are positive factors, but it is probably true that, in relation to the size of their populations, the Jewish communities of 1800 and 1880 were equally well served by institutions as strong. The question remains: will that generation which is now the heir succeed where its predecessors, at a comparable point in their histories, failed? Will the account of American Jewish religious life to be written a generation hence be a tale of great historic success in enjoying religious freedom and coping with it, or will it be an elegy?

The American Jew and His Religion   (pp. 101–119)

BY ARTHUR HERTZBERG

Notes

1. See my article, "Religion," *AJYB*, vol. 59 (Philadelphia, 1958), pp. 114–15.
2. See A. M. Dushkin and U. Z. Engelman, *Jewish Education in the United States* (New York, AAJE, 1959), pp. 39–44.
3. See M. Sklare and M. Vosk, *The Riverton Study* (New York, 1962), p. 11. In that community, three out of ten did not observe the High Holidays; only two out of ten came to synagogue on other occasions.
4. The most recent study of intermarriage is that of E. Rosenthal, "Studies of Jewish Intermarriage in the United States," *AJYB*, vol. 64 (Philadelphia, 1963), pp. 3–53. Jewish college students in relation to their religion have been studied recently in a survey

that appeared in *The National Review* (October 8, 1963), pp. 279–302. The survey came to the radical conclusion that "students raised as Jews tend to abandon the tenets of their faith, regardless of what kind of college they attend." This must be qualified by the fact that Jewish allegiance is not necessarily measurable by the kind of theological commitment that the editors of *The National Review* had in mind. It is nonetheless true that the intensity of Jewish concern has been lessening in the college community.

5. See the best study of a large Jewish community, S. K. Bigman, *The Jewish Population of Greater Washington in 1956* (Washington, 1957), pp. 114–15. This finding is consonant with what was discovered about the religious behavior of the leadership, i.e., the most committed part, of Conservative synagogues: see E. Lehman, *National Survey on Synagogue Leadership* (New York, n.d.), pp. 13–15. The members of Conservative synagogue boards keep *kosher* at home as follows: 37% "strictly," 27% "partially," i.e., they buy *kosher* meat but have no separate dishes, and 36% are not *kosher* at all. This survey found that a majority of the synagogue leaders did not attend Sabbath services. No question was asked regarding personal observance of the Sabbath. The best discussion of the current estate of Jewish observance is still that in A. Gordon, *Jews in Transition* (Minneapolis, 1949), pp. 71–147.

6. There is considerable conflict of scholarly opinion as to the size of the Jewish community in the United States in the Revolutionary period. The estimate that has generally been given is 2,500 to 3,000, for 1790, the date of the first census of the United States. See figures in S. Wolf, *The American Jew as Patriot, Soldier and Citizen* (Philadelphia, 1895), p. 12, and J. R. Marcus, *Early American Jewry*, vol. 2, p. 393. This estimate has been scaled down in more recent writing. The lowest figure is that given by I. Rosenswaike in "An Estimate and Analysis of Jewish Population in the United States in 1790," *PAJHS*, vol. 49, p. 34. He concludes that "in the entire country there were possibly 1,300 to 1,500 Jews."

7. D. de Sola Poole, *An Old Faith in a New World* (New York, 1955), pp. 258–301.

8. H. B. Grinstein, *The Rise of the Jewish Community of New York* (Philadelphia, 1947), p. 334.

9. Poole, *op cit.*, p. 459. Until 1700 the Sephardim were twice as numerous as the Ashkenazim. In the course of the eighteenth century the Ashkenazim grew to outnumber Sephardim. See also M. Stern, "Function of Genealogy in American Jewish History," *Essays in American Jewish History* (Cincinnati, 1958), pp. 79–81, 85; and the Preface to the same author's *Americans of Jewish Descent* (Cincinnati, 1960). Stern's researches have shown that by 1840 the early Sephardim had disappeared almost entirely as a

separate group, either through marriage with Ashkenazim or because of a rate of intermarriage of at least 15%. In re the provenance of the clergy of Shearith Israel, see Poole, *op. cit.*, pp. 158–210.
10. Poole, *op. cit.*, pp. 437–38.
11. R. Learsi, *The Jews in America* (Cleveland, 1954), pp. 64–78.
12. For a summary of the statistical information in this area, see U.Z. Engelman, "Jewish Statistics and the United States Census of Religious Bodies (1850–1936)," *Jewish Social Studies*, 9 (1947), pp. 127–174.
13. Grinstein, *op. cit.*, pp. 243–51.
14. M. Weiner, *Abraham Geiger and Liberal Judaism* (Philadelphia, 1962), p. 18.
15. D. Philipson, *The Reform Movement in Judaism* (New York, 1931), pp. 335–36.
16. C. Reznikoff and U. Z. Engelman, *The Jews of Charleston* (Philadelphia, 1950), p. 128.
17. One famous incident was the serving of *trefah* food at the graduation banquet in 1883 for the first four graduates of the Hebrew Union College. See M. Davis, *The Emergence of Conservative Judaism* (Philadelphia, 1963), pp. 219–20. See also Philipson, *op. cit.*, p. 379.
18. Davis, *op. cit.*, pp. 317–18.
19. J. R. Rosenbloom, "The American Jewish Community," in B. Menkus, ed., *Meet the American Jew* (Nashville, 1963), p. 8.
20. See the most recent discussion in N. Glazer and D. P. Moynihan, *Beyond the Melting Pot* (New York, 1963), p. 139.
21. Davis, *op. cit.*, p. 322.
22. The Schechter-Schiff controversy over Zionism is described by C. Adler, *Jacob H. Schiff: His Life and Letters*, vol. 2 (New York, 1929), pp. 163–69. Schiff wrote Schechter on September 22, 1907: "The political doctrine brought forth and advocated by Zionism has nothing in common with the Jewish messianic hope." Earlier Schiff had maintained that Zionism was incompatible with American patriotism.
23. Rosenbloom, *op. cit.*, p. 10.
24. See my essay, "The Conservative Rabbinate: a Sociological Study," *Essays in Jewish Life and Thought*, J. L. Blau *et al.*, ed. (New York, 1959), p. 331.
25. This description of the role of the rabbi in America agrees with that presented by M. Sklare, *Conservative Judaism* (Glencoe, Illinois, 1955), pp. 159–95, and by J. E. Carlin and S. H. Mendlovitz, "The American Rabbi: A Religious Specialist Responds to the Loss of Authority," *The Jews* (Glencoe, Illinois, 1958), pp. 377–414.

Bibliographical Note

There is, as yet, no monograph on the history of Jewish religion in America. The best recent statement is a long essay by Moshe Davis in *The Jews: Their History, Culture and Religion*, Louis Finkelstein, ed., I, 3rd edition (New York, 1960), pp. 488–587. Information and insights on various aspects of the subject will be found in the one-volume works on the Jews in America; in that mine of information which is the quarterly, *Publications of The American Jewish Historical Society;* in the several collections of documents published by Jacob Marcus and by Salo W. Baron and Joseph L. Blau; and in an early volume by Max J. Kohler, *Phases in the History of Religious Liberty in America* (Baltimore, 1905). The monographic studies of the various individual cities, some of which are mentioned in the notes, are rich in material.

On the history of Reform Judaism in America, the following two volumes are the most useful: David Philipson, *The Reform Movement in Judaism* (New York, 1931), and Sylvan D. Schwartzman, *The Story of Reform Judaism* (New York, 1953). The key figure in the history of American Reform Judaism, Isaac Mayer Wise, has been the subject of a recent biography: *Rabbi in America,* by Israel Knox (Boston, 1957).

Conservative Judaism has recently been treated by Moshe Davis in *The Emergence of Conservative Judaism* (Philadelphia, 1963). There is as yet no history of the Conservative movement after 1902. The career of Solomon Schechter has been described in a biography, *Solomon Schechter,* by Norman Bentwich (Philadelphia, 1938). Though in this bibliographical note only historical studies are listed, an exception needs to be made for one book that does not fit that category, the volume in which the Reconstructionist position was announced and defined: Mordecai M. Kaplan, *Judaism As A Civilization* (New York, 1934).

The greatest dearth of published historical writing is in relation to Orthodox Judaism in America. Its history is yet to be written. It is revealing that Leo Jung in *Guardians of Our Heritage* (New York, 1958) does not discuss a single American figure. The ultra-Orthodox community in Brooklyn has recently been the subject of study. The best book is Solomon Poll, *The Hasidic Community of Williamsburg* (Glencoe, Illinois, 1962).

THE NATION AND THE INDIVIDUAL

ABRAHAM JOSHUA HESCHEL

Disaster, Deliverance, Confusion — these three words mark the supreme issues of Jewish existence in our day. Yet though involving the heart and center of our existence, they remain at the periphery of our thinking. The memory of the Disaster is being effaced from our minds, the Deliverance we take for granted, and the Confusion we ignore. Since the day the Temple was destroyed there has been no age like ours. It is as if God had rolled up the centuries of Jewish history and placed it under our heads. What is the meaning of all this? What is the import of this hour? And where is the thinking of our day?

The Torah which God gave to Moses was "white fire engraved with black fire."[1] And this is the image of the events we experienced — the white fire of the upbuilding of Israel engraved with the black fire of ruin and disaster. The fire conceived and bore light. But if we are deaf to the cries out of the flames, who will understand the signs of birth? Horrible are the pangs. What will come into the world? We have grown used to the thought that six millions have been consumed. We live and think as if there had never been an Auschwitz or a Majdanek. How fast does the power to forget spread! I am told that some Jewish children in America say to their teacher who mentions these martyrs in class: "It could not have happened. You have imagined it!" Six millions were wiped off the face of the earth. And there is the danger that they will also be annihilated from our memories. Are they doomed to a twofold annihilation?

"The parchments are consumed but the letters soar aloft."[2] Who has heard a thing like this? Who has witnessed such a marvel? The return to Zion we had dared to yearn for is actually taking place. The hand of the Almighty was present in this deed, and who shall say, there is nothing new under the sun? Yet the heart does not comprehend what the eyes behold. We have not grasped the marvel, we have not felt the mystery, we seem powerless to speak, to illumine our lives in the light of events. At times we feel as if a deep slumber had descended upon us; the visions appear to us like the words of a sealed, enigmatic book. Some even shake their heads at all this and say, there is no wonder in the creation of Israel, no mystery, no marvel. We stand at a climax of Jewish history, and what we witness surpasses our power of comprehension and appreciation. We are a generation

---

This article is based upon an address given at the 1957 Jerusalem Ideological Conference. The translation is in part by Rabbi Simḥa Kling and the *editor*.

[1] See ירושלמי — שקלים פרק ו׳, ה״א, ב׳, ע״ד; סוטה פרק ח׳, ה״ג, ילקוט שמעוני, שמות ר״פ and cf. כ״ב, ע״ד: תורה שנתן הקב״ה למשה עורה של אש לבנה וכתובה באש שחורה . . . [ועם שכותב קנה הקולמוס בשערו ומשם נטל משה זיו הפנים].

[2] עבודה זרה י״ח, א: גוילין נשרפין ואותיות פורחות.

10

which has the evidence of the mystery of Israel, but we do not know how to testify.

To interpret our history in the light of mere facts is to distort it. To be literal is to be ludicrous. To be sure, from the point of view of practical reason and logic the efforts of the Zionists were doomed to failure. The Zionist vision was like a fable, or a dream, and in the eyes of practical people it was absurd to be a dreamer and to build the future of a people upon the flimsy grounds of fable. Yet where practical logic failed, visionary logic succeeded. Like a beacon in the darkness of history came the State of Israel. It is a haven of refuge for those in despair who cried for a sign that God is not forever estranged from the world of history.

Our vision must turn in four directions. "What is above? What is below? What is ahead? And what is behind?"

What is above? Know what is above.

What is below? Below is the abyss of evil.

What is ahead? Ahead are the generations that shall ask: What did they say, those who lived through the Disaster and the Deliverance? Let us not forget the words of our sages: "The things that a man does in his childhood return to blacken his face in old age."[3]

And what is behind? Behind are generations of Jews who kept faith with the God of Israel and his Torah.

The Holy One, blessed be He, took from under the throne of Glory a fiery coin, showed it to Moses, and said, "They shall give this. They shall give like this."[4] The thought of our days will be preserved only in one form, in one coin: in a coin of fire, of white fire and of black fire.

"The letters soar aloft." Ours is the task of putting together the letters which hovered over Majdanek and Auschwitz with the letters with which Zion and Jerusalem are being built. The secret of history is concealed in our destiny. Deep within history lie the wonder and the horror, the satanic and the sublime. We have seen civilization in its depravity, and a prophetic vision in its sublimity. It behooves every Jew to say: I am glory and ashes.

This is our tragedy. We live as if there were nothing unique about Jewish existence, as if all sufferings had been in vain, as if prophetic teachings were a misunderstanding. Our cardinal sin is that we do not grasp the sublime in our existence, that we do not know how to adjust our lives to the grandeur, our thoughts to the mystery, the single one in Israel to the Eternal One of Israel. What is sublime in the existence of Israel? The shrieks from the gas chambers, such as have never been uttered by man, somehow resound in our depths. They are too horrible to be conveyed. Woe to the generation in whose time man could become so debased. Never has the mystery of Jewish existence been as striking as in our time. Never has a sanctuary been hallowed

[3] שבת קנ"ב, א: דברים שאדם עושה בילדותו משחירים פניו לעת זקנתו.

[4] Cf. ירושלמי שקלים פרק א', מ"ו, ע"ב: דאמר רבי מאיר כעין מטבע של אש הוציא הקב"ה מתחת כסא כבודו והראהו למשה ואמר לו זה יתנו כזה יתנו.

with so much innocent anguish as that of the Jewish people. Every one of us alive is a spark of an eternal candle and a smouldering ember snatched from the fire. Without his knowing it, every one of us is crowned with the Holy. Let us learn to be aware of the majesty which hovers over our existence. Great is our sorrow, and great is our task. Let us rescue the heart of man, that heart which may reach up to the heart of Heaven. Let us regain a sensitivity to the Presence of God in the world.

We are Jews as we are men. The alternative to our existence as Jews is spiritual suicide, disappearance. It is not a change into something else. Judaism has allies but not substitutes. Every people has a religion that it has received from others. Only in Israel people and Torah are one. All of Israel, not only the select few, are the bearers of this unity. Let us look at our recent history. The talmudic statement, "A servant-girl in our day has seen more than sages and prophets,"[5] is true for our time. The life of a Jew is a sign and testimony that man hovers continually between the abyss below and the heaven above. The depravity of civilization is proof that a godless people is bound to become a satanic people. Man has become the enemy of God. The restoration of the land of Israel is a testimony to the world that the prophetic vision is not a dream, that the word of our God shall endure forever.

If We Do not Build a House for the Individual . . .

Much has been spoken and written in our midst about nation and society, about the community and its institutions. But the individual has been lost sight of. It is my task to write about this neglected subject. It is common knowledge that Judaism is not merely concerned with the individual. He who goes his own way abandons the Jewish way. To withdraw oneself from the community is to detach oneself from the God of Israel. However, it is a fact that the Jewish people to-day is like a tree from which many fruits are falling off. A tree does not bear fruit every day. Its yield diminishes, and the fruit that falls from it is bound to rot.

What was the status of the Jewish community in the Diaspora in the past? The Jew as an individual occupied a spiritual position in the world. His life had form, style, and inner dignity. He stood for certain ideas; he lived for a higher purpose. It was his national existence which lacked form and dignity. That was the purpose of the Zionist movement: to emphasize the distress of the Jews as a people, to proclaim that the problems of the individual were secondary to those of the people, that unless a national home were built the efforts and accomplishments of the individual, however great, would be like whirling dust.

With the rise of Israel as a country, the Jews in Israel found their solution to the national question. In the meantime the spiritual plight of the individual had deteriorated, especially in the Diaspora. He had cast off the traditional

---

[5] Cf. מכילתא בשלח ב׳: ראתה שפחה על הים מה שלא ראה יחזקאל.

forms but found no way to fill the void. Even those who are Jews publicly, cease to be Jewish privately. Jewish *belonging* is to substitute for Jewish *living*. If the individual is lost to Judaism in his privacy, the people is in danger of becoming a phantom. Every individual is a pillar on which the future of Judaism rests. There is no vicarious Judaism: no institution can discharge the responsibilities of the individual. Tradition is not the monopoly of an elite. Each Jew is obliged to say: "Into my hands has been given the future of the entire people." Just as every person is a microcosm, so is every Jew a miniature Jewish people. He carries within him the soul of the entire people. Most of the מצוות devolve upon the individual and are to be carried out by the individual. This is the greatness of Judaism: it makes the individual the mirror of the people.

The problem of the individual is the urgent issue of our time. If we do not build a house for the individual, we shall labor in vain in the building of the nation. There is nothing in the universal that is not contained in the particular. One stands aghast before the multitudes of our people: hearts without a Jewish thought, homes without a Hebrew book, books without Jewish content. A generation has risen that knows not the Torah, that knows not how to distinguish between the Sabbath and the weekday, between the sacred and the sensational. A grudge against Judaism still rankles in the hearts of many Jews; there are individuals who hate the very fact of their having been born Jews. Many who are anxious to study any of the world's cultures have a strange lack of curiosity in regard to the sources of Jewish learning. There are still, of course, guardians of the wall, Jews who keep the Law and scrupulously observe all its injunctions. But we are not speaking now of the pious but of the lost sheep of the House of Israel. Horrid is the desolation, and fearful the failure. But who is to blame? The flock or the shepherds? Judaism or the Jews?

It will be said: The trouble is that the will is gone and that one cannot coerce the dictates of the heart. The truth is that there is an embarrassment of the souls, and a silent cry for God. A cry that may turn to prayer. The stirrings of uneasiness are vague. Who will lend a language to the soul? Direction to the mind? The bodies are well-fed, but the tongue is parched. The triumphs of paganism have turned to calamities. A thirst has arisen in many hearts, and we see signs of a revival. Many who had strayed are trying to bring their children closer. Some parents are sending their children to All-Day Schools. And even among those who desecrate the Sabbath there is a desire to find a way back to its observance. Many lost souls are searching for a root and anchor, for a path to God. And if we do not open a way for them, many will go after strange gods. Let us not forget the danger of conversion which lies in wait for us in every country. The opportunity for a revival is glorious, and the possibilities numerous. But it is slipping through our hands.

Many leaders of our people do not know *the language of the soul*. A person goes to the synagogue. His mouth is sealed, his mind blocked. Who shall open his heart? Who shall set his soul aright? It is written in our Siddur, נשמת כל חי תברך את שמך, "The soul of every living thing praises Thy name," and shall the soul of the Jew not know how to praise? On every Sabbath multitudes of Jews gather in the synagogues, and they often depart as they have entered. The soul does not know how to pour itself out. There is a gulf between the soul of the individual and the atmosphere of the synagogue. There are those who have come from afar, from the depths of assimilation, with a vague yearning in their hearts. What they sought for was not given them, and what they already had was taken from them.

Many are the trials and temptations of the modern Jew. The doors of Western culture are open before him, and whenever he wishes to enter, he finds a welcome place. Why should he not assimilate? The worthwhileness of belonging to the Jewish people must not be taken for granted. Why should one not detach himself from the Jewish community and join another community? Can we in all sincerity say to every Jew: he who separates himself from Judaism commits spiritual suicide? Various efforts have been made in the Diaspora to plant a vineyard of secular culture to take the place of tradition: art, music, literature, theater, press. With what pains has that vineyard been cultivated, how much labor and energy have been sunk into it! And what happened? Like the קיקיון דיונה, the gourd of Jonah, it arose overnight and was lost overnight.

Technological civilization and secular culture are no answer to man's ultimate questions. Literature and language are only vessels, not the substance. This applies in particular to Jewish existence. Compared to world culture, our secular culture will, at best, be second rate. Is it conceivable that any secular idea will be a sufficient motivation for the Jews scattered in the Diaspora to preserve the bond and to take upon themselves the burden of a Jewish destiny?

Every human being is beset by personal problems. He is involved in perplexities and embarrassments, in loneliness and frustrations. There is a question which is uppermost in his mind: What aid, comfort and guidance do I derive from belonging to the Community of Israel? What does it mean to me personally? He will not affirm and appreciate that belonging, unless he is convinced that Judaism does bestow upon him the sort of guidance which no other source is capable of giving him; that living as a Jew will raise him to a plane which cannot otherwise be reached.

We who are gathered here have a concern in common: that Jews remain Jews. Every teacher of Judaism must ask himself whether he is doing the right thing in instilling loyalty to Judaism in the youth. לפני עור לא תתן מכשל[6], "Thou shalt not place a stumbling block before the blind." History has taught us that our existence as Jews often exacts a frightful price. Granted, no imminent danger threatens us at present. But who knows what the morrow will bring? Is our generation prepared? From the standpoint of personal

---

[6] Lev. 19.14.

security it is of course preferable for an individual to assimilate. The doors of assimilation, as I have said, are open to the multitudes of our people everywhere, and they may very well succeed in disappearing as Jews. Are we not being led astray and misleading others in our efforts to strengthen Jewish existence? To assess Judaism soberly and farsightedly is to establish it as a good to be preferred, if necessary, to any alternative which we may ever face.

For the Sin We Have Sinned in Disparaging the Spirit

We speak of the obligations of the individual to tradition. But what of the *rights* of the individual within the tradition? We have forgotten the love of God for Israel. We have forgotten that "the Holy One, blessed be He, does not ask the impossible of His creatures," that the ways of the Torah are דרכי נועם, "ways of pleasantness." "The Torah speaks in the language of men."[7] But in recent times many of the sages of Israel have overlooked the man in the Jew. They gained no insight into his difficulties, and failed to understand his dilemmas. Every generation has its own problems. Every man is burdened with anxieties. But the sages remained silent; they did not guide the perplexed and showed little regard for the new problems that arose. In the past, when a Jew's education was confined to the ד' אמות של הלכה, the four cubits of the halakhah, and categories of Abbaye and Rava shaped his thought pattern, his way of thinking and reasoning, he had but one criterion: is it permissible or forbidden, is it Kosher or not? He thought in the categories of הלכה and lived his life according to its standards. The הלכה determined not only his actions but the very mode of his thought.

A complete change has taken place in the field of education. For the most part Jews derive their knowledge not from talmudic but from secular sources. Halakhic ways of thinking and reasoning are strange to most people; they have no inkling of those concepts and values. The authors of the הלכה and the average man do not speak the same language. A divided generation has risen. A man does not understand the language of his neighbor. Each side claims to possess all the truth. Many know that Judaism is "a burden." But who knows that it is also "a joy of the spirit and the Paradise of the soul," that the Sabbath is a foretaste of the world to come? Is it a sin to derive joy from Judaism? For many of us tradition has become a dried-up tree. Its taste and sap are gone. There are many who speak in the name of our people who have studied neither our history nor our literature, who have never perceived the flavor of Jewish existence, who eat the shell and discard the substance. Our fallow land is known far and wide; our rich soil is the secret of the few. We have failed in that we did not know how to convey the imponderable, how to open the eyes of the heart, how to draw forth the light of the Torah from its wrappings. We have not cultivated the eye, and the eye is dim;

[7] ברכות ל"א, ב: דברה תורה כלשון בני אדם.

we have not cultivated the ear, and the ear has grown dull. We, the teachers, are of little faith. We skirt the problems; we do not reach the core.

The basic Jewish problem today is not שלילת הגלות, "the denial of the Diaspora," but the disparagement of the spirit, the disregard for Jewish thought. The eye of the heart is dim. Jewish thought is often neglected and cast aside like an unwanted vessel. Reflection, introspection, an intellectual movement, are all lacking. There is much noise, but the still, small voice is not heard; much promotion but little instruction. We busy ourselves with communal affairs and forget the life of the individual. We seem to believe that propaganda and promotion are the panacea, that beautiful edifices or public demonstrations can alleviate or cure the sickness of our generation. But spiritual problems cannot be solved by administrative techniques.

We have fought for political rights, established institutions, and organized political parties. But institutions and parties alone will not save the people. Jewish survival is a spiritual, and not only a political problem. An anti-intellectual climate, the neglect of thought, the evasion of the problems of the spirit may be our undoing. The modern Jew is on trial. The modern Jew is only an experiment. And who knows whether the experiment will succeed?

The avenues of communication between Judaism and the Jew, the channels of thought and understanding, are obstructed. There is little point of intellectual contact between them. The light of Judaism dwells in deep darkness.

There Is No Faith without Effort

Judaism is an answer to man's ultimate questions. The moment we become oblivious to ultimate questions, religion becomes irrelevant, and its crisis sets in. The primary task of religious thinking is to re-discover the questions to which religion is an answer. Without an intellectual effort, without an understanding of the questions, Judaism and its answers are like stale bread to a sated man, like a solution without the riddle.

Judaism declined not because it was refuted, but because it became irrelevant, dull, oppressive, insipid. When faith is replaced by creed, worship by discipline, love by habit; when the crisis of today is ignored because of the splendor of the past; when faith becomes an heirloom rather than a living fountain; when religion speaks only in the name of authority rather than with the voice of compassion — its message becomes meaningless.

Individuals detached themselves from the tradition when they ceased to perceive the connection between the problems which agitate the heart and the Torah and the commandments, between the landscape and the synagogue, between the setting sun and the evening prayers, between the Sabbath and the riddle of time. A Judaism confined to the limits of the הלכה, with all due respect be it said, is not exactly one of the happiest products of the Diaspora. Such condensation and parochialism has little of the sweep and power of the prophets. He who would restrict Judaism to הלכה will distort its image and deprive it of its grandeur. Those who cite the words of our sages: "Since the day of the destruction of the Temple God had no more than four cubits of the הלכה in His world,"[7a] forget that these words are not an expression of triumph but, on the contrary, an expression of pain and sorrow that the שכינה was expelled from the wide world of history and nature. The roots of religion lie in the depths of thought, in reflection that surpasses our power of expression, in awe and amazement before the wonder and the mystery beyond all comprehension or utterance. A religious revival will come from inner embarrassment, from the agony of the intellect as it stands overwhelmed in the face of the mystery which lies hidden in all things and the inscrutable mystery of the mind itself. It is from the despair that goes hand in hand with hope, from tribulation and perplexity, from yearning and song, that faith in God bursts forth.

Authentic faith is more than an echo of a tradition. It is a creative situation, an event. It is an act of the whole person, of mind, will, and heart. It is *sensitivity, understanding, engagement,* and *attachment*; not something achieved once and for all, but an attitude one may gain and lose, a flash of insight in isolated moments. But such experiences or inspirations are rare events, may come and go, penetrate and retreat. To some people they are like shooting stars, passing and unremembered. In others they kindle a light that is never quenched. The remembrance of that experience and the loyalty to the response of that moment are the forces that sustain our faith. In this sense, *faith is faithfulness*, loyalty to an event, loyalty to our response.

Faith comes out of awe, out of an awareness that we are exposed to His presence, out of anxiety to answer the challenge of God, out of an awareness of our being called upon. *Religion consists of God's question and Man's answer.* The way to faith is the way of faith. The way to God is a way of God. Unless God asks the question, all our inquiries are in vain.

Faith in the living God is, we repeat, not easily attained. Had it been possible to prove His existence beyond dispute, atheism would have been refuted as an error long ago. Had it been possible to awaken in every man the power to answer His ultimate question, the great prophets would have achieved it long ago. Tragic is the embarrassment of the man of faith.

"My tears have been my food day and night, while they say unto me all the day, where is thy God?"

"Where are all His marvelous works which our fathers told us of?"

"How long, O Lord! Wilt Thou hide Thyself perpetually?"

"My God, my God, why hast Thou forsaken me?"[8]

There is no faith at first sight. A faith that comes into being like a butterfly is ephemeral. He who is swift to believe is swift to forget. Faith does not come into being out of nothing, inadvertently, unprepared, as an unearned surprise.

[7a] ברכות ח', א: מיום שחרב בית המקדש אין לו להקב"ה בעולמו אלא ד' אמות של הלכה בלבד.

[8] Ps. 42.4: היתה לי דמעתי לחם יומם ולילה באמר אלי כל-היום איה אלהיך; Judg. 6.13: ואיה כל נפלאותיו אשר ספרו לנו אבותינו; cf. Ps. 44.2; Ps. 89.47: עד מתי ה' תסתר לנצח; Ps. 22.2: אלי אלי למה עזבתני.

Faith is preceded by awe, by acts of amazement at things that we apprehend but cannot comprehend. I am not speaking of perfect faith. There is perhaps no such thing in the world. I am referring to faith that goes hand in hand with uncertainty, perplexity, quest, struggle — even doubt is part of faith. We must never cease to question our own faith and to ask what God means to us. Is He an alibi for ignorance? The white flag of surrender to the Unknown? Is He a pretext for comfort, a substitute for prestige and intellectual search?

Ezra the Scribe, the great renovator of Judaism, of whom the Rabbis said that he was worthy of receiving the Torah had it not been already given through Moses,[9] confessed his lack of perfect faith. He tells us that after he received a royal firman from King Artaxerxes, granting him permission to lead a group of exiles from Babylonia: "I proclaimed a fast there at the river Ahava, that we might afflict ourselves before our God, to seek of Him a right way for us, and for our little ones, and for all our substance. For I was ashamed to require of the King a band of soldiers and horsemen to help us against the enemy in the way; because we had spoken unto the king, saying, the hand of God is upon all of them for good that seek Him."[10]

Many people will say: "Happy are those who have faith. As for us, we were not born with the capacity for it." Rejecting the idea that faith is a universal attitude, correlated to our situation as human beings, many maintain faith is a matter of luck, an innate psychological disposition. The paradox is that in rejecting religious faith they manifest an unquestioned faith in fatalism, as well as a disregard for the inner dynamics of religious existence. Such fatalism breeds, what may be called, *religious bashfulness*. The modern Jew is ashamed to live up to what is in his heart. It would look sanctimonious, if not hypocritical. He is too sophisticated; he is ashamed to pray; he is ashamed to confess that at times he is overpowered by an awe and a sense for the trace of God in the world. Bashfulness, in return, leads to a further alienation.

In the meantime a new religion is emerging throughout the world, a religion in which the body is the supreme object of worship to the exclusion of all other aspects of existence. The pursuit of its pleasures has grown into a cult; its masters are the venerated priests; for its ritual no efforts are spared. We have bartered holiness for convenience, loyalty for success, wisdom for information, joy for pleasure, tradition for fashion.

There is no faith except in the cultivation of the heart, in the depths of the soul, in the ennoblement of the mind. And this cannot be attained amid the vulgarization of life, or without sensitivity and strain, discipline, effort and contemplation.

There is no human being without faith. But some worship idols and others the God of Israel. We are free to choose. An idol is what man creates for himself, in his own image, in the image of his concepts, for the satisfaction of his

---

[9] סנהדרין כ"ב, ב: (אמר ר' יוסי) ראוי היה עזרא שתינתן תורה על־ידו לישראל אלמלא (לא) קדמו משה.
[10] Ezra 8.21–22: ואקרא שם צום על־הנהר אהוא להתענות לפני אלהינו לבקש ממנו דרך ישרה לנו ולטפנו ולכל־רכושנו: כי בשתי לשאול מן־המלך חיל ופרשים לעזרנו מאויב בדרך כי־אמרנו למלך לאמר יד־אלהינו על־כל־מבקשיו לטובה . . .

needs and desires. "Dwell in the land and cherish faith." (Psalm 37:3) — "Lig in der erd, un pasha dich mit emunah." (Rabbi Mendel of Kotsk).[11] God must not be described as a human need. On the contrary, man must be understood as a need of God. God is either of no importance or of supreme importance. Without Him all is vain: the state, civilization, the life of the individual and of society. What God means is expressed in the words: "For Thy kindness is better than life."[12] God is He whose regard for me I value more than life. Are we not the ones who spread the idea throughout the world that there is a God who judges the earth, who created heaven and earth, and who chose the prophets of Israel? If there is no God, it is not worthwhile to be a Jew. If there is no God, the work of the prophets of Israel is a scandal of world history.

I repeat: there is no faith without strenuous effort, effort in thought and in deed. Faith is not something snatched from mid-air, *creatio ex nihilo*, something absorbed in a fit of distraction. Awe precedes faith; the sense of wonder, amazement, and embarrassment precede faith. "Hidden are the things we have seen; we do not know what we see." We must free ourselves from glib phrases, from superficial explanations and ideologies, and should learn to behold "the miracles daily wrought for us, the wonders and the goodness, at all times, morning and noon." The way of Judaism is not to adjust God to our understanding but to adjust our understanding to God. The truth is that our religious problem is not a matter of faith but a matter of dread and fear before the awesome grandeur of Jewish existence; not a matter of sentiments or stirrings of the heart. On the contrary, the heart is opaque. "Do not be led astray by your hearts."[13] It is a matter beyond feeling, even beyond understanding. *God is in search of man.*

Man in His Greatness

We are in the habit of saying that the greatest contribution of the Jew is that he was found worthy to know God. Perhaps his contribution is that he was found worthy to know *man* in his greatness. Only he who grasps the grandeur of man knows the glory that is in Judaism. What is his greatness? His bold attachment to God, his unconditional loyalty to the covenant with God, despite the confusion, disappointments and God's hiding his face from us, the attachment to God in the acts of daily life.

It is an axiom with us that a Jew who abandons the people of Israel detaches himself from the God of Israel. But we are prone to forget that he who objects to the God of Israel, betrays the destiny of the people of Israel. Just as there can be no Jew without the people of Israel, so there is no people of Israel without God. Let us not withhold from our children the knowledge that we shall only endure in the covenant, with God. The fate of God is bound

---

[11] Ps. 37.3: שכן ארץ ורעה אמונה — ליג אין דער ערד און פאשע דיך מיט אמונה.
[12] Ps. 63.4: כי טוב חסדך מחיים.
[13] Num. 15.39: ולא תתורו אחרי לבבכם.

up with the fate of Israel. "Ye are My witnesses, and I am God."[14] "When you are my witnesses, I am God; and when you are not witnesses I am not God." We are witnesses, and we sin if we do not bear witness. It is impossible to utter the word Jew without recalling His name. There are two Hebrew names for Jew: יהודי, the first three letters of which are the first three letters of the Ineffable Name, and ישראל, the end of which, אל, means God. Judaism is not a matter of blood or race but a spiritual dimension of existence, a dimension of holiness. This dimension comes to expression in events and in teachings, in thoughts and deeds. Israel's strength lies in the knowledge that it is the people of the God of Abraham.

We are proud of the achievements of our technological civilization. But our pride may result in our supreme humiliation. The pride in maintaining, "My power and the might of my hand have gotten me this wealth,"[15] will cause us to say "our gods," to the work of our hands.[16] One shudders to think that involved in our civilization is a demonic force trying to exact vengeance on God.

After having eaten the forbidden fruit, the Lord sent man forth from Paradise, to till the ground from which he was taken. But man who is more subtle than any other creature that God has made, what did he do? He undertook to build a paradise of his own by his own might and to drive out God from His Paradise. For generations all looked well. But now we have discovered that our paradise is built upon the top of a volcano. The paradise we have built may turn out to be a vast camp for the extermination of man.

We are the bearers of the vision for all men. Shall we extinguish the vision? How can we forget that Habbakuk summarized all of the מצוות in one verse: "The righteous man shall live by his faith."[17] Jewish belonging entails the love of Israel, love of the present generation and love of all the generations. The past and the present are interlocked. Love of Israel is inconceivable without including those who fashioned our heritage; without love for our generation, we shall never succeed in relating ourselves to Israel of the past. It is incumbent upon us to walk with Moses and Isaiah, Rabbi Joḥanan ben Zaccai, Maimonides and the Baal Shem, just as it is incumbent upon us to enter into fellowship with our contemporaries. This does not mean that everything which bears the stamp of antiquity is necessarily the best. We have outworn many a garment. But by and large we are inclined to deny the relevance of the past and to exchange the old for what is up-to-date. We forget that it is not in the power of the individual nor of a single generation to erect the bridge that leads to truth.

If we agree that the existence of the people depends on the spiritual existence of the individual, then together with our concern for building and strengthening the State of Israel and Jewish communal institutions everywhere

[14] Cf. Isa. 43.10, 44.8.
[15] Deut. 8.17: כחי ועצם ידי עשה לי את־החיל הזה.
[16] Hos. 14.4: אלהינו למעשה ידינו.
[17] Hab. 2.4: וצדיק באמונתו יחיה.

we have the important concern for the individual and his problems. To the individuals we say: "Do not detach yourself from the community,"[18] and to the institutions we say: "Do not detach yourself from the individual." A Jew without commitment to the spirit, a Jew without faith, without a sense of the importance of Judaism, a Jew without any observance, is without Jewish substance. The attachment of the individual to the people is not of lip-service or financial contribution but a commitment in thoughts and deeds. We have no power to issue decrees. But it is our duty to teach and to proclaim: Guard the legacy of ages! Without the study of the Torah, without the Sabbath, without festivals, prayer and attachment to God — there is no Jewish existence.

We succeeded in establishing the State of Israel. The time has come to establish the House of Israel. The State is in the Holy Land; the house of Israel is to be found wherever Jews have settled, a house whose windows are open towards the Land of Israel. The consciousness of the people's unity is important for us. But this abstract thought alone is not sufficient to nourish our lives. Unity becomes reality only when translated into a way of living. Judaism is an historical reality, not only an idea in the mind or a sentiment of the heart. It is not a concept which hovers between heaven and earth but a fabric of living thoughts, deeds and sentiments, and hence neither static nor unchanging. It derives its glow and substance from the sparks of light in the soul of the Jew. Every Jew is bound to bear the eternal light, for the soul of man is called a light. Thus do we live in every generation. We derive our sustenance from one another. Just as one candle is lit with another and suffers no loss, so does a Jew draw renewed power from his fellowmen and teachers.

Even if a plain Jew performs one מצוה, it is as if he had rebuilt one room of the desolation of the House of Israel. We must not underestimate the value of modest achievements, even of a moment of reverence or an act of dedication.

The renewal of the intellectual bond between Jew and Judaism, between the people and its Torah, is the call of the hour. We would do well to realize that the negation of Judaism in the life of the individual has robbed him of his glory. The trouble is that the soul is in exile, that even the Torah is in exile. There is glory in our tradition, but so much has been done to hide it. Modern man is lonely. We cannot force everything upon him. But we must attain the power to reveal to him a life in which there is glory, and say to him: "In this shall you rejoice."

The Gates of Halakhah Are Closed

The gates of הלכה are closed. No one departs and no one enters. Those inside are not concerned with those on the outside. Those on the outside do not understand those who are within. The door has been locked to those who knock, and those who are anxious to enter grow weary looking for an opening.

[18] אבות ב:ד: אל תפרוש מן הציבור.

There are certain wide-spread notions which cry for revision. The depersonalization of Jewish thinking has inflicted upon us a negativist conception of הלכה. Jewish law has become "לא with an *aleph*." We speak of it as if it were only endowed with negative attributes. Even celebrations are regarded as restrictions, as if the primary function of הלכה were to restrict, to confine, to deny and to deprive. Forgotten is the joy and the guidance, the sense of divine relevance of human deeds, the affirmation of man's kinship with God to be experienced in Jewish observance. One does not have to be a scholar in order to experience the eternal majesty of the biblical words. One does not have to be a saint in order to sense that the Sabbath is a delight. חיי עולם נטע בתוכנו, "Eternal Life He planted within us." Judaism is an *anchor of ultimate significance to a tottering world*.

There is also the notion that either you observe *everything or nothing*; all the rules are of equal importance; and if one brick is removed, the whole edifice must collapse. Such intransigence, laudable as it may be as an expression of devoutness, is neither historically nor theologically justified. There were ages in Jewish history when some aspects of Jewish ritual observance were not adhered to by people who otherwise lived according to the law. And where is the man who could claim that he has been able to fulfil literally the מצוה of ואהבת לרעך כמוך, "Love thy neighbor as thyself?"

Maximalism is not the way to this generation. For since only a small minority of those who have forsaken the traditional way of living is prepared to accept the maximum, this notion drives away the overwhelming majority. It is unwilling to surrender a single iota of tradition, yet willing to surrender the multitudes of Israel. Is it the way of Torah to say to the majority of our people: "You have no share in the God of Israel"? Let us not trample on the heads of the people. We must not write off those who have left, those who are sunk in ignorance. Saving a soul sets aside the Sabbath, and the word soul has a double meaning. Let us bring in the estranged. Even those who have only a minimum of attachment have the capacity for greatness.

Torah as *a total way of living* has been abandoned by the multitudes of our people, and we cannot force it upon them. We must evolve *a pedagogy of return*; we must devise *a ladder of observance*. We have no right to abrogate the הלכה, but we have also no right to abandon the Jewish people. Extremism, maximalism is not the way. Elasticity, flexibility is the way.

Ben Azzai used to say: "Do not despise any man, and do not consider anything as impossible; for there is not a man who has not his hour, and there is not a thing that has not its place."[19] Even those who seem frivolous have moments of sensitivity, moments in which they will respond to those who combine אהבת תורה with אהבת ישראל, depth of appreciation with the power of thinking. Both wisdom and love are necessary to show a way how to return.

---

[19] אבות ד:ג: אל תהי בז לכל אדם ואל תהי מפליג לכל דבר, שאין לך אדם שאין לו שעה. ואין לך דבר שאין לו מקום.

THE NATION AND THE INDIVIDUAL

"Blessed is he who considers the weak."[20] One must have understanding and sympathy for those who are poor in spirit. Rabbi Isaac Luria said of his disciple, Rabbi Hayim Vital: "Sing, O barren one, who did not bear, . . . for the children of the desolate one will be more than the children of her that is married."[21] In our generation even a modest effort a person makes with כונה for the sake of God is more precious in the eyes of the Lord than the great deeds done in the generations of the past. "Sing, O barren one" — though the generation looks barren, and its spirit continues to abate. "For the children of the desolate one will be more than the children of her that is married."

What is the spiritual level of the multitudes of Israel? It is not on the heights of Torah but in the lowlands, in the valley. Like Ezekiel in his time, we also see the valley full of bones, and they are very dry. It is God who asks: "Son of Man, shall these bones be revived?" The answer is in our hands. Often we say in resignation: "Our bones have dried up." Indeed, we are spiritually poor. But despair means paralysis. Instead of indulging in the sorrow and admission of our failures, let us undertake a new effort to revive the dry bones. The mountain of full Jewish living is towering, and few are the men who know how to leap out of the valley to the top of the mountain. If we assert that a Jew has no status unless he lives at the top of the mount and fulfills all the details of all the commandments, the masses will remain in the valley. The sages said: "Not all men or all places nor all times are equal."[22] "The Torah spoke in the language of men."[23] "Come and see how the Voice goes forth to all Israel. Each one hears according to his ability. The old men, the young men, the women, and even Moses — each in the measure of his ability."

There is a way of Shammai of whom it is said: "He pushed him away with the builder's measure he held in his hand,"[24] and there is a way of Hillel who said, "Love peace, pursue peace, love man and bring him closer to God."[25]

If a man wrongfully takes a beam that belongs to someone else and uses it in building a house or a palace and then the owner of the beam demands that it be returned to him, what is the law? The House of Shammai says: He must demolish the whole palace and restore the beam to its owner. The House of Hillel, however, says that since demolishing the palace would entail too great a loss and prevent the owner from repenting, the owner of the beam can claim only the money value of the beam, instead of the actual beam being restored, so as not to place obstacles in the way of those who wish to repent. For if they had to destroy the whole building, they would not offer to make restitution.[26]

[20] Ps. 41.2: אשרי משכיל אל דל.
[21] רני עקרה לא ילדה . . . כי רבים בני שוממה מבני בעולה.
[22] יבמות ט"ז: ג' [ר' יהודה בן בבא אומר] לא כל האדם, ולא כל המקום, ולא כל השעות שוין.
[23] See note 7.   [24] שבת ל"א, א: דחפו באמת הבנין שבידו.
[25] אבות א:יב: אוהב שלום ורודף שלום, אוהב את הבריות ומקרבן לתורה [= למקום].
[26] Cf. ירושלמי גיטין פ"ה, ה"ה, מ"ז, ע"א.

119

For the benefit of those who are able to return, we should set up a *ladder* in the valley, *a ladder of learning, a ladder of observance*. To each individual our advice should be: Observe as much as you are able to, and a little more than you are able to. And this is essential: *A little more than you are able to*.

For such a pedagogy to be effective, it will be necessary to prevent the *tendency to minimalism*. The level of Jewish living must never be stationary. It is the task of religious pedagogy to instill an awareness that there is no standstill in the life of the spirit. We either *ascend* or *go down*. The law of Hanukkah requires that every man should light one lamp for himself and one for his household. Those who seek to fulfill the law in the best possible manner should, according to the House of Shammai, light eight flames the first night, and every following night one flame less. According to the House of Hillel the reverse is right: the first night one lamp, to be increased by one on each succeeding night. Most of us follow the path of regression. The right way is that of the House of Hillel.

The people will have the strength to ascend, if the leader himself continues to rise, if the leader himself retains his position at the top of the ladder.

Many of our people can afford to sanctify the Seventh Day. Many people can afford to set aside times for study, for prayer. One obstacle lies in the soul, and the other obstacle is due to the maximalist conceptions.

מצוה גוררת מצוה.[27] He who knows *how to begin* will also learn how to continue, *how to advance*. Provided he begins in the right spirit, provided he begins in reverence for God. "Thy word is a lamp to my feet, and a light to my path." Why is the Word compared to both a lamp and a light? The Psalmist, say the Rabbis, meant to say: When I begin to study the words of the Torah, my attainment is modest. But once I enter the words, many gates open up before me.

We are told that the Holy One, blessed be He, prefers the oil of the olive tree to all other oils. So also the sages of Israel. They yearn for the Jew to become pure olive oil. Nevertheless, we have no right to depreciate the other oils. What oils may be used to kindle the Sabbath light? And what oils may not be used? Rabbi Tarfon said: "Only olive oil is to be used." Upon hearing this opinion, Rabbi Joḥanan ben Nuri arose to his feet and said: "What shall the Jews of Babylon do who have only sesame oil? What shall the Jews of Persia do who have only peanut oil? What shall the Jews of Alexandria do who have only radish oil? And what shall the Jews of Cappadocia do who have no oil but naphtha?"[28]

The people of Israel are accustomed to miracles and know, as the sages taught, that "He who commanded the oil to burn may also command the vinegar to burn."[29]

The ladder will be flimsy unless its rungs consist of action as well as

---

[27] אבות ד:ב.
[28] See Shabbat 26a.
[29] תענית כ"ה, א: מי שאמר לשמן וידלוק הוא יאמר לחומץ וידלוק.

insight, of acceptance as well as appreciation. Without a return to reverence, without a revival of the sensitivity of faith, the call to discipline will sound hollow. It all depends upon the spark of longing for honesty, for meaning, for sanctity. We must learn how to initiate the Sabbath — and all Jewish acts — by kindling a light in the home and a light in the soul, by evoking an insight into the great love story between God and the Community of Israel.

There is a way of conveying not only information but also appreciation. The Lord said to Moses: "Each who is numbered in the census shall give this: half a shekel of the sanctuary."[30] Moses may have found it difficult to find a way of setting forth to the people what God demands of man. Indeed, it is sometimes more difficult to ask for half a shekel than for the whole shekel. So Rabbi Meir said: "It was as if the Lord had taken a coin of fire from under His throne of glory and, showing it to Moses, said: They shall give this. They shall give like this."[31]

The Torah is written without vowels. Yet the vowels are the soul of the words. The Torah consists of consonants; we are called upon to supply the vowels. What we need is a way of hearing the vowels while reading the consonants.

The Duties of Israel and of the Diaspora

Let us confess: there is no wholeness in the Diaspora. There are sparks but no flame, individuals but no community, schools, synagogues but no Jewish spiritual atmosphere. Only he who has been in the land of Israel knows what the Diaspora lacks. With the establishment of the State of Israel the whole Jewish world was filled with light. But we have still not learned how to use that light. It has not influenced the way of life in the Diaspora. The heart of the Jew everywhere is bound to the land of Israel with strong, deep ties. In times of crisis he feels that whenever any one touches Israel, it is as if he touched the apple of his eye.

The question of dual loyalty will soon be out-moded. A drastic change in political thinking is bound to bring about new concepts of international relations. We must think not in terms of "dual loyalty" but in terms of "dual residence." Technological developments will do away with geographical distance and separation. A Jew will say his morning prayers in New York and walk in the streets of Jerusalem at sundown. The Jews of the Diaspora yearn to hear a spiritual message from the mouths of the people living in the land of Israel. They have felt the dangers of assimilation in their own flesh, but they are also concerned with the dangers of assimilation in the land of Israel. The settlement of Israel was not a natural thing but a gift of God. We shall not succeed in repairing our house in the Diaspora without close relations with Israel, without the air of the land of Israel. The Diaspora Jew

---

[30] Ex. 30.13: זה יתנו כל־העבר על הפקדים מחצית השקל.
[31] See note 3.

has not only a duty to give but a right to receive as well: inspiration from Zion, faith from Zion.

Judaism stands on four pillars; on God, the Torah, the people of Israel, and the land of Israel. The loss of any one of these entails the loss of the others; one depends upon the other. And hence every Jew, wherever he may be found, is precious. The people of Israel is a tree whose roots are in Israel and branches in the Diaspora. A tree cannot flourish without roots. But how can it bear fruit without branches? Be careful with the branches!

Just as there are מצוות in relation to the land of Israel, so are there מצוות in relation to the people of Israel. We are bound to Israel with every fiber of our being and we desire to have a share in its upbuilding. In the near future these Jews will begin to look upon the State of Israel in the light of their own problems. What does the Jew in the Diaspora lack? An additional measure of faith in Judaism. The Lord made the sea a sea and the dry land dry land. Moses came and made the sea dry land. So is the life of Israel in the world: they walk on dry land in the midst of the sea. The survival of the Jew is as difficult as the splitting of the Red Sea. But the faith of the children of Israel that God will split the sea for them bore fruit. The Jew of the Diaspora has but a glimmer of awe for the generations, a seed of faith. The question which confronts us is: what will become of the seed?

Would that the redemption of Israel may go forth from Zion!

A Love-Letter To My Congregation
MANUEL LADERMAN

I FEEL I HAVE BEEN VERY FORTUNATE IN THE years in which I have been privileged to serve as your rabbi. You took me in as a green graduate of an orthodox Yeshiva, with no previous experience, with no practice in the running of a congregation, with only my ordination papers as supposed evidence of my Jewish scholarship and my college degree as a qualification. You accepted me on faith, and you undertook to follow my direction on matters of faith, about which many of you had more years of experience, a greater maturity of understanding and certainly far more wisdom.

In turn, I took you on faith. You were a new group of men and women who had just formed a congregation, with very little experience, except that which you had gained in the various other synagogues of which you had been a part, but never with the responsibility of creating your own and following a pattern of administration, financial responsibility, and a set independent purpose. I accepted your proffer of a pulpit which was very vague in your own minds, because you were relatively uncertain of what you were after, with only some rather hazy ideas of what Jewish education might possibly be, so that the religious education of your children might be improved and that their interest in learning the Torah might be stimulated.

You took me as an Orthodox rabbi without a beard, a relatively unheard of phenomenon in the America of the early 30's, and one which in our Denver community was looked on as something of a scandal. You accepted an English-speaking rabbi for an Orthodox congregation, when Yiddish was the usually accepted tongue of preaching and teaching. While I did preach in Yiddish too, and taught a Talmud class in Yiddish, the whole slant of the responsibility that I accepted was of a new cast.

I accepted your youthful enthusiasm for converting what was called, largely for lack of any specific definition, "The Building," and determined to turn it into a religious school, a synagogue with daily and Sabbath and festival services, and the host of related activities which would attract young people particularly, without estranging the elders from its influence.

Mutually we accepted two compromises which were determinative for the future of the congregation. One was that the traditional separation of men and women at worship would be maintained, although on a different pattern from what was the usual architectural plan, by having

MANUEL LADERMAN *is Rabbi of Congregation Hebrew Educational Alliance in Denver.*

the women on the same floor as the men, and not in a gallery overlooking "where the action was." Conversely, we agreed within the very first week, and quite inadvertently it turned out, that at social functions there would be a mixing of the sexes, and men and women would sit together at dinner and that there would be social dancing.

These were two significant innovations in an Orthodox synagogue. There are those who would not consider these developments of major consequence today. In 1932 they were revolutionary, and they set a tone, for our community and for others, that tradition has to be respected in worship, and that sociability was an integral part of an American way of life, which would include the easy mingling of the sexes.

I have a file, well guarded in a secret place, of the mistakes I know I made. Very likely you could add to that file ten-fold, in pointing out omissions and errors of which I was guilty in the early days and down to today. The file that I have is one which is a frank facing of the limitations which I was subject to, because of inexperience, because of being a tyro at the job, and because I was daring enough to step in where angels would fear to tread, often to my own discomfiture and chagrin. I do not intend to make this a personal revelation of my shortcomings and a confession of my thoughts. I am more interested in pointing out what I consider the significant areas for which I am grateful for the part you played in my life.

I am writing this not as a valedictory, because I pray that I shall be privileged to continue to serve you, nor as a thank you letter of appreciation for any special occasion. I do so as a testimonial because I am constantly aware of how many of my colleagues are unhappy in their congregational relationships. Many have found being in the rabbinate a cramping or a narrowing experience, and feel they would have done better elsewhere, and live in constant regret for the things they might have done if they had not been lost in the straits of the rabbinate.

I do not share such a view. I do not believe that I would have been happy in some other kind of work, and I do know that I have been blessed in many ways in the work that I was allowed to do. That is not to be a Pollyanna and say that everything was always just rosy. Being a rabbi has many, many difficulties, and there are a great host of times and of experiences which are extremely wearing to one's spirit and ambition.

I am only trying to suggest that, in an overall view, the satisfactions far outweigh the disappointments, and the sense of fulfillment, the periods of disillusionment.

I began to write to tell you that there are specific times about which I have been very proud and very appreciative of your attitude towards me as your rabbi. Without too many details, and because some would only awaken old wounds and are better left simply as matters alluded to and not pinpointed, a reference to them prompts this appreciative statement. Every clergyman sometimes goes off the deep end. He gets himself into a trap of thinking that all the wisdom in the world is his and, despite every kind of friendly caution and counsel, insists on making a public pronouncement for which later he would, as the phrase has it, have bitten his tongue.

I am no exception. I have said things from the pulpit which drew large attention from a wide audience, far beyond the walls of the synagogue in which they were uttered, because of their sensational nature. There have been a number of occasions in which the wrath of many was poured out on me. One was a matter of national concern, in which the repercussions were widespread, from many areas of the country, from every segment of the populace. People were outraged, and the demands for my scalp were many. Another was of a more limited scope, in which I said some rather harsh things about another segment of our Jewish population, in a surrounding where it was not only bad judgment but bad manners, and where again there was fury and anger as a result.

I am referring to two specific incidents. There must have been many others, in which your patience with me was heavily taxed. You might very well have followed the path of congregations which feel that under certain circumstances their rabbis have lost their worth and the respect of their community, and ought to be discharged, or whatever face-saving device can be concocted to ease the incumbent out of his position and his congregation out of their embarrassment.

You were aware of my failing and my fault. You were sensitive because you were a young congregation, trying to find a place for yourself on the religious map. You were concerned because there had been ample warning given to me, sufficient hints of the inadvisability of what I was about to say, so that I could not claim innocence or ignorance of what turned out to be the consequences.

In spite of the inadequacy and inadmissability of what I had done, you backed me, not in what I had said, but in my right to say it. You refused to countenance any of the suggestions that were universally made, that I had overstayed my welcome. You refused, at least formally, as far as I could tell, even to consider the question of termination of my tenure. You closed ranks, finally, solidly, to a man and woman, and accepted the vituperation and reprimand. You let it be known, in ways that were far too subtle for me to discern, but which the community here and country-wide soon learned was irreversible, that there would be no question of any kind of rebuke or effort at removing me from the pulpit because of the errors that you all felt I had made. I have carried in my heart for more than thirty years a great sense of pride at this universal strength you gave me. It has not made me think any more highly of my own thoughts, which I have regretted in many ways, but of your sense of loyalty and support which were exemplary and admirable.

I have two other areas of appreciation that I want to indicate. One when I was seriously considering appointment to a position as the head of an important Jewish institution. I was vacillating and undecided for a considerable time. It was tempting in many ways, and frightening, too. You gave me full leeway in making whatever decision I saw fit. There was no indication or implication that I was playing hard and fast with my responsibilities in the congregation, but only a patient waiting to see what the outcome of my deliberation would be. I made the decision to stay, and I did so out of considerations which were personal and complex. Your willingness to wait upon my final decision was another one of those signs of your thoughtfulness which make you all very precious to me.

The other element that I want to refer to is extremely personal. I had a period of serious illness, in which your helpfulness in every area in which I might find relief was a model. There was no intrusion upon the acute phase of illness, the convalescent period, the interval of simply regaining strength. Many who had no right to make demands upon me were far less considerate, and came to ask for advice and participation and entrance into public duty before I was ready for it. But not my congregation itself, who certainly had first claim upon all my services. Many men and women undertook responsibilities which were far beyond their calling or their desire, just so that they could be of help. There were substitutions and passings over gaps which must have caused a serious drain upon many congregational responsibilities for a period of some six months, with never a word of impatience or a suggestion of greater haste in my return to my duties.

I have been very fortunate since then in being able to carry on what I have felt, and what you have felt, were my responsibilities. I have never for a moment forgotten that I was given the privilege of quiet and peace and rest for an extensive segment of time, because of the goodness of your hearts and the consideration which you had for my family.

I have been dwelling on personal matters exclusively. Our relationship has had other stresses than those between an individual and a congregational family. We have lived through a period of war. We have survived a one-year interval when I took a leave of absence to seek to be of help to our fellow co-religionists in Europe and North Africa. We have had to accept a change in the pattern of neighborhood and of surroundings. We went through the crisis of creating a new sanctuary and edifice, and all the financial involvements and entanglements that it brings. We are faced with new challenges which the new world of the 70's brings to every established institution. We have had some turnover of lay leadership, although here, thanks to the providence of the Almighty,

310 : *Judaism*

we have been singularly fortunate in maintaining a very considerable proportion of the leadership with which this congregation began. Those who have passed on have left a heritage of devotion in their contributions, in their service, and in the loyalty of their children from which we continue to benefit.

How can we, you and I, who have begun together in a world which in many respects was different from today's world, continue to serve the purpose which is greater than any one of us? What new untapped sources of ancient lore for new inventiveness of a modern spirit can help us to be useful and effective in the itme that is upon us? I would like to suggest several areas of service.

We can never turn our backs, so I view it, upon the influence of tradition. There are many who would uproot and start afresh in every area of life. I have the feeling that it would be a mistake in an individual person's experience and a tragedy as far as a community or a congregation is concerned. None of us dares ever to forget that we are the handiwork of our forebears and the idealism which they implanted in us. Without that recognition, we are nothing; with it, we can be significant. No generation before ours has been so strongly tempted to turn its back on the past. No generation dare follow that pattern.

It is not alone that tradition speaks to us out of the hoary aspects of long ago. More important, as I have always tried to present it, tradition is significant because it is a part of our present-day life and can improve and enlarge and enhance and uplift the experiences of our own time. I have said it to you many times, and I hope you will bear with me when I am repetitious of it, that tradition is meaningful not only as a debt, as a mortgage which the dead past lays upon us, from which we cannot free ourselves decently. Tradition gives meaning to our own beings, and our own lives, and helps make our lives beautiful. Tradition simply unfolds for us the highlights of the experience of other generations. Its value is always to be judged in terms of its relevance. Its impact on us derives some glory from its age, but that is not sufficient to give it value. Its importance is in its application to our needs, for our time, of our relationship with God on high, and with the men and women amongst whom we live. Therefore, I say that our congregation must always be responsive to tradition, and be a vehicle through which it can be made significant to the day in which we live.

A new concept has entered into Jewish thinking in the re-establishment of the State of Israel. What was for all generations before us an ideal has become for us a reality and a challenge. No Jew, no Jewish group, no congregation, dare omit the reality of Israel from its overriding purpose. Whether it participates in one or a hundred of the programs which Israel projects for the Diaspora, there must always be a reflection of the importance of the rebirth of the ancient land.

A LOVE-LETTER TO MY CONGREGATION : 311

This is new, and its novelty is constantly upon us. Whatever synagogues may have done in the past about the Holy Land, they will have to rethink and revise, now and in the years to come. It is tragic that we have not learned sufficiently how to make the rebirth of Israel an integral part of our religious experience. We have a glimmer of a beginning in the observance of the Israel Independence Day on the 5th of Iyar. We have an even newer effort in connection with a "Day of Jerusalem" on the 28th of Iyar. Neither one of these can be said to be adequate to the grandeur and the glory and the sense of blessedness that the achievement of Israel ought to provide. Here is a challenge for the future, of which our congregation and all others, of every stripe and coloration, have to be aware.

We will have to respond to being in an era of transition. Nobody can possibly underestimate the differences in our world, in the thinking, in the permissiveness, in the feeling that all values are to be discarded. It will not be easy, and I am not sure that anyone of us has yet uncovered the secret ways in which to approach the matter, but that we will have to be conscious of the fact of transition is something I cannot overstress. In what way are we taking note of the complete revolution in outlook which is being brought to our attention with such sharp violence? I don't know that I have any real grasp on the situation, and perhaps it will take younger and newer people to see it adequately. But to be face-to-face with the problem is part of what all of us must do resolutely if we are to be adequate to the challenges of today and tomorrow.

No one of us who has spoken about peace in all its ramifications, and the word has its penumbra of glory since the most ancient times, can give adequate expression to the fervor which the word arouses today. I have the feeling that someday there will be a paean to peace which will outshine anything that was ever penned by any human being before, which will echo this tremendous underground of commitment that is present in our time. Those who deal in war apparently do not understand it. Those who think in terms of ongoing military adventures are quite obviously blind to it. The Synagogue, which has always been the house of peace, and in which the words and the prayers for peace have been echoed so often, cannot close its avenues of approach to the new and wondrous manifestations of our time. This will be, in my judgment, the residue of all the turmoil in which we live today. And a Synagogue ought to be adequate to, or at least responsive to, what this means for the world ahead of us.

The final thought I have about congregational-rabbinical responsibilities goes back to the most enduring word in our people's vocabulary, Torah. We shall have to learn to embrace the Torah, not only as a gesture of respect when it is carried in procession, not only as a service of the lips when we see it inside the opened Ark, but as the totality of Jewish individuation which separates us off from all peoples. We share with all humanity many, many great ideals. We differ from all the rest of humanity in our exaltation of the word and its influence on our lives. The word as written in the scroll, as expounded in the commentary, has given life in the experiences of individuals and families and is a Jewish contribution to civilization. No other can possibly approximate it or replace it. You and I together must give it reality, as fervent, as literal, as glowing, as was ever done in all history. This challenge we shall have to meet.

I close this love letter to you, my congregation, with the hope that where I have been at fault, you are generous enough to be forgiving, or where I have been of service, you are thoughtful enough to make your lives more beautiful. Every life that I have been privileged to touch, every mind that I have been allowed to enter, every experience of Jewish beauty which I have been permitted to enhance, every area of comfort which I have been privileged to assist, have brought me experiences more enriching than any that I have conferred. I am grateful that it was given to me to serve, to lead, to be helped, and to be loved by so many of you.

"Who Hast Not Made Me a Man": The Movement for Equal Rights for Women in American Jewry

by ANNE LAPIDUS LERNER

IN GENERATIONS PAST, a Jewish girl's life was relatively free of options. She moved from girlhood to womanhood, apprenticed to her mother as part of an extended family in which she learned enough to enable her to replay her mother's role. Some Jewish women did, it is true, go into business; many worked outside the home; some received a secular education. But their lives, while not entirely monochromatic, did not offer the wide range of choices open to today's women. The Jewish woman aspired to be worthy of her husband's praises extolling her as an *eshet hayil,* "a woman of valor" (Proverbs 31: 10), before the Friday evening *qiddush.* If, in her dreams, she wished to play a redeeming role, it was much more likely to be that of Queen Esther, carrying out Mordecai's orders, than that of Deborah the Judge, leading her people in war as in peace.

Many of today's Jewish women are less likely to be satisfied with the role of "woman of valor," combining business acumen and home-making skills with practical wisdom and a concern for the poor. The modern Jewish woman is more likely to regard as inequitable that division of labor, according to which the wife attends to all the physical needs of the household, while the husband "sits among the elders of the land."[1] Queen Esther no longer reigns supreme in the hearts of young Jewish women. More and more of them are admiring Vashti's spunk instead.[2]

Note: I wish to express my gratitude to my husband, Rabbi Stephen C. Lerner, editor of *Conservative Judaism,* for giving so generously of his time and energy. I also had the advantage of using the excellent files at the Blaustein Library of the American Jewish Committee.
[1]Proverbs 31:23.
[2]Mary Gendler, "The Vindication of Vashti," *Response,* Summer 1973, pp. 154–60.

Questioning the traditional picture of ideal Jewish womanhood is not entirely new. One might cite the power struggle between Abraham and Sarah over Hagar,³ or the complaint of the daughters of Zelophehad regarding discriminatory inheritance laws,⁴ as the first faint rumblings of Jewish feminism. But these and other isolated instances do not really constitute a major strand in Jewish tradition. In the past, protest has been either so isolated as to be ineffectual, or so rechanneled as to become part of the normative approach. Thus, in mishnaic times Beruriah's sarcastic use of the rabbinic injunction against excessive conversation with women did not become a force for change;⁵ and in this century Sarah Schnirer channeled her dissatisfaction with the situation of Jewish girls into the very Orthodox Beth Jacob movement.⁶ Organized dissent is a recent phenomenon.

Jewish feminism in its present form is essentially an outgrowth of the American women's movement. Betty Friedan's *The Feminine Mystique* (1963) and other works urging women's liberation, the bra-burnings and similar "violent" protests of the late 1960s and early 1970s—all these had their impact on Jewish women's views of their role in Jewish life. Such women, both here and abroad, had their satisfaction with their assumed roles as housewives and mothers shaken. Indeed, as a group, Jewish women were in the forefront of the new feminism, though Jewish women have traditionally been taught that they must be good nurturers, ever ready to sacrifice themselves for husband and children.⁷

Such questioning was not lightly undertaken, nor was its outcome predictable. One might have expected a weakening of commitment among Jewish women to a Judaism which, as Betty Friedan and other Jewish leaders of the feminist movement pointed out, had men daily bless God for not having created them women. One could scarcely have hoped for a sincere grappling with Judaism and, through this, a heightened sense of commitment.

For traditionalists, unsympathetic to feminist demands, it is hard to view challengers of established and sanctified Jewish mores as anything other than threats to the very fabric of Jewish existence. Yet concern with feminism did give rise to a specifically Jewish brand which, while questioning

---

³Genesis 21.
⁴Numbers 27.
⁵Avot 1:5; Eruvin 53b.
⁶Nisson Wolpin, "Jewish Women in a Torah Society: for frustration? or fulfillment?" *Jewish Observer*, November-December 1974, p. 15.
⁷Aviva Cantor Zuckoff, "The Oppression of the Jewish Woman," *Response*, Summer 1973, pp. 52–53.

many traditional Jewish assumptions, was frequently accompanied by growing respect for Judaism and Jewish values. The "growing assertiveness by women [on college campuses] to resist the ancient Jewish practice of male dominance in religious practices" reflects, in the words of Rabbi Norman Frimer, national Hillel director, " 'a unique combination of radicalism and traditionalism.' "[8] Rabbi Frimer's words are, in a sense, a good definition of a movement which includes both extremely Orthodox women who ask only that their parents allow them to go to college and women who want the right to have abortions. It is a complex movement, one that is not very cohesive, yet does move.

JEWISH FEMINISM

The movement, now loosely defined under the rubric of Jewish feminism, is relatively new. Its conscious beginning was as a series of isolated questionings in the shadow of the women's movement. Some Jewish women found each other in the anti-Vietnamese war movement, others in a consciousness-raising group or in the group involved in the *Brooklyn Bridge,* a self-styled "revolutionary Jewish newspaper." The first issue of *Brooklyn Bridge,* February 1971, contained the following statement:

> Jewish daughters are thus caught in a double bind: we are expected to grow up assimilating the American image of "femininity"—soft, dependent, self-effacing, blonde, straight-haired, slim, long-legged—and at the same time be the "womanly" bulwark of our people against the destruction of our culture. Now we suffer the oppression of Women of both cultures and are torn by the contradictions between the two. These contradictions take some curious forms. Jewish men demand that their Women be intellectual sex-objects. So Jewish families push their daughters to get a good education. The real purpose is not to be forgotten however. While PhD's do make Jewish parents proud of their daughters, the universities are recognized as hunting-grounds for making a "good" marriage. Grandchildren assure the race.
>
> We've been called "Jewish princess" and "castrating bitch," by the rest of the world and by our own men loud and clear. We've been defined as a "Jewess" and been the object of rape. As Jewish Women we are strong, but always the force *behind* our men. We were strong in order to survive, and kept things together for our families and our culture, and for this we are now attacked as being "Jewish mother," ridiculous and disgusting as that has come to be.[9]

At the same time that some women were protesting cultural and social oppression, others set about investigating the position of women in Jewish

---

[8]Irving Spiegel, "Equality Sought by Jewish Coeds," New York *Times,* April 20, 1975.
[9]"Jewish Women: Life Force of a Culture?", p. 14.

religious life. Ezrat Nashim, founded in September 1971, is "perhaps the first group publicly committed to equality for women within Judaism."[10] It was, and has remained, a small group of women devoted both to the study of Jewish and secular materials relating to women and to active attempts to effect change in Jewish life. They have served as a major resource for speakers, educational materials, and advice of all sorts. Although they are of diverse backgrounds, many are Conservative and have been to Ramah camps, the educational and religious camps sponsored by the Jewish Theological Seminary of America (JTSA). As a group, they are well-educated in Jewish and general culture, and committed to Judaism. As internal critics, or "loyal opposition,"[11] they are less vulnerable to accusations of self-hatred of the kind often leveled at such Jewish women as Betty Friedan and Shulamith Firestone, and others like them. Their appearance at the Rabbinical Assembly convention in March 1972, their first public act, brought the Jewish feminist movement to wide public attention.

The growing public awareness of Jewish feminism gave rise to the National Jewish Women's Conference in New York in February 1973. As Judith Plaskow Goldenberg, who was then finishing her doctorate in theology at Yale University, stated at that conference:

> We are not here due to some unfolding of the Jewish tradition, to the fact that it is a Jewishly appropriate moment for us to have come together. We are here because a secular movement for the liberation of women, of which many of us are members, has made it imperative that we raise certain Jewish issues now. We are here because we will not let ourselves be defined as Jewish women in ways in which we cannot allow ourselves to be defined as women. This creates a conflict not just and not primarily because the women's movement is a secular movement whose principles we are attempting to apply to an ancient religious tradition, but because the women's movement is a different community around which we might center our lives. The conflict between communities is the first level on which I experience the conflict between being a woman and being a Jew.[12]

The more than 500 women who participated in that conference discussed various Jewish and feminist concerns. Most were elated that they were not alone in questioning the attitudes and values of traditional Judaism and Jewish social norms but that there were others like them as well. Yet it was also clear that elation was not enough. Much had to be done.

The second conference, in April 1974, was different in scope and result. Discussing "Changing Sex Roles: Implications for the Future of Jewish Life," the conference was open to men and women, although they frequently met in separate sessions. This paradoxical arrangement, in which

---

[10]Martha Ackelsberg, "Introduction," *Response,* Summer 1973, p. 7.
[11]Susan Dworkin, "A Song for Women in Five Questions," *Moment,* May-June 1975, p. 44.
[12]"The Jewish Feminist: Conflict in Identities," *Response,* Summer 1973, pp. 11–12.

sexist role-typing was decried in groups which often were open only to one sex, gave rise to the establishment of the Jewish Feminist Organization (JFO). The preamble of its interim constitution reads, in part:

> We, Jewish feminists, have joined together here in strength and joy to struggle for the liberation of the Jewish woman. Jewish women of all ages, political, cultural and religious outlooks and sexual preferences, are all sisters. We are committed to the development of our full human potential and to the survival and enhancement of Jewish life. We seek nothing else than the full, direct and equal participation of women at all levels of Jewish life—communal, religious, educational and political. We shall be a force for such creative change in the Jewish community.[13]

JFO is becoming the umbrella organization of Jewish feminism, functioning through committees designed to include every interest and ability: a committee to "examine Jewish law to determine views on issues of concern to Jewish women," another to "publicly answer offensive ads, publications, media stuff with letters, calls, demonstrations, etc." JFO is divided into Eastern, Midwestern, Western, and Canadian regions, with sub-regions becoming increasingly active in some areas, and has recently hired its first part-time functionary.

Ferment among young Jewish women, whether or not they are directly connected to JFO, has become fairly widespread. Some are planning to publish *Lilith,* a journal devoted to Jewish feminism. The so-called Jewish counter-culture, young people involved in *Response, The Jewish Catalog,* and the *ḥavurot*—small Jewish fellowships devoted to prayer, study, and community—almost always stress egalitarian religious services allowing women a full measure of participation. Some of these men and women refuse on principle to participate in services which do not grant women's rights. Robert Lapidus, among the founders of one small Sabbath *"davening* group" in Boston, said that the wives, dissatisfied with their passive roles in Orthodox or right-wing Conservative congregations, were the driving force in the establishment of the group. The husbands had been largely satisfied with their active, participatory roles in established congregations.

Hillel Foundations are another place where changes are often made. Rabbi Allan Lettofsky reports that at the Orthodox service of his foundation at the University of Wisconsin, informed Orthodox graduate students ruled that women may have *'aliyot,* being called to the Torah, but only when women read the Torah. Thus, each Sabbath morning, at a certain point in the Torah reading, the male *gabba'im* and Torah readers are replaced by women, and women are called up for *'aliyot.*

At some campuses women's *minyanim,* quorums necessary for public

---

[13]*Lilith's Rib,* June 1974, p. 1.

worship, have been established.[14] At Brown University the women's *minyan* meets every Sabbath and addresses the Deity using feminine, rather than masculine, pronouns, although they do not consider God either male or female. Maggie Wenig, one of the participants, has explained other liturgical innovations: "There are blessings in Judaism for almost everything, including going to the bathroom, but there isn't one for menstruation or for a healthy pregnancy. These are the types of things we're developing."[15] The women involved in this group do not want to join a Conservative or Reform congregation where they may be allowed an active role, both because they want to do these things first in a female setting and because this type of group encourages relationships among the women. On balance, though, the women's *minyan* does not seem to be the "wave of the future."

Another interesting innovation is found in a somewhat less likely place, the Armed Forces. The Jewish Welfare Board's *JWB Circle* (October 1975) reports that Capt. Ellen S. Philpott is the Jewish lay leader in Crete, and Capt. Karen McKay Philips in Athens. These women, stationed in locations which do not have a full-time chaplain, organize religious services as well as educational and religious programs.

JEWISH RITUAL

A discussion of Jewish women today must perforce include the question of the woman's role in Judaism and Jewish ritual. Obviously, this is an area of many sharp disagreements within Orthodox, Reform, and Conservative Judaism. Before attempting to discuss current trends, one must sketch some of the background.

The position of women in the traditional Jewish *Weltanschauung* is about as elusive a matter as defining that *Weltanschauung* itself. A recent volume by Reuben Alcalay, *A Basic Encyclopedia of Jewish Proverbs, Quotations and Folk Wisdom* (New York and Bridgeport, 1973), divides its statements on women into categories: praises, strictures, and miscellaneous, with 14, 55, and 41 entries, respectively. When one considers that among the praises are to be found such statements as "woman is for children; woman is for beauty" and "women are docile," one can easily get the impression that the pedestal which traditional Judaism has purportedly maintained for women rests on a narrow base. The equilibrium is somewhat restored by the mate-

---

[14]Irving Spiegel, "Equality Sought by Jewish Coeds," New York *Times,* April 20, 1975.
[15]K.S., "Judaism is not for men only," *Brown Alumni Monthly,* February 1975, p. 19.

rial under the heading "wife." There the three subdivisions are "good," "bad," and "general," with 18, 10, and 45 entries, respectively. On balance, then, the traditional Jewish view of women is less than wholly favorable. Yet, this or any other method based on nonlegal material that tries to ascertain the traditional Jewish view of women is bound to degenerate into a quotation-matching game of "Can You Top This?" and proves little.

Although *aggadah,* nonlegal material, may be said to be the soul of Judaism, it is *halakhah,* Jewish law, which provides us with an accurate guide to the actual position and treatment of women in Judaism. Careful examination of the woman's position in the halakhic system, which was developed almost entirely by men, may lead one either to marvel at the consideration given women, or to recoil from the lack of it.

It is possible to divide Jewish laws affecting women that apply today into four categories: family status, testimony, private ritual, and public ritual.

Laws of family status were always among the most stringent in Judaism because an error here could cause problems affecting generations of unborn children. The traditional marriage ceremony, the foundation on which the family rests, would customarily have the bride circle the groom as a symbol of her submissiveness, but, beyond that custom, would have the bride say nothing and do very little. The *ketubbah,* marriage contract, was instituted in talmudic times to obligate the husband to support his wife and, in the event the marriage terminated in divorce or in his death, to arrange for her to receive a stipulated sum. Divorce could be initiated only by the man, so that the woman in an unsatisfactory marriage had little recourse. A man who abandoned his wife but refused her a divorce made her an 'agunah, "anchored" to him and unable to marry another. This was also the situation of a woman whose husband was believed to have died, but to whose death there were no witnesses, because he may have been lost at sea or missing in military action. Other laws which bore upon women and were particularly difficult for them were the laws of levirate marriage which, in biblical times, obligated a childless widow to marry her deceased husband's brother. If the brother-in-law refused, he and the widow had to go through a *ḥaliẓah,* release ceremony, in which she was freed to marry someone else by removing a special shoe from his foot and spitting before him. If the surviving brother was a minor, the widow had to wait, unable to remarry, until he attained his majority. In all these categories the woman was clearly hurt by her inability to initiate a legal action.

Another issue in family relations was family purity, the term commonly used to refer to laws dealing with menstruation. In brief, a menstruating woman was forbidden all contact with her husband for the period of her menstruation and for the following seven "clean" days. At the end of this time, if there had been no bleeding, she had to immerse herself in a *miqweh*, a ritual bath, before resuming normal relations with her husband.

A woman's testimony, like that of minors, the mentally impaired, and deaf-mutes, was generally not acceptable. This provision did not evince very high regard for women, a situation which was scarcely ameliorated by the fact that a woman's testimony regarding the *kashrut* of her home or her having been to the *miqweh* was acceptable.

In private ritual a woman had both more obligations and more options. There are three "women's *miẓwot*": lighting Sabbath and holiday candles, separating the *ḥallah* portion from bread dough and throwing it into the fire after reciting the appropriate blessing, and the laws of family purity. Of these, only the last was to be observed exclusively by women; for a man could light candles and in fact was obligated to do so if there was no woman in the household, and whoever, male or female, made the bread dough had to remove the *ḥallah* portion. There also are *miẓwot* which women shared with men.

In general a woman was exempt from performing most commandments enjoining one to do something at a particular time. Thus, although woman was exempt from the obligation to pray at the proper time, she was, according to many authorities, nevertheless obliged to pray. At any rate she was required to hear the *megillah* on Purim, might make *qiddush* on Sabbath and holidays, and might wear *tefillin*. For various reasons, women did not usually avail themselves of all the options open to them.

It was in the synagogue, the arena of public worship, that women were treated most differently from men. The seating arrangement, with a balcony, rear section, or separate room reserved for women, made it difficult for them to feel part of the service. Woman's exclusion from all prominent functions, such as rabbi or *ḥazzan;* her inability to be counted for a *minyan*, and her exclusion from an *'aliyah*, reinforced the differences in the roles of women and men.

To 20th-century sensibilities many of these laws may seem prejudicial to women. It is important, however, to consider them in the context of the periods in which they were promulgated. Thus, in the talmudic period, the *ketubbah* was devised to protect women from capricious divorce by tying divorce to a financial settlement. Also, in their attempt to ameliorate the condition of women, the rabbis sometimes circumvented biblical law, as they did in accepting the testimony of one witness, instead of the requisite two, to the death of a husband in order to free a woman from the crushing *'agunah* burden. In an assessment of the talmudic period as a whole, Judith

Hauptman, instructor in Talmud at the Jewish Theological Seminary, examined a number of issues, including divorce and inheritance, and came to the following conclusion:

> With these examples in mind, we renounce the view held by many, both men and women, that the Jewish tradition, having been shaped by men, is totally biased in their favor. It was the Rabbis, members of the very class of people who were more equal than others, who voluntarily extended some of their privileges to those who were not so fortunate.[16]

Orthodoxy

Within Orthodox Judaism, little has changed. Many Orthodox Jews would probably concur with Rabbi Wolpin's dictum that "the women's role is not the object of discrimination—just one of definition."[17] Although social attitudes now allow women to work outside the home, as they did, for example, in Eastern Europe, religious attitudes are not changing significantly.

The innovations have been outside the realm of religion. Some Orthodox Jewish women have organized a JFO chapter in Boro Park, Brooklyn's center of Orthodoxy. One of their aims is to strengthen the resolve of young Jewish women to pursue educational and career goals, often in opposition to family and community. One Manhattan Orthodox synagogue is struggling with the question of permitting women to be elected to its board. The rabbi is not opposed; some of the members are. The fact that discussions of the woman's place continue unabated in Orthodox journals and meetings is an indication of the strength of Jewish feminism and its impact upon elements within Orthodoxy.

Some change is inevitable. Rabbi Haskel Lookstein of Congregation Kehilath Jeshurun in New York, while maintaining that women should not be "public personalities," expects that they will become more active in the corporate aspect of Orthodox Jewish life in the next decade.[18] Possibly in response to the Jewish Women's Conference, there was, in early 1974, a conference at the National Young Israel in New York to consider the status of Jewish women.

Most Orthodox spokesmen discuss the issues only to arrive at the traditional conclusions and to skirt such knotty and virtually insoluble problems

---

[16]Judith Hauptman, "Women's Liberation in the Talmudic Period: an Assessment," *Conservative Judaism,* Summer 1972, p. 28.

[17]Wolpin, *loc. cit.,* p. 13.

[18]Enid Nemy, "Young Women Challenging Their 'Second-Class Status' in Judaism," New York *Times,* June 12, 1972.

as that of the *'agunah.* Thus, in an article in *Ms.,*[19] "Why I Choose Orthodoxy," Bracha Sacks raised some of the issues confronting Jewish women, but not that most painful one. And Rabbi Aaron Soloveichik, speaking to the Union of Orthodox Jewish Congregations in 1969 on the "Attitude of Judaism toward the Woman,"[20] emphasized the superior spirituality of women, but concluded with a strong plea for the sex-segregated prayer and family purity.

Still, according to Rabbi Sholom Klass, in "Women's Rights Fully Protected by the Torah,"[21] rabbis have attempted to help the *'agunah.* They have, he noted, consistently tried, where possible, to free *'agunot* whose husbands had disappeared and to aid women whose husbands refused them a divorce. Cases in which no solution is possible were not at issue here. Thus, Rabbi Klass cited a case in which Rabbi Moshe Feinstein annulled the marriage of a woman whose husband refused her a divorce "on the strength that the witnesses were not Sabbath observers and the wedding feast was held in a non-kosher hall and inasmuch as they didn't follow the tenets of our Torah at the wedding, therefore the latter requirement of a divorce according to our Torah also did not apply." But he did not discuss what would have happened had both the wedding feast and the witnesses been kosher. Contrary to its title, the article inadvertently supports the contention that women's rights are not "fully protected by Torah." Its opening sentence best shows the tenor of the argument: "The current Women's Liberation movement has generated many side issues which some people have used to malign our Torah." Surely, the *'agunah* issue cannot possibly be a "side issue" to the *'agunah* for whom there is no solution. If, as the Talmud states, the altar sheds tears when a man divorces his first wife,[22] what must happen in the case of an *'agunah*?

There are Orthodox leaders who respect the arguments of Jewish feminists. Professor Ze'ev Falk of the Hebrew University Law School, indicating that much *halakhah* relating to women was based on a society and a sociology which have since changed, hinted that new times call for new solutions.[23]

A most perceptive discussion of women's rights in Orthodox Judaism, by Rabbi Saul J. Berman of Stern College for Women, Yeshiva University,

---

[19] July 1974, pp. 82–83, 108–10.
[20] *Major Addresses Delivered at Midcontinent Conclave and National Leadership Conference, November 27–30, 1969,* pp. 21–32.
[21] *Jewish Press,* New York, April 21, 1972.
[22] Gittin 90b.
[23] "On the Status of Women in Jewish Law" (Hebrew), *De'ot,* Fall 5732, pp. 29–35.

touches three sources of discontent among Jewish women: "the sense of being deprived of opportunities for positive religious identification"; "the disadvantaged position of women in Jewish Civil Law, particularly areas of marriage and divorce," and "the Rabbinic perception of the nature of women and the impact that it has had on the role to which women are assigned."[24] Assailing past discussions of this issue, Rabbi Berman states:

> It is time to admit that we have attempted through our apologetics to make a virtue of social necessity. We have striven to elicit voluntary compliance by women to a status which men need never accept. . . . It is becoming increasingly difficult for Jewish women to accept the idea that their own religious potential is exhausted in enabling their husbands and children to fulfill *mitzvot* (p. 9).

The careful analysis to which Rabbi Berman subjected each of these areas is exemplary in that he never dismissed any of them as trivial.

When discussing possible solutions, however, Rabbi Berman was less than comforting. Recognizing "the reality of the religious quest of Jewish women," he suggested that his colleagues in the Orthodox rabbinate do likewise. He urged them, in particular, to design synagogues in such a way as to enable women to feel more a part of the service, and to expect of them the same decorum as of men. Emphasizing the importance of Jewish study, Rabbi Berman also suggested that Jewish women try to discover "customs expressive of their religious feelings in contemporary society." The traditional role of Jewish women must be examined, along with alternatives, to see what is more appropriate today.

Courageously unwilling to accept the *status quo* with regard to *'agunot,* Berman felt that the Jewish religious leadership must rectify this situation. Remedies proposed within Jewish law have not, however, proved acceptable to the Orthodox rabbinate as a whole. Rabbi Berman, therefore, suggested that the Jewish community press for legislation which would enable civil courts to enforce civil antenuptial agreements mandating religious divorce for those who obtain a civil divorce or annulment. All rabbis could then require couples to sign such agreements.

The proposal does nothing to help those already married. (Even among the Orthodox the rate of divorce is rising. Rabbi Samuel J. Fox of Boston has said that the Jewish Divorce and Family Relations Court of the Massachusetts Board of Rabbis handled twice as many Jewish divorce cases in 1975 as in 1974.)[25] Furthermore, Rabbi Berman's plan constitutes a critique of the efficacy of *halakhah* and of the ability of Orthodox religious leader-

---

[24]"The Status of Women in Halachic Judaism," *Tradition,* Fall 1973, pp. 5–28.
[25]*Jewish Advocate,* Boston, January 8, 1976.

ship to repair this glaring inequity to women. Is there no other recourse than to request civil authority to rescue Jewish women from Jewish law?

Dr. Trude Weiss-Rosmarin, editor of the *Jewish Spectator* and one steeped in Orthodox traditions, has long discussed the issue of Jewish divorce. Although in 1950 she defended separate seating and differences in education, she did urge that there "be some reinterpretation of Jewish divorce law making it possible for a woman to divorce her husband, instead of being divorced by him."[26] She then went on to claim that the inequities "do not prove that a wronged wife has no recourse to justice." Her recent position has been unequivocal. She has recommended transferring the power of issuing divorces to the rabbinic courts. "So as to liberate Jewish women from being chained as *agunot,* the Rabbinic Courts must be appointed as *bona fide* agents, acting on behalf of the husband, so as to grant divorces to deserted wives."[27] Dr. Weiss-Rosmarin has also urged that women be allowed to enter the rabbinate.[28]

A few noted examples of halakhically acceptable innovations have occurred. There have been Orthodox women's *minyanim,* groups consisting of ten or more women who could participate fully in a somewhat modified service. On Simḥat Torah, 1974, Rabbi Steven Riskin allowed a women's Torah service to take place in the building of the Lincoln Square Synagogue during the time of the Torah service in the main sanctuary. The 1975 women's service was held in mid-afternoon, when its impact was much less. Riskin has also allowed a woman to wear a *tallit* in his synagogue. According to Susan Dworkin, Rabbi Riskin, "who has never been known to permit any infraction of *Halachah,* gets himself a reputation as a raging liberal by allowing women to behave in ways they are nowhere forbidden to behave."[29]

On the other hand, the position of some elements in Orthodoxy with regard to women has hardened. Where once separate seating without a *meḥizah,* a physical barrier, was deemed adequate, the current generation has established *meḥizot* in congregations, new and old, or raised the height of existing *meḥizot.* One interesting technological innovation in this area was the purchase by a hasidic congregation in Brookline, Mass., of a 550-pound thermopane mirror-coated one-way panel, intended for the new Hancock Tower in Boston, for use as a *meḥizah.* It will enable the women to see what is going on, but will not allow the men to see them.[30] Married women whose

---

[26]"Jewish Woman in a Man's World," *Jewish Spectator,* May 1950, p. 12.
[27]"The Rabbi as Politician," *Jewish Spectator,* January 1973, p. 4.
[28]"Women's Liberation," *Jewish Spectator,* March 1973, p. 7.
[29]Dworkin, *loc. cit.,* p. 45.
[30]*Jewish Week,* New York, November 9–15, 1975.

Orthodox mothers walked around with uncovered heads are now expected, and often coerced by community pressure, to don a *tikhl,* kerchief, or *shaytl,* wig, on all occasions. An example of a new denigration of women is reflected in an editorial in Rabbi Bernard Levy's *Jewish Homemaker*:

> We have found in many of our . . . homemakers a sad lack of information regarding kashrus. And we ask the question: Does the fact that the master of the house is a Torah Jew automatically make his kitchen kosher? How many Torah Jews have taken an interest in the cupboard? They rely implicitly on their balleboste [housewife]: she knows what she may buy and what she may serve him. . . . His function is to see that the proper brocho [blessing] is made.[31]

Traditionally one accepted a woman's word that her home was kosher, but the *Jewish Homemaker* said that the housewife is not competent in this scientific age to know what ingredients among new chemicals and derivatives are kosher. It concluded with a plea that "Torah Jews" investigate their kitchens.

Another area traditionally the enclave of Orthodox Jewish women is the *miqweh* and the laws of family purity. *Miqweh* is a private matter, not for public discussion. Since a woman should not be questioned whether she goes to the *miqweh,* statistical data are hard to obtain. However, there is a fairly prevalent impression that the *miqweh* is more widely used today outside of strictest Orthodox circles. Many young modern Orthodox women whose mothers did not go to the *miqweh* go now. This is also true of some traditionalist Conservative women. A number of Jewish feminists, who have been urging the extension of women's public religious rights, were inspired by Rachel Adler's exposition at the first Women's Conference of the mystical value of the *miqweh* to begin to observe the rules of family purity. A look around the waiting room of the Jewish Women's Club, commonly known as the Mid-Manhattan *miqweh,* reveals styles from wigs and long sleeves to uncovered long hair and jeans. Some women seem to feel that if they ask to be included in rituals previously reserved for men, they should also accept those reserved for women.

Thus, while small but growing numbers of Orthodox women are reevaluating their traditional role in Judaism and asking for changes, others, perhaps a majority, are accepting more fully all the traditional demands made on them. Some even refuse to enter certain Orthodox synagogues where women's voices are heard in the congregational singing, because "the voice of a woman is impurity."[32] These women pose little threat to Or-

---

[31]"In Our Home We Keep Kosher," *Jewish Homemaker,* September-October 1974, p. 3.
[32]Berakhot 24a.

thodoxy. Orthodox Jewish feminists, however, are a disturbing element, for they will not indefinitely be satisfied to remain in a passive role in segregated sections of synagogues.

Reform

At the opposite end of the Jewish religious spectrum, Reform Judaism has long been concerned with enhancing the participation of women in public ritual. As Rabbi Sally Priesand, the first ordained woman rabbi, indicated, this was the gist of a statement by the *Rabbinerversammlung* (rabbinical conference) meeting in Frankfurt am Main in 1845.

> One of the marked achievements of the Reform movement has been the change in the status of women.... This conference declares that woman has the same obligations as man to participate from youth up in the instruction of Judaism and in the public services and that the custom not to include women in the number of individuals necessary for the conducting of a public service (a *minyan*) is only a custom and has no religious basis.[33]

A year later the Breslau Conference proposed that women observe all *miẓwot*, be responsible for their vows, and participate in public worship, and that the man's benediction to God, "Who hast not made me a woman," be eliminated. Despite the revolutionary nature of these proposals, one must note, according to Rabbi Priesand, that the conference neither mentioned the abolition of separate seating nor stressed encouraging women "to seek leadership roles within the synagogue structure."

American Reform Judaism further enhanced the position of women by introducing family pews, which did not obtain in Europe. Nevertheless, despite statements, including some by Rabbi Isaac Mayer Wise, urging the participation of women in the governance of Reform congregations, the gap between theory and practice, here as in Europe, has remained large.

> While most congregations have granted women the privileges of membership and voting, only about 5 percent of all Reform congregations have women serving as presidents and vice-presidents. And only about 4 percent of the members of the Board of Trustees of the Union of American Hebrew Congregations are women.[34]

The preamble to a resolution adopted in April 1973 by the New York Federation of Reform Synagogues underscores the problem:

> Historically, the Reform Movement was the first in Judaism to assert the religious equality of women. We are proud, too, that there are no logical impediments barring women from any post or office in Reform Judaism, and that women have

---

[33]Sally Priesand, *Judaism and the New Woman* (New York, 1975), pp. 30–31.
[34]*Ibid.*, p. 35.

made effective contributions in various offices, including the office of president in some congregations and the rabbinate itself. Despite this, inequities persist. Very small numbers of women are elected to our governing bodies. Very few are enabled to contribute in full measure of their skills, energies and creativity to a movement in which, by right, they should be full partners.

Further resolutions in 1974 and 1975 indicate a continuing need for action to achieve equality in the synagogue, the liturgy, and religious education.

Social attitudes are hard to change. Dr. Trude Weiss-Rosmarin reported that Rabbi Gerald Raiskin (Reform) "let it be known that women will not be called to the Torah at Temple Sholom [Burlingame, Cal.]. The reason, he explained, is that the Torah service is the last frontier of male religious functions. If it were shared with the women, the men would stay away from services."[35] Sex-segregation is also prevalent in the nonreligious sphere. Women do not serve as ushers during services, nor do men pour tea or coffee at the Oneg Shabbat.[36]

In a letter to the editor of *Ms.* (January 1975), Annette Daum, coordinator for religious action programs of the New York Federation of Reform Synagogues, praised Reform Judaism's achievements for women. She did point out, however, that Sally Priesand, the first woman rabbi, was not ordained until 1972, and that Barbara Herman, the first woman cantor, was yet to be graduated in June 1975. In closing, she remarked, "I speak as one who still bears the scars of her struggle (successful) to become president of her synagogue." Even in this, change has not been easily accepted.

Rabbi Priesand was not the first woman to study in a Reform rabbinical seminary, merely the first to do so and be ordained. In 1922 the Central Conference of American Rabbis issued the following statement: "In view of these Jewish teachings and in keeping with the spirit of our age and the traditions of our Conference, we declare that woman cannot justly be denied the privilege of ordination."[37] Nevertheless, when Martha Neumark was a student in the rabbinical department at Hebrew Union College in the 1920s, the board of governors voted six to two against the ordination of women. The only two rabbis present cast the two favorable votes. Martha Neumark left in the middle of her junior year, after almost eight years of study. Rabbi Earl S. Stone reported that in 1939 "the ordination class at the Jewish Institute of Religion was graduated with Helen Leventhal Lyons who

---

[35]Trude Weiss-Rosmarin, "Female Consciousness-Raising," *Jewish Spectator,* September 1973, p. 6.

[36]Myron Schoen, "Even Reform Is Slow On Women's Lib," *Jewish Post of New York,* January 10, 1975.

[37]Priesand, *op. cit.,* p. 62.

completed all of the requirements for ordination but, at that time, was refused this honor. She participated in our ordination exercises and was graduated with the degree of Master of Hebrew Letters."[38] Even the fact that these two women were the daughters of distinguished Jewish scholars and rabbis was not enough to carry theory into practice and provide for their ordination.

American Reform Judaism's first *de facto* woman "rabbi" was Paula Ackerman, widow of Rabbi William Ackerman, who after her husband's death was asked to replace him as spiritual leader of Temple Beth Israel of Meridian, Miss. At that time Rabbi Maurice Eisendrath said that there was no reason not to ordain women rabbis. Mrs. Ackerman, who after her retirement was asked to take another pulpit, said she hoped that her work would advance the cause of the ordination of women.[39] Similarly, Temple Avodah, a Reform congregation in Massapequa, Long Island, not long thereafter appointed a lay woman cantor, Mrs. Sheldon Robbins.[40] Twenty years elapsed before a duly trained woman was ordained as a rabbi or invested as a cantor.

Now that women are being ordained, though in small numbers, within the Reform movement, the question of their acceptance by congregations must be faced. Unfortunately, the move to open the rabbinate to women comes at a time when the Reform seminaries are producing more rabbis than can be placed in Reform congregations. At a workshop conference sponsored by the Task Force on Equality of Women in Judaism of the New York Federation of Reform Synagogues on March 2, 1975, Rabbi Priesand expressed the hope that seminaries attempting to adjust supply to demand would not eliminate women students first. Jane Evans, executive director of the National Federation of Temple Sisterhoods and secretary of the World Union for Progressive Judaism, feels that women rabbis will eventually gain acceptance, although, like the women pioneers in medicine and other analogous professions, the first women rabbis may find placements somewhat limited. Progress in this area depends not on religious law alone, but on social change as well.[41]

Clearly, if the Reform movement, which in many cases has abrogated such basic areas of Jewish observance as kashrut or the use of *tallit* and *tefillin*, has changed dates of holidays, has held Sabbath services on Sunday,

---

[38] Letter to the Editor, *Jewish Post of New York*, August 22, 1975.
[39] *Time*, January 22, 1951.
[40] New York *Times*, August 3, 1955.
[41] In a conversation with this author.

and has been equivocal about intermarriage, has taken so long to ordain a woman, the impediment was not religious in nature.

Conservatism

The situation of women in Conservative Judaism is decidedly more complex than in either Orthodoxy or Reform. Unlike Orthodoxy, Conservatism affirms change in Jewish law. Unlike Reform, it emphasizes fealty to tradition. Given its dual commitment, to tradition and to change, the movement comprehends a great diversity of opinion about the place of women in its religious life. Many congregations, as well as the national institutions of Conservative Judaism, are debating and arguing the issue.

It is fair to say that Conservative Judaism from its earliest years has granted new and substantial rights to women. The movement grew as it introduced mixed pews and the bat-mitzvah ceremony on Friday evenings, and as it emphasized equal education for girls in congregational schools. The Women's League for Conservative Judaism is probably the strongest lay arm of the movement, and the Teachers Institute of the movement's central institution, the Jewish Theological Seminary, has always had a sizable number of young women among its students.

With few exceptions, no further rights were effectively accorded women until the ferment of the past few years had set in, although the changes previously introduced led to an atmosphere responsive, in many cases, to calls for change. The initial impetus for the reconsideration of Conservative Judaism's position on women was probably the appearance of members of Ezrat Nashim at the convention of the Rabbinical Assembly, the organization of Conservative rabbis, in March 1972. These uninvited guests, "well mannered, earnest and honest, reared in our Conservative congregations,"[42] were allowed to hold an open meeting for the rabbis' wives, while their husbands were voting on resolutions. They also distributed handbills asking, among other things, that women be counted in the *minyan,* be granted full participation in religious observances, be recognized as witnesses in Jewish law, and be allowed to initiate a Jewish divorce.

In the wake of this action, the Women's League for Conservative Judaism; the United Synagogue of America, the association of Conservative congregations; the Committee on Jewish Law and Standards (CJLS) of the Rabbinical Assembly, and the Jewish Theological Seminary all moved in varying degrees toward a recognition of the merits of the feminist demand

---

[42]Selma Rapaport, "Two Worlds?", *Outlook,* Summer 1972, p. 24.

for increased women's rights. In effect, Ezrat Nashim had served to bring forth opinions and feelings which had been germinating beneath the surface.

Most significant in this regard was the CJLS's September 1973 decision, by a 9-to-4 vote, that women may be counted equally with men in the *minyan*. The nine men who supported the decision reasoned that "the contemporary position of women in society, the fact that we educate women and that they play a greater role in synagogue life, and that we encourage them to attend services require of us to count them." The minority position was that "there is no halakhic support. The *minyan* should consist of heads of household who support the community. There is no need for a *takkanah* [the form of rabbinic decision used by the majority], only a small pressure group wants it and it is a passing fad."[43]

The CJLS decision was deemed of sufficient weight to merit a front-page story in the New York *Times,* September 1, 1973. It raised a storm of comment, both positive and negative, and led to the rediscovery of favorable CJLS decisions in 1955 with regard to *'aliyot* for women. Many congregations began to discuss the issues. Others, in which discussions had started earlier, decided in favor of the feminists. Most congregations granted women both *minyan* and *'aliyot,* but some only one of the two—usually *'aliyot.*

The 1955 decision on *'aliyot* for women of the Committee on Jewish Law and Standards, like all its decisions, was not binding on rabbi or congregation, who may follow either the majority or a minority opinion. The majority decision then, supported by ten rabbis, allowed *'aliyot* for women only on special occasions, after the mandatory seven Sabbath *'aliyot.* The minority of five rabbis wished to allow women *'aliyot* on an equal basis with men. What is remarkable about those decisions is that only one member of CJLS felt he could support neither. In other words, all but one member of the committee supported granting women *'aliyot* on either a limited or a full basis. Nevertheless, during those relatively unruffled years the decision had had almost no impact.

In 1962 Rabbi Aaron Blumenthal, a former president of the Rabbinical Assembly and author of the responsum which had become the minority decision, conducted a survey on *'aliyot* for women for the Rabbinical Assembly.[44] Of the congregations which responded, 196 did not grant women

---

[43]Mayer Rabinowitz and Nessa Rappoport, "The Role of Women in Jewish Ritual: A Summary of the Committee on Jewish Law and Standards" (Rabbinical Assembly, January 2, 1975), pp. 2–3 (mimeo.).

[44]"A Questionnaire on Aliyot for Women and Bat Mitzvah: Results and Observations," 1962 mailing to RA members (mimeo.).

aliyot under any circumstances, eight granted *'aliyot* with no restrictions, and 50 with restrictions. Some of the restrictions are particularly interesting. The late Rabbi Louis Levitsky thought it should be granted to "only those to whom it has deep religious significance and who can recite the *berakhot* by heart easily—never more than one on any Shabbat." These are restrictions which are never applied to men. According to Rabbi Blumenthal, "a number restrict it to girls at their Bat Mitzvah." This is a rather odd approach to religious training, but one which recurs. The bar-mitzvah ceremony marks a young man's entrance into adult Jewish responsibility and privilege—the first, it is hoped, of many such occasions. But a bat-mitzvah would mark a young woman's *exit* from participation. It would be the only time she was permitted to go up to read the *haftarah*.

A conflict over the Rabbinical Assembly's decisions regarding women was launched by Rabbi I. Usher Kirshblum of the Jewish Center of Kew Garden Hills, New York, in May 1975. In a letter sent to many members, he accused the CJLS of announcing its decision on the *minyan* "through the orchestration of a front-page article of the New York Times," thus undercutting the position of the congregational rabbi as *mara de'atra*, halakhic authority for his congregation. Excerpts from letters received by Rabbi Kirshblum in support of his position, which he circulated, reflected similar concerns, rabbis objecting to being challenged by their congregants and fearing that the Conservative movement was approaching Reform.

Rabbi Kirshblum also sharply criticized both Rabbi Wolfe Kelman, executive vice-president of the Rabbinical Assembly, and Rabbi Seymour Siegel, chairman of the Committee on Jewish Law and Standards, in the Yiddish press. The tone of the attack by Rabbi Kirshblum and his associates in the Committee for the Preservation of Tradition and Diversity Within the Rabbinical Assembly, of which Rabbi Kirshblum is chairman, is that of a group suddenly finding itself embattled. Rabbi Kelman carefully answered Rabbi Kirshblum's charges.

In the summer of 1975 a questionnaire was sent by this author and her husband, Rabbi Stephen C. Lerner, to all Rabbinical Assembly members regarding the status of women's rights in their synagogues. Of 229 respondents, 114 (almost 50 per cent) indicated that their synagogues granted women *'aliyot*, at least on some occasions, and 85 (37 per cent), including some congregations not granting women *'aliyot*, counted them in the *minyan*. An additional 40 congregations grant *'aliyot* only to girls, mainly at their junior services where the age level occasionally extends through high school.

The answers also revealed something about the pace of change. In 64 of the 94 (68 per cent) congregations which indicated when *'aliyot* were first granted to women, this right had been instituted since 1973. Sixty-nine of the 85 (81 per cent) congregations counting women in the *minyan* had decided to do so since 1973. In other synagogues, discussion was either in progress or scheduled. Clearly, the *"minyan* decision" had triggered a movement, which seemed to be lagging only in Queens, N.Y., and in Canada.

One of the first issues concerning women discussed by the Committee on Jewish Law and Standards was their inability to initiate divorce proceedings, leaving them *'agunot*. As early as 1930 Rabbi Louis M. Epstein, chairman of the Rabbinical Assembly's Committee on Jewish Law and an expert on the status of women, proposed that the *bet din* be empowered by the husband at the time of the marriage to arrange for a Jewish divorce in the event he was granted a civil divorce or disappeared. Although there was considerable initial support, and CJLS approved the proposal in 1935, it was not implemented. Only in 1968 was the antenuptial agreement instituted, providing for the retroactive nullification of the marriage if the husband refuses to grant a divorce. Despite the psychological objections to discussing divorce just before marriage,[45] this agreement should go a long way toward alleviating problems in recent and future marriages. Unfortunately, it does little to help the women who married in the intervening 33 years. In cases where no agreement exists and the husband refuses to grant a *get*, a Conservative *bet din* will annul the marriage. Since such a procedure is not recognized by Orthodox Jews, it may not solve the problem of a woman who wishes to marry one.[46]

Regarding the ordination of women, Rabbi Mordecai Waxman asserted in the presidential address opening the 1975 Rabbinical Assembly Convention that "the question of entry of women into the Conservative rabbinate is not a question of whether, but when." In an interview at that time he predicted that "properly ordained and educated" women would be admitted "to membership in the Rabbinical Assembly."[47] No action has been taken on this matter except for a little known CJLS decision, on June 10, 1974, in which a majority of nine held that women should serve neither as rabbis nor as cantors, and a minority of three,

---

[45]Simon Greenberg, "And He Writes Her a Bill of Divorcement," *Conservative Judaism,* Spring 1970, pp. 92, 135; cf. Aaron Landes, "The Ante-Nuptial Agreement," *ibid.,* Spring 1972, pp. 61–63.

[46]See the soul-searching article by Simon Greenberg, *loc. cit.,* pp. 75–141.

[47]Irving Spiegel, "Conservative Rabbi Sees Woman in Pulpit Soon," New York *Times,* April 21, 1975.

that they should.⁴⁸ A growing number of women, some of whom would have preferred studying at the Jewish Theological Seminary, have been preparing for rabbinic ordination at Hebrew Union College and the Reconstructionist Rabbinical College, the latter sponsored by a movement which issued from Conservatism and has vigorously emphasized women's rights.

Waxman's prediction has yet to be fulfilled. No woman has been accepted for study in the rabbinical department of the Jewish Theological Seminary, the only institution specifically designed to ordain Conservative rabbis. Women studying in other schools at the Seminary, however, are allowed equal access to classes in the rabbinical department. They may study at the Seminary's College of Sacred Music, but not at the Cantors' Institute which confers the title of ḥazzan. There are some women on the faculty, although none on the prestigious Graduate Rabbinical School faculty. Women also hold high administrative posts, among them Sylvia C. Ettenberg, dean of educational development.

The issue of women at the Jewish Theological Seminary surfaced in 1903, when Henrietta Szold asked permission to attend classes at the institution, newly reorganized by Solomon Schechter. Permission was granted "only after she had assured its administration that she would not use the knowledge thus gained to seek ordination."⁴⁹ The question of the ordination of women was raised again in the 1970s. In 1972 Professor Gerson D. Cohen stated:

> I, for one, would urge serious consideration if a woman applied [to the Rabbinical Department] who was qualified academically, characterologically and religiously, and I would urge the faculty and my colleagues in the Rabbinical Assembly to consider it.⁵⁰

Some time later, as chancellor, Professor Cohen further expressed himself on this subject in the publication of the National Women's League of the United Synagogue:

> . . . anyone who has considered the matter dispassionately will concede that admitting her [an applicant] to candidacy for ordination *at this time* would hardly reflect the consensus of the Conservative Movement, whether of its laity or its professional leadership. . . .
> . . . the quest for full equality with men on the levels we have been discussing [the rabbinate] has not been echoed by those young women who have been studying at the Seminary. . . .⁵¹

---

⁴⁸Mayer Rabinowitz and Nessa Rappoport, *op. cit.*, pp. 2, 3.
⁴⁹Susan Dworkin, "Henrietta Szold," *Response,* Summer 1973, p. 43.
⁵⁰Nemy, *loc. cit.*
⁵¹Gerson D. Cohen, "Women in the Conservative Movement: 1973," *Women's League Outlook,* Winter 1973, pp. 5, 32.

Some women and rabbinic colleagues disagreed with Cohen's later statement. The members of Ezrat Nashim, two of whom were then teaching at the Seminary, declared:

> For a woman to aspire vocally and actively to a role which is barred to her takes a great deal of courage, for she risks mockery, frustration and doubts, by her society, of her femininity. Despite this, several women have requested admission to the rabbinical program and have been turned away. Many more women might have applied were it possible to be admitted, several signatories to this letter included. How many gifted spiritual leaders has the Jewish people done without because one-half of the Jewish population is biologically ineligible?[52]

Another respondent, Tziporah Heckelman of Waterbury, Conn., vice-chairman of adult education of the Women's League for Conservative Judaism, praised the chancellor's statement:

> Your *Outlook* article on women in the Conservative Movement was an important statement on an inflamed issue. In all likelihood, it will be viewed as "reactionary" by men and women who are caught up in the groundswell of erasing all role distinctions in Synagogue life. I, for one, applaud its statesmanship and its reintroduction of perspective on an issue too much considered from the narrow vantage point of what's good for the modern American Jewish woman, to the exclusion of concern for what's good for the family, the fabric of Jewish law and the Jewish people as a whole.[53]

Rabbi Aaron Blumenthal, while praising Cohen, concluded that "his faculty is opposed overwhelmingly and that there is nothing he can do about it. That is both sad and unfortunate."[54] Chancellor Cohen and the JTS faculty continue to grapple with the problem of a suitable role for women in rabbinic and other religious leadership.

In one area, the Seminary's network of Ramah summer camps, the status of women has changed. In 1974, without any fanfare, JTS, which is responsible for the educational and religious supervision of Ramah, issued a directive mandating *'aliyot* for women. By and large, this change has been successfully incorporated into services at the camps. However, camps do offer a choice of nonegalitarian services where needed.

Essentially, the Seminary synagogue has been the congregation of the senior faculty. As such, its bent is decidedly right-wing in religious orientation. It is one of the few United Synagogue congregations in which separation of the sexes is maintained, although without a *meḥiẓah*.[55] Of late an

---

[52]*Ibid.,* Summer 1974, p. 29
[53]*Ibid.,* p. 11.
[54]"Is Seminary Opposed to Women Rabbis?", *Jewish Post of New York,* January 3, 1975.
[55]Shaare Zion of Montreal, one of the last Conservative synagogues to maintain separate seating, is considering change. In January 1976 its board of trustees voted to establish mixed seating, subject to a vote of the congregation in the spring. A poll indicated that 78 per cent of the membership approved the contemplated change.

occasional woman student has donned *tallit* and *tefillin* at week-day services, although no participatory rights are extended to women. But even here, small changes have occurred. On *Simḥat Torah* 1975 women at the Seminary were allowed a separate Torah service, at which they recited blessings, albeit modified, when called to the Torah.

At the present time the Seminary is proceeding slowly. Requests for more religious rights at its synagogue and for admission to its rabbinical department are not likely to abate.

At the 1973 biennial convention of the United Synagogue of America, the congregational arm of Conservative Judaism, three resolutions concerning women were adopted. These were the strongest statement for the equal participation of women in public ritual ever to be issued by any body in the Conservative movement:

THE ROLE OF WOMEN
A. The Place of Jewish Women in Synagogue Life Today
Whereas, it is demonstrably evident that women have the same concerns and commitment to their synagogue as do men; and

Whereas, it is also demonstrably evident that women have not, generally, been accorded equal opportunity commensurate with their ability to serve as officers and trustees and members of congregational committees; and

Whereas, we recognize the justice of extending equality of opportunity to Jewish women in synagogue life; therefore

Be it resolved that the United Synagogue calls upon its member congregations to take such action as will insure equal opportunity for its women congregants to assume positions of leadership, authority and responsibility in all phases of congregational activity.

B. The Role of Women in Ritual
Whereas, the United Synagogue of America desires to encourage and foster the availability of creative Jewish identity and experience to all members of the Jewish community; and

Whereas, women are, and have been, an integral part of synagogue life, generously contributing their energies and resources to its growth and development; and

Whereas, the Committee on Jewish Law and Standards of the Rabbinical Assembly has determined it is halachically permissible for women to participate in synagogue ritual; and

Whereas, the United Synagogue of America believes that the concept of full and equal opportunity and participation by women in religious as well as secular roles is an idea whose time has come; therefore

Be it resolved that the United Synagogue of America looks with favor upon the inclusion of women in ritual participation, including but not limited to participation in the *minyan* and *'aliyot*, and looks with favor upon its member congregations adopting such programs as will meaningfully implement this resolution.

C. Admission of Women in the Rabbinical School of the Jewish Theological Seminary of America

> Recognizing the growing role of women in the life of our congregations, the United Synagogue of America, in convention assembled, wishes to note that it looks with favor on the admission of qualified women to the Rabbinical School of the Jewish Theological Seminary of America.[56]

Despite the adoption by the United Synagogue of these proposals for greater women's religious participation, they were not implemented in the United Synagogue Youth (USY) movement, the most active arm of the organization. Neither at its national conclaves nor in its nationally sponsored programs, did USY accord women *'aliyot* or count them in the *minyan,* although some regional gatherings did so. A meeting of the National Youth Commission, the body charged with supervision of USY, voted in fall 1975 not to change its policy. A list of Youth Commission publications offers one article about Judaism's attitude toward women. Written by Nina Freedman, the wife of the USY director, the article is a paean to the traditional role of Jewish women.[57] This created the unlikely situation of the parent organization having endorsed more "radical" positions than those practiced by the children. As an ever-growing number of young women and men become accustomed to egalitarian services in their congregations, the official USY stand will experience further pressure for accommodation.

In the sisterhoods of the Conservative movement and among the leadership of their parent organization, the Women's League for Conservative Judaism, there has been a great deal of ambivalence about Jewish feminism. Sisterhood leaders have traditionally been dynamic volunteers who have been content to be the "power behind the throne," generally reflecting the acceptance of the traditional women's roles. Thus in the *Women's League Outlook,* national leaders, despite their important and coveted posts, are listed by their husbands' names, not their own.

In 1970 Evelyn Henkind, then League president, discussed the impact of women's organizations on Judaism, saying that there was

> ... no danger of feminizing religious life because women are not asking to take on traditional religious roles of the male—nor are they trying to become rabbis. Most of our work has to do with educating the Jewish woman to continue the Jewish traditions in the home—as a mother and wife, in addition to being responsive to issues in the community and in the world.[58]

---

[56] *Proceedings of the 1973 Biennial Convention of the United Synagogue of America, November 11–15, 1973,* pp. 108–109.

[57] *The Jewish Woman: A Liberator, Already Liberated* (United Synagogue: Atid, College Age Organization), 4 p. (mimeo.).

[58] Quoted by Doris B. Gold, "Jewish Women's Groups: Separate—But Equal?" *Congress Bi-Weekly,* February 6, 1970, p. 11.

Ezrat Nashim's appearance led to reconsideration of these historically sanctified attitudes. Selma N. Rapaport, Mrs. Henkind's successor, viewed the group of young women sympathetically. After first placing them in the context of the women's liberation movement, she characterized them as members of the family, "reared in our Conservative congregations, graduates of our religious schools, products of our Ramah Camps, our LTF [Leaders Training Fellowship], our USY, some of them enrolled for studies at our Jewish Theological Seminary." She then inserted much of their flyer, "Jewish Women Call for Change," into her column.[59]

The result of an opinion poll conducted at the 1972 Women's League Convention, which preceded the Rabbinical Assembly "*minyan* decision," indicated 99 per cent of the participants in favor of allowing women to serve on congregational boards of directors; 98 per cent, of enabling them to initiate divorce proceedings; 70 per cent, of permitting them to read from the Torah; 66.5 per cent, of calling them for *'aliyot,* and 61 per cent, of counting them in a *minyan*. Averages of response to all five questions, correlated by age group, showed, not unexpectedly, that the desire for change decreased from 92 per cent among those 21 to 30 years old to 71 per cent among those over 60.

The 1974 Women's League convention participants voted by secret ballot on the following resolution:

> Women's League for Conservative Judaism endorses the recent decisions of the Committee on Jewish Law and Standards of the Rabbinical Assembly which allow women to assume a more equal role in ritual and Synagogue life, and understanding that the Rabbi is the final religious authority in his Congregation, to explore and discuss the implications of these decisions, and to implement them as individual circumstances permit.[60]

This resolution was obviously weaker than those passed by the United Synagogue the previous year, but it was clear. Though it passed by six to one, it made no headlines in *Outlook*.

Featured in a subsequent issue were the results of a questionnaire sent to the presidents of the 800 affiliated sisterhoods, eliciting information about current practice with regard to women in administration, ritual, and education. In this survey 26.4 per cent belonged to congregations giving women *'aliyot*, in addition to the bat-mitzvah, and 23.8 per cent to congregations counting women in the *minyan*. The conclusion Zelda Dick drew from the survey was that

---

[59]Rapaport, *loc. cit.,* pp. 4, 24–25.
[60]Celia Goldstein, "Business Unusual," *Women's League Outlook,* Winter 1974, p. 24.

... these figures strongly suggest an overwhelming "Silent Majority" which appears to be somewhat unmoved by the Resolution of the Committee on Law and Standards of the Rabbinical Assembly..., or by the hue and cry which seems to be emanating from what is evidently a small percentage of our Conservative women.... To say that, as a result of this survey..., a mandate has been called for a more liberalized women's role would be to interpret these figures in a manner that could be in violation of the trust of a majority of our membership.[61]

There is plainly a large gap between the Women's League convention vote and replies to the *Outlook* questionnaire. Whether it justifies Zelda Dick's conclusion is another question. She failed to record that many synagogues have significantly enlarged the religious rights of women over the past few years. Also, a questionnaire on synagogue practice indicates nothing about a "silent majority." In congregations, men too vote on ritual matters. Besides, the rabbi, as *mara de'atra,* has a veto power over religious innovations, although he cannot alone compel any new, non-traditional practices. Finally, it has been estimated, about 20 per cent of the rabbis in Conservative congregations are Orthodox rabbis, having little sympathy for Rabbinical Assembly legal decisions; and a minority of Conservative rabbis are in accord with them, at least on women's rights. Thus in perhaps 30 to 40 per cent of the congregations, the rabbis are opposed to religious rights for women.

Zelda Dick's striking conclusions and recent *Outlook* articles by Rabbis Morton Leifman and Henry Sosland seem to represent an attempt to slow the extension of rights to women in Conservative Judaism. It may be that Sisterhood leaders are beginning to sense that the full integration of women into the administrative and religious life of the congregations poses a threat to the continued viability of women's organizations.

JEWISH EDUCATION

Intertwined with the question of the religious role of Jewish women is the issue of their religious education. The famous dictum, "He who teaches his daughter Torah, teaches her lechery,"[62] generally excluded Jewish women from observing the highest commandment—Jewish learning. As Paula Hyman, now assistant professor of history at Columbia University, pointed out, "the *dominant* theme in Talmudic and rabbinic literature is not to educate women to the same level as men. Men and women, after all, were

---

[61]"Light from Our Poll on Women's Role," *ibid.,* Summer 1975, p. 15.
[62]Soṭah III, 4.

educated for different purposes and different roles. So the *yeshiva* and *bet-midrash* were male monopolies."⁶³ Rachel Adler added that "there is no continuous tradition of learned women in Jewish history."⁶⁴ Traditional Jewish education for a girl, according to Susan Dworkin, "succeeded when it helped her 'enable' everyone else to reach God."⁶⁵ Great changes have taken place in this century, however.

Conservative and Reform Judaism teach their boys and girls the same things, although women, as indicated above, are not accepted into the Conservative rabbinical school.⁶⁶ Among the Orthodox, even the liberals usually maintain real differences in education. The principal of a leading modern Orthodox day school in New York City recently told this writer that boys are given extensive training in Torah reading, whereas girls are taught only the "theory" and use the rest of the time for cooking and crafts. It would not be sensible, as he logically argued, to give girls the same training as boys, since the girls could not use it in their Orthodox synagogues.

"Right-wing" Orthodoxy often provides entirely separate schools for boys and girls. Rabbi David B. Hollander, vice-president of the Rabbinical Alliance of America, reported that boys in Orthodox day schools engaged in "deeper academic study," while girls focused on such subjects as typing, stenography, and kashrut in the home.⁶⁷ Rabbi Nisson Wolpin, writing about the ultra-Orthodox Beth Jacob schools for girls, granted that they had "succeeded in salvaging" the post-World War I generation of Jewish girls, but questioned how realistically these schools educate women. "Schooling educates for education," and women will have no time for that. Therefore, schools for Jewish girls should stress the intellectual less, and teach them how as women to help other Jews.⁶⁸ His article evoked both disagreement and praise. In a letter to the editor, Eve Roth of Lakewood, N.J., wrote that "once more, perhaps the finger should be pointed at the Torah society for failing its responsibility to its women, rather than at the women for seeking

---

⁶³Paula Hyman, "The Other Half: Women in the Jewish Tradition," *Conservative Judaism*, Summer 1972, p. 16.
⁶⁴Rachel Adler, "The Jew Who Wasn't There: Halacha and the Jewish Woman," *Response*, Summer 1973, p. 79 (reprinted).
⁶⁵"A Song for Women . . . ," *loc. cit.*, p. 44.
⁶⁶The report by the Women's League for Conservative Judaism of its "Survey of Women's Activities in the Synagogue, 1974" (unpublished) indicated that 98.8 per cent of synagogue schools have the same curriculum for girls and boys.
⁶⁷Eleanor Blau, "Rabbis See Women's Rights Measure as Threatening Orthodox Practices," New York *Times*, April 4, 1972.
⁶⁸*Loc. cit.*, pp. 15, 16.

that elusive fulfillment wherever it might be found."[69] Rabbi Benyamin Field of Phoenix, Ariz., elaborated on Rabbi Wolpin's suggestions for a practical education: "Aside from giving practical suggestions regarding how to set up and maintain a kosher kitchen (leaving technical halachic questions to the rabbi), there is a need for direction on how and where to shop, what to look for, and so on."[70]

The view of women in Jewish textbooks casts them in markedly stereotyped and old-fashioned roles. Naturally, if all girls were being educated for a home role only, this would be reasonable. However, since many Jewish women now work outside the home, receive an extensive education, both Jewish and secular, and participate actively in public worship, the gap between children's literature and reality is quite noticeable.

Melvin and Miriam Alexenberg's *Alef-Bet Picture Dictionary* (New York, 1963), in which the level of Hebrew does not indicate that it is directed at a day-school readership, is a good example. "Man" is shown standing, dressed in a business suit, hat, and tie, holding an attaché case; "woman" is shown bent over, her dress covered by an apron, sweeping the floor. Rayzel Berman's easy reader, *Hafta'ah likhvod shabbat* ("A Surprise for Shabbat")[71] shows Sabbath preparations being made by a woman, with the help of her son and daughter, while the father comes in at the last minute. *World Over,* a popular children's magazine published by the New York Board of Jewish Education, heavily emphasizes the role of men. One story, "Last Shabbat,"[72] views the new controversy in an interesting light. Its author, Barbara M. White, discusses a boy's reaction to his parents' exchanging roles for candle-lighting and *qiddush* on the Sabbath, i.e., that he is perfectly willing to have changes made in the synagogue, as long as they do not upset the home situation, in which he is comfortable. As the liberal-minded young man puts it: "So I said that I'd agree that it was okay for Mom to do anything if she didn't actually go and do it." Finally they agree to recite the appropriate blessings together, and alternate lighting the candles and holding the *qiddush* cup.[73]

In "Sexism and Jewish Education,"[74] Susan Rosenblum Shevitz, then

---

[69]*Jewish Observer,* January 1975, p. 4.
[70]*Ibid.,* p. 28.
[71]New York: Board of Jewish Education, 1968 (Hebrew).
[72]December 6, 1974, p. 11.
[73]Rabbi Wolpin *(loc. cit.)* used a picture from that story (p. 13) to illustrate his words about the dire effects of women's liberation. This emphasizes the importance of sociological patterns, even among the ultra-Orthodox, for, according to *halakhah,* it is legal for a woman to make *qiddush* and for a man to light candles.
[74]*Response,* Summer 1973, pp. 107–13.

educational director of New City Jewish Center, New City, N.Y., remarked that there were few role-models with which a young woman interested in developing a religious sensitivity could identify: "The textbooks unanimously choose to depict a rigidly defined family structure... and strenuous sex-role differentiation.... Women are depicted almost exclusively in domestic scenes and men in spiritual and ritual ones." Girls who might want to be rabbis or cantors, she continued, are never shown a woman in that role:

> Women are barred from Conservative rabbinical and cantorial schools. Furthermore those women who choose Jewish education as a profession are encouraged to be teachers, while the overwhelming majority of supervising personnel is male. This seems especially strange when one recalls that education is the only professional Jewish field which is truly open to women....
>
> The girl's *rite de passage* is presented as marriage and motherhood—in stark contrast to the boy's bar mitzvah. Whereas bar mitzvah is ideally a measure of independent religious status, marriage marks the change of the female's status *vis a vis* her primary male relationship.

Deborah Grand Golomb, speaking about the Reform educational system, came to a similar conclusion.[75] While secular children's literature and textbooks show increasing awareness of these problems, Jewish publishers and writers do not. At the present time, Jewish textbooks and children's literature will not provide the Jewish school girl with a sense of the variety of life options increasingly available to her.

ORGANIZATIONS

Jewish communal and philanthropic work has not been free of sex-typing either. Professor Daniel Elazar recognizes the contributions and importance of Jewish women's organizations, particularly Hadassah. He notes, however, that "with some exceptions, women function in environments segregated from male decision-makers within the Jewish community." The exceptions are "very wealthy women who have a record of activity in their own right," who are occasionally "admitted to the governing councils of major Jewish institutions and organizations. So, too, are the top leaders of the women's groups in an *ex officio* capacity which is sometimes translated into meaningful participation but frequently remains *ex officio.*"[76]

---

[75] Workshop Conference of the Task Force on Equality for Women in Judaism, New York Federation of Reform Synagogues, March 2, 1975.
[76] "Women in American Jewish Life," *Congress Bi-Weekly*, November 23, 1973, p. 10.

Women, volunteer and professional, often do the actual job of running Jewish communal activities, leaving the higher, decision-making posts to men. With the exception of Naomi Levine, executive director of the American Jewish Congress, and Charlotte Jacobson, chairman of the World Zionist Organization—American Section, women do not head major "coeducational" organizations. There was a recent breakthrough, which, however, was reported in the old, prejudiced fashion: "The Conference on Jewish Social Studies is the first of the Jewish scholarly organizations to have a woman president, Jeanette M. Baron, wife of the eminent historian Dr. Salo Baron."[77] Women usually are the secretaries, men the presidents.

The *General Assembly Papers,* summarizing the sessions of the National Committee on Women's Communal Service of the Council of Jewish Federations and Welfare Funds (CJFWF), are revealing. In a 1970 address, Mrs. Howard Levine, chairman of the committee, alluded to women's liberation in her address, but in rather perfunctory fashion. The question of "integration" referred to integrating the "Young Matrons" into the Women's Division. Young Matrons (aged 21 to 35) were "girls," and the participants were called by their husbands' names. In 1971, though names remained unchanged, the participants seemed to be much more aware of the importance of involvement in policy-making. Mrs. Leonard Bernheim, the session's keynote speaker, declared:

> Yet, while I am sure that a few women in this room have had top jobs, there are thousands of women around the country who are not invited to play a *major* role in Federations, Welfare Funds and other community organizations. I am not a member of Women's Lib, but there are many things this movement is saying which we, as Jewish women leaders, must listen to and do something about. . . . There may be times when we ought to have a sit-in in the Federation president's office or in the office of the Distribution Committee, or in any other functional office where we can make our views known and our opinions felt.

In 1972 Mrs. Levine, then national president of the Women's Division of the American Jewish Congress, addressed a plenary session of CJFWF. Her talk, on "The Changing Role of Women in the Jewish Community," raised many of the issues which had been of growing concern in the Jewish community. She reported on the results of a survey conducted that year of women's participation in federation boards of directors and committees in 1965 and 1972. The percentages had risen, but the highest, 28.4, was for officers and members of Federation committees in small cities, with the corresponding figure for large cities only 16.2 per cent. Speaking as a "token woman," Mrs. Levine urged expanding the decision-making role of women

---

[77] *Jewish Week,* June 21, 1975.

in federations. In answer to the argument that men were more valuable on boards, she pointed out that if that was the only consideration, boards were not representative:

> Yes, there must always be members who are large contributors. There must also be board members who are involved, who are activists, who are committed community leaders able to inspire others. Women may be any or all of these.

In closing, she urged that an affirmative-action program be undertaken to include women.

By 1974 the participants in the CJFWF Women's Communal Service sessions had all taken to using their given names, but the UJA and federations were nonetheless under attack from the Jewish Feminist Organization. JFO of Baltimore-Washington stated that its members "will submit their pledges this year, but that they will not be paid until women are equal to men, regardless of their choice of career, and 'the existing situation of separate women's and men's divisions has been changed.'"[78] In some places challenges were unnecessary. Frances Green and Mrs. Laurence Weinberg (as she prefers to be known) were chosen to head the federations in San Francisco and Los Angeles, respectively.[79]

In 1973 the American Jewish Committee established a National Committee on the Role of Women. In a June 1974 memorandum to the members of that group about women's activities in the agency's various chapters, Ann G. Wolfe, adviser to the new committee, reported on a series of interreligious workshops called "Institute for Women Today," in which the Committee is participating, along with Church Women United and the National Coalition of American Nuns. She also reported that groups of chapter members across the country had conducted surveys of the role of women in Jewish community organizations. The finding of the Washington, D.C., survey, "that women are dramatically underrepresented in proportion to their numbers in leadership positions in Jewish communal organizations," was corroborated in other cities. A salutary effect of this activity, said Mrs. Wolfe, was that those who developed questionnaires in various cities have had their own consciousness raised, and that the mere act of answering these queries has helped respondents understand the problems. The surveys served, too, as starting points for affirmative-action programs.

Other Jewish organizations have begun to find it advisable to alter their basic structure to obviate opposition and encourage growth. B'nai B'rith, which had long maintained sex-segregated groups, has experimented with

---

[78] *Jewish Post of New York,* August 1, 1975.
[79] *Jewish Advocate,* Boston, May 15, 1975.

"co-ed" units, as a way of reversing a decline in membership among young adults (25–35). Fifty-three such units, enrolling 4,000 members, have included single men and women, young married couples, members of a specific industry or profession, single parents, and persons isolated in small towns. These members manifest an unusually high degree of involvement. B'nai B'rith president David M. Blumberg, stating that "nine out of ten ... have no interest in joining voluntary groups that are segregated by sex," maintained that this new arrangement offers potential for growth.[80] Similarly, a newly chartered Machar group of Hadassah in Cleveland is for married couples.[81]

Among a number of outstanding American Jewish women's organizations, Hadassah has been the most influential and probably the most potent force in the lives of its members. Its more than 300,000 members are heavily involved in raising money for Israel and in study. Many would agree with the contention of Rose Feinberg, past president of the New England region and a member of the national board, that Hadassah has helped women feel themselves to be "worthwhile, active individuals."[82] Although she had no objection to Hadassah members serving coffee and cake to male delegates at the first Brussels World Conference on Soviet Jewry (February 1971), she felt that Hadassah members had long been liberated. Among Hadassah's achievements are its lowest per capita operating cost among Jewish organizations and its members' high individual contributions to Israel, second only to UJA.

If the women's movement, with its rejection of sex-segregation and volunteerism, begins seriously to challenge "women only" organizations, the American Jewish community will have a major task in providing for their creative reconstruction. Coed chapters may be the way.

ROLE IN SOCIETY

All Jews, except those living in almost self-contained, isolated communities like the hasidic village of New Square near Spring Valley, N.Y., realize that women are aware of the women's liberation movement. Although the synagogue or Jewish school may be shielded from its impact, the family and other societal structures are generally affected. Jewish women are increas-

---

[80]Irving Spiegel, "B'nai B'rith Gains with 'Coed Units'," New York *Times,* August 3, 1975.
[81]Bernard Postal, "Postal Card," *Jewish Week-American Examiner*, May 24, 1975, p. 17.
[82]Elaine S. Cohen, "Hadassah Ladies and Liberation," *genesis 2,* March 25, 1971, p. 4.

ingly choosing roles other than that of wife, mother, and home-maker. Recent figures for Greater New York indicated that only "four to five out of every ten Jewish women (16 years of age and older) are housewives."[83] Conversely, just over half of those women are either employed or students. A young woman today is likely to view her work as more important than did her mother or grandmother who may also have worked outside the home. Bracha Sacks, who is Orthodox, speaks of wanting "a fulfilling career,"[84] a concept which was probably foreign to her grandmothers, whether or not they were gainfully employed. If one can derive fulfillment from both career and family, one must value both.

Dr. Trude Weiss-Rosmarin has long claimed that a significant part of the problem of Jewish women derives "from the fact that the importance and dignity of the home-maker and mother are not sufficiently stressed in our civilization . . . ."[85] While proclaiming that sex-roles as defined by Judaism make sense, Dr. Weiss-Rosmarin would like women to be given an equal opportunity in the rabbinate, education, and communal and professional work, if they desire it.[86] Although the importance of home-making and mothering is not to be underestimated, one doubts that any profound shift in public attitudes will take place in the near future.

One is constantly besieged by alarms which purport to signal the breakdown of the Jewish family, and the subsequent breakdown of the Jewish community as a whole. This is not a new situation. According to Professor Gerson Cohen, "even before [Jewish] emancipation, when the stability of the Jewish family could be more effectively enforced by social controls, families seemed to totter from time to time."[87] The idyllic picture of the Jewish family of the past is a myth which, as Paula Hyman indicated, will not convince women to leave their jobs, but "may provide a group of angry and guilty Jewish working mothers who feel that their community is not supportive of them."[88] Rabbi Wolpin, on the other hand, felt that the home should occupy all of a woman's time:

---

[83] Fred Massarik, "Basic Characteristics of the Greater New York Jewish Population," AMERICAN JEWISH YEAR BOOK, Vol. 76 (1976), p. 248.
[84] *Loc. cit.*, p. 108.
[85] "Jewish Woman in a Man's World," *Jewish Spectator*, May 1950, p. 9.
[86] "Women's Liberation," *Jewish Spectator*, March 1973, pp. 4–7, 31.
[87] "Dr. [Gerson D.] Cohen Talks of the Jewish Family," *The Jewish Theological Seminary of America Bulletin*, November 1975, p. 1a.
[88] Paula Hyman, "The Jewish Family: Looking for a Usable Past" (unpublished paper for Conference on Changing Life Styles in America, sponsored by American Jewish Congress); see also Charlotte Baum, "What Made Yetta Work?," *Response*, Summer 1973, pp. 32–38, and I. Epstein, "The Jewish Woman in the Responsa," *ibid.*, p. 24 and *passim*.

When a woman does focus her interests, activities and designs for fulfillment outside her home, this can become a factor in the destruction of the family as a viable unit in society. Statistics need not be cited.[89]

But all Jewish women will not be restricted to their homes; therefore, it is reasonable to expect the Jewish community to move toward meeting the new needs of women. In the New York area some YM-YWHAs are beginning to offer expanded programs for the pre-school children of working parents, which may be extended to infants and school-age children. It would be appropriate for the National Council of Jewish Women, which has done much in the field of day care for disadvantaged minorities, to initiate some Jewish programs as well.[90]

There are also increasing numbers of Jewish women who are not married —never married or formerly married, single-parent or childless, young or old. Their situation results from extended schooling, challenging careers, a growing divorce rate, and prolonged widowhood. Their far less numerous predecessors of earlier generations had usually found a niche under the protecting shelter of the extended family. Today, as Rosa Felsenberg Kaplan pointed out, family seating and family-centered activities make single persons feel out of place. She suggested as "a possible option . . . the development of co-educational or non-gender-specific and non-marital-status-specific educational and community action groups which meet at times convenient for most working people."[91] The need for such programs is underscored by the near-universality of Dr. Naomi Bluestone's personal experience that "there is virtually no place in my Judaism for an unmarried woman over twenty-five."[92]

Though they accept many feminist strictures with regard to the need to restructure communities, Jewish feminists can differ from the others on problems of direct Jewish concern—e.g., zero population growth for Jews:

> No one inherits the Holocaust as pointedly as the Jewish wife who . . . is still getting pregnant long after it is safe, in a mighty effort to right the Jewish population deficit. The Jewish feminist is the only feminist who is told by mentors who are feminists too, that the abortion option is not for her.[93]

Married Jewish women also have their own special problems of adjustment, especially after their children no longer need baby-sitters. Pauline Bart, who has carefully examined the problems of middle-aged depression

---

[89] *Loc. cit.,* p. 13.
[90] *Impact,* National Council of Jewish Women, Biennial Report, 1973–1975.
[91] "The Noah Syndrome," *Davka,* Winter 1975, p. 32.
[92] Naomi Bluestone, "Exodus from Eden: One Woman's Experience," *Judaism,* Winter 1974, p. 96.
[93] Susan Dworkin, "A Song for Women . . . ," *loc. cit.,* p. 53.

in Jewish women, found that it is because of the demands made on the Jewish mother that she is more likely to be depressed once the "mothering" role becomes attenuated:

> The literature on the Jewish mother is practically unanimous in painting her as "supermother" especially vulnerable to being severely affected if her children fail to meet her needs, either by not making what she considers "good" marriages, not achieving the career aspirations she has for them or even by not phoning her every day.[94]

Many of these women have been so conditioned to define themselves in terms of their husbands and children that they cannot see any value in their own independent existence.

Divisions among Jews regarding feminism have spilled over into the political world. In the fall of 1975 many Orthodox spokesmen argued against the proposed Equal Rights Amendment to the state constitutions of New York and New Jersey, contending that the amendment would destroy the fabric of family life. One outstanding Orthodox rabbi, Rabbi Emanuel Rackman, implied that it was related to a Marxist view of the family; that despite First Amendment guarantees, its adoption might force religious schools to compromise their principles regarding separation of sexes for the sake of government grants, and that "the amendment might be used against rabbinical courts," which "exist by virtue of corporate charters given by government and enjoy tax exemption." To try to bring about the equalization of Jewish women in divorce by resort to the amendment, however, would be counterproductive in that it would only make the rabbinical courts more intransigent. Mrs. O. Asher Reichel, a well-known Orthodox *rebbitzin,* claimed that "all laws which segregate the sexes in places such as private schools, prisons, dormitories and rest-rooms will be stricken from the books," and intimated that it would be difficult to obtain single-sex accomodations in hospitals.[95] While many Jewish organizations relied on the First Amendment to protect Jewish religious law and supported the amendment, there also was significant non-Orthodox opposition to it.

Many people perceived the women's movement and its Jewish feminist subdivision as threatening, overly strident, and destructive. While many men and women have come to accept the movement's assumptions, a significant proportion of Jews have reservations about one or another part of its program, and a small minority remains in total opposition.

It seems clear, however, that the feminist movement is not likely to

---

[94]"Portnoy's Mother's Complaint," *Response,* Summer 1973, p. 133.
[95]*West Side Institutional Review* (publication of West Side Synagogue), October 1975.

disappear. Since the founding of the National Organization for Women (NOW) in 1965, the movement has grown in both organized and unorganized support. It has changed the perceptions of many women and men. In Jewish life, courses on the Jewish woman have been given in universities, free universities, Hillel Foundations, and adult-education programs. The best-selling *Jewish Catalog* contains a chapter on Jewish women. There are now Jewish women who are rabbis and Jewish women who are terrorists.[96] One might hope there would be more of the former than of the latter, though movements are not easily controlled. The image of Queen Esther is becoming less persuasive. Professor Leo Pfeffer sees in "the feminist revolution . . . not an enemy of the Jewish people [but] a challenge that can be met and lived with."[97] Judaism has always survived by evolution, never painless. The "new" Jewish feminism must be confronted and accomodated to ensure the survival of American Jewry.

---

[96]Elenore Lester, "What Drives a 'Nice Jewish Girl' into Life of Guerilla Violence?" *Jewish Week*, July 26, 1975.
[97]"Feminism and Judaism," *Congress Monthly*, June 1975, p. 14.

Jews By Choice
Their Impact on the Contemporary American Jewish Community

DR. EGON MAYER
Associate Professor
Department of Sociology
Brooklyn College

There is, I believe, an ancient Rabbinic saying that God does not send a *makah*, a scourge, into the world before He has given His people the secret of its cure. My topic this evening addresses what many in the Jewish community today believe to be one of the social *makahs* of American Jewish life, namely, intermarriage, as well as what a growing number of thoughtful people believe to be one of its possible "cures," namely, conversion.

If I am, indeed, correct in my recollectin of the Rabbinic maxim, then I would suggest that the purpose of my presentation is to explore some of the possible side effects of the cure. Since I am a sociologist, not a rabbi, I hope you will allow me to gloss over or ignore halakhic issues pertaining to conversion, which are properly in your province. My focus is on some of the demographic, social psychological, and behavioral consequences of the "Jews by choice" phenomenon. If those consequences are judged to have implications for Halakhah or Rabbinic practice, I believe those are judgments that rabbis will have to make. My task here is solely to serve as an analyst, not to serve as an advocate.

It was in 1972, with the first publications of the National Jewish Population Study, that America's Jews were first jolted into the realization of the massive dimensions of the intermarriage problem. That study revealed for the first time, on a national level, that the rate of Jewish intermarriage had risen dramatically: from about 7% in the 1940s to about 17% in the early 1960s, and again to about 32% by the early 1970s.

These numbers resounded like a thunderclap throughout the organized Jewish community, raising the spectre of large scale assimilation and the potential of major Jewish population decline to the level of serious statistical speculation. I am sure many will recall here the article by Elihu Bergman, published in *Midstream* in 1976, in which the Harvard demographer calculated that at the current rate of intermarriage the American Jewish population might diminish within the next one hundred years from its current size of five and one-half million to as few as ten thousand. It was an intentionally alarmist piece of calculus which, regardless of its correctness, served to raise the community's awareness of the potential long range consequences of uncontrolled intermarriage.

Throughout the 1970s, amidst the general alarm over the increased rates of intermarriage, relatively little attention was paid to a related and equally rapidly rising phenomenon, namely, the entry of non-Jews into the Jewish fold. The National Jewish Population Study had found that approximately one-third of intermarriages involved the conversion of the non-Jewish partner to Judaism. In that study, incidentally, it was found that women converts outnumbered men converts by about 10-to-1. Subsequent demographic surveys by Floyd Fowler in Boston(1975), by Albert Mayer in Kansas City(1977), and by Bruce Phillips in Denver(1982) all show that the rate of conversion has not only gone hand in hand with increases in intermarriage; it has, in fact, surpassed them. These studies, as well as my own survey of 446 intermarried couples, conducted on behalf of the American Jewish Committee(1979), show that the rate of conversion *into* Judaism during the past thirty years has increased by about 300%.

To concretize these percentages with some actual numbers there is, for example, the research of Rabbi David Eichhorn, published in 1954, which estimated that conversion under Reform and Conservative auspices was making between 1,500-1,750 new "voluntary" Jews annually. In recent personal conversation with Rabbi Sanford Seltzer, director of the outreach program of the UAHC, I have been informed that somewhere between 7,000-8,000 new students have passed through that organization's "Introduction to Judaism" course each year during the past several years. Since that course is the formal gateway to conversion under the auspices of the UAHC, Rabbi Seltzer estimates that there are now somewhere between 7,000-8,000 "voluntary Jews" entering the fold annually through their portals.

A survey of Orthodox rabbis in 1965 (Ehrman & Fenster, 1968) suggests that there had been an increase of about 50% in the number of candidates for conversion under their auspices. While Orthodox rabbis in the U.S. apparently deal with far fewer applicants for conversion than do Reform and Conservative rabbis, according to that survey Orthodox rabbis converted at least one thousand people to Judaism during the period 1962-1965. There is every reason to believe that the rate at which they have participated in enabling Gentiles to become Jews has not diminished.

I have not been able to locate any published or attributable data on conversion rates under Conservative auspices. Informal conversations with reliable observers of the movement suggest that there are between 3,000-4,000 new Jews entering the fold of Judaism each year under its auspices. In the Conservative movement, as in the Reform and the Orthodox movements, there is also acknowledgement that the rate of conversions has increase greatly during the past decade or two.

While a firm estimate of the total number of converts presently in the American Jewish population is difficult to come by, it is possible to make some very caution estimates based on all the available survey data. Based on those data, the most conservative estimate I would make is that there are *at least* 100,000 "Jews by choice" or converts in the U.S. today. I would not be surprised or very vigorously doubtful if someone argued that their number is actually twice as large.

There are three main points to note about all of these numerical speculations:

> Conversion into Judaism has increased very significantly in America during the past thirty years, more than keeping pace with the increases in the rate of intermarriage.
>
> The increases in the rate of conversion into Judaism have occurred more or less similarly in all three of the major branches of Judaism.
>
> When all the increases in rates are finally taken into account, converts or "Jews by choice" still remain a very tiny minority —somewhere between 2-4% of the total American Jewish population.

These observations concerning the sheer quantitative distribution of converts in the general Jewish population give rise to several more substantive questions:

> Does conversion, in fact, serve its sociological purpose of safeguarding Jewish identity?
>
> What, if any, are the qualitative differences between "Jews by choice" and "Jews by birth" in their expressions of Jewishness?
>
> What difference does it make whether "Jews by choice" enter the fold through the portals of the Reform, the Conservative, or the Orthodox movement?

What are the implications of widespread conversion for the American Jewish population in general?

What are the possible implications of "Jewishness by choice" on the part of those who have chosen *not* to convert under any formally religious auspices?

These questions by no means constitute an exhaustive list of things we might want to or need to know about the phenomenon under discussion. But they represent a set of important questions about which enough empirical information has begun to accumulate so that we can attempt enlightened answers to them.

Two comments are often heard made about conversion in the present day American Jewish community. One is: "Converts are our best Jews." Rabbis and others active in synagogue and Jewish organizational life seem to have no lack of examples of converts among their members who have "made good," so to speak. From synagogue presidents to chairmen of local UJA-Federation campaigns, Jewish community leadership, apparently, is a rich store of examples of "Jews by choice" who are living testimonials to the great potential benefits that conversion can bring to the Jewish people.

But there is another comment that is heard almost as often as the laudable examples of *gerei tzedek*: "Converts become Jewish only to please their spouses and/or in-laws, or to insure the fact that their children will be accepted in the Jewish community as Jews." In other words, it is often suggested that most conversions into Judaism are more a matter of social conventionality than of religious conviction. Therefore, by implication, it is suggested that the Jewishness of converts is apt to be shallow and inauthentic at best. Consequently, while conversion may be effective in producing more people who go by the Jewish label, it cannot prevent the erosion of Jewishness which follows as a result of intermarriage.

Which of these two images of the convert is closer to the truth?

My own claim to expertise on this subject comes from a survey, completed in 1979, which I conducted on behalf of the American Jewish Committee. We interviewed 446 intermarried couples throughout the United States. One hundred of the couples we spoke with, a little under 25% of our sample, were couples in which one partner in the marriage had become Jewish by choice through conversion. I might add that in another eighty cases, or about 18% of our sample, we found non-Jews who professed Jewishness and the practice of Judaism in some form, even though they had not gone

170

through any form of recognized religious conversion. I should like to return to this group a bit further along in my presentation.

In order to determine whether there are any measurable differences in Jewish affinities between those partners in an intermarriage who have converted and those who have not converted, we constructed what sociologists call indicators of Jewishness. One of them, a set of Jewish behavior indicators, included seven items: praying, attending synagogue services, bringing only kosher meat into the home, lighting candles on the Sabbath, making *kiddush* on the Sabbath and/or on holidays, fasting on Yom Kippur, and lighting Chanukah candles. While one can quibble with the adequacy of these indicators, they were sufficient to provide us with an overall measure by which we could detect the influence of certain background variables.

The other measure of Jewishness was a set of statements designed to tap what we consider to be some of the major attitudinal aspects of being Jewish: Being Jewish is very important to me. American Jewry and Jews in Israel are parts of one people. It is important to me that there should always be a Jewish people. A Jew has a greater responsibiity for other Jews than for non-Jews. I would be quite surprised and upset if my children did not regard themselves as Jews when they grew up.

These two indices were used to measure our respondents' "behavioral Jewishness" and their "attitudinal Jewishness."

The average score of our entire sample on the Jewish behavior index was 2.9 (on a range of possible scores from 0 to 7). When we compared non-Jews who were married to Jews with the converts married to born-Jews, however, there was a striking difference in their scores: 1.7 for non-Jews, 4.5 for converts who were converted under Reform auspices, and 7.0 for those who were converted under Conservative or Orthodox auspices.

In other words, our findings suggest that there is a very clear positive association between conversion and Jewishness as measured by a set of behavioral indicators. I should add that converts were far more likely than non-converts to have their sons circumcised according to Jewish ritual (72% vs 43%). They were also far more likely than non-converts to have their children become Bar or Bat Mitzvah (71% vs 30%). And they were more than twice as likely as non-converts to have given their children a Hebrew name (82% vs 36%). Similarly, about 60% of our convert respondents indicated that they are providing or are planning to provide their children with some type of formal Jewish education. By contrast, only about 20% of our non-convert respondents were providing or planning to provide their children with some type of Jewish education.

Of course, comparing the relative degree of Jewishness of converts and non-converts in intermarriages does not tell us anything about the relative degrees of Jewishness of converts as compared to born-Jews. However, based on a variety of local and national surveys regarding the behavior of American Jews, it appears that converts, on virtually all measures of Jewish behavior, are barely distinguishable from those of their brethren who are Jewish by birth.

Let me emphasize that in the foregoing comparisons I have constantly referred to *behavioral* aspects of Jewishness. I did so because when we turn our attention to the *attitudinal* aspects of Jewishness we are led to slightly different conclusions.

The five statements mentioned above which we used to create an overall measure of attitudinal Jewishness, produced an average score of 1.5 for the sample as a whole (the full range of possible score was from 0 to five). Non-converts had an average score of 1.2 while converts had average scores of 1.9, 2.5, and 2.8 depending on whether they were converted under Reform, Conservative, or Orthodox auspices respectively. These scores also show a greater sense of Jewishness on the part of converts than on the part of non-converts, which is also true of the behavioral measure of Jewishness. The relative difference between the two groups, however, was not quite as large on the attitudinal measure as it was on the behavioral measure.

We were also struck by another difference between the behavioral and the attitudinal measures of Jewishness. Since the same questions were asked of the born-Jewish partners in our sample as of their born-Gentile mates, we were able to see how similar or how different the two groups of marriage partners were on the two types of measures. Converts generally achieved higher scores on the behavioral measure of Jewishness than did their born-Jewish partners. On the other hand, in the attitudinal measure of Jewishness, the born-Jewish spouses consistently achieved higher scores than did their born-Gentile partners, whether the latter had converted or not.

In short, it appears that at this point the greatest impact of conversion is on the Jewish behavior of persons who become "Jews by choice" and on how they bring up their children so far as Jewishness is concerned. These aspects of Jewish acculturation also tend to be more religious in character, rather than ethnic or peoplehood oriented. Conversion, it seems, has a substantially lesser effect on the molding of the social worldview of the person. Indeed, given the great importance of Jewish fellow feeling among typical American

Jews, it might be argued that "Jews by choice" are probably far more adept at acting like Jews in matters of religious practice than they are at feeling or thinking like Jews when it comes to social relationships.

Similar findings were reported by Huberman in 1978 in his study of several hundred converts who were graduates of the Reform movement's "Introduction to Judaism" course in Boston. As he put it, "we infer from the reported trends that converts as a group define (their) Judaism in religious rather than in communal-ethnic terms. To converts, Judaism is basically a *religion* like their former faith."

To what extent the discrepancy between a religious sense and an ethnic sense of Jewishness produces any inner psychological stress within the convert, or perhaps between the convert and born-Jews in the family or in the wider community, can only be guessed at. But it is certainly an issue that neither rabbis nor other communal workers can afford to ignore.

It should be noted, and emphasized, that the discrepancy we have found between the behavioral-religious and the ethnic-attitudinal dimensions of Jewishness among converts cannot and should not be attributed to any lack of sincerity or good faith on their part. Rather, I believe that the nature of the Jewish conversion process, as it is presently organized, and the social expectations of the Jewish community in general, place a greater emphasis on the behavioral socialization of the convert than on his or her acculturation into the everyday ideology of contemporary American Jewish life. This latter dimension of Jewishness, as we know, is probably far more important to the large majority of American Jews than is a purely religious conception.

As numerous studies of contemporary Jewish life have shown, the functional ideology of the great majority of America's Jews is far more secular than it is religious. The issues which weld us together as a community tend to be such matters as the fear of anti-Semitism, the concern about the security of Israel, the desire to live among and associate with one's fellow Jews, and charitable activities to meet the needs of the Jewish community. The commitments of the great majority of America's Jews to these issues constitute what we might call the Jewish social ethic.

If our measure of attitudinal Jewishness is correct, it would seem that *Jews by choice share to a lesser extent in the ethos of the Jews than they do in the practice of Judaism.* Of course, I am aware that from the point of view of rabbis, who are, after all, religious specialists, this tendency on the part of converts may be seen as a virtue rather than a shortcoming. I am afraid, however, that unless "Jews by choice" are

173

socialized to share in the Jewish *ethos* as much as they do in the *practices* of Judaism, there is reason to expect that conversion can produce considerable stress within the converts themselves as well as between them and their born-Jewish brethren.

Looking back on the Jewishness of converts as it has emerged from our data, and bringing it to bear on some of the questions I had outlined earlier in this presentation, I am led to a number of conclusions concerning the possible impacts of the "Jews by choice" phenomenon.

> The great fear of the 1970s, that intermarriage would lead to the erosion of the Jewish population and to the ultimate assimilation of the Jews, should be considerably tempered by the available facts on conversion. There is every reason to believe that if the current rate of conversion into Judaism continues, even with the high rate of intermarriage, the size of the Jewish population should not be adversely affected.
>
> While conversion might well offset the demographic impact of intermarriage on the Jewish population, it doesn't produce the same type of Jews as does natural increase. Because "Jews by choice" learn to be Jews primarily through religious practices, their Jewishness tends to be somewhat more religious than ethnic, and more behavioral than attitudinal. This, of course, could be of great benefit to organized religious life. But it could also lead to a sense of estrangement between Jews by choice and born-Jews. Moreover, in the long run, it could lead to a rupture between religion and ethnicity which have hitherto been very closely intertwined in American Jewish life.
>
> The more behavioristic and religious orientation of "Jews by choice" can and, I believe, has led to strengthening of the role of the rabbi. As religious specialists, rabbis have suffered gradual loss of influence among American Jews as the community has become increasingly secularized. Ironically, as secularization has led to the increased incidence of intermarriage and the attendent rise in conversion, the rabbi is emerging as the important dispenser of the skills and the rituals through which non-Jews can become Jews, and through which intermarried families can remain within the fold.
>
> Finally, our study suggests that there are, indeed, significant differences between converts who become "Jews by choice" under Reform, or under Conservative or Orthodox auspices. For example, on a 21 point scale which we developed to measure the extent to which intermarried families were socializing

their children as Jews, we found that non-conversionary families achieved a score of 5.6. In conversionary families where the conversion had been under Reform auspices, the score was 10.5. Where it had been under Conservative auspices, the score was 14.7 and where the conversion was under Orthodox auspices, the score was 16.0. Virtually all our measures of Jewishness showed the same pattern. Converts differ from non-converts significantly in their expressions of Jewishness. But the difference in the degrees of Jewishness between those who converted under Conservative or Orthodox auspices and those who converted under Reform auspices is nearly as great as the differences between non-converts and Reform converts.

Up to this point my presentation has focused on the possible consequences of conversion on the Jewishness of the converts themselves and on the overall population size of the Jewish community. At this point I would like to shift the focus to a somewhat more subtle but no less important an issue: the potential impact of conversion on the psyche or worldview of the typical American Jew.

It is, I think, one of the most well established facts of American Jewish sociology that Jewish culture in America has evolved largely by a process of accommodation to the demands of living as middle-class Americans in a rational, scientific age. As a result, beliefs and practices (be it the story of Creation or the rules of *kashrut*) which could not be reconciled with the outlook and lifestyle of the dominant cultural majority have been abandoned by all but the most religiously stalwart. The reason for this accommodation is generally considered to be the very condition of Jews as a minority. Wishing to be accepted as equals in the wider arena of political, economic and social exchange, it is thought that Jews have had to become more or less like their neighbors—denominationally separate, but culturally equal.

This accommodationist stance of the minority *vis-a-vis* the majority has been based on at least one fundamental assumption: that members of the majority cannot and would not accept the minority on its own terms. As social psychologists have also shown through experiments, when one finds himself in a minority it becomes increasingly difficult to take one's own self seriously the longer the condition of minority *versus* majority persists. This is particularly true in situations where a minority holds beliefs which are not believed in or, worse still, are actively denied by the majority.

Historically, Jews have been very much in the position of what Peter Berger has called "cognitive minorities," i.e., groups whose worldviews are at odds with that of the dominant majority. Such groups, Berger has suggested, can sustain their beliefs and practices only by huddling together into tightly knit sectarian groups which offer mutual support in the face of overwhelming disconfirmation from the outside, or by making substantial compromises with the majority. The alternative is madness or disappearance. It is fair to say that the great mass of Jews in the United States and elsewhere have sustained their faith and their Jewish lifestyle through the strategies of compromise.

However, the long established relationship between "cognitive minorities" and the majority has undergone considerable alteration as a result of widespread cultural pluralism. The proliferation of and the tolerance for a great variety of lifestyles and belief systems is one of the distinguishing features of our highly modern, highly mobile and highly changing society. In such a society, virtually all people tend to belong to some community of beliefs and practices which are not shared by the majority. Alternate lifestyle groups, food faddists, and born-again Christians all share with the Chasidim the condition of being "cognitive minorities" in modern-day America. Ironically, while the great spread of cultural pluralism has made minorities more acceptable, the great advances in communications and the large scale intermingling of groups on the urban landscape has made it increasingly more difficult for members of minorities to remain untouched by the ideas and practices of one another. Thus, the beliefs of each group are constantly challenged, not so much by one dominant majority culture as by a great variety of alternative minorities.

The plausibility of one's own truth claims is continually at odds with the truth claims of others, who are forever present in one's environment. Thus, even the most ardent believer must continually reconfirm to himself that his way is, after all, to be preferred to the ways of others. No belief system or lifestyle can become so fully taken-for-granted and routine that it should not require constant reaffirmation in the face of enticing alternatives.

As Peter Berger, a Lutheran and one of the foremost American sociologists of religion, put it in an article in *Commentary* in 1979, "the believing individual is always both inside and outside of his commitment to his own faith." Then Berger added, "and one can only convince himself (of his own commitments) if he can at least in principle convince others."

In other words, under the conditions of a kind of free market cultural pluralism a conversionary stance becomes necessary, not so much to actually win converts from the outside as much as to reconfirm the commitments of those who are already within the fold—of those who are Jews by birth. As a matter of fact, it is all too common to find that when a Gentile woman becomes a "Jew by choice" she makes two people Jewish: herself and her spouse, who in many cases has long neglected taking his Jewishness seriously.

In short, under the conditions of a free-market model of cultural pluralism, where many minorities must continually affirm their claims and lifestyles against one another, so to speak, "Jews by choice" can have the most profound effect on the larger Jewish community. Their very presence in the community greatly enhances the plausibility of the Jewish way—not just for non-Jews, but for born-Jews as well.

By having voluntarily chosen to become Jews under religious auspices, in a society where most born-Jews have grown rather lackadaisical towards their religious precepts and regulations, and where there is a vast array of other lifestyle and belief choices which are equally available and certainly no less well-packaged, "Jews by choice" proclaim to the world unabashedly that *am Yisrael hai*, that the God of Israel and the people of Israel are their preferred alternative to all other beliefs and ways of living.

Whether one shares Rabbi Alexander Schindler's activist stance towards attracting converts to Judaism or not, it seems to me that one cannot ignore the great potential of the proliferation of "Jews by choice" in the community as a way of reaffirming the plausibility of Judaism. By voluntarily choosing Judaism as their religion, converts can, and to some extent have, set in motion the gradual reversal of a century of secularization and religious decline among Jews in America. In fact, I find it surprising that the various bodies of organized Jewry have not made much greater use of "Jews by choice" in helping to reaffirm the loyalty of born-Jews. I suspect that as "Jews by choice" increase in number and become more visible in the community their example will serve to strengthen the religious commitments of all Jews.

As I think is clear from my presentation, I believe that on the balance the conversion of non-Jews to Judaism has many great benefits for the Jewish community as a whole, not to mention the benefits it has for the converts themselves and for their jewish families.

However, such a sanguine conclusion should not distract anyone from a number of subtle yet profound problems raised by "voluntary Jews" in the midst of a community which historically has not been a voluntary one. I would like to sum up this presentation by briefly sharing some of these challenges.

The Challenge of Integration All minorities have difficulty being accepted as full-fledged equals in their host cultures, as we Jews, of all people, should know. This problem is all the more true for "Jews by choice," who must be integrated into Jewish culture and society which has not had the experience of integrating any outsiders for nearly two thousand years. The strategies of Gentile-avoidance which permeate Jewish culture cannot be easily overcome, nor can they be internalized by the erstwhile Gentile, no matter how sincere. Given the depth of this problem, the organized leadership of the Jewish community must address it with as much forthrightness and vigor as we have addressed other prejudices in the past. Neither the denial of the problem nor appeals to simple human good will are likely to be sufficient to deal with it.

The Challenge of Ethnicity The Torah, or the faith of Israel, and the people Israel are one. For better or worse, Judaism has always been largely an ethnic religion. It has been particularly so in the U.S. The collective identity of our people has been forged as much by beliefs and religious practices as by collective experiences of persecutions and triumphs. Therefore, even the most spiritually inspired of converts who come to Judaism as a result of a long and serious religious quest, will have a great deal of difficulty internalizing the collective memories of persecutions, migrations, accommodations to various host cultures, and the collective yearnings for Zion. Can we, or should we, even try to impart those collective sentiments to "Jews by choice"? On the other hand, if we do not or cannot impart those sentiments to them, can we be sure that we will be able to impart it to subsequent generations of born-Jews?

The Challenge of Divorce The problem of divorce is clearly on a different plane from the problem of integration or the problem of Jewish ethnicity. The latter touch the lives of the entire Jewish community, while the former, we hope, is a problem only for a small group of individuals.

While there are no statistics available at this point on the number of conversionary marriages that fail, there is no reason to suppose that the divorce rate among that group is any different from the divorce rate among Jewish families in general. In other words, we can expect a substantial number of conversionary marriages to end in divorce. In fact, experience tells us that such, indeed, is happening.

Because a disproportionately large number of converts are women who, in the overwhelming majority of cases, still desire and win custody of their children, the Jewish community can look forward to increasingly large numbers of women converts and their children who are cut off from their Jewish family connections by divorce. The community's concern for the continued Jewishness of converts and their children will probably require the helpful intervention of Jewish organizations into such situations, though what form such intervention might take I cannot say at the present.

The Challenge of "Self-Chosenness" Finally, the euphemism of "Jews by choice" leads us to consider a relatively small group of non-Jews and their children to whom I referred earlier. These are the spouses and offspring of intermarrieds who "pass" as Jews, who act as Jews, and who may even believe themselves to be Jewish, but who—for one reason or another—have not formally converted.

As I have indicated in my statistical discussion before, somewhere between 15 and 20% of all intermarriages will include at least one non-Jew who professes some blend of Judaism without conversion. If there are children in the family, which is true in most cases, there is an excellent chance that those children will be raised as Jews, sent to Hebrew school, become *b'nei* or *b'not* mitzvah and, as likely as not, will marry Jews.

Given the open and voluntary nature of the American Jewish community, it is unlikely that such "passing" into the community can be prevented. Moreover, I suspect that most of us would be at least ambivalent as to whether we really would want to discourage such "self-chosenness." Perhaps we would want to identify such individuals and families, and encourage their legitimization, so-to-speak, through formal conversion.

Whatever we would wish to do about this phenomenon of "self-chosenness," it alerts us to the fact that becoming a "Jew by choice" may mean something quite different to some Gentiles than to others. Those who have chosen to become Jewish through legitimate forms of conversion (and we have yet to reach a consensus as a community on just what that means) have agreed to make their choice of Jewishness through the established rules of the organized community. They implicitly endorse the establishment, so to speak. The others, who choose to define themselves as Jews by personal acclamation alone, are in effect trying to appropriate a legitimate identity through non-legitimate means.

The question for the community, as in any instance of social deviance, is to determine how to treat this phenomenon: to ignore it, to try to suppress it, or to try to find in it an opportunity for creative social change.

My personal preference would be to reread an article by Rabbi Adam Fisher, published in the *Reconstructionist* of May, 1973, in which he makes the case for the reapplication of the category of *ger toshav/ger toshevet*.

After many centuries of ghettoized existence, the Enlightment threw open the portals through which Jews could exit from their culture into that of the majority. It is the curious twist of modern pluralism, especially in the United States, that those portals of exit have now also become portals of entry for large numbers of non-Jews as well as for those Jews who wish to return. The challenge ahead, I believe, will be to keep those doors wide open to the traffic that now wishes to enter. Who knows? Perhaps the Messiah himself might yet come through those doors.

SELECTED REFERENCES

Berger, Peter L., "Some Sociological Comments on Theological Education," *Perspective* 9:2 (Summer, 1968).

――――――― "Converting the Gentiles?," *Commentary* 67:5 (May, 1979).

Ehrman, Albert & Fenster, C.A., "Conversion and American Orthodox Judaism," *Jewish Journal of Sociology* 10:1 (June, 1968).

Eichhorn, David M., (ed.), Conversion to Judaism: A History and Analysis (New York: Ktav, 1965).

Fisher, Adam D., "Ger Toshav and Mixed Marriage," *Reconstructionist* (May, 1973).

Fowler, Floyd J., *1975 Community Survey: A Study of the Jewish Population of Greater Boston* (Boston: The Combined Jewish Philanthropies, 1977).

Herberg, Will, *Protestant, Catholic, Jew.* (New York: Doubleday, 1955).

Huberman, Steven, *New Jews: The Dynamics of Religious Conversion* (New York: UAHC, 1979).

Kukoff, Lydia, *Choosing Judaism* (New York: UAHC, 1981).

Mayer, Albert, *The Jewish Population Study of the Greater Kansas City Area* (Kansas City: Jewish Federation, 1977).

Mayer, Egon, *Intermarriage and the Jewish Future* (New York: American Jewish Committee, 1979).

National Jewish Population Study

Phillips, Bruce A., *Denver Jewish Population Study* (Denver: Allied Jewish Federation, 1982).

AN EXPERIENCE OF PRAYER

JACOB NEUSNER

"WRITING is more than an instrument of communication. It is an instrument of thought." This is the judgment of Professor Edmund S. Morgan, of Yale University, which he expressed to the Yale freshmen in an address, "Curiosity and Communication." In thinking about a moment of prayer, I found it useful to write down, and share, the following thoughts.

The requirement of daily prayer brings the individual into a painful tension. On the one hand, he is to pray. On the other, he is to pray to God, and the awareness of God is not always available; and, if available, not always at the particular moment that calls for prayer. Thus a man is brought into conflict between the form of prayer and its content, between the requirement and the object of worship.

I have found the resolution of this tension not difficult; the alternatives, either to pray without genuine devotion, or not to pray until the advent of true commitment, are neither of them distasteful, for the escape into hypocrisy and "religious behaviorism," on the one side, or into habitual non-observance, on the other, is readily available. For my part, guided by the teachings of my faith that out of lack of feeling but observance, will come observance with deep feeling, I choose to pray daily, but seldom, alas, with an authentic prayer.

This had been my situation before, and so it is now, but in a rare moment, the memory of which I cherish, I prayed with awareness of the meaning of the words I was saying, and with a sense for their immediate truth: I prayed in the presence of God.

The day was early in April. It was warm and sunny; spring-light had come back, and from my window I could see daffodils and young hyacinth budding in the gardens of a neighboring garden-apartment. A parapet surrounds a small balcony outside my room, and for the first time, I decided to go outside to say my morning prayers. Jewish worship begins with the recitation of several psalms, and even in my dullest and most brutish moments, the words of these psalms convey the reality of a genuine religious experience, not my own but nonetheless someone's authentic encounter with God. On this particular morning, I found myself reading the Psalms with a slow and considerate interest. I discovered words and ideas that seemed new, even novel, and the record of an experience and of religious perceptions almost embarrassingly true and intimate. I regarded myself as an intruder on the intensely private religious experience of another man. I did not, however, regret this.

Jacob Neusner, a graduate of the Jewish Theological Seminary, is a member of the faculty of the University of Wisconsin.

AN EXPERIENCE OF PRAYER

The following prayers consist of the proclamation of the unity of God, preceded and followed by blessings. The preceding blessings acknowledge God as Creator of light and darkness, of the natural universe, and as Sovereign of man, as teacher of His will for His creatures. The following blessings acknowledge God's intervention into human history at the Exodus. The key is the declaration that God is one, which means both unique and united. It was here that I found for perhaps the first time an awareness that words of prayer convey reality. I stood in the sun, looked to it and beyond it, and contemplated the truth, incomprehensible it seemed then although in less serious moments it is almost common sense, that the Being who made the sun made me. The word אחד sustained itself, and in it spoke of the oneness of the light of the sun and the heart in my breast before God. Nature and I are one family, brothers before one Father. My mind thought to beyond the sun, that is as far as I could think into infinity, and to beyond that; and I perceived that 'way out there', beyond the universe whose infinity man can scarcely measure, is אל קנא: a Passionate God.

I believe this encounter with the meaning of my prayers, had it lasted, bore the potential of my becoming an atheist. The terror of the thought, its incredible assertion, appalled me. To think that the Sovereign of man's affairs, who hears and welcomes prayer, who searches the heart and soul of man, and the Creator of the universe whose vastness is not yet measured, is one and the same Being, struck me then with particular amazement. This extraordinary claim and alien conception, perceived in the full light of the sun and in the deep warmth of day, made sense.

The following prayer, the silent "eighteen benedictions," sustained the sense of amazement and wonder. The words "Blessed are Thou, O Lord, our God, God of Abraham, Isaac, and Jacob..." puzzled me. He, beyond the infinity of time and space, Who cannot be expressed in the most sublime equation of science, nor in the subtlest touch of art, will He be praised by me? And further, He Who cares in a majestic, abstract sense for man, did he concern himself for three men, my fathers? The words that followed meant what they meant. They were more than words: statements of belief. They did not, however, convey the sense and seriousness of the earlier prayers. I felt tired, brought my eyes and mind downward, to the gardens below, to the people, and was glad to be among them.

I realize that I have described this moment in its intellectual dimensions, which were and are important to me. Of its impact upon my self, my soul, I would only say that I became, for this moment, transcendant of my soul, a part of a grander, adoring universe, pointing toward an incomprehensible and inelectable Silence beyond. I did not begin to be at one with this Being. I did not come away with greater "faith," or deeper conviction, but only with a memory that the words I say by habit not only convey, but also contain, a perceptible meaning. I came to the reality of prayer.

JUDAISM IN THE SECULAR AGE

by

JACOB NEUSNER

Professor Harvey Cox defines secularization as "the movement of man's primary interest and attention from other worlds beyond or above this one and to this world. This includes the loosing of this world from its dependency on mythical, metaphysical, or religious dualism of any sort. It means therefore taking this earthly realm, with all its health and hope, with all its sickness and sin, in utter seriousness.[1] What is the meaning of the new age for Jews? for Judaism's relationships to the world? and to Christianity?

I. SECULARIZATION AND THE JEWS

No religion may be adequately compared to another. Each has its particularities which render comparison a distortion. Judaism cannot be compared to Christianity, for example, as if each component of the one had its functional or structural equivalent in the other. Christians understand by "religion" a rather different phenomenon, for it seems to Jews, perhaps wrongly, that Christians lay far greater stress upon theology and matters of belief as normative and probative than does Judaism. A Christian is such by baptism or conversion, by being called out into a new and sacred vocation of faith. A Jew is never *not* a Jew according to Jewish law. He is *born* into the Jewish situation. There was never a time that he was a man but not a Jew. There can be no time when he will cease to be a Jew, for, as the Talmud says, though he sin, he remains "Israel." The Jewish ethnic group is never perceived by Jewish theology to be a secular entity, therefore, and therein lies the root of much misunderstanding. Christians speak of "secular Jews," by which they mean Jews divorced from the profession of Jewish faith and the practice of the *mitzvot*. But Judaism does not, and cannot, regard such Jews as "secular," for they are all chil-

---

Professor Jacob Neusner teaches in the Department of Religion at Dartmouth College, Hanover, New Hampshire. He is author of *History and Torah: Essays on Jewish Learning* (New York, 1965), *A History of the Jews in Babylonia, I. The Parthian Period* (Leiden, 1965), and *II, The Early Sasanian Period* (Leiden, 1967), and other books.

[1] "Secularization and the Secular Mentality: A New Challenge to Christian Education," *Religious Education* 61, 2 (1966), 83.

dren of Abraham, Isaac, and Jacob. Their forefathers stood at Sinai and bound them for all time by the terms of a contract to do and hear the word of God. That contract has never been abrogated, and though individuals may forget it, its Maker can never forget them. A Jew who does not keep the Covenant still has its imprint engraved in his flesh. His children do not require conversion if they choose to assume its responsibilities. The world, moreover, has understood the indelibility of the covenant, for it has persisted in regarding as Jews many who regard themselves as anything but Jewish; and it has murdered the seed of Abraham into the third generation.

These remarks by no means represent the universal judgment of the Jewish community, which has mostly lost a theological understanding of itself. The larger part of Jewry regards being Jewish—"Jewishness"—as mostly an ethnic affiliation, and prefers to understand that affiliation in a this-worldly and secular way. Judaism, that is, the corpus of Jewish Tradition from biblical and Talmudic times onward, has a very different view, one more familiar to educated Christians from their studies of religious history, but less familiar from contemporary observation. It should be clear that I understand Jewish existence within the norms of classical Jewish theology. We are a people called forth to constitute a kingdom of priests and a holy nation, to serve as God's suffering servant and to bear upon ourselves the burden of humanity. Our collective vocation began with the call to Abraham, Isaac, and Jacob, carried us to Sinai, and will at the end of days reach fulfillment. "Secular" Jews do not see things this way, but however they see themselves, this is, I believe, how Judaism sees *them*.

It is a fact, moreover, that Jews quite alien to the Torah retain a very vivid sense of being part of a historical, if not of a supernatural, community. They yearn to see their children marry other Jews, though this may represent no more, in the eyes of the world, than an ethnic loyalty. They insist that their children associate with other Jews, even though association may have what Christians will regard as a wholly secular setting. But Judaism cannot regard the Jewish group as a secular enterprise, as I said, for it advances a very different view of what it means to be a Jew. It lays great stress upon community, upon the chain of the generations, upon birth within the covenant. As Professor Monford Harris writes: "The secularized gentile is precisely that: a secularized gentile. But the secularized Jew is still a Jew. The Jew that sins is still a Jew, still a member of covenantal Israel, even when he denies that covenant."[2] One cannot stress this fact too much: *there can be no Judaism without Jewishness,* that is, without ethnic identification. Judaism cannot be reduced to its "essence," whether that be construed as ethical, theological, or even behavioral. We know full well that there can be Jewishness without Judaism, and against this many of us struggle within the Jewish community. In our effort to keep the issues of Judaism to the fore, we may criticize the ethnic emphasis of the community as it is. But we struggle within that community precisely because it is what it is: all that is left of the remnant of Israel in this world. Its worldliness is a challenge. But the ethnic-Jews are right, and we are wrong, when they see as quite legitimately *Jewish* welfare activities of no particular Jewish relevance, and when they stress the value of association with other Jews for its own sake. They want thereby to preserve the group. Our regret is that they seem to have forgotten why. But the instinct is fully sound, and we critics must never forget it.

And who are these Jews, who cannot despite themselves achieve secularization? They are the bearers of an unbroken myth, a this-worldly group affirming the world and joining in its activities with religious fervor, yet regarding themselves, whether they be religious in the Christian sense or not, in terms the objective observer can regard only as preposterous, or religious. These Jews see themselves as a group, though their group should have ceased to hold them when the faith lost its hold upon them, and that is a paradox. They see themselves as bound to others, in other lands and other ages, whom they have never seen, and with whom they have practically nothing in common but common forefathers. This too is a paradox. They see their history as one history, though they are not everywhere involved in it. They reflect upon the apocalyptic events of the day as intimately and personally important to them. They died in Auschwitz. They arose again in the State of Israel. They respond passionately, no matter how remote they are from Judaism, to the appeal of the flesh, of Israel *after the flesh,* and see themselves in a way that no religious Jew can call secular, however secular they themselves would claim to be. This too is a paradox: They bear fears on account of the past, though that past is nothing to them except that it is the Jews'. They have nightmares that belong to other men but are not within their personal experience at all, except that they are Jews. They see themselves as

---

[2] "On Marrying Outside One's Existence," *Conservative Judaism* 20, 2 (1966), 64.

brands plucked from the burning, though they never stood near the fire. The classical faith demands that each man see himself as redeemed at Sinai from bondage to Pharaoh. The modern Jew, secure in America or Canada or Australia or the State of Israel, persists within the pattern of the classical faith, but in a far more relevant form of it. He was saved from Auschwitz and rebuilt the land. The ties that bind other groups of immigrants within the open societies in the West have long since attenuated. Despite the decline of faith, the ties that bind the Jews are stronger than ever, into the third and fourth, and fifth generation and beyond. Nor can one ignore the mystery of Soviet Jewry, of whom we know so little and understand nothing. They persist. They ought not. All we know is that almost fifty years after the Bolshevik revolution, young people, raised in isolation from their Tradition and from the Jewish world, trained to despise religion and above all Judaism, profess to be Jews, though they need not, and accept the disabilities of Jewishness, though these are by no means slight. Before this fact of contemporary Jewish history we must stand in silence. We cannot understand it. No worldly or naturalist explanation suffices to explain it. In my view, it is not a secular phenomenon at all, though it can be explained in a worldly way to the satisfaction of the world.

This is the paradox of the secular age. The Jews have said for almost two centuries that they are a religious group, and have accepted, by and large, the Christian world's criteria for religion. They have told the world they are different by virtue of religion, though they claimed that religion for them means what it means to others. And yet the secular world sees Jews who are not different from itself, for they have no professed religion. By their own word, such Jews, and they are very many, should have ceased to exist. Yet they are here, and they are Jews, and "Jewishness" is important to them in terms that the Christian and secular worlds alike find not at all "religious."

A second paradox is that the Jews have allied themselves with secularizing forces from the very beginning. Claiming to be merely Germans, or French, or Canadians, or Americans of the Jewish faith, they have chosen for themselves a place among those who struggled for the secularization of culture, politics, art, and society. The reason is, alas, that they had no choice. The forces of religion, meaning Christianity wherever it was established, invariably allied themselves to those of reaction, in opposing the emancipation of the Jews. Rarely do we find an exception to the rule: the more he was a Christian, the more he hated Jews. It is therefore no paradox at all that Jews have favored the secularization of institutions and of men, for if they hoped for a decent life, it was only upon a secular foundation that emancipation was possible. Even today, moreover, Christians would still prefer to use the institutions of the common society to propagate their faith. The public schools are still supposed to celebrate the great events of Christian sacred history, and Jewish children must still confront, and deny, the Christian message once or twice a year.

Christian opposition to secularization is by no means a mere vestige of earlier days. It is rather, I think, a fear of the need to believe *despite* the world, a fear of faith itself. For many centuries it has been natural to be a Christian. The world was mostly Christian, and where it was not, it was the realm of the devil and the Jews. Christians could aspire, therefore, to the creation of a metaphysic and a natural theology which, from the bare artifacts of the world, would rise, in easy stages, to the heights of Calvary. Metaphysics, religious philosophy, natural theology —these are naturally Christian enterprises, for only a Christian could conceive so benign and friendly a vision of the world that he might ask the world to strengthen, even to provide reasonable foundations within experienced reality for, his Gospel. It is no accident that Judaism has produced only a highly parochial metaphysic, very little natural theology, and a religious philosophy whose main task was to mediate between Judaism and the world. Judaism has had to stress revelation, and not a worldly apprehension of faith, because the world for two thousand and more years has offered little solace. Judaism has had to say *no* to many worlds, though it is not therefore a habitually negating tradition. It has had to say to pagans that God is not in nature; to mighty empires that the King of Kings alone is king; to Christians that redemption is not yet; to Bolshevism that Israel lives despite the "laws" of history. It has had to say no because of its first and single affirmation: We shall do and we shall hear. The result is that Judaism has looked, as I said, for very little help from the world. It has not presumed that the artifacts of creation would lead to Sinai; that a natural theology would explain why a Jew should keep the Sabbath or refrain from eating pork; that a communicable, non-mythological metaphysic would show Israel in a rational situation. In its early centuries, Christianity comprehended the Jewish situation. The apostle Paul offered not a reasonable faith, beginning with worldly realities and ending at the foot of the cross. He offered a scandal to the Jews and foolishness to the Greeks, and said it was faith, and faith

523

alone, which was demanded of the Christian; and it was by virtue of that faith, for it was a very difficult thing, that the Christian would be saved. Scandal and foolishness are sociological realities. From the fourth century onward, to be a Jew was a scandal to the Christians and foolishness, later on, to Islam. It was faith despite the world, and not because of it, that Judaism required, and received. This is the kind of faith with which Christianity begins, and, I believe, which is demanded once again. The Christian today is called to choose between Christ and the world, for the world is no longer his. I do not say it is a better world on that account, but it *is* a different world. I do not think however Judaism has suffered for its recognition and acceptance of the situation of *Golah,* of exile not only from the earthly land, but also from the ways of the world. If Christianity is entering a time of exile, it need not fear greatly, if Christians are prepared to affirm their faith through faith, and not merely through a reasoned apprehension of reality, which is not *faith* at all. As Christianity enters the Jewish situation, it need not, therefore, fear for its future. *Golah* is not a situation to be chosen, but to be accepted at the hand of God as a test of faith and an opportunity for regeneration and purification. We did not choose to go into exile, any more than the Christians would choose to abandon the world. Having gone into exile, having lost the world, Jew and Christian alike may uncover new resources of conviction, new potentialities for sanctity, than they knew they had. We who witnessed the destruction of an ancient temple learned of new means of service to the creator, that God wants mercy and not sacrifice, in Hosea's terms—deeds of loving kindness in those of Rabban Yohanan ben Zakkai. It is the world, and not the temple, that became the arena for God's work. Having lost the world, or wisely given it up, Christians too may recall that "the whole earth is full of His holiness," and that every day and everywhere the world provides a splendid opportunity for witness.

Finally, the advent of secularization offers still another welcome challenge to both Judaism and Christianity. In the recent past, exponents of both traditions have accepted the world's criteria for the truth or value of religion, both Judaism and Christianity. In its grosser form, this acceptance has led to such arguments for religion as those that claim religion is good for one's mental health, or important as a foundation for ethical behavior, and valuable as a basis for a group's persistance, or a nation's. In all instances religion has been evaluated for its service to something else, to health, to decency, to group solidarity. In its more refined form, the worldly argument in behalf of religion has stressed man's need of religion in the face of the absurd; or his dependence upon religion as a source of cogent and unified world-views. We have been told that religion is an answer to human needs. We are supposed to conclude that we ought therefore to foster it. These arguments represent the final blasphemy, the affirmation of faith for worldly purposes. Though Cox does not necessarily suggest it, secularization represents an inquisitorial judgment: the world does not *need* religion. It can provide a sound basis for mental health, a reasonable, though tentative, foundation for ethical action, even—as the Jewish community seems to prove—an adequate basis for group life, without faith in any form. Man does not need religion to overcome the absurd, for he can accept the absurd with the same enthusiasm and life-affirming vitality that he accepts the other artifacts of reality. He can meet his needs elsewhere than at the holy altar.

We who affirm that God made the world need not claim in his behalf that he needs to have done so. We who hold that God acted freely and out of love need not deny that love and that freedom in the name of worldly rationality. Mankind does not need religion. The worldly uses of religion have far more acceptable, secular surrogates. Man does not need to believe in God to avoid insanity, or absurdity, or social disintegration. He does not need to accept revelation in terms that render revelation the result of worldly ratiocination. Mankind is challenged by the world's own power to accept or reject revelation, to affirm or deny God, upon judgment of the real issues. These issues are, Did God make the world? Does Providence govern history? Is Torah, meaning truth, from Heaven? The world cannot resolve them for us, and in the joyful acceptance of its perquisites, Jews and Christians alike are much enriched. They regain the opportunity to believe, as I said, and to assent with rejoicing to the imperative of Sinai, to accept in submission the yoke of heaven, to love God with all our heart. These have been the classical paradigms of Jewish existence. This world once more renders them vivid.

II. Secularization and Judaism

Judaism is both admirably equipped, and completely unprepared for secularization.

It is well equipped to confront an uncomprehending world, as I have said, because of the exigencies of its history. It is, moreover, able to face this world with something more constructive than ungenerous disdain. It has always regarded the world as the stage upon which the divine drama may be enacted. The world presents Judaism with its highest challenge, to achieve sanctity within the profane, to hallow the given. For this task, Judaism comes equipped with Torah and *mitzvot*, Torah which reveals God's will for the secular world, *mitzvot* which tell us how to carry out that will. Through *mitzvah*, we sanctify the secular, not in a metaphysical sense, nor through theologizing intractible givens. One sees the setting sun and lights a candle, the one a natural perception of the course of the earth upon its axis, the other a perfectly commonplace action. But he adds, "who has commanded us to light the Sabbath light," and the course of nature becomes transformed, and a commonplace action transforms it. We don a piece of cloth with fringes, and say, "who has commanded us concerning fringes." That cloth is no longer like any other. It serves as a means of worshipping our Creator. We build a frail hut of branches and flowers at the autumn season, an act of quite natural celebration of the harvest. But we say, "who has commanded us to sit in the Sukkah," and those branches become a sacred shelter. Our table becomes an altar, and the commonplace and profane action of eating food becomes the occasion to acknowledge the gifts of Him who gave it. We speak of our people's humble happenings, of their going forth from slavery to freedom, but doing so is rendered by the commandments into a sacred action, a moment of communion. We open our minds to the wonders of the world, and this too is Torah and requires a benediction. A man takes a wife, and we proclaim the blessings of Eden, the memories of besieged Jerusalem, and the hope for future redemption. Our Tradition leads us not away from the world, but rather into it, and demands that we sanctify the given, and see it as received, commanded from Heaven. All things inspire a sense of awe and call forth a benediction. Nothing is profane by nature, nor is anything intrinsically sacred, but that we make it so. The heavens tell the glory of God. The world reveals his holiness. Through *mitzvot* we respond to what the heavens say; through Torah we apprehend the revelations of the world. Judaism rejoices, therefore, at the invitation of the secular city. It has never truly known another world; and it therefore knows what its imperatives require.

Judaism has always, moreover, understood history, or social change, to be in some measure exemplifications of divine sovereignty. It has understood daily affairs to reveal more than commonplace truths.

The destruction of a worldly city was understood from prophetic times onward to be a call for penitance and *teshuvah*, return to God. The sorrows of the age were seen as the occasion for renewed inwardness, prayer, repentance, and doing deeds of compassion, so that men might make themselves worthy of the compassion of God. It has at the same time recognized a tension between event and divine will. Judaism has never merely accepted history, any more than it accepted nature, but sought rather to elevate and sanctify the profane in both. History does not speak God's will in unequivocal terms, for history is to be interpreted, not merely accepted, by means of the Torah. We have seen in revelation a guide to understanding events, and have never uncritically accepted events as themselves bearing unexamined meaning. All things are seen under the aspect of Sinai, and all events must be measured by the event of revelation. We are not, therefore, at a loss to evaluate the changes of an inconstant world. We have, moreover, demanded that God, like ourselves, abide by the covenant. In times of stress, we have called him to account, as much as ourselves. To offer a most recent example:

The journal of Chaim Kaplan contains the following passage:

> There is a rumor that in one of the congregations the prayer leader came and dressed himself in a *kittel* [shroud] and prepared to lead his poor and impoverished people in the *Neilah* [closing prayers for the Day of Atonement] service, when a boy from his congregation broke in with the news about the ghetto. At once the Jew dispensed with Neilah, took off his *kittel*, and went back to his seat. There is no point in praying when the gates of mercy were locked. . . .[3]

We have taken events so very seriously that we are prepared to call God to account, and even to remind him, as did Ezekiel, that his good name and ours are one and the same. What happens to us happens to him; the covenant measures the loyalty of both its signatories.

Judaism has offered a worldly understanding of man's part in the achievement of God's kingdom. Man is the partner in the building of the kingdom. He is needed to perfect the world under the sovereignty of God. Just as the commonplace may be profane or sacred, but the *mitzvot* consecrate, so too the world, society, may be sanctified. That sanctification is of a most practical sort. We are told to heal the sick, free the captives, loosen the bonds that enslave men. A starving world is an affront to God. All the technical skills of men possess the

---

[3] Quoted by J. A. Isaacson in *Conservative Judaism* 20, 2 (1966), 87.

potentiality to achieve holiness, therefore, and all the vocations of men may serve to sanctify the world. The secular city, Professor Cox writes, requires the skill of men. The kingdom of God cannot do without men's abilities. The kingdom of God is meant to find a place in the history of this world, moreover, according to the eschatological theory of significant Jewish thinkers. The only difference between this world and the world to come, or the age to come, will be the end of subjugation to paganism, so said Samuel, the third-century Babylonian master. Israel is meant, furthermore, to live in this world, to bear witness to God in the streets of the city. For centuries, and most immediately in modern Judaism, Jews have seen themselves as bearers of the kingdom, as witnesses to the rule of God over the world. One need hardly stress, therefore, that Judaism is ready and eager for the worldly encounter.

That encounter, however, is by no means neutral. Judaism has seen itself under a very special vocation, as I said, to say *no* to the lesser claims to divinity entertained by this world. It has told the world that sanctity inheres in it, but denied that the world as it is is holy. It has offered the world the promise of redemption, but denied that redemption is just yet. It has borne unflagging testimony to the unredemption of mankind, and insisted upon a radical criticism of the status quo. These are the vocations, too, of the secular city, which denies ultimacy even to religion, all the more so to lesser structures. Judaism has insisted that the world is ever secular, both so that it may be sanctified and so that it may not lose the hope for ultimate redemption.

And yet Judaism is utterly unready for secularization in the current sense. Professor Cox writes that secularization is "the loosing of the world from religious and quasi-religious understandings of itself, the dispelling of all closed world-views, the breaking of all supernatural myths and sacred symbols. . . ." Nothing in my understanding of Judaism suggests that Judaism can accept, or even comprehend, "the loosing of the world from religious . . . understandings of itself." If from my perspective there can be no "secular Jew," there can surely emerge no "secularized Judaism." Judaism begins with the affirmation of a supernatural apprehension of reality, however we may courageously try to formulate that apprehension in naturalistic or humanistic terms. It begins with the proclamation of the unity and sovereignty of God. It offers to the world the spectacle of a people bound to God's service and governed by his will. It tells the world that this people serves as the heart of humanity, the barometer of its health, and that its history becomes paradigmatic for the human condition. Judaism may cope with the world, may indeed affirm this age in the terms I have outlined; but it can never turn away from itself and its primary assent. Our prophets have offered the world the belief that at some times God may hide his face from man. This may be such an age. We can never confuse, however, our own difficulties in belief with ontological or anthropological Godlessness. Sinai has happened. We may not have seen his face, but we have the record that his glory passed before us. Not every age has an equal apprehension of the glory. A handmaiden saw at the Red Sea what was not given to the prophets to see. We know through Torah, and can never, therefore, claim ignorance, only frail forgetfulness. We may, as Rabbi Abraham J. Heschel says, be messengers who have forgotten our message. But we can never forget that we once had a message. We may comprehend the hiddenness of God; indeed, we are those who have most suffered in his absence. We can never confuse that comprehension of *our* condition with the illusion of *his*. We have lived for a long time within the gates of the secular city. Our Tradition has prepared us for, and our condition has taught us the imperatives of, its discipline. We have aspired to its liberties. But these imperatives we accept, these liberties we demand, *upon our own terms*. We are not secular within the secular city, but we are Jews, *yehudim*, upon whom the name of the Lord has been called. We cannot change our name, either to add to his discipline that of the world, or to win for ourselves the blessings of the world. In the city of this world, or in the world to come, we can only be ourselves, Jews. This is the final paradox of our current situation: we who have confronted the data of secularization long before our neighbors now rehearse our ancient response to these data. We who first told the world of its secularization need now remind it of its consecration.

III. Judaism and Christianity in the Secular Age

It is frequently said that we live in a post-Christian age, by which is meant that we live in an age no longer characterized by the normality of Christian vocation. How are the two traditions to cope with the new situation? What are its promises? Both faiths clearly meet parallel challenges. Indifference to religion, disbelief, a wholly worldly view of man—these are problems faced by all men who strive for religious faith. Jews and Christians have much more in common than they ever had. The world has given them a common struggle.

Jews need not, however, find the disestablishment of cultural-Christianity the occasion for rejoicing, nor, quite obviously, for gloating. Christianity understood us as Jews, and gave us the privilege of martyrdom as Jews. When the new age sees us, it does not see us in the perspective of sacred history. To the Christian, our Scriptures are revealed truth. To the secularist, they are literature. The Christian finds us a question to his faith. The secularist sees us as curiosities. The Christian understands our professions. The secularist interprets them. The Christian sees in us a mystery. The secularist reduces the facts of our existence to an anomaly in the laws of sociology. Whether or not we were well off in a Christian age, we are not better off in a post-Christian age. Both are ages of unredemption, but we can say so to the Christian.

This is not, however, a time to forget the past so that we may work together in the future. It is a time to remember the past and reconsider its lessons. Christians must not ask us, nor surely themselves, to gloss over the inhumanity of Christianity toward Judaism, and the indecency of Christians toward Jews. If we now turn a new page in history, it is not because we shall never review the pages already written. Jews preserve the memories of the past, because in them are enshrined consecrated hours of our loyalty to our Tradition, even at the gates of death, of our capacity for piety, of our ability to love God. We can no more forget the destruction of European Jewry than we can erase from our Scriptures the destruction of Judea by the Babylonians. It is no exaggeration to say this: The Temple of our spirit that was razed at Auschwitz is no less sacred to us than the Temple of Jerusalem. It is nearer; it is a greater tragedy; and these we loved, our flesh and blood. If however Christians choose to take seriously the Hebrew Scriptures and the Jewish people, if they wish to achieve a reconciliation and a better way for the future, as it is clear they do, then they too need to remember. Their memory is not, however, meant as an act of guilt or penitance—for if it is, a Jew cannot say so,—but rather, I think, an act of completion. If the anguish of Auschwitz is not a Christian anguish, as much as a Jewish anguish, then Christians by their indifference cut themselves off from the human lessons of Auschwitz, and retrospectively accept a measure of the burden of Auschwitz. More broadly phrased: if the Christian regards the Jewish people as the children of Abraham, Isaac, and Jacob, as he does, then he must want to know the story of his cousins. He must need to bear their pain, for the sake of a whole and complete apprehension of sacred history.

For their part, Jews must enlarge the dimensions of their memory. We know our own pain, but we too easily forget that we were not alone in bearing pain. At every stage in Jewish martyrdom under Christianity, many men suffered with us, Christian, Moslem, and pagan. We are all too easily enticed into the sin of judging Christianity by the deeds of Christians, and Christians by the actions of some Christians. It is not our task to lay the blame for Auschwitz. The judge of all flesh will also have to come to judgment. It is not for us to say that Christianity is morally and spiritually bankrupt, as has been said by a Jewish theologian. It is not for us to accuse others of bearing "a criminal past." We believe, moreover, in man's capacity for atonement and regeneration. We affirm, not merely for ourselves, the call to repentance, and we believe that the children's children of Haman taught Torah in Israel. We do not believe that guilt inheres in blood. And we do not claim to have the right to apportion guilt. All men stand in need of God's mercy and forgiveness, and we are not the least of them.

We Jews cannot ignore, moreover, the varieties within Christianity as a religious tradition, and among Christians. If the record of German and Polish Christianity is unsavory, that of Danish, Dutch, and Italian Christianity is not. The same "Christianity" which produced so many centuries of anti-Semitism gave the world men of conscience and of charity as well. The same Scriptures which say, "His blood be upon our heads" say also "Forgive them, for they know not." Christians hold that the world, and they within it, are redeemed, and we, in our error, measure them by that claim. We Jews however hold that the world is unredeemed, but awaiting its redemption. Shall we therefore judge, or even understand, it according to others' counsels of perfection? If within the Churches men compromise the right because of political realities, ought we not to see it, with sadness, to be sure, as yet another testimony of worldly unredemption? It is part of our task to suffer the world, in the certain hope that we bear its sorrows. We cannot repudiate that task, though we may sorely regret the occasion for it, by a mere this-worldly response to our suffering.

Our task is quite different. We Jews have to come to a further understanding of Christianity's, and Islam's, place in sacred history. We need to ask ourselves the question, Are Christians merely "sons of Noah," or are they, as they claim to be, sons of Abraham, Isaac, and Jacob? Sons of Noah, that is, all mankind, are expected to keep the commandments not to murder, not to worship idols, not to blaspheme the name of God, not to commit adultery, not to rob; to establish courts of justice, and not to be inhumane to animals. Christians affirm these laws, but much else. It is through Christianity and Islam that the Name of the God of Israel has come to vast parts of mankind. It is through Christianity and Islam that the Torah has reached distant places on earth. And the contrary needs to be said: it was *not* through Judaism. One can, of course, provide a historical explanation, that Judaism was prevented by Christianity and Islam from carrying out its sacred mission. But Judaism affirmed that prohibition, and abandoned its mission, or revised its concept of it so that in effect, Christianity and Islam were regarded as preparing the way for Monotheism among men. Medieval Jewish thinkers said exactly that. If so, one must reflect upon its implications.

In the new age, Jews are enabled to reflect upon the old. For long centuries Christians and Jews had no serious desire to talk together. Jews were held to be eternally cursed. Christians were seen as persecutors only. The task of dialogue was merely self-justification, denial of the other's claim to truth, and exchange of proof-texts to support one's own claim and destroy the other's. It now seems to some, including this writer, that another kind of conversation is possible. We seek not the disintegration of dogma, as H. J. Schoeps puts it,[4] but rather "real understanding . . . of spirit and truth." Two Jewish thinkers in the modern mode have come to grips with the reality of Christianity, Franz Rosenzweig and Martin Buber. Rosenzweig wrote:

> Our recognition of Christianity rests, in fact, upon Christianity, namely, upon the fact that Christianity recognizes us. It is the Torah . . . which is spread abroad by Bible societies. . . .
> What Christ and his Church mean within the world—on this point we are agreed. No one *comes* to the Father except through him. No one *comes* to the Father—but the situation is different when one need no longer come to the Father because he *is* already with him. That is the case with the nation of Israel. The nation of Israel, elected by its Father, keeps its gaze fixed beyond world and history toward that last, most distant, point where he, Israel's Father, will himself be the one and only . . . At this point, where Christ ceases to be Lord,

---

[4] *The Jewish Christian Argument* (New York, 1963), 126f.

Israel ceases to be elect. On this day, God loses the name by which Israel alone may call upon him; God is then no longer Israel's God. But until this time it is Israel's life to anticipate this eternal day in confession of faith and in action, to stand as a living symbol of this day, a nation of priests with the law, to hallow the name of God through its own holiness....[5]

Martin Buber wrote:

> If we want to express in a simple formula the difference between Jews and Christians, between Israel and the Church, we can say: The Church is grounded upon the belief that Christ has already come, redemption has been granted to men through God. We as Israel are unable to accept this belief. The Church views our position either as unwillingness to believe, a hardness of heart in a very dubious sense, or as a constraint, a fundamental limitation of ability to perceive vis á vis reality.... We as Israel understand our inability to accept this proclamation in another fashion. We understand the Christology of Christianity throughout as an important event which has taken place between the world above and the world below. We see Christianity as something the mystery of whose coming into the world we are unable to penetrate. But just as we know that there is air which we breathe into our lungs, we know also that there is a space in which we move; more deeply, more genuinely, we know that the history of the world has not yet been shattered to its very core, that the world is not yet redeemed. We feel the unredemption of the world.... For us the redemption of the world is indissolubly one with the perfecting of creation, with the establishment of a unity no longer limited in any respect, no longer suffering contradiction, realized in all the multiplicity of the world, one with the fulfilled kingdom of God....[6]

As Schoeps points out, what is important in Buber's statement for our problem is that he is prepared to say, Christianity must be understood as an "important event which has taken place between the world above and the world below." Buber speaks as "we as Israel."

Buber and Rosenzweig were attempting to formulate a *Jewish theology of Christianity*. I find it difficult to recognize how they have succeeded, although I can offer no better way. It is not enough to affirm that Christianity has brought, though in a form we do not always approve, important Jewish theological and moral teachings to the nations of the world. That is merely a sociological fact, which may

---
[5] Cited in Schoeps, p. 141.
[6] Cited in Schoeps, p. 150f.

or may not yield a theological affirmation. Rosenzweig does not help us when he says that "others" come to the Father through the Son, first, because he ignores the even more impressive role of Islam; second, because Judaism cannot be either relativized—as good only for the Jews, or ethnicized—as good for the Jews alone; and third, because Christians themselves could scarcely agree. So we have gained nothing. Buber does not explain adequately what he means by "an important event . . . between the world above and the world below." Buber seems in the end to have come to Rosenzweig's view, for he stated, "The gates of God stand open to all. The Christian need not go through Judaism, the Jew need not go through Christianity, in order to come to God." I find Schoeps' criticism wholly valid:

> Israel and Christianity *must* assert the exclusive and ultimate nature of the revelation granted to each on the grounds of the truth of revelation itself; for in fact God cannot transcend his own word, which is absolute truth, if he does not wish to make a mockery of human belief. . . .[7]

A Jewish theology of Christianity must begin, therefore, with a recognition that Christianity has played a role in the history of human redemption. But the meaning of this role must remain a mystery for Jews. Schoeps points out that the two faiths come together in their eschatological expectation of God's rule on earth. In the meanwhile, they may agree to disagree. What is it that forms the foundation for their common conversation, even for their disagreement? I think it clear that the *Bible* provides that foundation. Is it possible that Christians have a better understanding of its imperatives than Jews, or that the contrary is the case? Is it possible that we may illuminate the Scriptures for one another, out of the experience that each has had in history? These are not questions posed to scholarship, but posed to faith by faith. They may well form the agenda for our future conversations.

At the same time, it is important for Jews to specify their expectations. We ask, in brief, for Christians to take our existence seriously, just as we must theirs. We ask that they learn about our faith, just as we must learn about theirs. Jews are afflicted with vast ignorance about Christianity; they speak of it, frequently, as if Marcionism and Manichaeism were normative and not heretical; as if the New Testament had not been studied for close to two centuries by critical and

---

[7] Pp. 152-3.

penetrating scholars; as if Jesus' claim were either interpreted when his words are attested in rabbinic literature, or ignored. Jews must overcome much ignorance. Christians, for their part, must abandon the well-worn contrast, in the words of Rabbi Robert Gordis,[8]

> between the "Old Testament Lord of Justice" and the God of Love of the New Testament.... Closely related to this unwarranted distinction is the widespread practice of contrasting the primitivism, tribalism, and formalism of the Old Testament with the spirituality, universalism, and freedom of the New, to the manifest disadvantage of the former. Another practice which should be surrendered is that of referring to Old Testament verses quoted in the New as original New Testament passages.... Finally the dialogue between Judaism and Christianity can be mutually fruitful only if it always is kept in mind that Judaism is not the religion of the Old Testament, though obviously it is rooted in it....

Beyond the neo-Marcionism to which Rabbi Gordis raises objection lies the ancient presupposition that with the advent of Christianity, Judaism became a dead religion. I know of no facts adequate to refute such a theological opinion. It would be futile to point to the achievements of the Jewish spirit, achievements of Scriptural study, of Talmudic application of law to life, of theological inquiry. The only fact that should carry weight is this: The Jews today live to deny it, and they live as Jews. If we Jews need, as I said, to take seriously the whole record of Christianity, Christians similarly need to reckon with us, and to cease to look upon us ignorantly or malevolently, surely to cease ignoring our part of sacred history. I realize the difficulty is no less than that we face. It seems to me that the apostle Paul was first to face it, for to him are ascribed, in Romans, chapters 9 through 11, reflections upon Israel "after the flesh." Not competent in New Testament studies, I cannot, quite obviously, venture an exegesis of these passages. But I am struck by Paul's affirmation that God has not rejected his people, but rather

> Through their trespass salvation has come to the gentiles, so as to make Israel jealous. Now if their trespass means riches for the world, and if their failure means riches for the gentiles, how much more will their full inclusion mean!... For if their rejection means the reconciliation of the world, what will their acceptance mean but life from the dead?... As regards the gospel they are enemies of God for your sake; but as regards

---
[8] *The Jewish Frontier.*

> election they are beloved for the sake of their forefathers. For the gifts and the call of God are irrevocable. Just as you were once disobedient to God but now have received mercy because of their disobedience, so they have now been disobedient in order that by the mercy shown to you they also may receive mercy. For God has consigned all men to disobedience, that he may have mercy upon all. . . .

In the early generations, Jews and Christians, both weak before the power of pagan gods, spoke angrily to one another, but they spoke. The Jews reflected very little about Christianity. Rabbi Tarfon merely said, for instance, that the Jewish-Christians were to be despised because they knew God and then abandoned him. The Christians offered more thoughtful comment upon the Jews. In time, as we have seen, the two groups moved far away from one another. No longer did anger, and thus, deep concern, characterize their relationship. No longer did they see one another as erring brothers, surely not as mysteries to one another. The world has brought them back together, through the disestablishment of the daughter, and the untold suffering of the mother. The daughter once more weeps for the hurt of the mother. The mother once more seeks the welfare of the daughter. It is this last, least expected event of the age of secularization which may prove, in time to come, the earliest event in the new redemptive drama.

We Jews have still another expectation. We ask not only to be taken seriously, we ask that our apocalyptic history be taken seriously. We have lived through our darkest and our brightest days. From 1933 to 1945, we suffered total destruction. At the portal of Auschwitz in 1945 the path did not lead to what was then Palestine. It seemed to lead nowhere. Yet within three years, the nations of the world voted, and the Jewish people created, the State of Israel. To non-Jews this is merely a political event. To Jews it is a miracle. It is no less the work of Providence than the cleansing of the Temple by the Maccabees, than the return to Zion under Joshua and Zerubabbel, indeed than the freeing of the slaves of Egypt. We see it as a mystery in the drama of redemption, and not merely—though in all honesty, it would have sufficed—as worldly balm for worldly suffering. If the exodus from Egypt is seen by Christians as a moment in sacred history, they ought to understand why we see the exodus from Auschwitz as another. If the one is sacred, so is the other. If the State of Israel is seen merely under the aspect of a secular world, then so is the entry into Canaan. We do not ourselves pretend to fathom the mystery, or to know the meaning of these days. We ask only that Christians remain open to the possibility that something of great importance has happened.

Is there no way forward? Are we to be left paralyzed by the categories of traditional theology, understood in a fundamentalistic way? I think not, if we recognize, as I have implied, that Buber and Rosenzweig do not, in the end, provide very relevant guidelines. They make it clear that Judaism and Christianity are mutually contradictory when looked upon from the perspectives of the beginning, or the end, of time. But, as Rabbi Jacob Agus pointed out to me (in a letter, August 22, 1966), "In regard to what lies between beginning and end, that is, the actual course of history, Judaism, through Maimonides, accepted Christianity as a 'preparation for the days of the Messiah,' and Christianity, through St. Paul, accepted the existence of Israel as a providential act 'until the fullness of the gentiles will be gathered in.' In detail, both Judaism and Christianity are complexes of ideas and judgment, which differ sometimes radically, sometimes only in nuance, and sometimes not at all." Rabbi Agus rightly stresses the importance of focussing "upon the living people behind the official facades." He sees the error in the preceding paragraphs as "the attempt to continue a fundamentalist concept of history in a non-fundamentalist universe of discourse. The history of ancient Israel is used by us and by Christians as a *text* of religious instruction. It is an illustration of the way in which the values of faith spring out of events. This illustrative value is frankly homiletic, being independent of the objective truth of the historical event. It is our duty so to use the *text* of Scripture as to serve the ends of religious humanism. It can easily be used for opposite purposes. In the case of the New Testament, which contains in some places hostile polemics against Jews, it is the duty of Christians to interpret their text in the spirit of religious humanism. This result emerges almost inevitably from the confrontation of Christians with the kind of living Judaism that explicitly incorporates the thrust of religious humanism."

Rabbi Agus stresses that as non-fundamentalists, we need to see in history both the values of faith and its distortions. "History is placed under judgment in terms of the values of our faith," he says, adding, "So the history of the Christian conquest of the West provides illustrations aplenty of every kind of sin and of every type of heroic ardor.... We do regard the Christian faith as a great extension of 'ethical monotheism,' and we deplore its numerous failings, as being due in part to human nature and in part to the ambivalence of every religious heritage. Are Christians 'Israel of the spirit' as they claim to be? Yes and no, in the same way in which no Jew can claim by his descent alone to be part of 'the remnant of Israel.' For 'God looks to the heart,' and only He can tell who his saints are. . . ."

It is in this spirit that Rabbi Agus replied to the essay of Rabbi Eliezer Berkovits, "Judaism in the Post-Christian Era" (JUDAISM, winter, 1966). In his letter to the editor (JUDAISM, summer, 1966, 359-60), Agus says, "To my mind, genuine, living religion is in a perpetual state of tension between the questioning of the objective mind and the subjective faith of the individual and the community. Insofar as the objective realm of ideas and values forms part of the very being of religion, a perpetual dialogue is not only desirable— it is essential to the life of faith. However, a version of religion exists that either limits severely or eliminates entirely the place of objectivity in the realm of faith. For that kind of believer, be he Jewish, Catholic, Protestant . . . any kind of interreligious dialogue is obviously anathema."

It seems to me that the plurality of choices in the secular city renders such an objectivity accessible. Living in the confines of an all-Jewish, or an all-Christian world, Jews and Christians alike once found it easy to see "the other" as the outsider, to look upon history through the prism of faith alone. His task then becomes that of the apologist, who needs to justify, or explain away, what clearly conflicts with the demands of contemporary conscience. And yet, is he now better off when he succeeds? Does he more profoundly apprehend his own faith, having defended it against unintended secular criticism? I think that Gavin Langmuir's contribution to the CONTINUUM symposium on Father Edward Flannery's *Anguish of the Jews* (in press for fall, 1966), suggests otherwise. Langmuir sees Flannery's treatment of the history of anti-Semitism in Christendom as *theologically* (as well as historically) unsound, and proposes what I understand to be a rather more penetrating and realistic way to come to terms *theologically* with the facts of *history,* be they concerned with anti-Semitism or some other failing of Western Christendom. Langmuir's "Majority History and Post-Biblical Judaism" (JOURNAL OF THE HISTORY OF IDEAS, 27, 3, summer, 1966, 343-64), similarly demonstrates, as did his "The Jews and the Archives of Angevin England: Reflections on Medieval Anti-Semitism" (TRADITIO 19, 1963), that by a one-sided and mostly apologetic treatment of painful matters, one may close off an understanding of what was actually *happening* and why, and may prevent a deeper perspective upon the eternal realities of faith. Indeed, the apologetic path, upon which one is forced by fundamentalism to tread, may prove in the end to lead away from true religion, whether Christian or Jewish. I can think of no more striking example of that fact than Rabbi Berkovits's article, referred to above, which bespeaks a spirit of triumphalism and hostility that is anything but authentically Jewish. His bitter, nasty words, "Judged in the light of our own experience and under the aspects of the Messianic history of the *am olam* [eternal people], we are confronting a morally and spiritually bankrupt civilization and religion. . . . We reject the idea of inter-religious understanding as immoral because it is an attempt to whitewash a criminal past," and the like—these seem to me the opposite of the truth, not because they are wholly wrong, but because they are only partially right. And here Rabbi Agus's warning becomes crucial, that we must look backward, and forward, upon the realities of human beings who were Jews, some good, some bad, and Christians who were similarly a mixture of the good and evil impulses, and upon Christian civilization and religion, where they survive, which have much still to do to render men human and humane, and have other important tasks ahead. Who is to judge whether one or another segment of mankind is "morally and spiritually bankrupt," and when is such a judgment to be made, and before which tribunal, and to what end? Our own experience includes ambiguous memories, but we surely can not *yet* claim to make judgments from the perspective of "eternity" or from the viewpoint of an as-yet-unfulfilled "Messianic history."

So in the end I think we are not helped by the fundamentalistic formulation of the question, whether by Buber and Rosenzweig, or by Rabbi Berkovits, or by Vatican II for that matter. On the contrary, a measure of nominalism seems in order, invariably the counsel of one who, like myself, sees things mostly as a historian, and all too little as a theologian. So far as the world contains faithful Jews and faithful Christians, these today constitute "Judaism" or "Christianity," for *this* hour and in *this* place; perhaps they represent a segment of an "eternal people" or "the Church," but surely only by their own temporal professions and measured only by their own partial witness. "Judaism" and "Christianity"—and other traditions must be seen in a similarly extreme-nominalistic way—are all too complex in their ordinary realities to be understood so cosmically and so one-dimensionally, as monolithic constructs facing one another. It is not these, but rather the faithful Jew and the faithful Christian who once again are meeting, each in the integrity of his tradition, each in his own uniqueness, but each also bearing in his soul and spirit and flesh the stigmata of a common humanity and also of uncommon faith. As people they meet to be sure, but as special kinds of people, who find one another different, for particular historical and theological reasons, from the rest of humanity, and reckon with one another differently on that account.

With these expectations met, and with the necessary theological enterprise undertaken both among Jewry and within Christendom, what is the dialogue we seek? We seek an exchange of mutual respect, a respect which will be earned, and not bestowed by either upon the other. We seek to merit one another's esteem because of the intrinsic worth of each. Men of differing traditions seek to understand one another, and, recognizing our differences, to live together in harmony. In these words I have paraphrased those of Moses Hadas, in his introduction to *Aristeas to Philocrates*.[9] Hadas thus describes the exchange between the "King of Egypt" and the High Priest of Jerusalem. When the Jews assemble at the table of the king—a table, incidentally, prepared according to the dietary laws of Judaism, but without great éclat—what is it that takes place? What is the result of mutual respect? They ate together, and discussed great questions. How might the king preserve his kingdom unimpaired to the end? What is the best course in all actions? How might the king keep his friends like-minded with himself? How might he obtain a good report even from those disappointed in their suits? How might he be invincible in warfare? What is the highest good for life? How could he endure whatever befell with equanimity? What is the goal of courage? One could go on at considerable length. It is clear from these questions—and I have not quoted the replies—that the purpose of the dialogue was mutual illumination.

What are equivalent questions for today? I think it is obvious that the issues of secularization, confronted by both traditions, provide a meaningful agenda. What does it mean to affirm faith in a relativistic, pluralistic society? What does it mean "to take this earthly realm ... in utter seriousness"? How may Israel and the Church alike carry out the task of bearing witness? of healing? of affirming the humanity of man? How indeed may we speak of God, separately or together, among men who cannot hear us? Just as the secular age has permitted us to come together, so it provides us with a purpose for our meeting.

---

[9] New York, 1951, p. 61.

540

We cannot, however, disregard our past. We are not new to this world. Our respective traditions have much, much more to say than the secular world is able to comprehend. We can, however, resume the discussions cut off so tragically at the outset of the common era. What is the meaning of revelation? What is the purpose of man? What is the role of law in piety? Of faith? What is the nature of salvation? What does Scripture mean? And what does Scripture want of us? We are, therefore, not limited to the agenda of today. We have a long agenda of our own, one which has been neglected far too long. If we come together once again in a neutral, secular city, which is equally indifferent to us both, we still hope together, praying each in the way he has been instructed, to see the kingdom of God, when the secular city will become His dominion, and may it come speedily and in our own time.

SYNAGOGUE AND CENTER

The Symposium in Retrospect

JACOB NEUSNER

THE symposium on the relationships between the synagogue and the Jewish Center movement, published in our last issue, generated lavish quantities of heat, but also, fortunately, a little light.* We intend here to review the discussion of the issue which was raised, quoting liberally from the various newspaper and magazine comment and speeches, few of which have reached a wide audience. If, for the purpose of discussion, we reduce the response to the symposium to broad categories, we find that three main groups emerge: the unyielding "pro-Center" opinion, the unyielding "anti-Center" opinion, and that opinion focused on thoughtful discussion of issues, which, in the current fashion, we might call "the dialogue."

Those who argued that the present Centers constitute the best agency for Jewish leisure-time activity, broadly construed, made two main points which would appear to contradict each other: On the one hand, advocates of the Center maintained that Centers are not meant to be "religious." On the other, they asserted that Centers today are in fact "Jewish," growing progressively more so, funcioning creatively and affirmatively in a Judaic and Jewish-cultural setting; that Center staff members are increasingly concerned with improving their Jewish education and training; and that, on the whole, the movement is toward the goals held implicitly or explicitly by the participants in the symposium.

This view was advanced, for example, in letters to the editors of the National Jewish Post and the Congress Bi-Weekly, the latter (from Graenum Berger of the Jewish Welfare Board in the issue of June 25, 1962) saying:

> ... what the writers of *Conservative Judaism* deliberately obscured, is that the "creative Jewish revival" that has come to American Jewry has not found a "holdout" in the Jewish center but one of its most ardent advocates.
>
> Any close student of the Jewish community centers in this country will note the substantial attention it pays daily to every aspect of Jewish life. There are well-attended Jewish educational programs for children, youth and adults. It is within the center walls that the Jewish aged had the first opportunity to associate with their elderly brethren and to continue their

---

* Considerable correspondence has been received on this subject, which we plan to consider in a future issue. Ed.
Dr. Neusner, a research fellow at Brandeis University, is a member of the editorial board of *Conservative Judaism*.

abiding Jewish interest, often ignored by other Jewish institutions that found them no longer useful.

Has the writer been aware that it is precisely the Jewish community centers that has been the intellectual oasis for Jewish speakers, thinkers, artists? Has he seen the special Jewish art exhibits, the displays of Jewish books, the concerts with Jewish themes, the dances with Jewish choreography? Does he know that many of our centers even have Hebrew schools and religious services, and they are prepared to extend such program if they did not meet with clerical opposition? . . .

Mr. Manuel G. Batshaw, executive director of the Jewish Community Center of Essex County, New Jersey, made the same point in an article in the Newark *Jewish News,* in which he described his own center and its Jewish programs. A third such view was expressed by Herbert Millman, associate executive of the National Jewish Welfare Board, in a commentary on Rabbi Harold M. Schulweis' article, printed in *The American Rabbi,* November, 1961, and worth quoting here *in extenso*:

By now, the Center field can enunciate a role that is not less than serving as a fortress of Jewish life, sharing the task with the synagogue, the Jewish school and the Jewish home, and other Jewish institutions and agencies. The Center is admittedly not a "house of prayer" nor is it primarily the locus for the formal instruction in Judaistic teachings. Yet, it can and increasingly does, address itself to motivating the pursuit of Jewish knowledge and the deepening of Jewish understanding.

The typical Center program includes many types of experimental elements which are beneficial to the social, cultural, physical and moral development of the participants. There is opportunity for people to discuss the meaning of God; to study the Bible as history, literature and the source of morality; and to consider the value of synagogal affiliation. It can and does help people of all ages to appreciate the Judaistic alternatives to man's hostility to man. Center boards and staffs are manifesting great interest in contributing to a Jewish cultural rebirth and already have just cause, in many communities, to be proud of their work to this end. The role of the JWB-sponsored Jewish Book Council of America, National Jewish Music Council and Lecture Bureau have been significant in this regard.

Their problems during this period have substantially been those with which the synagogues have struggled—overcoming the influence of indifference, conformity with the behavioral system of the larger society, preoccupation with the material, and entrancement with the achievements of modern day technology—factors which Rabbi Schulweis has effectively analyzed.

The Center of today is the child but not the image of the "Y" of the "Americanization" era. The modern Center does not view itself as a cafeteria which operates on the level of "give them what they want," nor even that of "keeping them off the streets." It applies the knowledge and methods of social work to helping people toward self-realization as human beings, as Jews and as socially-responsible individuals and groups. It is not pleased that a relatively high proportion of Jewish individuals in the community are not affiliated or active in the synagogue, or in other aspects of Jewish life, and it shares the concern of rabbis and responsible Jewish leaders over the fact that this is the state of affairs.

This is a condition which the Center must and does deal with realistically. Into the doors of the Centers come people of all ages with a variety of outlooks on Judaism, ranging from worshipful to marginal or rejective. Beginning with people where they are and guiding them toward self-fulfillment through significant group experience are the twin pillars of practice of the social group worker. He is guided by the established social principle that groups which mean the most to individuals and with which they voluntarily affiliate have marked influence on behavior, attitude and outlook . . .

Contactual Jewishness — to treat with a phrase employed by Rabbi Schulweis—has its important place in the Center, but is admittedly not sufficient by itself. A simple dictionary definition of contact is to "put in touch." The Center is indeed a place where Jewish people—representing all types of affiliation and non-affiliation—are put in touch with each other, relate to an institution which is one expression of the Jewish community, and avail themselves of opportunities of helping them in their quest for answers to the meaning of being Jewish. Contactual Jewishness need not, therefore, be underrated to make the point that this is insufficient reason for the existence of a Jewish agency. As implied by Rabbi Schulweis, the deliberate introduction of Jewish substance in the program (i.e., Jewish content) is also essential, as are defined Jewish objectives to which the leadership has deep conviction and commitment and can, therefore, transmit to the membership.

Leisurism, the word employed in the title and elsewhere by Rabbi Schulweis, appears in his usage to suggest a vacuous filling of people's free time at the expense of synagogue attendance and worthwhile educational pursuits. Responsible Center leadership abhors this concept as much as does the rabbi. Leisure is a condition which varies from generation to generation and from culture to culture. Today, it increasingly represents both an opportunity and a peril to the individual and to society. To the employed, it is a condition of more hours free from required labor; to the retired person, it is days on end to fill disconsolately or happily; to many a modern day professional or business man, it is not necessarily hours free from the tensions of responsibility, but is time to devote to parenthood and communal duties and only lastly to relaxation or cultural enjoyment; to the child, it is doing what you want to do when not required to attend public or religious school, take piano lessons, or keep dentist appointments. Updating a usable definition of leisure is a concern of social science, as well as of religion.

Knowing what we do of the choices available and attractive to Jews as well as non-Jews of all ages and economic levels in the use and abuse of free time, even those Center activities listed by Rabbi Schulweis warrant a *dayenu*. To assume, however, that this is all that the Center represents is akin to judging the synagogue by the men's club bowling league or the sisterhood's fashion show.

The Center worker who is uncommitted Jewishly is to all intents and purposes an anachronism. Jewish self-acceptance and acquisition of Jewish knowledge are recognized as being as essential to the success of a Center worker as is professional training. More and more Center workers are pursuing carefully developed programs of Jewish study. Just to cite two

examples: in New York City, a large number of Center workers has participated in annual courses for Jewish social workers conducted over the past seven years by the Jewish Education Committee in cooperation with the Metropolitan Section of JWB. Led by outstanding rabbinical scholars and Jewish educators, these courses consist of two semesters of study covering 20 to 24 weeks. Some students have attended for three to five years, or longer. Similarly, workers at the Los Angeles Jewish Centers Association are encouraged to take specially designed courses at the College of Jewish Studies of that city. JWB institutes in all parts of the country and agency in-service training programs have demonstrated the eagerness and diligence with which workers seek to obtain and apply knowledge in enriching the Jewish quality of programming. Completion of such courses is noted in the personnel records of Center workers.
Active participation as worshippers, board members, officers and volunteers in the synagogues of their choice is a well-developed trend among modern Center workers . . .

Another such statement on the affirmatively Jewish and Judaic commitment of the Center movement was made by Rabbi Isaac N. Trainin, advisor on religious affairs of the Federation of Jewish Philanthropies of New York, at the National Conference of Jewish Communal Service in Atlantic City on June 3rd, 1962. Because of the source of this statement, it is worth, again, quoting extensively:

. . . How did this entire rift begin? First, synagogue centers do fear the competition of the Y. Second, a number of the Sabbath programs initiated by Y's throughout the country are of questionable nature in terms of their being in consonance with the Sabbath. Third, the question of non-sectarianism in Y's has aroused the indignation of religious leadership. This is understandable. Fourth, the non-Jewish oriented staff people who do work in Y's have raised serious questions as to how the Y can function as a Jewish agency. The Y movement must face some of the following boldly:
1. It cannot and must not ignore the Rabbinate, for it is the guardian of our traditions.
2. The Y is in a quandary in trying to satisfy its membership, but as a Jewish institution, it must raise the level of Jewish standards rather than to cater to the lowest common denominator.
3. While rabbis should not pretend to be group workers, group workers should not pretend to be rabbis. There is an unfortunate phenomenon developing in the Y field, to wit, that by simply acquainting oneself with the biblical text, one becomes an authority and gains the right to interpret Jewish law . . .
4. In considering Sabbath programs, we must guard carefully against the violation of the Sabbath. When we respect the Sabbath, we respect ourselves as human beings. It is no accident that the Bible talks about remembering the Seventh day because we were once slaves in the land of Egypt. Are we not slaves to our own materialistic world today? Should we not differentiate between the weekday and the Sabbath?
While we may stand for open-door policies, we must guard zealously our purpose and our philosophy. We must ask ourselves what the "H"

in the YMHA stands for. Are we talking about centers under Jewish auspices or Jewish centers under Jewish auspices. What a difference there is. What commitment do we have to the past, the present and the future? Judaism cannot be imbibed by vitamin pills. It must be experienced, it must be lived. The greatest threat to Judaism is the Am Hooretz.

If there is room for a steam room, let's make room for a Jewish library. If we insist on professional standards for group workers, let us insist on good Jewish background for the group workers. Can you blame rabbis for questioning the influence of group workers on Jewish children, if so many group workers are ignorant of their Jewish heritage? If we have room for table tennis, we should have room for communal Talmud-Torahs. I deplore the fact that we have seen the end of communal Talmud Torahs. In my opinion, it is the responsibility of the Y to revive that movement in Judaism . . .

Let us now talk about the possibility and the urgency for cooperation between the Y movement and the synagogue world. We must give thought to how synagogues and Y's work together in order to prevent intermarriage, divorce, separation, delinquency and other social problems. There is no question that such cooperation can be achieved. The Commission on Synagogue Relations of the Federation of Jewish Philanthropies of New York has been able to establish a dialogue between the rabbi and the group worker. More and more Y's are offering group guidance at the request of synagogues. More and more Y's are calling upon religious leaders for assistance in enriching their Jewish programs.

I want to re-emphasize the last point because very often there is an indifferent attitude towards religious leadership on the part of Jewish communal institutions which is uncalled for. I recall that in 1957, I addressed the executives of the larger Jewish federations in this country. My remarks were met with cynicism and indifference. I got the feeling that many of them were not interested in seeking cooperation from their religious leadership. This is wrong. This attitude must be overcome, if we are to work together for the betterment of the Jewish community.

This is the age of status seeking. Can we not translate and sublimate this into Jewish channels? Can we not make Jewish learning and Jewish knowledge the sine qua non of Jewish living? In addition to, if not instead of basket ball and hand ball tournaments, how about bible contests? All of this can be achieved, if synagogues and Y's work together, instead of apart . . .

In support of these contentions, moreover, the *Connecticut Jewish Ledger's* news editor, Mr. Bert Gaster, published a survey of the Jewish Community Centers of that state—there are five—in which rabbis and center workers affirmed that the Center movement there plays an affirmative and useful role in building Jewish life, one worker asserting that "Religious Jews have special reasons to feel proud of this great institution and its manifold achievements . . . " and another expressing regret that the Center is not (yet) above criticism.

We have cited the above discussions at length because they represent an important and apparently authoritative affirmation of the under-lying assumptions of the symposium itself, namely, that every Jewish communal activity should be engaged in building Judaism and in realizing the religious and social teachings of the Jewish religion. If this proposition were not acceptable to the men cited above, they would not find it necessary to cite so elaborately the affirmative Jewish programs being conducted today by Jewish Centers.

At the same time, however, these same defenders of the status quo took a wholly contradictory line, and one that is difficult to harmonize with this positively-Jewish position. They held that the Center is not and was never intended to be "a religious institution." This view was expressed, perhaps somewhat grossly, by the Wisconsin Jewish Chronicle in an editorial on the symposium, but, more significantly, Trainin makes this point in the speech cited above:

> Y's are often attacked for conducting secular activities. Let us recall the Talmudic dictum, that one of the duties of a father is to teach his children how to swim; that physical activities are not non-Jewish. Furthermore, let us remember that the Y is not a religious institution. Who said it has to be? It can and should be a Jewish institution. If our synagogue leadership would take the trouble, they would find that in many Y's Jewish cultural programs of the highest order are an integral part of the programs of those institutions. All over America, Y's and bureaus of Jewish education are cooperating in improving the quality of Jewish programs and of training staff for a better understanding of the Jewish heritage.

We are not entirely clear what is meant by "not a religious institution" *in the Jewish context*. The opposite of "religious" is "secular," and yet Trainin's speech emphasized a wholly "unsecular" position, so far as we understand it.

There is a Jewish secular position. It was explored by the Bundists, some early Zionists, and others. It was most recently advanced by an advocate of the Center movement as an affirmation of "the cultural values" of Eastern European Ashkenazic Jewry, such values running the gamut of virtues generally approved by liberal opinion. Whatever the merits of the secularist position in Jewish life, however, Trainin and the others do not advance it, and probably do not hold it. (We doubt, in fact, that any Jewish social or communal worker would dare to confront the Jewish community with a fully articulated and completely honest statement of the secularist-Jewish position as the rationale for Jewish Community Center activities.) Yet this is precisely the implication of the distinction, which we can not admit, between the "secular" and the "religious" in Jewish life.

The issue is, then, whether Judaism recognizes such a distinction in human enterprise between "religious" and "secular." Historically, it has not. The distinction between "religion" and the rest of human "culture" was introduced into Western Civilization at a specific time in Western history, namely, as a consequence of the bloody wars of the Protestant Reformation. It has no roots in much of Protestant thought, or in Roman Catholic, or Islamic thought, and none whatever in Jewish thought.

If this is so, one must wonder what Trainin means by the statement, "The

Y is not a religious institution." If it is a Jewish institution then it is *eo ipse* a *religious* institution, and must regard itself as of a potential sanctity equivalent to every Jewish institution, including the Synagogue, and, like all Jewish institutions, consecrated to the spiritual and ethical endeavor summarized by the word "Torah." It is more likely, however, that "not a religious institution" simply means "a place where the issues of Judaism are not allowed to impinge," for frequently in the discussion of the symposium the point was made that the Center is the sole meeting ground for all the Jewish "sects" (that is, Orthodox, Conservative, and Reform Jews). Whether this is true or not we cannot say, but we know of no walls of sectarian self-segregation within American Jewry that are sufficiently high or impregnable to justify the following statement of Trainin:

> We talk about Klal Yisroel? I believe that the Y has a historic responsibility in this direction. It is the only agency in American Jewish life that can serve all religious ideologies. When one goes to rabbinical conventions it becomes evident that the concept of Klal Yisroel does not really exist. The question now is not are you a Jew, but what kind of a Jew are you, Conservative, Orthodox or Reform? We speak about adjective Judaism. There is a danger that the adjective may remain and the noun will be lost.
> It may be possible that if there were one Judaism, there would be no need for a YMHA. After all the synagogue once did house within its walls all of the activities of the community. But we know that this is not possible in Judaism today.

"Intermarriage" between Jews of Orthodox, Conservative, and Reform orientation is quite commonplace, so that we wonder whether such a "responsibility" as this really needs to be taken seriously. Moreover, religious Jews of the several movements have far more in common than Trainin appears willing to admit. The real division is between religionists and secularists, in our opinion.

Another, and less expected, line of argument was a spirited attack on synagogues and synagogue-centers themselves, apparently based on the assumption that some of the symposiasts ignore formidable motes in their own eyes. Most assuredly the Synagogue warrants at least as searching and dispassionate study, but it seems that the issues posed by the symposium on the essential character of American Jewish culture are hardly illuminated by comments such as these (again Trainin, but not untypical of others):

> First, it is unfortunate that religious life in America seems to have evolved a philosophy that God can be worshipped only in the multimillion dollar edifices. This means tremendous budgets with the accent put on fund-raising.
> Second, a great number of synagogue centers unwittingly have become catering paradises with the emphasis on gastronomical Judaism.
> Third, a very serious evil facing some synagogue centers is the emphasis on bingo, which is neither Jewish nor ethical in a house of God.
> Fourth, let us face the fact that there is a paucity of standards in Jewish

SYNAGOGUE AND CENTER — THE SYMPOSIUM IN RETROSPECT

education. More than a few rabbis seem to be lackadaisical toward their responsibility to take a greater interest in what is going on in their schools. One rabbi recently told me, that he hasn't visited his Talmud Torah in sixteen months. He leaves that problem entirely to the principal of the school and yet this school has 850 school children.

Fifth, let us be concerned with the great number of unaffiliated Jews. Even in suburbia where synagogue membership is relatively high, one is appalled by the tremendous number of Jewish families who do not affiliate with synagogues. In one Long Island community, there are four synagogues with a total membership of 2700 Jewish families. The total Jewish population in the community numbers 7500 Jewish families.

Sixth, we must be concerned with the religious orientation and practices of synagogue leadership. It is unfortunate that so many of them officially maintain the need for Kashruth and Sabbath observance, but in their personal lives disregard both. Recently I was invited to supper by a prominent synagogue leader. He was abashed that I would not eat with him in a treif restaurant.

Seventh, we must be concerned with the ignorance of synagogue leadership in the most fundamental aspects of Jewish history and tradition.

Eighth, let us not look away from the fact that in so many synagogue centers, the gyms are empty and the youth programs are deplorably run.

Nine, let us be concerned with such non-Jewish activities as card games in synagogues.

Ten, let us be concerned with the poor and minimum attendance at synagogue services.

Eleven, let us evaluate the number of non-religious programs conducted in synagogues which it is inherently not equipped to handle. Let us not fool ourselves—so many of the synagogal activities today add no value to the Jewish purpose of the synagogue.

Finally, we note a wholly unexpected line of defense, namely, that the Jewish Community ought to support Jewish Centers whether these centers serve Jews (let alone Judaism) or not. Samuel D. Freeman of the Jewish Center Lecture Bureau wrote, in a letter to *The Reconstructionist* of June 1, 1962, that the *Jewish community* ought to provide Centers as a part of its humanitarian obligation:

> I have read your editorial on Jewish Community Centers and I wonder: "Now that Jews have by and large moved away—having become full-fledged members of the affluent society," shall they now forget their own experience when they occupied the very same apartments now occupied by Puerto Ricans, Shall they say, "We are only concerned with our own needs, let the total community concern itself with Puerto Ricans?" Does education encompass study and learning or does it also include living what we learn? I submit that it is the concern of the synagogue to concern itself with a totally Jewish membership, but even there we find some of the more enlightened taking stands and considering issues which face the total community, and taking stands as Jewish institutions.
>
> As it happens the condition you describe is hardly characteristic of the national picture with regard to Centers, but those very few urban locations where this situation exists are hardly justification for the impression

you leave that what you describe is the current problem in Centers generally.

In those few Centers where Puerto Ricans are being served, Jews have an extremely valuable service they can render, for they too have gone through such a similar experience that they can set an example for the rest of the community in assisting the acculturation process of these newcomers and helping build a favorable image on the part of the rest of the community. And to do this as a Jewish institution is noteworthy. Israel with all of its problems still finds room, in true Jewish spirit, to aid the new emerging nations with their technical problems. They don't say "Let the UN do it."

Jewish values and specific Jewish interests still find a place in these Centers (you have but to visit the Educational Alliance on the East Side and the Hebrew Educational Society in Brownsville, to see this) but these Centers "live" their Jewishness by the way in which they contribute to the welfare of the total community. As you know there are still many Jews in urban settings who choose not to move to suburbia or who are economically unable to. The social scene is varied, varied for the Jew too, and the way in which he is served and educated varies with the setting. No blanket prescription will be effective for all Jews.

It is considerably easier to summarize the comments approving the viewpoint of the symposium *in toto,* as there were fewer of them. We cite one, that of the May, 1962, *Jewish Spectator*:

Jewish Community Centers no longer can fill any real need in the suburbs and in the smaller cities where Synagogue Centers and Temple Centers "have taken over." Instead of adjusting itself to these "sweeping sociological changes," the Jewish Community Center movement competes and duplicates by building Jewish Centers in communities where Jewish and recreational needs are adequately served. Many white elephant Jewish Centers dot the American landscape as monuments to a "rigid personality pattern" one would least expect in leaders with a "social work philosophy." If not for the elaborate "health club" facilities of these Centers, offered at a mere fraction of the cost of reducing courses at professional establishments, and the "baby sitters" services of the Center nursery schools and day camps, provided as an almost free gift to families who can well afford unsubsidized care for their young children, most Jewish Community Centers would stand deserted.

As for Jewish Community Centers in the "old neighborhoods" (and some "new neighborhoods") of the large cities, the majority now serve a predominantly non-Jewish clientele. It is certainly in harmony with Jewish ethics to succor the non-Jewish poor "together" with the Jewish poor. According to Jewish law, charity must be extended to all non-Jews who have no recourse to other assistance. It is eminently proper that the wards of Federation-supported Jewish hospitals in New York now care for more non-Jewish than Jewish patients (as the result of "sweeping sociological changes," Jews occupy semi-private and private rooms), but it is improper, we hold, that Jewish Federation support is extended to recreational programs in Jewish Centers with a predominantly non-Jewish clientele.

The Rabbinic contributors to the *Conservative Judaism* symposium are outspoken in their criticism of the un-Jewishness of the Jewish Community Centers, though not more so than Mr. Urbont. But this criticism is irrelevant since the Centers have become so unimportant in the total pattern of American Jewish living that it hardly matters what transpires in them, although it is of major concern to our community to put a halt to the waste of funds this entails.

The real issue at this juncture is not whether Jewish Community Centers offer or do not offer Jewish programs, in keeping with the recommendations of the Janowski Report, but whether there is altogether still a need for them. Rabbi Mordecai S. Halpern, reporting on the Detroit area, writes, in *Conservative Judaism,* that the new Jewish Center in his community (Oak Park, Mich.) "has not met with success. Apart from a few classes of the United Hebrew Schools that meet there, there is little to justify the building of this edifice." As in many other places, the Oak Park Jewish Community Center was "catapulted" upon the community. According to Rabbi Halpern, "often a community becomes aware of a new Center only *after* a Board of Directors has completed final plans for the building and the shovel is already in the ground."

It is frequently argued that the Jewish Community Centers are the only "non-denominational" ground where Jews can and do meet. Is this still true at a time when religious-ideological differences in American Judaism have almost disappeared, and when the Allied Appeals of the Federations and Welfare Funds have become the rallying place (and the rationale, alas) for most members of the Jewish community, not excepting the "secularists?" As we see it, the Jewish Center is no longer needed as a prop of awareness of "Klal Yisrael." The State of Israel, and work for Israel, is the force which now makes for unity in the American Jewish community. American Jewry has numerous organizational fossils. Organizations are still sending Matzoh to Israel, which is exporting Matzoh to this country, and organizations still plead for "food packages" to Israel containing the foods which Israel overproduces. The American Zionist Council and its constituents (except the Zionist Women's Organizations with "projects" in Israel) provide another melancholy exhibit in the growing collection of American Jewish fossils in which the Jewish Community Centers are now the most costly item.

The *Congress Biweekly* (May 14, 1962) added:

We have had increasing occasion to note the mounting evidence of religious, cultural and educational advances in the American Jewish community. While all the various manifestations of this most welcome phenomenon do not yet add up to that Renaissance so crucial to what is generally termed "creative Jewish survival," the signs do afford a measure of encouragement. More children than ever before are receiving a Jewish education. More books on Jewish themes are being published and hopefully, being read. Adult education courses everywhere are drawing an enthusiastic response. The synagogue, of course, is enjoying a well-publicized revival. And finally, more and more American Jews are being exposed, through their organizational affiliations and commitments, to the intellectual treasures of the Jewish storehouse.

A prominent holdout to the general trend is the Jewish Center movement which, by and large (there are notable exceptions, of course), restricts its services to the recreational and the athletic. Now, basketball, dramatics and the like are certainly fine in themselves, building character, broadening the personality and accommodating the leisure of both youth and adults. The question, however, persists whether such a limited, hardly specialized range of activities is justified by institutions calling themselves *Jewish* Centers. To be sure, the Jewish Centers helped fill an important function *in their time,* aiding in the Americanization and integration of immigrant Jews. But that was decades ago. The Jewish Centers, the critics argue, must begin to seek a new role to satisfy the new needs of third-generation American Jews.

While we share many of the views of the Conservative rabbis regarding the shortcomings of the Jewish Centers, yet we do not agree that Center and Synagogue be made synonymous in name and function. Diversity is still an ideal to be cherished; and the Jewish Center, like the Synagogue, will always have a place in the community spectrum. There are still Jews who will not join a synagogue but will join a center. Such Jews can be neither ignored nor neglected. Nor can responsible Jewish leadership abdicate its responsibility to them, particularly to the youth.

The task, therefore, of our leaders, lay as well as rabbinic, is to keep urging a new course upon the Jewish Centers, one that gives primacy to Jewish values of the spirit and intellect. This, of course, is no easy task. Center boards of directors must be persuaded; funds must be made available; a corps of center-workers qualified to carry out the new program must be trained; fresh attitudes must take hold. Can we dare to hope that some day—soon—those Jews, young and old, who come to the Jewish Centers to play will remain, so to speak, to pray?

In the group of comments which we characterized as "dialogic" one must include the thoughtful remarks of Philip Slomovitz in the Detroit J*ewish News* of May 11, 1962. Slomovitz recognizes that the discussion is not purely ideological, but touches upon the matters of budget and prestige, for which men are willing to shed blood. He points to the problems that would follow the "re-Judaization" of Centers:

> This immediately marks an exit from ideological discussion on the very vital Center issue. We must commence the search for a solution to this vital problem by securing a general agreement that Jewish Center programs must be thoroughly Jewish in content. It is subject to question whether it can be turned into a religious agency. If that becomes our aim, then we shall have to reckon with the secularist element in Jewry—and that group, while it may have diminished in numbers, has not vanished completely. The fact is that in our own Center there functions an educational group that substitutes an activity of its own for the Hebrew and Sunday schools. It provides a minimum of Jewish knowledge to its children, but it persists in its secularist ideas. Would we eliminate such a group from Jewish life by demanding that it should accept the four- or five-day Jewish school, thereby driving them out entirely from communal participation?
>
> On the basis of Rabbi Halpern's appeal, what are we to say to Jews who desire to support the Center in its present form of sponsoring minimalized Jewish programming and who "tolerate" the priorities given to the overall educational system which receives allocations even larger than those made to the Center? What are we to say to the group—small as it

may be—that is still antagonistic to Israel and Israeli institutions, but which concurs in gifts to Israel in order that their own hobbies that are included in the Allied Campaigns should be cared for?

Are we prepared for a complete revamping of our communal structure and a total revision of fund-raising procedures so that each contributor may be free to select the cause he favors while he rejects what he disapproves? Doesn't that threaten the shattering of the existing all-inclusive campaign machinery which has existed for more than 30 years?

A good beginning has been made through current discussions and studies to make the Jewish Centers genuinely Jewish, to encourage Jewish content in programming, to strive for a revitalized spiritual Jewish existence. But in doing so let us also keep in view the truth that synagogues, too, are also guilty of transgressing in sponsoring programs that often fail to reach the high standards we must always aim for. A local synagogue group only recently conducted a fund-raising event that was marked by low level entertainment.

The Synagogue, too, must look to its laurels. Its traditional status as a Beth Tefilah and Beth Medrash—as a house of study and as a house of learning—has diminished. Some synagogues have difficulty enrolling daily minyanim, and in studying improvements in our Jewish contents we must consider the needs of all institutions, the Synagogue as well as the Center. This is said only for the sake of indicating that even the religiously-oriented elements in our community are not guiltless in their programming. Therefore we must be realistic. The major claim, in the Conservative Juda- merely a fun-providing agency, that it functions to make available sport and sociability facilities, and that it is otherwise un-Jewish in spirit and in content. Therefore, what are we to do? Close up the Centers and tell those who use its facilities to go to the synagogue? It is admitted that most people already are affiliated with the Synagogue. Are we, therefore, to tell those who seek sociability and fun and sports to go to the YMCA? Or, will the Synagogue install gymnasiums and swimming pools to fill the need? We have just spent more than $3,000,000 for the functioning Detroit Jewish Center. Should we put it up on the auction block and say we have washed our hands with the Center Idea in Jewish life?

That would hardly be reasonable. No community is prepared to abandon its Center or Centers and to transfer everything in the established community gathering place to the Synagogues. Therefore, admitting that in searching for faults we have found them, the solution lies in cures, in making the available facilities effectively Jewish, while at the same time retaining their traditional American links, so that the existing social-recreational agency will be a source of pride for Jewry.

Criticism is good for the soul. Now let us utilize it for the perfecting of our communal spiritual structures. It would be sheer folly to try to make of the Center a scapegoat that would in the end result in a complete split in whatever communal unity exists in American Jewry. Make the Center more Jewish and let it be utilized for the highest ideals in Jewish life. Perhaps it is possible, even in the midst of a struggle between Synagogue and Center, to perfect so cooperative a spirit between the two that it will effectuate the noblest aspirations of a culturally productive communal program.

Comments in a similar spirit were made by the Connecticut *Jewish Ledger* on May 31, July 19, and July 26, 1962:

... The Center has served great purposes; and it can once again. But at the present time, some centers in some places destroy Jewish values rather than to sustain and to realize them ...

For example, a Jewish Center which conducts a completely profane program on the Sabbath day does not build the American Jewish community, but destroys one of its central institutions. Yet there are Centers which make no effort to recognize the existence, let alone the sanctity, of the Sabbath. When Jewish youth, coming from the synagogue school and given the impulse to participate in Jewish activities by the synagogue, witness such activities, they must learn that the Sabbath is not taken seriously by the Jewish community and hence may be violated as it is in the Center. It is this kind of destruction of Jewish values that was criticized in *Conservative Judaism*.

... We believe that the Jewish community center may be, and in some areas, is in fact, one of the most effective and constructive means or building truly Jewish lives in the American Jewish community. We hold that Centers carry out programs that cannot be effectively done by any other institution, and serve unique and vital functions. We believe that the Center may be as sacred and consecrated an instrument as the synagogue itself in the realization of the ideals of Judaism. We also think that some centers are presently not sacred but profane, and terribly, unnecessarily destructive of Judaism.

The issue is simply whether every Jewish community needs a Jewish center or YMHA or not. Surely many, including ours, do. But we wonder whether it is a matter of doctrine, or a dogma of the faith, that wherever there are Jews, there must necessarily be a Jewish center, as in truth there must be a synagogue.

In one particular area, the YMHA and Federation invested close to a half-million dollars in a large tract of land for a new center building. This land was purchased secretly, so that the half-dozen neighboring congregations, Reform, Orthodox, and Conservative, were uninformed and unconsulted. So we are told by a rabbi in the neighborhood.

The excuse for the new project was an allegedly scientific study made by "professionals." This study, of leisure time facilities available to a rather wealthy suburb, similar to Westchester or Fairfield counties in average income, concluded that insufficient leisure time facilities existed in this area, and hence a center was required.

In the survey, however, none of the local synagogues or rabbis was consulted. No questions were asked about available synagogue facilities, or about youth activities, young adult programs, etc. Apparently some "scientists" do not consider the program of the synagogues to be part of "leisure time" facilities; nor do they take seriously the "leisure time" value either of Jewish study or of Jewish worship.

It seems to us that it is ludicrous to build a Center where it may not be wanted or needed; or to plan a center where its services are in part superfluous (country clubs exist in the suburbs under discussion), or duplicate presently available and successful programs of a variety of synagogues and temples.

It seems to us that it is either irresponsible or simple-minded to plan such a center without study and fair evaluation of all local facilities and leisure time activities.

It seems to us that it is undemocratic to carry out such plans secretly and surreptitiously.

The continuing discussion of the relationship between the Jewish community center movement and the American synagogue has emphasized the need for mutual cooperation. Indeed, the rabbis have been criticized bitterly for daring to raise some rather basic questions about centers' goals and purposes. But these questions should be answered precisely and honestly, and those who have raised them should be admitted to a gentlemanly and respectful dialogue. We fail to see how this story illustrates the desire of some Center officials for democratic cooperation, open-minded discussion of common concerns, and mutual respect.

The same question was discussed by Herbert Millman in his article cited above:

> A section of Rabbi Schulweis' article is devoted to questioning the validity of support of the Center by central community funds as against the non-support of the synagogue and other organizations. He bases his position in part on the thesis that the Center as an autonomous body should receive its financial support solely from those who believe in it.
> There are substantially well-defined criteria employed by Jewish federations and other central financing bodies which are applied to decisions around appropriateness of support. The emergence of the Jewish Community Center as an agency of the total Jewish community reflects the field's progressive acceptance of these criteria.
> For one, it is general today that the decision to establish a new Center or to replace an existing one is a community decision, involving federations and representatives of different points of view in the community. Rabbis have been active on survey committees to determine the need for a Center and what its program should be. Community planning and reevaluation is a process which is normal to social agencies. Contrari-wise, in a pluralistic society, it is expected that synagogues and churches become organized and supported as groups develop the will to do so.
> Another criterion met by the Center is the inclusive character of its membership and leadership. By definition, membership is open to Jewish individuals of all shades of opinion. Similarly, Center boards are representative of different points of view. On the other hand, to the writer, who has been an active synagogue lay volunteer for many years, commitment to the branch of Judaism represented by his synagogue is *aleph* in the profile of a suitable board member (along with regularity of worship, participation in learning, willingness to serve on one or more committees, willingness to provide and obtain financial support and ability to participate intelligently in board deliberations).
> A third is financial accountability. A quid pro quo for central support is attesting to the expenditure of funds on an agreed-upon basis through periodic reports to federations and other bodies representing the stewardship of the total Jewish community. Such accountability goes beyond finances alone, but also includes a review of program and consultation in connection with the establishment of new services. Whether synagogues should or would submit to such review is a basic question that must be answered, if they are to seek community support in general. The writer notes that Rabbi Schulweis refers particularly to the school aspects of the

synagogue's program in warranting community support. This is certainly an area that merits, and is receiving consideration, in some cities, through bureaus of Jewish education and other instrumentalities.

By and large, Centers are seeking to fulfill their function as agencies of the total community. In this regard, as in others, progress is substantial in some cities and relatively laggard in others.

As to the symposium itself: it was frequently criticized for raising the issues it did, and the motives of the symposiasts were questioned. In some places, the writers were accused of "making a power play," and in others, of sinning by asking embarassing questions in public and by "unstatesmanlike" editorial policy (*Reconstructionist*). To such comments, Rabbi Jack J. Cohen (former rabbi of the Society for the Advancement of Judaism) may have been referring in his *Jerusalem Post* article of June 22nd:

> The debate should be joined, because the controversy is more than a competition between institutions, indigenous to American Jewry, for the support of the Jewish community. It touches at the heart of the spiritual problems that beset American Jewry. How is American Jewry to be organized so that its differing ideologies do not disrupt its unity? How are the secular and religious aspects of Jewish life to be treated institutionally and educationally? How can Jewry provide for the Jewish background and commitment of its civil servants? The answer to these and similar questions calls for sweeping changes in both the center and the synagogue.

To this we may add: what price Jewish unity? Are embarassing questions to be stifled, are abuses and corruptions to be ignored in the name of "Jewish unity"? Slomovitz's questions are troubling, but for that very reason, should not be ignored but answered. The answers may not be any more pleasing than the alternatives they themselves will pose, but surely the editors of *Conservative Judaism* would have done a disservice by ignoring the unJewish character of too many Centers, the profanation of the Sabbath in too many (one is too many, and there are more than one), the anti-religious and atheistic attitude of too many social and group workers who influence Jewish youth today, and the entirely plausible possibility that communal funds are being wasted.

We refer, finally, to the essay "Wasting Communal Funds" by Dr. Esra Shereshevsky (former Education Consultant to the Joint Distribution Committee and present Consultant for Secondary Education and Assistant Professor of Rabbinics and Hebrew at Graetz College, Philadelphia) and published in the May, 1962, issue of the *Jewish Spectator,* in which the author describes the center-versus-Jewish-education struggle for priority in communal funds on an international scale, and its tragic consequences.

> With the launching of every UJA Campaign the drama and tragedy of Jewish existence in many lands is projected anew. The Jewish tragedy, however, is not only one of precarious physical existence and threatened Jewish continuity. Judaism is fundamentally a religious civilization predicated on education. The news from North Africa and the South of France is disquieting indeed. But the severe spiritual and cultural crisis faced by

the North African immigrants in France is no less a cause for worry. Reared in an atmosphere of Jewish tradition and strong family ties, they are suddenly flung into the secularist culture of France. Jewish life in France is attenuated and the Jewish educational system is feeble. As a result, many of the new Jewish refugees fall victim to missionaries and Communist propaganda. The extent of mixed marriages among the new immigrants has reached high proportions.

Why is the French Jewish Community, the largest of Continental Western Europe so ill prepared for the absorption of refugees? For many years the American Joint Distribution Committee has been pouring into the French Jewish Community about $1,000,000 annually to cover two-thirds of the yearly budget of the local Community Organization. Of this sum $320,000 are ear-marked for "Jewish Education and Culture." In the last ten years, millions of dollars have thus been placed at the disposal of the French Jewish community. Yet, only 10% of all Jewish children in France obtain any kind of Jewish education. The French Community Organization, (Fond Social Juif Unife) is neither equipped for nor interested in Jewish education. Why then, is *this* group used as the body through which "Joint" Funds are channelled for Jewish education in France? Who keeps an eye on the proper use of the funds? For years the FSJU has been requested to set up a communal agency for Jewish education to which "Joint" is ready to give professional and technical aid, and for years this request has been "postponed." In the meantime, the French Jewish educational system and facilities move from bad to worse. The total number of children attending FSJU-controlled schools (day schools and supplementary) does not exceed 2500. The physical conditions of the schools are appalling. Light and ventilation are insufficient, facilities for relaxation are practically nonexistent. There are no curricula, text books and training facilities for teachers. The monthly wages of a supplementary Jewish school teacher are $35.

The bulk of the funds earmarked for Jewish education in France is spent in Metropolitan Paris. The country communities are neglected, although it is there that the poorer Jews and many refugees from North Africa have settled. FSJU is not interested in the small and poor communities as very little income for other FSJU projects can be expected from them. Marseilles, now the second largest Jewish community on the Continent of Europe, has neither adequate Jewish educational facilities for its own children nor for those of the refugees who settled there. When three years ago a group of Marseilles Jews applied to the FSJU for help for the construction of a Day School for 200 children, who were ready to enter such a school at once, their application was ignored and rejected. At the same time, large sums were spent for lavish Community Centers. In Lyons, a five-story modern Jewish Community Center remained locked for three years, while a stone's throw away children were attending Hebrew School in a dilapidated garage. All attempts to get some rooms in this Center for a few hours a week were blocked. In Paris a million-dollar Jewish Community Center is now being planned under the auspices of FSJU, while Hebrew Schools occupy cellars.

"Joint" and the small contributions of the French Jewish Community are however not the only financial sources for Jewish education and culture in France. The Jewish Claims Conference, too, has made sizable allocations. In France all applications for Claims Conference Funds are screened by the Cultural Committee of the FSJU, prior to anrsmission to the Rapporteur of the Claims Conference in New York. The Cultural Committee is primarily an arena for politics. The meetings are tugs of war of personal power politics rather than sessions devoted to an evaluation of the applications. Year after year the Claims Conference and their Rapporteur have been appraised of this shame—and year after year the Claims Conference has made allocations without attempting to see to their proper use. Year after year the Rapporteur of the Claims Conference visits France and other countries, only to return to New York with the most unsound and unprofessional recommendations.

The French Jewish Community Organization has proven itself incapable and unwilling of assuming the responsibility for the education of their youth. It stands to reason, then, that the Claims Conference should have enlisted other organizations in France for reconstructing Jewish cultural and educational life. But this is not the case. On the contrary, a few efforts by some sincere groups and individuals are stifled by chicaneries. Thus one regulation stipulates that any capital investment project for Jewish education requires at least 50% of financial participation by the applicant or sponsor. As a result, children of communities that cannot raise their 50% share are taught in out-of-repair buildings or left without Jewish education at all. For years the only Jewish Day School in Brussels could not receive a Claims Conference allocation because the Jewish Community of Brussels was unable to raise its 50% quota of the building costs. At the same time, the Jewish Community of Brussels received the total amount for the construction and equipment of a lavishly equipped Jewish Community Center, while Claims Conference allocations, earmarked for the Jewish education of children who live in about 100 widely scattered villages in Belgium, was cancelled because the Brussels Jewish Community could not raise its share of the budget. Many similar examples could be cited. The saddest case of all is that of the Jewish Day School in Marseilles where the Claims Conference demanded a substantial contribution from a poor and struggling community. Finally a compromise seems to have been found by accommodating the Jewish Day School classes in the new Jewish Community Center.

The request of the Claims Conference for local participation is defended by the fact that German Funds will not be available forever (until 1965). Communities must be "educated" to assume their own responsibilities so as to be prepared for the years following the cessation of Claims Conference Funds. What utter non-understanding of educational needs! Yet, while Jewish education languishes, a little empire of Jewish Community Centers, financed by the social welfare arm of the Claims Conference and equipped with the latest gadgets of the American and European entertainment industry, has sprung up. These centers are to attract the Jewish teen-agers and young couples for leisure-time activities in a Jewish atmosphere. But who looks to Jewish content in these Centers? The FSJU has little concern and less acumen for this task. Millions of dollars have been channelled by the social welfare department of the Claims Conference through the FSJU for the construction of Community Centers, but the Claims Conference has done nothing to insure that these Centers are not 'amusement places' but bases of some Jewish religious and cultural values.

Another area where much valuable Jewish education work could be performed are the summer camps. About 6000 children attend approximately

50 Jewish summer camps in France. More Jewish children can be reached through these camps than through the Jewish schools. "Joint" subsidizes most of these camps through the FSJU and the Claims Conference has allocated about $55,000 as a subsidy for an experimental summer camp at Herbey, near Grenoble. In most of these camps, however, kosher food is not available and there is no Jewish educational program. To meet the shortage of properly trained personnel for the French-Jewish summer camps, some French-speaking American Jewish students volunteered as counselors without pay. Only transportation costs were requested. The project is still awaiting approval . . .

Another organization concerned with the education of Jewish youth in France is ORT. Some 40,000 teenagers, principally of North African origin, receive vocational training in the ORT schools. Many of these youngsters are separated from their families. It is deeply disturbing that no Jewish education whatsoever is provided for these young people who mostly stem from traditional families. Three years ago Dr. Azriel Eisenberg of the New York Jewish Education Committee was invited by ORT to conduct a survey of its institutions with a view to introducing and planning Jewish educational programs. The survey was completed under the most trying circumstances, at a time when it was already dangerous to visit certain areas in Algeria and Tunis. Suggestions were submitted but not acted upon. . . .

All of us willingly contribute to UJA. But with giving alone the duty of the contributor is not fulfilled. We also must see to it that the funds we provide be properly spent. Instead of permitting that large funds earmarked for reconstruction of Jewish life in Europe be handed over to community officials who are neither interested nor versed in the needs of Jewish education, we should insist that American organizations entrusted with the administration of these funds exert more control in the right direction.

In the end, the issue is how best to organize the community. Our contention has been that whatever *forms* the Jewish community may experiment with, the *substance* must always be the same, namely, the Jewish faith in all its ramifications and nuances. We gladly take issue with those who do not share our conviction that Judaism and Judaism alone must hold the central and dominant position in every Jewish undertaking. The alternative is illustrated in a mundane sense by the situation in French Jewry described by Shereshevsky. The alternative in an ultra-mundane sense is unthinkable.

THE PASSING OF JEWISH SECULARISM IN THE UNITED STATES

HERBERT PARZEN

Conscientious secularists in the American Jewish community are faced with a dual impasse: in separating themselves categorically from the Synagogue —the basic institution of the historical tradition as the inevitable instrument for the survival of organized Jewish life in America, they are committed to foster a substitute—a secular Jewish culture sufficiently resourceful to reward them with self-fulfillment and to assure group survival. This is no easy enterprise, especially in this country where the climate is not congenial to the task. The plain fact is that American civilization deprecates and discourages such ventures. Indeed, the dominant historical trend in this country is becoming progressively impatient with competing cultural patterns.

Secondly, while Jewish secularism was destined to flourish temporarily and artificially in this country it is now in the process of disintegration. Actually it is beyond therapy and can no longer serve as an agency for self-fulfillment and survival. The secularist remnant—comprising for the most part the middle-aged and the immigrants unable and unwilling to adapt themselves to reality—have substituted for their *Weltanschauung*, their life purpose, a nostalgic dream woven of the stuffs of past achievements. So they live in the past and despair of the future. At last they recognize what has been clear to most Jews for years— that American culture is unitary and national, by design and intent. The only exception is religion. And though there is a clear-cut contemporaneous tendency to de-emphasize this tradition, the separation of Church and States is, nevertheless, a regnant rule in American thought and life; it decisively directs, likewise by design and intent, that the religious phases of American civilization shall be diverse, discrete, and, necessarily, pluralistic. Thus, religious pluralism is the law of the land. Cultural pluralism, on the other hand, despite the conceit of a certain group of American intellectuals including Jews, has not taken root because it is not en rapport with the American historical pattern.

In this respect America is not incom-

Whether a native viable Jewish Secularism is possible, given American social conditions and mood, is a question on which a distinct shift of opinion towards the negative has taken place in the recent past. The author indicates the sources, ideological and social, of such secularist Jewish groups and their present plight. The rapprochement with the Synagogue on the part of some whilom secularist elements, the tentative gropings of others towards a more positive incorporation of the Tradition in their basic Jewish alignment, and the intransigence of still others, form an instructive and predictive picture of modern America Jewry in ideological transition.

parable to Western Europe. There modern nationalism as embodied and envisioned in the State has excluded competitive cultures and insisted that every citizen comply with the patterns of its culture as an integral part of his loyalty to the State. Consequently, the Jewish communities, during the stormy struggle for emancipation and enlightenment in the nineteenth century, achieved adjustment to the general social order on the primary basis of religious tolerance. That is to say, while every State has had an established or preferred church it also recognized non-conforming religious bodies, often with reluctance, as functioning institutions within the body politic. The Synagogue was, accordingly, the prime instrument of adjustment to modern life, and acknowledged as the center of Jewish loyalty and identification. Its internal dissents resulted, in the main, from theological differences, from conflicting conceptions of Judaism as an historical organism, and disagreement about the status of the Jewish people in the modern world. By and large, West European Jewish communities agreed that the language and the culture of the nations of which they were a part must be accepted, shared in and cultivated in addition and as part of political allegiance. This consensus explains why many Jews in those lands were affiliated with the *gemeinde* or *Kehillah*—religious organs in the eyes of the law—even though by conviction they remained outside of the Synagogue. It also accounts for the fact that in Western Europe up to the time of Theodor Herzl (the end of the 19th century) secularism was unknown as an organized force in Jewish life, as a programmatic goal of Jewish culture. Potential secularists there undoubtedly were; but they remained ineffectual. Since they had no constructive program for the preservation of Jewish communal existence they just drifted into assimilation. Only Zionism guided many of them to nationalism.

In Eastern Europe the situation was utterly different. Persecution of Jews was rife up to the Revolution of 1917 when they were "emancipated" by the Kerensky Government. Religious tolerance during the Czarist regime was unknown. For the church was not only established by law but was monolithic by ukase, and willingly supported, in its turn, the despotism of the Czars.

The result of this black reaction was the cohesion, in large measure, of the Jewish community; the determined stand of the Synagogue against all proposals for adjustment to modern life and thought, and its resistance to the modernization of its educational system. The status quo was upheld by the plea that even the most innocuous innovation would play into the hands of the Government, one that sought to destroy the Jews. So, Haskalah and subsequent manifestations of Jewish life, adapted to European cultural standards, were overtly indifferent or inimical to the Synagogue and, whether bourgeois or radical, passively opposed Czardom or entered upon open revolt. Thus, secular nationalism was born; it offered concrete programs not only for the adaptation of Jewish life to Western culture but also for the perpetuation and rejuvenation of Jewish society—without concern for the Synagogue, with anchorage in Jewish nationalism. While the language and culture of the dominant population were acquired by these people as a matter of course and for the sake of life itself, they demanded that the State as part of its constitutional function recognize Jewish

THE PASSING OF JEWISH SECULARISM

culture—Yiddish or Hebrew—and nationality, and actively enable them to flourish.

In due course, secular nationalism expressed itself in two viable viewpoints: Zionism and National-Cultural Autonomism or Galut nationalism. Zionism came to the fore because its adherents denied that Jewish nationalism could be sustained in any social order wherein Jews remain a minority; they, therefore, sought to create a Jewish state in the Land of the Fathers so that the Jewish people would constitute the majority population and fashion its own intrinsic civilization. Others, Marxists and middle class, insisted that cultural-national autonomy is entirely feasible in the lands of their domicile when guaranteed by a democratic and progressive social order. The historical fact is that all the positive parties—the Bund, the Folkists and the Zionists (with the exception of the Mizrachi) were secularists who formulated a constructive program for Jewish survival with manifold creative activities as a substitute for the traditional status quo of the Synagogue.

It is important to indicate that the assimilationists among East-European Jews were not secularists. They like the assimilationists of the West had no affirmative program for Jewish living to replace that of the Synagogue. Accordingly, secularists must be differentiated from assimilationists. The first planned to preserve Jewish peoplehood and its culture, the second sought absorption or "integration" in the dominant civilization.

Thus, Jewish secularism originated in Eastern Europe, and was imported to this country as part of the social baggage of East-European immigrants. Just as the religious newcomers proceeded to implement Judaism on American soil so the secularists moved to promote their secular Jewish culture. And, during the immigration epoch, they were successful due to compelling circumstances, independent and transcendent of ideologies. For the vast majority of immigrants, during the era of Americanization, were interested in fostering a friendly cultural atmosphere in order to feel "at home" in the new environment, and to assure themselves essential social and intellectual, recreational and esthetic satisfactions. As a matter of fact, all groups —religionist, secularist and indifferentist —shared, to a considerable extent, in the building of that cultural structure and were braced by its benefits. As the immigration wave waned and Americanization had its effects, that culture began to crumble; today it is a wraith.

For an initial period these masses were not expected to—nor could they— participate in American cultural enterprises. In time, as Americanization influenced the immigrants they voluntarily and, to a degree by pressure, began to shed their "greenness" for American coloration. Indeed, Jews were eager to become Americanized. They readily recognized that their economic wellbeing, social advancement and even family solidarity depended on the incisive impress of the Americanization processes.

As "Americanism" inundated immigrant life, transforming its patterns, imposing and inspiring imitation of American mores and ideas, habits and customs, the secularists—consciously or unconsciously—faced a critical and fundamental problem. They stood committed to the creation of a secular Jewish culture in this country and, at the same time, they became aware that their course countered the mainstream of American history.

During the immigration years the problem was sidestepped with ease, and with impunity. The stream of newcomers prolonged the need for the immigrant culture and restored the ranks depleted by Americanization. As the flow of incoming migrants diminished due to the First World War and its effects including the restrictive immigration legislation of 1922-24, and as the Americanization processes speeded up, the fate of Jewish secular culture assumed commandingly critical dimensions.

Simultaneously, the generation of secular culture builders among the immigrants aged and died. Their successors —whether their children or newcomers to this country—faced a different Jewish community, American and Americanized. As this community mastered the English language and accommodated itself to American civilization; as it imitated the popular patterns of American life; and as it conformed to the dominant syndromes of behavior, it increasingly satisfied its cultural, social and intellectual requirements in the general cultural surroundings, and forsook the immigrant cultural institutions. As the number of their adherents progressively diminished and increasingly slaked their intellectual interests from American sources, the leaders were unable to preserve the intensity and the color of the culture nor its position as a creative current in the community. Even the zealous secularists, who ignored the laws of American development which have evoked and enforced a national and homogeneous culture, felt frustrated. They found themselves in the unenviable role of shepherds whose flock was dying out despite their utmost care and watchfulness.

To-day this crisis is central. The effects of Americanization have been cumulative and have run their course. The offspring of the secularists are, in the main, second or third generation. The vast majority no longer patronize the cultural institutions—whatever shreds still exist—fostered by their forebears. They no longer use the Yiddish language nor read its press and literature, nor visit its theatre and music halls. They are Americans sharing in American culture and enriching it.

A recent letter, vivid and rather tragic, *In the Drama Mailbag*, of the New York Times, is to the point. The writer is the daughter of Annie Tomashefsky and a niece of Boris, former stars of the Yiddish stage, and a kinswoman of the Edelsteins—father and sons—erstwhile producers on Second Avenue. She writes: "Of recent years I have thought a great deal about the Yiddish theatre. "The Second Avenue" (the theatre by that name) has been out of the family's hands for a long time, and we are thankful that it is so. I was sad in the later years of its existence to walk in on a Saturday night and see a handful of actors struggling valiantly to create a make-believe world for an apathetic audience made up of people who were there simply because they had bought benefit tickets. On the other hand, it is good to know that the necessity for it no longer exists, that we American Jews no longer have the need to be entertained in a little corner set apart from the rest of the country by custom and language."

The trickle of newcomers since the end of the Second World War are powerless to retard the normative currents of Jewish living in the United States. A residue of the older secularists still guard the old ramparts as professionals, servicing institutions—many of them with provisions for eleemosynary and mortuary benefits—in use by recent immigrants and the last patrols of intellectual Yiddishists. Attempts have been made to buttress these organizations by encouraging the younger generation to organize English-speaking branches. Surely this is not the stuff from which culture emerges. It is rather a gesture of despair to hold on to a forlorn hope.

In order to perceive the perilous position of present-day secularists in the United States, it is essential to sketch in some detail their groupings and their dilemmas.

Among the General Zionists there survives a hard core that is secular-nationalist, the "old guard" leadership and a younger group of intellectuals, mostly European trained. Prior to the establishment of the State of Israel, in consonance with the doctrines of European Zionist theoreticians, with whom incidentally the notable American Zionist thinkers disagreed, their program was clear. The purpose of Zionism was to found a Jewish State in Palestine wherein the Jewish people could develop their Hebraic life untrammelled by an inimical environment. They, accordingly, negated the Exile: no Jewish community outside of the Yishuv was capable of survival, in the long run. Just as anti-Semitism, they argued, had driven Pinsker, Herzl, Nordau and their confreres to nationalism, almost immediately channelled into Zionism, to plan for a Jewish State wherein they would be rid of that perennial plague, so will the hate and contempt of the nations drive all self-respecting Jews to settle in that commonwealth, once established, for the sake of safety, freedom, and creative survival. There is no alternative for the manly Jew.

With the establishment of the State these secular Zionists, logically and psychologically, should have "gone up" to Israel. They declined to resettle. They have remained in Exile, voluntarily. They justify their refusal to "go up"— the duty of the leading Zionists if not of the rank and file, according to preponderant public opinion in Israel—by various arguments to the effect that they still have vital political and economic functions to perform on behalf of the State. The retort is simple: these functions have become the responsibility of the entire Jewish community, and it has actually assumed them, and not only of Zionists.

These Zionists, by choosing to remain in the *Golah*, have in effect abandoned their pre-state doctrinal position. Hence they are forced to search for a new set of principles to replace the old to justify their anchorage in the Diaspora, in the American Jewish community. Indeed, they confess that they are probing for a reinterpretation of Zionism to enable them, ideologically, to take part in the task to secure the permanence and the creative revival of Jewish life in this country. They plan for Zionism to take the lead in rallying American Jewry to a program which will impregnate Judaism in this country with creative impulse, with historical continuity, with an Hebraic framework and modern dynamism. They further grant that the revamped program must recognize that American Jews, by and large, are identified with the Synagogue and interpret that identification as their central Jewish loyalty and are, at the same time, firmly ranged at the side of Israel in the herculean effort to solve its complex of problems and to insure its integrity.

Recently, the Zionist Organization of America has taken steps to actualize this plan. To this end it has enlisted the help of Dr. Mordecai M. Kaplan, the founder of Reconstructionism and in many respects the outstanding interpreter of Judaism in this country. He has accepted the chairmanship of a Commission to prepare studies for a course of action. It will necessarily approximate the ideas which he developed in his *New Zionism* —the unity of the Jewish people requires a definition of its relationship to Israel and the Diaspora; the religious character of the Jewish civilization must be recognized to achieve Jewish survival in America as throughout the *Golah*; Jewish religion must be revitalized to make the Jewish civilization dynamic and relevant to modern society; the Hebraic framework of the Jewish civilization must be reenforced with the help and influence of Israel, and finally, under these circumstances, Jewry will flourish and be spiritually creative. At all events, the Miami Convention of the ZOA, in October 1958, instructed the incoming Administration to give attention and consideration to the work of Professor Kaplan's Commission. Obviously, the moment this sort of Zionist platform is projected secular nationalism is repudiated together with its concomitant corollary of negating the Diaspora.

The Labor Zionists (Poalei Zion) have constituted, in the past, a strong organized secular segment in the community. Their historical program, an amalgam of Socialism and Zionism, proposed a democratic Socialist society in the contemplated commonwealth; as Zionists they pledged themselves to settle there in order to build it with their brains and brawn. Their life in the *Galut* was conceived as a sort of preparatory period for *halutziut* in the Yishuv.

With the cumulative effects of the Americanization processes on the younger generation and the founding of the State, the Party has faced a number of the same problems which has confronted the secular General Zionists. While the last of the immigrant leaders are dying out, or retiring to Israel, the rest, certainly the major portion, have been attracted by the allurements of American life. They are content to remain in America and there has been no rush to "go up" even by those American leaders of Labor Zionism though Ben Gurion as well as the Mapai Party deem this country "exile" and urge "aliyah." So, the ideology of the party in the United States is of necessity undergoing pragmatic revision, though formally it is a reluctant revision. As part of this adjustment a goodly number of its adherents have affiliated with the Reconstruction movement; others have joined the staid synagogues. Their children, in considerable numbers, receive the routine religious education in nonparty schools. Even the party schools are teaching traditional concepts and observances in accordance with the *mores* of American Jewry.

In fact, the Labor Zionist constituency, like most groupings in the Jewish community, has imitated the American abhorrence of strictly-defined ideologies and party discipline. It, accordingly, is no longer ideology-minded, class-conscious or party-partisan. A substantial segment, if not a substantial majority, of the membership of the Farband, the Pioneer Women and, to a somewhat lesser extent, of Poale Zion itself, consists of stereotype American Jews—neither secularists nor Socialists and certainly not Marxists; their Zionism is as pallid as that of the General Zionists. In sum, their behaviour patterns and social attitudes differ little from other American Jews. Enrollment in these organizations is not unlike the membership-procuring processes in other Jewish or American societies or orders—through friends or accident. Ambitious "joiners" prefer them because of the comparative ease with which it is possible to forge to the front, to gain recognition and assume leadership. Another attraction is undoubtedly the glamor accruing to these organizations because of their official association with the governing party in Israel, augmented by the opportunity to mingle on occasion with Israeli emissaries and Histadrut representatives.

As indicated, the ideologues continue to theorize that the Diaspora including the United States must be considered Exile and as such negated—with the consequence that Jewish life outside of Israel is, inevitably from a long-term viewpoint, impermanent. But they have realistically designed and approved a pragmatic program that, excepting the specific interests in organized labor and the special relations with Histadrut and Mapai in Israel, is so viable and inclusive that large sections of American Jewry of various shades of opinion—excluding the American Council for Judaism and the Orthodox religionists—can affirm it without scruple.

Historical necessity forces the party to declare in its platform its rededication "to organize American Jewish participation in *Kibbutz Galuyot* by steadily increasing *aliya* to Israel, and its loyalty to the "concept of *halutziut*." All Zionist parties in this country assert the desirability of these ideas!

Essentially, however, the program seems to negate secularism and follows, in certain respects, the lead of Reconstructionism. A few details are in order: The Labor Zionist is urged "to belong to at least one major local institution, such as a *synagogue* (italics supplied) community center, etc. . . . to send his children to a Jewish school; if at all possible to a private Jewish day school." His home should have "a Jewish atmosphere—Jewish books, art and symbolic (ritual) objects should occupy a prominent place" in its decor. Please note: "The observance of Jewish holidays, the practice of Jewish customs, the singing of Jewish songs, and discussion of Jewish subjects should be an important feature in his family life." Obviously, the sting of secularism is blunted.

Moreover, Labor Zionism is committed "to strengthen Jewish group life in America by constant attention and devotion to Jewish education... "And is dedicated to the building of Jewish morale and self-respect and to the promotion of affirmative Jewish living everywhere."

More than that—the party "aims to advance the moral standards and add to the human dignity of the Jewish individual both as a Jew and as a citizen of his native land. It seeks to improve the cultural, social and economic status of all Jewish communities and that of the lands of which they are a part."[1] The Exile is expected to be quite permanent!

In summary, it is no exaggeration to

---

[1] See the pamphlet "Labor Zionism in America" by C. Bezalel Sherman, published by Labor Zionist Organization of America—Poale Zion, New York.

insist that Labor Zionism in this country has undergone definite Americanization in the sense that it tends to be indistinguishable from middle class Jews, though perhaps a mite more liberal in economic and social affairs. It is an American brand of Poale Zionism which decisively differs from the doctrines of Mapai, Mapam or Ahdut Avodah, the three Socialist parties in Israel. Obviously, Labor Zionism plans to function indefinitely in America; it is encouraging interest in and loyalty to the religious tradition; it accepts the Synagogue as an institution of personal Jewish identification; it has gone a long way toward abandoning its secular character. And America certainly in practice, is no longer Exile; the Jewish community is not negated; it is urged to plan for permanence.

Another secularist group, largely radical or Marxist in its social orientation and Yiddishist in its cultural outlook, is clustered about the Jewish Labor Committee and its cognate social and cultural associations. The Committee is a "defense" organization presumably speaking in the name of the Jewish trade unions, of the Jewish "working class." It "aids Jewish and non-Jewish labor institutions overseas; it helps victims of oppression and persecution and seeks to combat anti-Semitism and religious intolerance abroad and in the United States in cooperation with organized labor and other groups." The cultural organs affirm "nationhood without Jewish statehood," are opposed to "assimilation" and promote "secular Yiddish culture and the Yiddish language."

One historical datum must be noted which accentuates the doctrine of "Jewish nationalism without a Jewish state."

In September 1943, at the initial session of the American Jewish Conference—the organ that mobilized Jewish organized opinion in this country for unified action with regard to the problems which confronted World Jewry as a result of the Second World War—the Jewish Labor Committee abstained from voting on the Palestine resolution calling for the establishment of a Jewish Commonwealth. Subsequently, the Jewish Labor Committee joined the American Jewish Committee in withdrawing from the Conference. This action scuttled the Conference, to all intents and purposes.

In sum, these secularists constitute the remnant of Yiddish intellectuals in this country: journalists, artists, scholars, whose stem is rooted in the ideology of the "Bund"—an East-European Jewish revolutionary party dating back to the Czarist regime. Its classic program, as indicated, proposed the overthrow of the Romanov dynasty and the establishment of a Socialist state in which there would be provisions for national cultural autonomy in its Yiddish frame of reference for the Jewish people. This party was liquidated in Russia after the Bolshevik Revolution. It wielded considerable influence in the turbulent in-between-the-wars era in Poland. After the Second World War, a number of these people came to the United States as refugees. They have fortified intellectually and socially the remnant of their American confreres.

Though historically the "Bund" combatted Zionism, its members, with the founding of the State of Israel, have become non-Zionists, more precisely, pro-Israel. Accordingly, the Jewish Labor Committee has joined the informal association of the presidents of the sixteen major American national organizations, under the aegis of the Jewish Agency, for the purpose of assuring the security and the integrity of Israel and counteracting Arab propaganda in this country. Though they have made peace with the existence of the State they are troubled and critical because of the neglect of the Yiddish language and culture in Israel.

They seem to be unaware that history has passed them by, has defeated them. Yet, consciously or unconsciously, they cannot surrender or submit to the inevitable. Despite their persistence and determination, their way of life is fading out, and is becoming an eccentric and an esoteric phenomenon in the Jewish community. They refuse to recognize that the course of history has overrun Yiddish culture in this country because it could be no more than an adjunct of the immigration epoch. Since creative achievements are indestructible, Yiddish culture is all too rapidly becoming an historical monument. Its custodians constitute an indomitable band of "romanticists" who encourage each other, console each other, and together lament their destiny. As for their influence on the contemporary Jewish community it may truly be said that it hardly ripples the surface.

In the interim there has developed in this country a native brand of Jewish intellectualism that is often designated secularist because it is decidedly hostile to the Synagogue. It has for the most part, been nourished in the avant-garde climate of American intellectualism and bears its mark.

If Jewish secularism denotes a movement that seeks to provide an alternative or substitute for religionism these people cannot be placed in the secular category at all. For they have not formulated a program for Jewish living nor proposed an imaginative idea with power to inspire the creative survival of the Jewish community. We have seen that East European Jewish secularism and the immigrants who brought it to the New World presented such programs and proposed such ideas.

This new order of Jewish "secularists" tends to resemble in part the West-European Jewish intellectuals of the nineteenth century—before Theodor Herzl appeared on the scene. They, too, were opposed to the Synagogue and held aloof from the constructive currents coursing through the Jewish community. Because they were indifferent to Jewish strivings for survival and had no proposals for Jewish creativeness, they necessarily remained unorganized for Jewish purposes. On the other hand, they depended on European civilization for the satisfaction of their cultural needs and, in turn, enriched it with their talents. With the resurgence of anti-Semitism in the last decades of the nineteenth century they were content to join the liberal political parties in the hope to stem it or to affiliate with Marxist organizations in the belief that the contemplated New Order would have no room for racial and national hatreds.

Our American Jewish intellectuals are, in fact, neither secularists nor assimilationists in the historical sense. They reject assimilation because it evokes a heinous and banal image. Recognizing the error of classical assimilationists who drifted into desertion of their spiritual heritage and abandonment of their cultural patrimony, they prefer to be known as integrationists. They adhere to a kind of "ethnicism," a biological survival, with stress on group security, without concern for the fate of the historical values of the Jewish people. They, accordingly, aim to transform themselves into integers in the American culture. To this end, they emphasize the preservation of Jewish rights and the enhancement of human equality at home and abroad. Their primary purpose is to preserve the position won by emancipation and the status acclaimed by enlightenment.

Inevitably, this type of life-philosophy is sterile and not conducive to intellectual or spiritual self-esteem. Hence, of late, a number of these intellectuals, after harsh experiences as a result of anti-Semitism and bitter disappointment with the personal freedoms in their attempts to become "integrated" in the radical milieu of their first choice, have returned to the Jewish fold for self-fulfillment. As a result of their frustrations and accompanying traumata they desperately want the "home" environment to be therapeutic. That is not an easy task because, basically, they have remained unresponsive and inimical to middle-class culture and the Jewish community is middle-class. Consequently, some hesitatingly explore existing institutions with which to affiliate in the hope that they would prove at least minimally satisfying; numbers prefer to remain on the periphery, perplexed and egocentric, hyperagnostic and in conflict; others have unreservedly selected to become associated with Judaism.

It is understandable that a goodly percentage are attracted to Reconstructionism for several reasons. One, it is undeniably a rational and intellectual discipline. Two, it teaches that American Jews need to learn to live in both the American and Jewish civilizations—a distinctive form of "integrationism." Three, Reconstructionism recognizes secularists as a legitimate grouping in the American Jewish community. And four, its religious *Anschauung* is devoid of supernaturalism; it is naturalistic and humanist. Accordingly, they are not subjected to an organic contradiction with their makeup.

Nevertheless, a segment of them, after scrutiny and study, has rejected Reconstructionism because of its doctrine that Judaism is a religious civilization and its contention that the survival of Judaism in the Diaspora is dependent upon the beneficent influence of Israel. This group cannot become reconciled to religion and Zionism, however construed.

Indeed, not a small percentage ignore the religious and the Zionist significations of Reconstructionism, and remain within its ranks. Theirs is, thus, the typical attitude of American Jews—derived from the American environment—not to emphasize the ideological content of organizations or movements of which they are a part. In this respect they resemble middle class Jews and, more generally, the middle-class in the United States.

Those who are still in the process of exploring Judaism and are not yet ready to become committed to any institution prefer the role of the critic. They appear to recognize the Synagogue as the religio-cultural institution of the community and its potentialities for improving the cultural calibre of Jewish life. Their criticisms, on the sidelines, seem to suggest that the Synagogue at present is stuffy and levelling; it lacks the strength and the dynamism to foster a creative culture. Apparently, they expect the Synagogue to conform, somehow, to their specifications. In the interim they plan to watch, to observe and criticize from the outside. They are unable or unwilling—is it lack of courage?—to aid in the realization of their expectations from within. Since life refuses to function and certainly cannot thrive in a vacuum, they are left with their *"credenda"* and carpings; and they remain alienated, without moorings.

The more emotional and venturesome have accepted Orthodoxy. They are the penitent, the mystics and the cravers of unquestioned orderliness in life. They are weary of rationalism and intellectualism. They have turned to religion in a desperate attempt to attain a secure and saving anchorage. Feeling betrayed by reason and self-reliance, they lean on the irrational and the supernatural. Thereby they want to erase from memory or the sub-conscious the "broken reeds" on which they hitherto relied. Quite naturally, they feel that the salvation for which they hunger inheres in the opposite extreme to the one which they formerly acknowledged. They are, therefore, prepared for the "leap in the dark."

As for the rest they remain "integrationists" without the means of attaining a soteric standpoint, goal or aim. Despite the fact that their experience has demonstrated the folly and futility of not facing reality, they persist in pursuing a phantom, unable to cope with what faces them. Affiliating with one or another of the existing "defense" groups or campaign organizations may give scope to their talents but not to their need of "belonging." Judging by their writings they have not found the *gemütlichkeit* inherent in spiritual anchorage, nor are they likely to. Their "activities", by their very nature, cannot earn self-fulfillment. So they live in a sort of no-man's land, on the periphery of Jewish life and on the margin of American culture, discontented, dismayed, disjointed.

History, as a rule, is faithful to its organic forces and dynamic currents. In the long run, it ignores the romantic fancies of men and bypasses their introversive formulas; for they are foreign to its structural web of patterns. The men who persist in defying history's abiding directions or in disregarding the constitutional course of its currents, are quixotic. Life laughs at them and, in the end, repudiates them. Jewish tradition depicts these types as *nishmatin artilain,* "naked souls", meandering about the world without balance and without consistency! This, it seems to me, is the fate of Jewish secularists in the United States.

Power in a Midwestern Jewish Community

KENNETH D. ROSEMAN

In any group, some individuals are bound to possess greater power than their fellow-members. Jewish communities are no exception, and within them an identical phenomenon is apparent. Some men are more powerful than others — so powerful, in fact, that they can determine the basic policies and directions of the entire communal entity. Students of this pattern must ask, of course: Who is included in the power structure, and who is excluded from it, and, in either case, on the basis of what criteria? What are the personal characteristics of those who constitute the power structure, and how does that structure operate in the community? What are its goals, its achievements, its problems? The writer's answers will necessarily be conditioned by the data he has gathered from a sample Midwestern Jewish community, but it seems to him reasonable to assume that his conclusions may, with some reservations, be applied to any metropolitan Jewish community.

There are certain limitations the writer has chosen to impose on himself. The Jewish community only in its most "parochial" sense has been subjected to investigation here. No attempt has been made to analyze Jewish relations with or influence on the general community, nor has there been an effort to interview every leader or power figure — but only a representative cross-section of such individuals in the particular Jewish community in question. Finally, the writer has undertaken to examine the power structures of past generations only to the extent that historical information appeared necessary for a proper understanding of the contemporary situation.

Rabbi Roseman is Acting Dean of the Cincinnati School, Hebrew Union College - Jewish Institute of Religion.

DEFINITIONS

Certain terms call for definition at this point — "Jewish community," "power," and "power structure."

One hesitates to define "Jewish community" in terms of any agreed-upon or shared values, as even the most casual observer will note that Jews in any city differ considerably on a variety of issues. The often profound ideological, social, economic, and ethnic splits evident among American Jews militate against such a definition. Whatever kinship, religious, cultural, or other ties unite the community, they are certainly highly attenuated. Still, there are two generally-shared convictions which form the basis for a concept of the "Jewish community" in any ideological sense. On these two points there exists, as it were, a consensus. In the first place, nearly all Jews share the conviction that Jews must survive as a distinct group. Some may place greater emphasis on the religious aspects of Jewish survival; others may stress cultural forms; still others may hold that the philanthropic aspects of Judaism are most important. Regardless of their differences, however, they will, with few exceptions, agree that Jews must survive. A second area of wide, if not quite unanimous, agreement relates to the need for communal services — that, given the necessity of Jewish survival, Jews must be provided with certain social, health, recreational, and religious services by their own "sectarian" organizations.

Beyond this minimalist definition of "Jewish community," there is another way in which one may define the term — the institutional structure which forms the pragmatic and functional basis for a concept of the Jewish community. It constitutes, indeed, the only formally structured Jewish community, having replaced any type of *kehillah* organization. The central Jewish welfare agencies of the community, that is to say, operate *as if* there existed a Jewish community. The leadership, too, presumes that such a pragmatic, functioning community exists; it is within this structure and based on the consensus of values previously mentioned that any policy and financial decisions will be determined. Therefore, when we speak of the Jewish community, we shall mean the total Jewish population of the city and the organizational and institutional structure, as well as the consensus of shared values upon which the entire organization must ultimately rest. The writer, however, will not use the term "Jewish community" to designate the total community of Jews in America; he will always intend it to refer to the Jewish population of a particular city.

We are convinced that, within this Jewish community, there is no definition of an overall communal purpose other than the two shared values of survival and service which have already been mentioned. A typical expression of the position held by the leaders of the power structure is this statement: "One does not think up purposes for the Jewish community. Rather, purposes are determined by needs."[1]

There are, however, those who express a different view. They define the goals of the Jewish community in terms of certain specific values — knowledge of Jewish tradition, participation in religious activities, or working for social welfare causes. A moderate statement combining both these viewpoints is found in a report emanating from our sample city's Jewish welfare fund:

On the basis of these group deliberations a Committee consensus was reached on the rationale for Jewish communal services. It must be understood that while the four principles which comprise the rationale are each applicable to every Jewish agency or institution, the orientation of the agency or institution determines the means by which and the degree to which these principles are followed.

I. Jewish Community services should meet the felt needs of the Jewish community.
II. Jewish Community services should serve to reinforce and preserve the Jewish Community.
III. Jewish Community agencies should have a responsibility for service to the total Community.
IV. Jewish agencies should reflect the ideals of social justice which is a major part of the Jewish heritage.[2]

So much for the term "Jewish community." The second term which must be defined is "power." The concept of "power" carries

---

[1] Statement made by an interviewee.

[2] Associated Jewish Agencies of Cincinnati, *Report to the Coordinating Committee from the Committee on "Why Jewish Agencies?"* (January 29, 1965), pp. 3–4.

with it, of course, many diverse connotations. There often appears in works dealing with the subject an aura of the surreptitious and mysterious — which seems to attract individuals to the study in the lurid hope of uncovering something clandestine, a conspiracy of some sort. Such notions, the present writer is convinced, are to be avoided, and the concept of power is to be viewed as morally neutral in all respects. That is to say, power *per se* will be considered neither bad nor good. It is only with reference to specific applications of power that moral judgment may be justified, although we shall endeavor here to avoid even this form of criticism.

One may, of course, advance many definitions of the concept of "power," but for our purposes Floyd Hunter's statement seems most functional and inclusive: "Power is a word that will be used to describe the acts of men going about the business of moving other men to act in relation to themselves or in relation to organic or inorganic things."[3]

It will be noted that there are three necessary elements in this definition. First, power must be understood as requiring participation and involvement in community actions. Thus, individuals who possess the potential for power may choose never to realize this power by avoiding manifest behavior in power situations. A second consideration is that power is never exercised in a vacuum, but always in relation to a specific issue or object. Finally, we shall note that power inheres in men, although it may be manifested through institutions or other channels. Consequently, if we are to discover the elements of power in a community, we must understand how men act in specific situations.

Not only is it necessary to ascertain the location of power in the community, but any description of it must depend on the type of power which is manifested:

Three major forms of power may be distinguished in terms of the type of influence brought to bear upon the subordinated individual. The power-holder exercises *force* when he influences behavior by a physical manipulation of the subordinated individual (assault, confinement, etc.); *domination* when he influences behavior by making explicit to others what he wants

[3] Floyd Hunter, *Community Power Structure: A Study of Decision Makers* (Chapel Hill: University of North Carolina Press, 1953), pp. 2-3.

them to do (command, request, etc.); and *manipulation* when he influences the behavior of others without making explicit the behavior which he thereby wants them to perform.[4]

In a voluntaristic community, such as the Jewish community is, power is generally exercised by domination or manipulation, and usually by a combination of the two. Although threats of coercion or force may in some attenuated manner underlie both dominance and manipulation, it is rare to find them overtly attempted as means for influence over behavior.

We would also remark that, while the total community is never called upon to approve or reject the policies of the power structure, there are ways by which it acts as a check against the development of unlimited power. In a voluntaristic community, there is no taxing power; all funds must come from the citizens by way of donation. Consequently, there exists the threat, at times quite explicit, that contributions will be withdrawn if a certain policy is or is not followed. This fact is, in our opinion, frequently responsible for the large measure of compromise in the Jewish community, although, we hasten to add, some compromises are reached through an honest desire to cooperate among the leaders of the community. Only under extraordinary circumstances is there a willingness to take the risk of antagonizing large contributors or large segments of the population. Therefore, in this regard, we may say that *vox populi, vox dei* — at least, as we shall later see, the voice of *some* of the people!

It will be helpful at this point if we distinguish between "power" and some other concepts with which it is frequently confused.

Most men are encouraged to assume that, in general, the most powerful and the wealthiest are also the most knowledgeable or, as they might say, the smartest ... The powerful and the wealthy *must* be the men of most knowledge; otherwise how could they be where they are? But to say that those who succeed to power must be "smart," is to say that power *is* knowledge. To say that those who succeed to wealth must be smart is to say that wealth *is* knowledge.

These assumptions do reveal something that is true: that ordinary men,

---

[4] Herbert Goldhamer and Edward A. Shils, "Types of Power and Status," *American Journal of Sociology*, XLV (September, 1939), 171–72.

even today, are prone to explain and to justify power and wealth in terms of knowledge or ability. Such assumptions also reveal something of what has happened to the kind of experience that knowledge has come to be. Knowledge is no longer widely felt as an ideal; it is seen as an instrument.[5]

If power is not knowledge and if it is not wealth, neither is it a number of other things. We agree with Bierstedt that

> Social power has variously been identified with prestige, with influence, with eminence, with competence or ability, with knowledge (Bacon), with dominance, with rights, with force, and with authority... Prestige would seem to be a consequence of power rather than a determinant of it or a necessary component of it...
>
> Similar observations may be made about the relations of knowledge, skill, competence, ability, and eminence to power. They are all components of, sources of, or synonyms of prestige, but they may be quite unaccompanied by power. When power does accompany them the association is incidental rather than necessary.[6]

Power should also be distinguished from leadership, although the two frequently overlap. In general, we would understand leadership to include the active assumption of responsibility for the execution of a policy previously determined by those in power. What this means is that a power-figure may, for one reason or another, never take the subsequent step of assuming a position of leadership.

Finally, the term "power structure" needs some discussion. It is obvious to even the most casual observer that, within any community, there is a hierarchy of authority and power. At the very lowest level, there are those individuals who are charged with the execution of policy, but who are never consulted about its formulation. These persons cannot legitimately be included in the power structure of a community. Above this level, there are various other strata in which individuals exercise more or less influence on the development of community policy. These individuals constitute the power structure. As Hunter has written, "it is obvious that a social order, or a system, must be maintained... Broadly speaking,

---

[5] Irving L. Horowitz, ed., *Power, Politics and People: The Collected Essays of C. Wright Mills* (New York: Oxford University Press, 1963), pp. 605–6.

[6] Robert Bierstedt, "An Analysis of Social Power," *American Sociological Review*, XL (December, 1950), 730–31.

the maintenance of this order falls to the lot of almost every man in the community, but the *establishment of changes* in the old order falls to the lot of relatively few."[7] This small group of men in the community from which emanate the basic policy orientations and decisions about how the community is to operate stands at the apex of the power structure. These men are usually, although not necessarily, placed at the top of the community's organizational structure.

To be precise, then, the term "power structure" means all the individuals and institutions in a community who or which play a role in the determination of community policy. As we stated before, the power structure is stratified, so that individuals will be found to have more or less power, depending on a number of factors. This writer's primary concern will be with the relatively small group of individuals at the top of the structure.

As a general rule, the power structure has achieved success if "it utilized commonly available resources at a much greater rate and with considerably more skill than its opponents."[8] We shall have later occasion to notice the particular factors and resources which may be strategically used by the power structure of a Jewish community to achieve preeminent position. We shall also notice that there is some opposition to the power structure, both by individuals and by organized groups.

METHODOLOGY

In any survey of this sort, methodology is of crucial importance, as it may in some ways produce a bias in the results. Floyd Hunter's reputational survey method was selected as the most efficient and satisfactory way of isolating and interviewing the power elite. According to the Hunter method, a number of knowledgeable individuals in the community are asked to list those whom they consider powerful. By comparing the lists submitted by these respondents, a consensus is achieved concerning the membership

---

[7] Hunter, p. 9.

[8] Aaron Wildavsky, *Leadership in a Small Town* (Totowa, N. J.: Bedminster Press, 1964), p. 278.

of the power structure. These names constitute the basic interviewing list, although the interviewer may wish to add some names to assure adequate representation of all elements in the Jewish community.

In addition to the interviews based on this list, we would also urge the incorporation of some case-study techniques. We mean by this that power may also be analyzed through determining the roles which individuals have occupied during the resolution of various community issues and problems. While costly in terms of time and effort, this technique is an effective way of reducing the risk of distortion, a risk inevitably present when one deals with the elusive matter of reputation.

Our final list of interviews was restricted to twenty-four individuals. This cross-section of the Jewish community's power elite was found to be both manageable and productive of worthwhile results.

Going Through the Chairs

The writer was most concerned with the question, "How does one enter the power elite?" A number of factors emerged as possible answers to this question.

It appears that there are two ways of entering the power structure: vertically or horizontally. The most common way is vertical mobility, so that a young man begins his career of community service in fundraising, then assumes a committee or board assignment, progresses to the presidency of an individual agency, and finally achieves a top position in one of the central organizations. It is at this last stage that the individual either achieves permanent power or falls out of favor. As Jennings states, "In most organized endeavors, there is a series of steps that those at the apexes have traveled, barring lateral introduction . . . In non-profit organizations, the process is popularly known as 'going through the chairs.' "[9]

Horizontal mobility, on the other hand, means entering the

---

[9] M. Kent Jennings, *Community Influentials: The Elites of Atlanta* (Glencoe: Free Press of Glencoe, 1964), p. 181.

power structure near the top without "going through the chairs." Because this is not the "normal" way of entering the power structure, it is usually reserved for several special types of individuals. There are, of course, high-prestige persons who can be used for publicity, but it must be remarked: these people do not achieve *bona fide* power; they remain subservient to the desires of the true members of the power structure. The second type of individual who achieves power by horizontal mobility is the large or potentially-large donor who feels that power and prestige are due him by virtue of his money. Finally, horizontal mobility may be used to induce an older man who has money, prestige, and capability to become active in community work. Such an individual cannot, obviously, be asked to start at the lowest levels; he must begin nearer the top.

Not every job in the Jewish community is open to the horizontally mobile individual. Generally, this type of appointment is limited to the top jobs of individual agencies or to second-level positions in the central bodies, although very infrequently it may be used for the top positions. Since such appointments are resented bitterly by those who have entered the power structure vertically, they are used sparingly and only when the desired results cannot be otherwise achieved. The leaders of the power structure are also somewhat wary about appointing someone to a top position without previously testing him on jobs of lesser responsibility. The horizontally mobile individual is often an unknown quantity.

Regardless of which method of entry an individual uses, he must have certain personal qualities which legitimize his power. Analyzing what qualities or attributes are necessary to achieve lasting power, we found two partially conflicting hypotheses. Although neither is correct in all respects, we tend to agree that the latter is more nearly representative of the way in which the men currently at the top of the power structure achieved their power.

The "democratic view" presumes that any young man can achieve a position of top power if he works hard and successfully, gives generously within his means, and is reasonably "presentable" and well-liked by the power structure. Our research would tend to confirm this idealistic, egalitarian hypothesis to a certain extent. We are convinced that anyone can rise, for example, to membership on the board of an individual agency or even to the board of the central organizations, provided he follows the pattern outlined above.

On the other hand, although our research indicates that personal effort and generosity may secure a measure of power, the conclusion is inescapable that money, family tradition, and a number of similar factors are usually more influential in the final analysis. In our study, we discovered that, of the funds raised during a recent Jewish welfare fund campaign, 60.4 percent of the money was donated by only 3.7 percent of the donors. Quite obviously, this places the large giver in a highly strategic power position. And, as the need for additional funds increases in Jewish community enterprises, one may expect to see an increased concentration of power in the hands of the very wealthy whose gifts alone will determine the success or failure of many communal projects.

It is appropriate here to note some of the ramifications of the financial crisis in the Jewish community. According to most reliable estimates, the cost of preserving the present agencies and programs will continue to rise at about 5 percent per year, assuming that government and community chest contributions also remain constant or increase. This latter assumption is not necessarily valid, especially in view of the rapidly increasing demand for funds in the new governmental welfare programs. Should there be a sizeable diminution of the money available to the Jewish community from such external sources, a very real crisis would materialize.

In many cities, the awareness of the impending crisis, as local fundraising struggles to keep pace with rising costs, has engendered serious reconsideration of the programs of the Jewish communal agencies. One suspects that the leaders of the power structure are already beginning to consider seriously the elimination of agency programs and welfare fund beneficiary agencies. Such changes require profound alterations of attitudes and organizational allegiances and, to be accomplished, must be set in motion well in advance. To a degree, this reflects the inefficient and cumbersome decision-making process in most Jewish communities.

Although the financial outlook would seem to be somewhat dark, there is no need to be altogether pessimistic. If some agencies can be eliminated, immediate pressures will be considerably reduced. A change of only a few thousand dollars is unusually significant in welfare fund budgets. Perhaps the most realistic hope is that an attractive "cause" will capture the imagination and enlist the efforts of the community. If, for example, a large number of Jews were permitted to emigrate from the Soviet bloc, we believe that the morale and the financial contributions of the American Jewish community would rise to the occasion, much as they did after the founding of the State of Israel. It is unfortunate that crises must be depended on to mobilize and vitalize the Jewish community, but there seems to be no other reasonable expectation.

In addition to financial contributions, the aspirant to power must be willing and able to devote a great amount of time to Jewish community work. This, of course, implies that he is able to afford to neglect his occupation, another fact leading to the concentration of power among the wealthy.

One hypothesis expressed frequently would have it that one should be of the "German," old-line Reform Jewish aristocracy to achieve a high position of power. Our research tended to confirm this, but not without qualifications.

The first qualification is that one must consider the history of a particular Jewish community. Who were the earliest Jews in the community, and what were their religious affiliations and principles? The fact that so many American cities were first populated by German Jews who became, at a relatively early date, both Reform and wealthy tends, of course, and not surprisingly, to confirm the hypothesis. Nevertheless, there are some cities in which Orthodox Judaism and its laymen have gained a sizeable measure of power.

A second qualification is that the aspirant to power may indeed come from an Orthodox Jewish background; but, before he can gain power, he must accept the behavioral norms of the dominant group, in this case, usually the norms of the Reform Jews. It is true that most of the men in the top levels of power are descended from older families which have had traditions of power. As such, they assume that they will continue the family tradition and power; and the simple assumption itself is often responsible for creating "real" power. Still, belonging to an old-line, Reform Jewish family is not a *sine qua non* for gaining power. Children of Orthodox Jewish parents may achieve top-level power, provided they become sufficiently acculturated to upper-class, Reform Jewish mores. The proof of this contention is that a few of the top men in the power structure are first-generation Reform Jews, but their appearance in no wise distinguishes them from, for example, a fourth-generation Reform Jew.

It would be our contention, then, that while religious affiliation and length of residence are important, they are not nearly so crucial as is usually assumed.

Leaders from the Periphery

During the course of his research, this writer has been struck repeatedly by the fact that the families which rose to positions of community domination during the early years of the twentieth century have generally relinquished their leadership.[10] To be sure, some of their descendants have continued to be active, but typically their power and influence have by now been severely limited. There are, of course, exceptions, and we may find one or two families which seem to have preserved their inherited status.

Nevertheless, we were led to ask, "Why, given all the necessary advantages, such as wealth, leisure, prestige, and a family tradition of service, have these families been disinclined and/or unable to continue at the top of the power structure?" A number of suggestions may be advanced. None of them will suffice to describe all the cases, nor will they all be operative in any one instance. Together, however, they form a general picture of the diffusion of the older Jewish leadership of any community.

In the first place, it is clear that public service is an exhausting and taxing avocation. As a consequence, it would appear, there is the phenomenon that, after an extended period of communal service, a family may become tired. Its energies, creativity, and competitive

---

[10] As a historical note, it should be pointed out that leadership of the Jewish community in its earlier phases tended to be concentrated in the hands of several family groups; that is, the "men at the top" were usually related to each other — which is why it seems legitimate to speak of families.

Photo by George Stille, Cincinnati
Courtesy, Jewish Hospital, Cincinnati

A favorite of the power structure:
Cincinnati's Jewish Hospital adds a new building

Courtesy, The Jewish Community Center, Cincinnati

"The felt needs of the Jewish Community":
The Jewish Community Center of Cincinnati

drive expended, its responsibilities and activities may be undertaken by new and more ambitious families and individuals. With this, of course, goes the assumption of added power for the new group.

To this, of course, must be added the fact that some of these upper-class, assimilated Jews found it convenient to pass into Christianity, thereby removing themselves from all contact with the Jewish community. Others merely moved out of the city.

A third consideration is that the older families were engulfed in a tidal wave of new residents. For a while, of course, they maintained their position, but, after several decades, the force of a mass of new immigrants striving vigorously to improve themselves was felt. More infertile than these newcomers, the older families could no longer provide adequate leadership personnel. As a result, a number of new families appeared in the power structure, and, eventually, gained precedence over the older members.

There is another, and attractive, explanation. When the immigrants from Eastern Europe first arrived in America, the assimilated Reform Jewish leadership — the patricians, we may call them — saw that it was their self-appointed task to "Americanize" the newcomers. The patricians devoted themselves to this end with great fervor, teaching the immigrants English and trades, preparing them for citizenship, blunting the adverse effects of their unusual dress and manners, and providing them with charity as long as money, clothing, lodging, and recreation were needed. It was a consummate shock to these "Lady Bountifuls" when the flow of immigration ceased. Their raison d'être vanished, for the people they had once so vigorously and ably assisted had now moved into the middle class, and some had even become wealthy. They no longer needed a dole, and no new immigrants arrived. What was now necessary, under these changed conditions, was a planned communal structure which would provide a richer Jewish life for all the members of the Jewish community. Many a patrician, however, could not adjust to the new task. When the settlement house became the luxurious community center, the exemplars of the old "Lady Bountiful" approach found themselves technologically unemployed, as it were, and many of them disappeared from the Jewish communal scene. They preferred, instead, to transfer their skills to activities within the general community where they could continue uninterrupted in their traditional charitable philosophy.

Typically, the leadership of the power structure is lax concerning Judaism and Jewishness. A historical note is valuable here. Before 1880, Jews of the upper classes appeared to be very secure. There was no excessive need to assimilate, as they were well-accepted by the "Protestant Establishment." By the 1910's, however, mass immigration of Jews and Catholics had occurred in many areas of the country. The direct effect of this immigration was a change in status for the Jews, for now the immigrants were seen by the "Establishment" as a potential threat to its political and social power. As a consequence, there appeared a systematic program of exclusion and discrimination. In this situation, the upper-class Jews were faced with a clear choice. Either they could seek entry into Christian society, by open conversion or by merely avoiding anything Jewish, or they could retreat to the Jewish community and there develop the power and prestige denied them in the general community. With a few exceptions, the Jews chose the latter alternative.

Since this time, the position of the Jew in American society has improved, although he still encounters social exclusion from certain circles. There is a renewed feeling of security among the leaders. They are more comfortable with their Judaism, as long as it is minimal and does not interfere with their "more important concerns." In general, they tend to be observant of only the few "required" practices, such as temple membership and holyday synagogue attendance. While determined to combat anti-Semitism, they are at pains to carry on the battle without publicity, fanfare, or exposure of the fact that they still feel marginal enough to be threatened by anti-Semitic attacks. The "sha-sha" policy is also predicated upon the belief that more can be accomplished by informal and behind-the-scenes efforts than by public demonstrations and outcry. Almost all of these men are abysmally ignorant of anything but the most elementary information about Jewish history, theology, and practice or about the Bible and Hebrew. This, however, is not seen as a detriment to their leadership or power, for their community service is based totally on a secular ethic.

Underlying their activity, we sense, is still the goal of achieving prominence in the general community. Consequently, they may be what Kurt Lewin calls "leaders from the periphery." As he puts it,

In any group, those sections are apt to gain leadership which are more generally successful. In a minority group, individual members who are economically successful, or who have distinguished themselves in their professions, usually gain a higher degree of acceptance by the majority group. This places them culturally on the periphery of the underprivileged group and makes them more likely to be "marginal" persons. They frequently have a negative balance and are particularly eager to have their "good connections" not endangered by too close a contact with those sections of the underprivileged group which are not acceptable to the majority. Nevertheless, they are frequently called for leadership by the underprivileged group because of their status and power. They themselves are usually eager to accept the leading role in the minority, partly as a substitute for gaining status in the majority, partly because such leadership makes it possible for them to have and maintain additional contact with the majority.

As a result, we find the rather paradoxical phenomenon of what one might call "the leader from the periphery." Instead of having a group led by people who are proud of the group, who wish to stay in it and to promote it, we see minority leaders who are lukewarm toward the group, who may, under a thin cover of loyalty, be fundamentally eager to leave the group, or who may try to use their power outright for acts of negative chauvinism. Having achieved a relatively satisfactory status among non-Jews, these individuals are chiefly concerned with maintaining the status quo and so try to soft-pedal any action which might arouse the attention of the non-Jew.[11]

There can be no doubt that presenting a good public image to the non-Jewish community is crucially important to these men. They are in close daily contact with the business, professional, and governmental leaders of the non-Jewish community. No suspicion can be permitted that, in their own Jewish communal sphere, they are unable to maintain control. Consequently, the appearance of harmony and peaceful cooperation must be preserved, even at the expense of sacrificing or compromising principles. The leadership also maintains explicitly that a good public image is necessary to

---

[11] Kurt Lewin, "The Problem of Minority Leadership," in Alvin W. Gouldner, ed., *Studies in Leadership* (New York: Harper & Bros., 1950), p. 193.

the fulfillment of its goals within the Jewish community. Even so, preserving a good image is not the entire explanation for the insistence on communal harmony. Even apart from the public relations problem, the top men in the power structure are committed to the idea that, at all costs, the organizational structure must function smoothly and with as few disruptions as possible, and there is a pragmatic basis for this. A disgruntled group within the Jewish community might not contribute to the welfare fund campaign. Funds being at a premium, it is extremely important that no group be alienated so completely that it withdraws or threatens to withdraw its donations. As a result, it is *sh'lom bayis*, communal peace, which has become the cardinal virtue in community operation, often at the cost of fundamental and necessary social planning.

While the marginality of the men at the top of the power structure is quite beyond doubt where it touches strong manifestations of Jewishness, we may seriously question the last part of Lewin's allegation — that these leaders engage in "acts of negative chauvinism." This writer has found no occasion on which the top level of leadership has attempted to gain status in the general community by sacrificing the interests of the Jewish community. Men may, however, gain status by neglecting Jewish activities and restricting their communal service to organizations which are nondenominational or secular. Our findings lead us to the conclusion that, quite to the contrary, the top leadership is zealous in its desire to make the Jewish community an exemplary community — if only to prove to the general community that Jews can do better than others and that they can take care of their own problems! Nor should we neglect the fact that many of these men are, at least partially, motivated by genuine humanitarian concerns.

FIREBRANDS AND POLICY MAKERS

Finally, we wondered whether it was necessary to have certain personal characteristics in order to enter the top levels of the power structure. Our research would show that these men are, on the whole, genteel, sophisticated, and worldly. It would also indicate that these qualities are not necessarily connected with power, although they are frequently associated with it. Younger men attempting to gain power, however, must manifest the "proper" traits of character, and these would normally include pleasant personality, good appearance, business or professional success, and movement in the proper social circles. On the few occasions when an individual was dropped from the power elite, personal factors would seem to have been largely responsible for the reversal of his fortunes. In general, individuals whose power status declined abruptly had had quarrels with those already at the top of the power structure. These disputes did not concern their capabilities or efficiency in jobs to which they had been appointed; rather, as one interviewee put it, they were "too rich for the blood of the ... leadership which uses them. They were too emotional, talk too much, are firebrands and controversial rabble-rousers. They are also too Jewish. They lost leadership by bucking the crowd."[12] The men who lost power did so, we believe, because the power structure considered them uncontrollable. In general, they were characterized — and not without good reason, at times — as dissenters, troublemakers, and hotheads.

None of this should be understood to imply that the policy-making level of the power structure is completely closed to dissent. What appears to be true, however, is that such discussion and controversy as may arise are also controlled by the top men. No issue, that is to say, will be raised for action until the top level of the power structure has agreed that it should be discussed. When the power structure is ready to discuss and to attempt solution of an issue, its members' control and management are not suspended — what is to happen must happen on *their* terms only, for it is their basic desire to preserve their former policies insofar as possible. As Hunter states,

When new policy is laid down it must be consistent with the general scheme of old policy and should not radically change basic alignments of settled policy. This does not mean that structural alignments do not undergo drastic overhauling on occasion, but consistency is a prime virtue which must not be passed over lightly, so that the basic equilibrium in the

---

[12] Statement made by an interviewee.

social systems of the community may undergo as little disruption as possible.[13]

The example of the generally ill-fated Jewish Community Council movement of the 1930's may illustrate the strong desire of the power structure to maintain control over the processes and results of planning and decision-making. Jewish community councils were usually established as explicit attempts to democratize local Jewish communities. They were structured so that each Jewish organization in the city would be entitled to equal representation in the council. This structure, however, led to two difficulties. In the first place, too many people and organizations, often with conflicting objectives, were involved; the arrangement was unworkable and inefficient. A second problem was that the Jewish community council allowed dissident elements in the Jewish community a forum in which to stir up trouble. The leadership of the power structure felt that such open channels of communication could only frustrate what they took to be their more efficient and benevolent functions. Consequently, Jewish community councils, while they may still retain a paper existence, are altogether bypassed by the leadership.

The desire to maintain control over the policy and functioning of the community is also demonstrated by the power structure's summary neglect of social planning. Hunter has summarized the possibilities in the following statement:

Planning ... becomes a ritualistic panorama engaged in by reasonably well-paid under-structure personnel whose plans more often than not fail to reach the point of action. Action results when a plan fits the relatively narrow interests of the policy-makers, but on many issues there is community paralysis and inaction ...

If the professional in one of the social agencies is too zealous in searching out the basic causes of disorganization and social malfunctioning, he is liable to suspicion and censure. If he does engage in fundamental social research which turns up elements pointing to social reform or change in existing community alignments and structure, his materials may be presented to a limited group of persons who profess interest and who dutifully place his report with many like it in the files of the organization.[14]

[13] Hunter, p. 209.
[14] *Ibid.*, pp. 240–41.

It is not at all difficult to explain the reluctance of the power structure to permit extensive planning. The primary objection is that plans, once made and publicized, demand a degree of commitment on the part of their formulators. Extensive, long-range social planning would severely restrict the power structure's ability to improvise solutions to current problems in keeping with the demands of their overall value orientations. Furthermore, the lay leadership has consistently demonstrated an inability to function, both emotionally and financially, within the confines of a long-range plan.

In general, then, a continued weakness is to be anticipated in this area of community organization. It is unfortunate, of course, as successful planning could result in more efficient uses of both the human and the financial resources available; it would solve many community problems, although not always along lines most acceptable to the power structure. Rather, one expects that the power structure will continue to operate on a crisis-to-crisis basis, with only a vague and haphazard idea of the goals and values which should be pursued. Planning will continue on an informal, conversational, and nonaccountable basis, at least for the foreseeable future.

Nevertheless, a qualification is in order. Informal planning, for all its deleterious effects, does not represent the "smoke-filled room" image of conspiracy usually associated with power by the public. We would agree with Hunter that

The popular notion of men plotting behind the scenes is a fictional illusion except when one gets into the area of organized crime. The men of power usually operate openly with one another and on equal terms ... If the little fellow comes out on the short end of affairs, or if he is "not in the know," as the popular expression goes, it is for reasons other than fraud.[15]

We attempted, during the course of our research, to discover if there is in our sample city one individual whose power is so extensive that he controls the entire Jewish community structure. Our unavoidable conclusion is that there is currently no such person, but this conclusion needs qualification in two respects.

[15] *Ibid.*, p. 180.

First, effective control over policy formation in the Jewish community can be and is maintained by a loose coalition of members of the power structure. With a few salient exceptions, these men will be found on the board of the welfare fund. The exceptions are men of great economic power who have chosen, for one reason or another, not to serve on the board. Their opinions are well-known, however, and they are consulted before any decisions of magnitude are reached. Only in the most extreme cases would the desires of these men be ignored. On the other hand, it happens not infrequently that a policy decision proposed at lower levels is reversed in view of the opinions of the few men at the top of the power structure. The second qualification is that, in limited spheres of interest, there are individuals who do exercise preeminent power.

It would also be our observation that, although there appear to be many separate centers of power, all the most powerful men cooperate freely and frequently with each other. The practical result of this high degree of interrelatedness is that the power of each individual is enhanced within his specific sphere of interest and that, taken together, these men constitute a massive and powerful group.

In summary, we may say that a man may realistically aspire to "real" power in the Jewish community if he is wealthy, willing and able to devote considerable amounts of his time and energy to communal work, and comes from an old Reform Jewish family (or has completely accepted the mores of this group). Whether he actually achieves such "real" power depends partly on his personality and partly on a number of other factors, not the least of which may be chance.

POWER AND THE PROFESSIONAL

The high standards and capabilities of Jewish communal agencies must, in large measure, reflect the high caliber of their professional executives. The current professional leaders of the Jewish community continue to manifest the same elevated competency which marked their predecessors. While there may be individual deviations, the modern professional is technically well-trained and able to operate programs well above the level of comparable programs outside the Jewish community.

One observes, however, that there has been a considerable and growing antagonism between the religious and the philanthropic centers of Judaism. Each of these structures is attempting to gain preeminent power and prestige at the expense of the other. In this competitive situation, the professionals appear to have elected a policy of militant secularism — making as few concessions as possible to Jewishness. The feeling among the professional executives seems to be that for them to identify themselves with overt Jewishness would somehow constitute both a defeat at the hands of the temple or synagogue and a dilution of their professional standards. It might be noted, in passing, that the tide of battle has been uniformly in favor of the philanthropic structure — to the extent that religious institutions are now threatened with the very real possibility of becoming vestigial.

There is sustained pressure, however, on the part of the laymen, who insist that community agencies must openly manifest their attachment to Jewish practices and ideals if they are to continue receiving support from the Jewish community. One report advocated "a need for greater Jewish commitment among Jewish social work professionals ... Jewish institutions need to clarify their roles in the perpetuation of Jewish group life."[16]

It is this writer's observation that the power of the Jewish community professional is growing considerably. There appear to be several reasons for this development. In the first place, the increasing complexity and specialization of modern communal service mean that the average layman cannot attain the same understanding of agency problems and needs as he formerly could. Inevitably, then, he must place more reliance upon the testimony of the expert, in this case, the professional agency executive.

The importance of the trend must not be minimized. As the layman comes to rely more heavily on the advice of the professional, the power of the latter is extensively broadened, and this applies in

---

[16] Associated Jewish Agencies of Cincinnati, *Report to the Coordinating Committee from the Committee on "Why Jewish Agencies?"*, p. 2.

particular to policy formation and planning. As a general rule, we may assert that the effective limits on the professional's power are now determined only by his ability or inability to present information which would justify his recommendations and to withhold data which would controvert his plans.

The power of the professional executive in the Jewish community is further increased by another factor which is not altogether unconnected with the first. This is the matter of board member selection and tenure. As the demands of specialization increase, the ability of the layman to contradict the professional decreases proportionately. The professional who wishes to establish a firm basis for his power must recognize this fact and the inevitable conclusions which derive from it. Thus, it is obvious that, in the selection of board members, the professional will be careful to handpick for nomination those individuals who are interested in the work of the agency, but who are neither powerful, aggressive, nor too-well informed. These persons can be "educated" along the lines which the professional chooses. They must also, if possible, be connected with interests whose favor the professional wishes to cultivate. The professional, by so structuring his board, may preserve his expertise and, consequently, his power. Needless to say, this tactic is not always successful. Lay nominating committees have shown themselves determined to preserve at least a measure of independent judgment. Parenthetically, it is to be noted that laymen use different criteria in nominating individuals for board membership. To them, social acceptability, friendship, wealth, and interest are more important.

Another fairly recent development has, paradoxically, helped to secure the power of the professional. In an effort to be more democratic, some boards have limited the terms, both of membership and of office, to approximately four years. The supposed consequence of this was to have been a more representative membership and the advantage of a variety of different opinions. It was also held that, by demanding a turnover in board membership, new people could be involved in agency work, and good workers could be rewarded. Above all, the specter of the "self-perpetuating board" would be banished from communal life.

The effect of this policy has been somewhat unexpected. Before the democratic system was instituted, boards were frequently self-perpetuating; members had life tenure, even permanent occupancy of specific offices. Under this system, it was possible for the individual layman to develop knowledge and expertise enough to act as an effective check on the professional. Now that tenure on boards is limited, the layman is denied this possibility. As soon as he begins to develop a depth understanding of the nature, functions, and problems of an organization, he is forced to leave his office and, on occasion, the board. In practice, this means that the checks on the professional are considerably diluted and that, as a consequence, his power is enhanced.

Still, it must be noted that the professionals in the Jewish community have not taken advantage of the far-reaching potential of power-seeking and empire-building. In general, they have worked closely with the laymen and have shown themselves dedicated to the highest professional standards. They have consistently placed institutional and program success above their personal advantage, although, as is obvious, the two may be tightly intertwined.

Rabbis in the Power Structure

Our sample community is perhaps somewhat atypical in that its rabbis, especially those serving Reform congregations, do not occupy the same high status in the power structure as their counterparts in many other cities. Nevertheless, we are certain that, within broad limits, one generalization may be allowed. It is our observation that the lay leaders of the power structure operate with only a minimal regard for the opinion of the rabbis. Their ethic is entirely secular and relates to Jewish religious norms only as an afterthought, if at all. The rabbis are consulted out of deference to their position and stature and with the knowledge that their cooperation is necessary for the execution of many policies, but we seriously doubt whether a lay leader would relinquish his own vital interests or change well-established community policy on the advice of a rabbi.

We are aware that, in many communities, rabbis have headed

the local welfare fund drives and other communal projects. Such an occurrence would be impossible in our sample community, where the laity is so firmly entrenched in power.[17]

CATHOLIC ISRAEL

We have, throughout this essay, attempted to describe the composition and activities of the power structure of the Jewish community, based on generalizations and abstractions from the data gathered in a sample study. We suggested that the power structure does exist, although not as a monolithic structure. It is composed, primarily, of Reform Jews — many now of East European rather than German background — who, by reason of their wealth, effort, and social position, have gained power in the Jewish community. This group, while it controls both the policy and the finances of the Jewish community, is not unopposed. Various individuals and groups have challenged its power, sometimes with an unexpected degree of success. In general, however, the power structure can assert effective control in cases which it considers important.

We believe that the efforts of the power structure have been honestly directed toward the best interests of the entire Jewish community. Its members have shown themselves willing to compromise and have held fairly consistently to a theory of "catholic Israel" in which all segments of the Jewish population have legitimate and unalienable rights. Perhaps the best demonstration of the beneficial aspects of the power structure is the high quality of communal service rendered by the individual agencies. This beneficial work will continue, especially if the power structure admits the value of long-range social planning and commits itself to accepting the results of such studies.

---

[17] The various circumstances which have permitted rabbis to gain such positions of eminence elsewhere require explanation and analysis in the light of the particular situation in other cities. This explanation falls outside the scope of this article, although we would expect that the answer in the case of other cities would be found in the failure of the laymen to exert their power effectively and in the personality of the individual rabbi.

We suggest, finally, that the power structure will become more flexible and diffuse in the future as religious, social, economic, and ethnic divisions within the Jewish community weaken. On the other hand, the growing homogeneity of the Jewish community may not be sufficient to offset the increased power of the few large financial contributors, especially in view of the increasing shortage of funds. Within the next generation, we shall know the answers to these questions. And upon these answers depends the future of the Jewish community.

THE INTELLECTUAL AND CONTEMPORARY JEWISH LIFE

RICHARD L. RUBENSTEIN

It is difficult to be involved continuously in the life of a University community without giving serious thought to the relationship between the Jewish intellectual and the Jewish community. There are many deeply committed and loyal Jews who make their contributions to cultural and intellectual life without affecting a studied indifference to Jewish life and practice. Yet, the conclusion is inescapable that a very significant number of Jewish intellectuals and academicians have only the most tenuous sort of relationship to Jewish life. This is all the more surprising when one sees continuing evidence that their gentile counterparts do not share their lack of concern with religious life and its values. In Cambridge leading academicians play an important rôle in the life of the Protestant and Catholic churches around Harvard Square. But the three synagogues in the Cambridge-Belmont area do not have a single academician among their leaders and almost none among their members. This is not because Jewish academicians are not to be found at Harvard and M.I.T. A recent survey of the student body of Harvard College estimated that twenty-five per cent of the students were Jewish and this figure is known to be higher in the Graduate School of Arts and Sciences and the Law School. The number of Jewish faculty members is high although no survey has been taken.

It is difficult to say whether the Harvard experience is typical of American colleges and universities. It will be assumed here that it is. Even if the Harvard situation is not entirely typical, it is certainly influential.

The disinterest of a large class of Jewish intellectuals in Jewish life and thought is all the more puzzling in view of the renaissance of theology as a humanistic discipline within American culture since the mid-1940's. People like Niebuhr, Tillich, Barth, and Buber are listened to today by intellectuals. They are discussed and what they have to say is of extreme importance. There has been a special concern with their critique of much that is self-defeating and inequitable in our society and with their radical analysis of the human predicament. Psychologists and psychoanalysts have been quick to recognize the immense relevance of this work to their own disciplines. An example of the recognition by psychologists of the relevance of theology to the contemporary assessment of man was the invitation extended to Martin Buber to lecture at the William Alanson White Institute of Psychoanalysis in the spring of 1957. This school was the scene of much of the work done by Harry Stack Sullivan in the interpersonal theory of psychiatry. It was recognized that the new theology had enormous significance for contemporary

Rabbi Rubenstein is, at present, Director of the Hillel Foundation at the University of Pittsburgh, and was Associate Director at Harvard Hillel when he wrote this article.

40

culture not merely for its doctrine of God, but because of its anthropology, its *logos* of man.

It should be stressed that the doctrine of man rather than the doctrine of God was taken most seriously. No attempt has been made by intellectuals to accept the whole body of religious thought and practice, Jewish or Christian, uncritically. Yet, with the abandonment of the illusion of the possibility of a future-oriented utopian fulfillment in the 1930's and '40's, attention was turned to assessing the "now" of human possibilities. As long as intellectuals took seriously the future-oriented political myths of the thirties, the stress of concern had to be focused upon the gradual or violent alteration of external socio-political conditions as the real problem of man. As soon as it was realized that in the best of all possible worlds, the human situation would be limited by irreducible moral, physical, and spiritual dilemmas which would make human existence tragic and ironic in any circumstance, the problem necessarily shifted to a greater interest in the actual life situation and the limits of possibility available to man. In a world of fixed and inescapable necessities, men sought knowledge of how best to assess and live with their limitations. The enormous interest in the psychological disciplines in our times has been, in part, a concommitent of the decline of an earlier and easier optimism with human possibilities. There is little surprise in the hostility of the Soviet Union and Marxist theoreticians with psychoanalysis. Where the official philosophy remains a future-oriented myth, any attempt to allow man to make the most of his *present* possibilities must be seen as reactionary.

The renaissance of interest in theology is directly related to the cultural scene. Psychic realities existed and were comprehended long before they were systematized and conceptualized in the nineteenth and twentieth centuries. Religious rite, myth, and practice have received a new assessment in our times. An age which was quick to penetrate beneath the surface in psychic phenomena, soon realized that religious thought and practice had long ago dealt with the realities of the human situation, albeit without the conceptual structure of contemporary depth psychology. The result has been a far-reaching renewal of interest in religious and theological literature and the problems implicit in them, though not necessarily a renewal of religious commitment or religious practice.

This renewal of interest should have offered the synagogues and the Hillel Foundations an enormous opportunity to reach and to enlist defected Jewish intellectuals. Yet, by and large, it is agreed that this has not happened. Occasionally, Jewish leaders, engaging in the healthy catharsis of self-criticism, blame themselves for what has happened. They claim that had they not succumbed to the demands of an uninformed laity for ever more leveling popularization or even vulgarization of their programs they could have secured the loyalties of Jewish intellectuals. Certainly, there is much in contemporary Jewish life which might offend sensitive Jews, but our self-criticism may be too harsh. A brief comparison of even the so-called popular programs of our synagogues with the programs of local churches will demonstrate that in many communities there would be no cultural offerings of any sort, save the movies, were it not for the adult education programs of our synagogues. By any standard of comparison the Jewish community offers the most intellectual program to its laymen of any of the religious groups. The reasons for the continuing defection of Jewish intellectuals go far deeper and they do not stem primarily from the admitted inadequacies of the synagogue.

One of the reasons why the renaisance of theological concern has not affected a significant change in attitude on the part of the Jewish intellectual has been its almost exclusively Protestant character. Even the Jewish leaders of the new theological endeavor, Buber and Herberg, have not been committed to the *life and practice of the synagogue*. Both have shared significant elements of the Protestant polemic against both the Law and the creative relevance of rabbinic Judaism whose primary institution is the synagogue. In this they differ from Jewish secularist groups whose rejection of synagogue life and practice is more deeply rooted in the Jewish experience. Now, Protestantism is and remains polemic to Judaism on its insistence that the Christ-event is the central event in human history. For Protestantism, Judaism is the religion of those with eyes "that see not" and ears "that hear not." There is no way of mediating the issue on their side, and Rosenzweig's attempt to mediate the issue on our side avoids the issue of the truth of the Christ-myth. When I was a rabbi in Natick, Mass., I had very often the task of taking non-Jewish children from the local churches through our sanctuary. They would always ask questions in such a way that it was obvious that what they were really asking was "Is this the way it was done in Jesus' time?" They didn't want to see a modern synagogue. They wanted to understand, and quite rightly, the birth of their own tradition. This attitude which begins at Sunday School carries over into adult cultural life. Jewish life and religion are seldom seen in the context of their present reality. Judaism is something "overcome," "superseded," or "antedated." Few religious traditions have been as misrepresented as that of rabbinic Judaism. The theological distortion has also fathered a cultural distortion. One does not have to go to racial anti-Semites to discover blatant misrepresentations of Judaism. Within the *Geisteswissenschaft* tradition, Judaism has been falsely identified with the spirit of alienation and the middle-class, bourgeois ethic. It is impossible to take a humanities course in any of our universities without this misrepresentation intruding. Toynbee is not an isolated phenomenon, but part of a tradition in Western culture which starts with Paul, is continued by the Patristics and Augustine, is accepted by Spinoza, and finally is bequeathed to the twentieth century by Hegel, Schelling, and nineteenth century German philosophy.

This tradition has nourished much of contemporary culture. It has certainly been strongly felt by the theologians. Kierkegaard's debt to Hegel is well-known. Thus the most important single figure who gives rise to the contemporary renaissance of theology is part of this tradition. Unfortunately, the contemporary Jewish intellectual has been as much influenced by this negative evaluation of Judaism as his Christian colleague. Furthermore, he has had an ever diminishing opportunity to acquire an impartial understanding of Judaism and its real character. It is foolish to describe the American university education as secular. In the humanities, the Christian polemic against Judaism is all-pervasive. Law is contrasted to love, the new covenant is seen as the herald of a new dimension in human existence, the "old" covenant as man's spiritual bondage. The Jewish intellectual does not have to read Paul, Hegel, or Toynbee to be influenced by this attitude. The very cultural air we breathe identifies Jews and Judaism with bourgeois society, the middle class ethic, conformity in spiritual matters, and a basic lack of genuine, open, religious spirit. Without a Jewish education, the Jewish intellectual is almost inevitably alienated from himself and from the traditions of the synagogue.

But the alienation of the Jewish intellectual goes far deeper than the theological alienation. As an intellectual, he is a part of another tradition in American letters which makes it difficult for us to reach him. He is part of the alienation which the American intellectual has felt towards the American people at least since the time of Jonathan Edwards. Examples abound. Henry James finally renounced his American citizenship. Ralph Waldo Emerson was more concerned with the unavailability of good books in Massachusetts than with the struggle between the states which was about to begin. T. S. Eliot turned his back on our shores for the Anglican and Royalist shores of England. The insane poet, Ezra Pound, wrote his cantos in Europe in an atmosphere of high treason. Not all American intellectuals have been alienated from the surces of American life, but there has been a tension between the practical do-abilities of the American people and the highly verbal culture of the American intellectual.

The Jewish intellectual shares this both as an American and, doubly so, as a Jew. In addition, he very often experiences a real tension between the middle class life of the majority of American Jews and his own life. This is very likely coupled with the tensions of the Oedipal problem, since the Jewish intellectual's parents are most likely to be of the middle class. He tends to reject Judaism, identifying it with that which is cultic, provincial, and with what he would deny in order to find freedom of expression and freedom of thought. Although the Jewish intellectual is more often than not the product of a middle class environment, he is as intellectual doubly estranged from that environment.

When we look at the contemporary Jewish scene, we behold that the institutions of Jewish life are almost entirely supported by, addressed to, and a product of the middle class. Marshall Sklare and Nathan Glazer have told us what in any case we already knew. The American Jewish synagogue has grown with the growth of suburbia. Today, the synagogue is largely a reflection of its suburban environment. No place is more middle class in spirit than suburbia. In addition, no place is as anti-intellectual in the deepest sense.

In this situation, it would be folly for the synagogue to commit itself irrevocably to the ideals and the ethos of *any* special class or interest group even where the majority of Jews belong to it. The synagogue is that institution in which the community of Israel expresses its ultimate concerns as they are occasioned by the passing of time, the crises of life, the aspirations for self-improvement, and the fate and destiny of Israel. It can never accept uncritically any class or social structure. This does not mean that the task of the synagogue is primarily the work of social reform. Nevertheless, there are and have been for a very long time sufficient inequities in our social system that we can not uncritically accept its values in totality. The prophetic function of the synagogue is certainly to identify the ever-changing idolatries of every age. Yet, this does not mean that the synagogue can or should identify its aspirations or values with those of the defected intellectuals. There can be no such thing as a program primarily for intellectuals in either the synagogues or the Hillel Foundations. This would be neither wise nor possible, nor would it help either the intellectual or the non-intellectual.

The program of the synagogue cannot be a program which excludes either group. What is basically required is a *fundamental seriousness and authenticity* about everything we do. Really great issues need not be so hidden within a web of concepts that their relationship to our life situation is obscured. The synagogue is the institution in which all men can express their ultimate concerns about situations through which all must pass. The intellectual suffers pain and guilt as strongly as the non-intellectual. The intellectual has the same problem of unravelling the ambiguities of Jewish identity in a non-Jewish world as the merchant. Both must come to terms with the passing of time and the final limitations of human existence. These are issues which concern us as *men*, not as special groups. *The final appeal of the synagogue is to the life realities which all experience in common.*

The task of the synagogue is therefore a mediating task. It must continue to make apparent each man's need for a community of ultimate concern. Its literature and its rite have a classic appeal. The only way that great world literature has ever been preserved has been because of the fact that its appeal and its character were multi-dimensional. Had *Oedipus Rex* appealed only to an *avant-garde* in Greece, it would not have survived to our times. It survived because it touched every man most deeply in an area which no man can escape or ignore. Furthermore, it reached levels of the psyche which are impenetrable to much that is superficial. Religious literature and rite have the same character. It is addressed to every man and it reaches levels of the psyche which are unavailable to areas of less concern. Goethe communicated the universality of the classic in his Prologue to *Faust*. The poet, the director, and the comedian discuss what each wants out of the play. Each wants and gets something different. The director wants his profits which only mass support can assure; the comedian wants an adequate vehicle for his performance; and, the poet wants to create something which will be of eternal value.

The fact of the matter is that really great issues have been those which can be universally communicated not only to the intellectual but to those who claim that they are not intellectuals as well. The life situations of each are not that different. Judaism is not concerned with the periphery of concern which varies in any case. It is fundamentally concerned with the realities of the life situation in so far as they are appropriate to community expression. Birth, guilt, death, time, and a meaningful integration of values lie within the preview of its concern.

We must therefore avoid two things. On the one hand, we must avoid pandering to the vulgar tastes of people who basically don't want their vulgar tastes pandered to, no matter how much they protest that they do. Judaism is an extraordinarily serious matter. It begins with the pangs of birth and ends with the separation and tragedy of death. These are not things which can be taken lightly. Nor are they matters to which the techniques of self-avoidance and the gimmicks of an acquisitive managerial society can be adequate. It is only in a fundamental and authentic seriousness that the great moments of life, as well as the moods and emotions which attend the passing of time, can be met. It is precisely for this reason that those who ask for gimmicks don't really want them. They themselves can see through their own deceptions. There is enough cheapness in their lives without vulgarizing the sanctuary as well.

On, the other hand, we must have a religious maturity sufficient in its depth not to fall into the trap of erecting a hierarchy of personality types in which we posit the intellectual as the ideal type towards which all others must strive. By the very nature of our world, we cannot all be intellectuals. Some are born in families where the sheer struggle for existence must be the only concern. Why take a person like this and rub salt on wounds by postulating a hierarchy of religiously approved personality types. Why make any man feel this sense of inferiority. Judaism cannot accept the Greco-Aristotelian conception that the noetic virtue is man's highest excellence. Each person is a peculiar soul unto himself and must develop his own special excellence whatever it may be. We must have sufficient maturity and love both to be serious enough to withhold from the non-intellectual what will be harmful and self-defeating and, yet, to recognize the necessity of the choices life has thrust upon him. His life, with its defeats, compromises, and victories must be just as precious to us as the others. We must recognize and accept a variety of personality types.

It is in this way that we can serve both groups. The rabbinate is not and cannot be exclusively concerned with either group. Representing Judaism, we must stand for the fundamental reality, the reality of man as thinking, but also as suffering, feeling, striving, and failing. We stand for this totality as it is expressed within the community of Israel. Our task and responsibility is that of utter seriousness to the *total* community of Israel. The gimmick is the worst thing we can offer the non-intellectual. By the same token, the worst thing we can do for the intellectual is to flatter his ego and allow him to feel that when he abstains from meaningful commitments within the community of Israel, he has been justified and that we have implicitly given him our approval.

Quite the contrary. We must never forget that every religion demands its peculiar form of sacrifice. In actual fact, no matter how diverse the range of Jewish affirmations may be, there is one sacrifice demanded of every-Jew. Catholicism demands the surrender of personal freedom to obedience of the hierarchical system. Protestantism — the Kierkegaardian variety — demands surrender of the intellect to the absurdities of faith. Judaism's sacrifice is not so obvious and, in a sense, it is much more difficult. Judaism demands that we sacrifice our pride so that we never see ourselves as intrinsically superior to any human being and certainly not to any human being within the community of Israel. This is a most difficult sacrifice for many intellectuals. They see themselves and their way of living as intrinsically superior to that of the middle class. It is for this reason that they are often unable to join in the life of the synagogue. In terms of acuteness, scholarly attainment, and sophistication much of what they see in the synagogue is far below their level. Yet, they fail to see the common realities which they share in any case and could share meaningfully within the context of the life of the congregation.

We must continually demand of the intellectual that he make his sacrifice. We must make him aware of the fact that he also is a member of the community of Israel without either praise or reproach. And when he tells us that the other people vulgarize the synagogue, we must not commiserate with him. We must insist that the responsibility of Israel is his responsibility, as well as those who now accept it. No man who stands for or serves the community of Israel can identify himself with, glorify, or attach himself to any special class or group.

There is only one technique adequate to the problem of involving both the intellectual and the non-intellectual in contemporary Jewish life. Whatever is done in the synagogue or the בית מדרש must be authentically Jewish. People are like honor in the old proverb. The quickest way to loose both is to run after them. Authenticity may not gain every Jewish intellectual. It will certainly gain those who have the slightest sensitivity to the realities of Jewish life. In contemporary cultural life, much lies beyond our control. That does not excuse us from doing what we can. There are no panaceas and this problem will undoubtedly always be with us. Yet never was the saying from Pirke Avot more appropriate:

לא עליך המלאכה לגמור
ולא אתה בן חורין להבטל ממנה׃

Is the Synagogue Becoming a Church, The Rabbi a Priest?
Religious and Secular Aspects of Jewish Community

HENRY SIEGMAN

IT HAS BECOME FASHIONABLE IN SOME PARTS OF the Jewish community—including, oddly enough, certain quarters of the rabbinate—to level the charge of "clericalism" against the religious establishment.

Jewish religious leadership, it is maintained by these critics, while preaching "Judaism is more than religion," is actually practicing "Judaism is religion only." Unique circumstances have projected American Judaism as an equal partner in a three-faith corporation of Protestant, Catholic, Jew. In their desire to exploit this situation, synagogues are assuming the role of churches and rabbis are transforming themselves into priests. They are accused of tampering with the historic character of the Synagogue, of the rabbinate, and of the *kehillah*, the traditional Jewish community, which embraced all of life and did not distinguish between the religious and the secular. Furthermore, this "un-Jewish" dichotomy between the religious and the secular is being asserted at the very moment when Christians, in their quest for a rediscovery of the Jewish roots of Christianity, are abandoning their old hostility to the secular world.

The charge of clericalism and the arguments for the "uniqueness" of Judaism are pressed most often by secular Jewish organizations, particularly those which have a large investment in interfaith activities. Until recently, their claims to spokesmanship vis-à-vis the Church went largely unchallenged, for Jewish religious organizations approached the interreligious enterprise with considerable ambivalence and caution. (Thus, while representatives of several defense agencies were busily engaged in lobbying in Rome during Vatican II, religious organizations refused to become similarly involved.) More recently, however, Jewish religious organizations have shown a new—if still qualified—openness to certain interreligious relationships, while spokesmen for both the Protestant and Catholic Church have shown a decided preference for dealing with the Synagogue and the rabbinate. In response to this challenge, professional Jewish ecumenists with the secular organizations have been impressing on Church leaders that the Synagogue is not the counterpart of the Church, and that to limit Judaism to the sphere of religion is a distortion of its true character.

One could observe that even if this argument were granted, it cer-

---

HENRY SIEGMAN *is Executive Vice-President of The Synagogue Council of America.*

tainly does not follow that rabbis and synagogues suffer some special disability which makes them *less* qualified than secular organizations to speak for the Jewish community. By sheer numbers alone, if nothing else, the Synagogue organizations are vastly more representative than are the defense agencies. Indeed, the Synagogue constitutes the only genuine grass roots institution in American Jewish life.

Furthermore, one could also observe that it is the secular organizations which are themselves most guilty of the sin they attribute to the religious organizations. If their argument against the preeminence of the Rabbi and the Synagogue is that Judaism does not recognize the distinction between the religious and the secular, then why the need for special interreligious departments within their organizations to be in charge of relations with the Church? Apparently, when they speak to the Church (or, for that matter, to society at large and to governmental agencies) they assume a religious face and unabashedly take advantage of the perquisites that accrue from the three-faith mythos.

Institutional considerations aside, it remains to deal with the substance of the charges, particularly since they have a very strong surface appeal. Everyone recognizes that Judaism *is* different, that its notion of religion is unlike that of the Church, that the realm of the secular was never consigned to the devil in Jewish thinking, and that the rabbinate never exercised a sacramental role. These feelings were summarized not long ago in an editorial in the *Reconstructionist* magazine: "In our vocabulary," the editorial declares "secular agencies are religious, they perform *miẓvot,* they serve to channel Jews' sense of moral responsibility to their neighbors. Just because Jews are identified with 'religious'—in the category of Catholics and Protestants—is no reason to overlook the uniqueness of Jewish existence. Jewry is not a church, but a people with a culture and a civilization."

There is something attractive about these words. And yet, they could not be more misrepresentative of the reality of Judaism, of its authentic worldview and self-understanding.

What follows is an attempt to delineate the fundamentals of the historical Jewish community and its ideological foundations, a task which in a time of radical institutions and ideological dislocation is of more than academic interest.

Synagogue and Community

A good place to begin such an inquiry is at the actual beginning, i.e., the historical origins of the Jewish community. As Salo W. Baron states, in his classic three-volume study of the Jewish community, these origins are to be traced to the Synagogue. More accurately, they go back to the religious gatherings that were held by the Jewish exiles in Babylonia. The term used for these meetings, *edah,* originally meaning simply a gathering, "came to be identified only with a worshipful gathering of Jews."[1] These gatherings, at first convened for the purpose of worship and religious instruction, gave their attention increasingly to the social needs of the community as well. Thus, "from its inception, the Synagogue was more than a mere sanctuary. . . It served everywhere as the center of all communal and many private affairs."[2] Synagogue and community became identical—so much so that congregational officers, as a matter of course, served as officers of the community as well. The *rosh haknesset* (archisynagogus) was at the same time the chief of the Synagogue and of the community. The same was true of the other Synagogue officials, the secretary (sofer) and the ḥazzan (who, unlike his modern namesake, was an assistant to the *rosh haknesset*). It was to the Synagogue, therefore, that the Jew turned, not only for worship, but also for social relationships and communal needs. For the Jewish people who emerged from the great crisis of exile stripped of state and territory, the Synagogue became the focal institution of their lives and the new instrument for national survival.

Given this identity of community and Synagogue, it is not surprising that the promotion of religion, with all that it embraced in the way of worship, education and judicial action "towered above all other (communal) activities." The community, thus, assumed an essentially religious character, which received powerful reinforcement from the fact that the traditional community's authority rested on its religious courts, the *battei din*. Indeed, religious alliance became "the main criterion of Jewishness and of membership in the Jewish community."[3]

Baron observes that, though the term Synagogue came to mean a Jewish house of worship, just as in Christianity *Ecclesia* came to connote a Christian place of worship, both terms "retained also their original significance, inasmuch as the Synagogue and Church continue to represent the aggregate of their respective communities."[4] *Indeed, the use of the term Synagogue to connote the total community and as a symbol of Jewish life and unity has no greater historical justification than in Judaism.*

The Role of the Rabbi

With the disappearance of the active priesthood and the downfall of Sadduceeism, rabbis and scribes made "insistent claims to exclusive leadership in public life." The rabbinic leadership that emanated from the Talmudic centers in Palestine and Babylonia was heeded throughout the Jewish world. There developed a submissiveness to this leadership

---
1. Salo Baron, *The Jewish Community: Its History and Structure, to the American Revolution* (Philadelphia: Jewish Publication Society, 1942), Vol. I, p. 61.
2. *Ibid.*, Vol. I, p. 87.
3. *Ibid.*, Vol. II, p. 124.
4 *Ibid.*, Vol. I, p. 87.

70 : *Judaism*

"greater than ever greeted the edicts of kings and high priests who ruled in Zion."⁵

An early practice of using lay judges in certain legal proceedings—a practice which might have strengthened the principle of lay religious leadership—was discontinued in the face of the growing complexity of the rabbinic legal structure. Lay judges were replaced by permanent judges, qualified through rabbinic ordination, which they received from central rabbinic authorities. As religion embraced with increasing exclusivity all walks of Jewish life, ordained judges gradually assumed functions going far beyond the administration of justice. "Soon they become the main leaders of the community, rivaling or exceeding elective officers in power, where they did not altogether replace such officials by their own appointees."⁶

In theory, at least, there existed some sort of distinction between municipal and religious responsibilities. Nevertheless, rabbinic scholars increasingly asserted themselves in the former area as well, and served as members of municipal councils in Roman Palestine. To be sure, this was resisted by the lay leaders, but they were unable to halt rabbinic supremacy in Palestine, and even less so in Babylonia.

Rabbinic hegemony raises serious questions about the democratic character of Jewish communal leadership. Here Baron offers a pertinent insight:

> Although not democratic in the modern electoral sense, rabbinic leadership cut across class and party lines and was, in some respects, more truly representative of the masses of the population than many an elective body. With forceful insistence, the talmudic sages opened wide to members of all social classes the gates to their own class, the aristocracy of learning.⁷

Rabbinic supremacy had first become a reality with the establishment of the Palestinian Patriarchate, which exercised supreme authority over the Jews of the Roman Empire. The patriarch (*Nasi*), as the recognized chief of world Jewry, appointed and deposed communal officers in Palestine and in the Dispersion. The Babylonian Exilarchate (*Resh Galuta*), which came into its own after the decline of the Patriarchate early in the fifth century, had more of the aura of a hereditary monarchy than that of a rabbinic office. Nevertheless, it, too, was essentially a religious office, as is suggested by the title, *Rabbana,* by which the exilarch was addressed.

The power of both Exilarchate and Patriarchate found its limitations only in the prestige and authority of the rabbis at the leading Talmudical academies. In describing this phenomenon, Baron remarks that "the grandeur of the political as well as spiritual power wielded . . . by a number of rabbis gathered around certain more or less permanent

---
5. *Ibid.*, Vol. I, p. 117.
6. *Ibid.*, Vol. I, p. 129.
7. *Ibid.*, Vol. I, p. 135

seats of learning is really amazing."⁸ These Talmudic sages welded Jewish life into a common pattern which was to last until the breakup of the ghetto in modern times. Centered in the Synagogue and the *bet hamidrash,* "the Jewish community was eminently equipped for its subsequent struggle for survival. . ." Not until the industrial revolution and the rise of modern science "was the pharasaic-rabbinic doctrine and way of life discarded or even modified in any essentials. The Jewish communities of seventeenth century Frankfurt or Cracow . . . bore an uncanny resemblance to those of Tiberias and Nehardea at the beginning of the third century."⁹

A brief survey of Jewish history following the post-Talmudic period reveals that, in Spain, rabbis held high rank in all communal councils and thoroughly dominated the courts. Italy, characterized by lay supremacy, was an exception. Yet, even here, "the rabbi remained the intellectual leader, the preserver of historic continuity and interterritorial integrity, and, hence, the chief protagonist in the drama of Jewish communal survival." In Franco-Germany, England and Poland, "rabbis were from all angles the leaders in communal matters." In Poland, however, questions of civil law were in the hands of lay elders.

To summarize, rabbinic leadership was always recognized in the traditional kehillah—in the breach no less than in practice. "No matter how many powers the communal plutocracy concentrated in its own hands, no matter how well it succeeded in making local rabbis and other officials subservient to its needs, the theoretical precedence of the scholar remained uncontested."¹⁰ It is in this uncontested leadership of the rabbinate that "the religious, educational and judicial control of the community had reached its climax. . . It was in the great elasticity, uniformity and continuity of this leadership that were focalized all the centripetal forces of the community."¹¹

Judaism and Christianity

In the light of the historical record, it is clear that many of the popular distinctions that are made between Judaism and Christianity are inaccurate. To be sure, there do exist real and important differences. There is no ecclesiastic authority in Judaism—hierarchically structured or otherwise (the hierarchical character of the ecclesiastic structure of the Church, almost always emphasized in these polemics, is not the relevant distinction) —which mediates the encounter between divinity and humanity, as there is in classical Christianity. (The validity of even this limited assertion must be qualified by an explanation of the role of the Temple priest-

---

8. *Ibid.*, Vol. I, p. 150.
9. *Ibid.*, Vol. I, p. 156.
10. *Ibid.*, Vol. I, p. 181.
11. *Ibid.*, Vol. I, p. 243.

hood in the area of worship and of the *zaddik* in Hasidic Judaism.) However, precisely because religion in Judaism is not limited to the human-divine encounter in the formal act of worship, but is expressed in the larger area of societal existence as well; that is to say, because Judaism, unlike Christianity, finds its fullest expression in a comprehensive system of religious legislation (*halakhah*) rather than in sacraments, the preeminence of the rabbinate, as the authoritative interpreter of the halakhah, was clearly recognized. While the internal hierarchical character of this authority was never clearly defined, its effective preeminence was never in doubt.

It should be noted that, in Palestine, there existed a clear hierarchical line of religious authority, from the local three-man *bet din* to the twenty-one man *sanhedriah ketanah* to the seventy-one man *sanhedriah gedolah*. Furthermore, the supreme authority of the local *marah d'atrah* is clearly established in Jewish law. As Immanuel Jakobovits, Chief Rabbi of Great Britain, states, rabbinic authority derives not from wisdom and learning alone, but from communal appointment. "As expressed so forcefully in the incident on fixing the date of Yom Kippur, a Rabbi Joshua, however superior his scholarship, must submit to the rulings and decrees of a Rabbi Gamliel as the practicing office holder. There can be no substitute for a challenge to an official and legitimate incumbent of a rabbinical post."[12]

From the above it should be clear that if by "clericalism" is meant the leadership of the rabbinate in every area of communal life, then Jewish history is an unbroken record of clericalism, in spite of the popular notion that "Judaism is inherently an anti-clerical religion." The role of the priest, of the Patriarchate and Exilarchate, and of the rabbinate in the various *kehillot* until the Enlightment cannot be understood in any other terms.

The difficulties created by the term clericalism are, ultimately, of a semantic nature. These semantic problems must not be allowed to obscure a central fact. If there is an irreducible imperative that emerges from Jewish history, it is that communal structures and leadership—be they lay or rabbinic—have always been based on the preeminence of religious purpose and commitment. In the struggle for power between layman and rabbi in various periods of Jewish history, the issue was never "the role of religion." Laymen, no less than rabbis, could not conceive of a basis or purpose for the kehillah other than a religious one, i.e., the working out of God's will in the daily life of *knesset yisroel*.

This point comes through with particular force in Jacob Katz's excellent work on the kehillah, *Tradition and Crisis—Jewish Society at the End of the Middle Ages*, where he stresses that the competition between

---

12. Immanuel Jakobovits, "Survey of Recent Halakhic Periodical Literature," *Tradition*, Vol. 8, No. 2, pp. 74–75.

rabbinic and lay leadership, which at times characterized organized Jewish life, must not obscure the fact that the kehillah was governed by the principles of religious law, which laymen championed no less than did the rabbi. In this they shared a common objective: "the (lay) wardens assisted in ensuring the dominance of religion in public life; and they were assisted by the rabbis, the paramount representatives of religion, in maintaining the regulations in other spheres"[13]

Defining Judaism

For those who oppose what they see as the self-aggrandizing role of the Synagogue, the central ideological issue is that Judaism, unlike Christianity, is more than religion. The implication of this assertion is clearly that religion does not define Judaism, and that religion is, therefore, *less* than Judaism, for Judaism includes culture, nationalism, ethnicity, and other such "civilizational" components in addition to religion.

To be sure, everyone may define Judaism in any way that is personally meaningful. It will be granted, however, that an historical definition of Judaism, no matter how difficult to arrive at, should not depend on anyone's personal values and beliefs. Furthermore, any redefinition that flies in the face of the mainstream of tradition and history—while it may be an action to which individuals are impelled by their own thinking and conscience—amounts to a rejection of that history and tradition and of the continuing identity which that tradition developed.

If, historically, the term Judaism did not suffer the limitations of the Christian concept of religion, this was not because Judaism includes elements other than religion, but rather because the Jewish concept of *religion* encompasses areas not included in Christianity. While, in Christianity, religion classically pertained to the spirit life of the individual, as distinguished from his societal concerns, in Judaism it extended to both. In other words—culture, ethnicity, nationalism are all concepts that in Judaism are very much a part of *religion*. Those who argue against this notion, and insist that these various components are not part of religion, but elements of a larger civilization entity called Judaism, of which religion is but one element, are limiting religion to worship in the synagogue, to dogma and to ritual. It is therefore they, and not religionists, who are adopting Christian categories in defining the Jewish concept of religion.

The Secular and the Holy

Because Judaism did not distinguish between the spiritual life of the individual and his societal concerns, there are those who conclude that what distinguishes Judaism is its championing of the secular society.

---

13. Jacob Katz, *Tradition and Crisis—Jewish Society at the End of the Middle Ages* (New York: Free Press of Glencoe, 1961), p. 126.

They argue, therefore, that it would be unforgivable if, at the moment that progressive Christian theology has discovered the secular city, the Synagogue should create a dichotomy between religious and secular areas of life.

Actually, what has, in fact, distinguished Judaism is its preoccupation with every aspect of life in society, *not with the secular quality of that life*. Indeed, in its societal orientation, Judaism always had a very specific direction and goal: to sanctify that life and to imbue its very aspect with holiness; in other words, to transform it from a secular to a sacred one. Rabbi Abraham Kook noted that Judaism knows only of the holy and the "not-yet-holy." In its effort to shape reality, Judaism "stands opposed to the secular movements which deprived the real world of transcendental meaning even more radically than to those religions which draw a sharp line between faith and the actual world.[14]

Judaism never suffered a secularist dimension, and the issue of secularism never distinguished it from Christianity. In its profoundest sense, religion in Judaism is precisely what it is in Christianity—only more so, as it were, for, unlike Christianity, the quest for salvation in Judaism always encompassed the broader area of the individual's life in society.

It has already been pointed out that the modern Jewish habit of disparaging the inward value of faith—a phenomenon not unrelated to that of Jewish secularism—is probably largely an unconscious defense mechanism in the face of the Christian challenge There is nothing authentically Jewish in such an attitude; clearly, "there is no performance of mitzvot without Jewish faith."[15]

The direction of the new Christian theology is antithetical to Judaism no less than to traditional Christianity. It seeks to desacralize religion through an accommodation to secular reality, and asserts that, in our modern technological age, man no longer lives his daily life with reference to transcendental goals and values. His life in society is self-contained and self-sufficient in a very material sense; God is no longer invoked in the life of modern society. As Cox states, in *The Secular City,* secularization represents a movement to bypass religion and to go on to other things. "It has convinced the believer that he could be wrong . . . and that there are more important things than dying for the faith." In the secular city, religion provides for few "an inclusive and commanding system of personal and cosmic values and explanations." The new theology celebrates this state of affairs; secularism is seen as a fulfillment of Christianity.

Of course, the Jew owes much to secular liberalism. It produced democracy and his political emancipation. Moreover, there is an impor-

---

14. Nathan Rotenstreich, "Judaism in the World of Our Day," *Forum,* Vol. IV, *Proceedings of the Jerusalem Ideological Conference* (Jerusalem, 1959), p. 50.
15. R.J.Z. Werblowsky, "A Note on the Relations Between Judaism and Christianity," *Forum, loc. cit.,* pp. 54–59.

tant sense in which Judaism is out-of-phase with Christianity and very much in phase with secular liberalism. Traditional Christianity holds a profoundly pessimistic view of man and society. Its principal theme is an infinite separation of evil man, in a world of sin and death, from a just God. The chasm is finally bridged only by Jesus. By contrast, Judaism's optimistic view of man and society is far more congenial to the optimism of modern secularism and its faith in education, science and technology.

However, this congeniality obscures a critical difference. Jewish optimism is rooted in a transcendent Creator who fashioned man in His image, who addresses him, and who also stands in judgment over him. Secular liberal optimism is rooted in man himself, and is thus always in danger of being transmuted into an *avodah zarah,* into idolatry. Emil Fackenheim expressed the skepticism of the post-Auschwitz Jew when he asks whether a secular liberalism that reigns supreme can be counted upon to remain liberal. Can it be counted on to respect the Jew's right to his Jewishness? Might it even be perverted into a demonic tyranny that denies the Jew's very humanity?

In any event, for the Jew, the new theology isn't really all that new. The Haskalah literature is full of the death of God and of religion because we have reached the age of science. Our Yiddishists and Hebraists substituted culture for religion, Zionists enshrined nationalism, and Bundists championed socialism. While all of these movements have their admirable qualities, none could have seen the light of day except for generations who lived as devout religious Jews.

The American Experience

Admittedly, a meaningful contemporary definition of Synagogue and community must take into account not only Jewish history, but ever-changing realities. This brings us to the role of the Synagogue under the new conditions of American Jewish life. Salo Baron, for one, does not discern any radical divergencies. "In Western Europe and America, the religious factor has retained its preeminent position in the scale of communal values . . . *the religious congregation has been the mainstay of all organized Jewish life*"[16] (emphasis added). Indeed, the evolution of community from, and its identity with, the Synagogue on these shores was virtually identical with the development of communal institutions in Babylonia.

From its very inception, American Jewish life centered around the Synagogue. The first Sefardim who came here in the middle 1600's set about reconstituting the European-type religious community to which they were accustomed. "Its central institution on these shores was the synagogue."[17]

---
16. Baron, *Op. cit.,* Vol. I, p. 4.
17. Jacob R. Marcus, "Background for the History of American Jewry," in *The Ameri-*

"Before 1820, the disciplined synagogue-community had claimed —indeed demanded—the loyalty of all Americans who called themselves Jews... Since 1820, ... American Jewry has been held together, if not by the synagogue, then by socio-cultural bonds and by the nourishing influences of a powerful subterranean current of religion and religious institutions."[18]

Daniel Elazar observes that even though the identity of Synagogue and community which had existed in early American Jewish life no longer obtained after the large wave of immigration from Central Europe, Jewish organizational life continued to be basically congregational. Though social service and educational institutions were nominally independent, "In fact, however, they tended to be dominated by leaders of particular congregations wearing different hats."[19]

It is interesting to note that the very earliest and, according to some observers, the closest approach which American Jewry has ever made to a national representative body was the Union of American Hebrew Congregations, which did not start out as a Reform institution, but sought to represent and speak for all American Jews. "Through its Board of Delegates it reached beyond purely congregational concerns into the areas of defense and relief, and even attempted to settle the early East European immigrants in colonies on the Western plains"[20]

What impact has the centrality of the Synagogue had on the self-image of American Jews? The sociologist, Bezalel Sherman, reports that:

> All surveys and population studies that deal with the attitudes of the Jews towards their group existence in this country report that the Jews regard themselves as constituting primarily a religious community, *whose ethnic character stems from the fact that the Jewish religion is the faith of the Jewish people exclusively...* (emphasis added) The new Jewish generation accepts the concept of Jewish peoplehood but it cannot comprehend a Jewishness that is completely divorced from the Jewish religion. Jews regard the Synagogue as the center of Jewish identification and see it as the institution in which American patterns of living and the search for Jewish self-expression converge.[21]

I propose that it is time, finally, to lay to rest a shibboleth that has been part of the conventional intellectual baggage of all observers of the American-Jewish scene, professional sociologists and amateurs alike, that Judaism, defined in predominantly religious terms, is a "churchy" phenomenon, the result of an accommodation to the three-faith syndrome of American society. Of course, one does violence to the traditional character of Judaism by limiting it to matters of faith. *But that is begging*

---

can Jew, A Reappraisal, edited by Oscar I. Janowsky (New York and London: Harper Bros., 1942), p. 5.
18. *Ibid.*, pp. 9-10.
19. Daniel Elazar, "Dynamics of the American Jewish Community," JUDAISM, Summer 1971, p. 337.
20. Marcus, *Op. cit.*, p. 18.
21. C. Bezalel Sherman, "Demographic and Social Aspects," in *The American Jew*, p. 47.

the question, for that is not what a religious definition of Judaism does. Quite the contrary, it broadens the purview of religious faith to embrace all aspects of life in society.

It is time that religious leaders stopped apologizing for their "accommodation" to the notion of Judaism as one of the three great faiths. It is those whose definition of Judaism empties that concept of the centrality of faith and of its all-embraciveness who are, in fact, accommodating themselves to secular realities in a way that totally distorts the historic character of Judaism.

To the extent that the new secular orientation of Christianity seeks to infuse general societal concerns with religious meaning and purpose, it approximates the traditional Jewish definition of religion. To the extent that this new orientation denudes life of transcendental meaning, as it all too often does, it could not be more hostile to Judaism.

The traditional definition of Judaism and of Jewish community does not argue for rabbinic hegemony. It does argue for the preeminence of religious character and purpose in our communal institutions and leadership. It is fatuous to argue that our secular defense agencies embody this character and purpose. They do not. Neither they, nor the social service agencies, invoke Jewish religious commitment and values on their own merit, or use them as the basis of their activities. Their orientation has been, and remains, a secularist one.*

One interesting aspect of the secularist orientation is the subtle way in which these agencies have historically misapplied the Church-State separation principle to eliminate religious influence from American public life—as distinguished from the institutions of government. This they have done on the assumption that Jews are most secure in a secularized society in which religious differences are least visible. (Of course, within the past year or two, all Jewish organizations seem to have joined the bandwagon of ethnic assertiveness. Whatever the motivation, it is clear that it is not the result of a religious renaissance.)

Such a view is wholly antithetical to traditional Jewish values. A policy aimed at weakening the influence of religion on society—in its public no less than its private manifestations—is a perversion of Judaism. Furthermore, the assumption that a Jew would not stand out in a secularized society is based on a conception of religion as a compartmentalized aspect of life, something to be expressed only in the privacy of a person's home and synagogue. It should be clear that nothing could be as foreign to Judaism as such a view. The distinctiveness of a religious Jew should be most strikingly conspicuous in a secular setting.

---

* Only recently, one of the major Jewish defense agencies sponsored a Conference on "Political Violence" jointly with Catholic University. The Conference was held on the Sabbath! One may be certain that this Jewish organization would not have scheduled the Conference on a day that might offend Catholic sensibilities. Their intensive involvement in ecumenical activities, no doubt, sensitized them to such gaucheries.

78 : *Judaism*

It should be stressed that no matter how one formulates a religious definition of Jewish community, there is no definition which reads any Jew out of that community. It is an old Talmudic principle that *yisroel, af al pi sheḥatah, yisroel hu*—no matter how far a Jew may have deviated from religious faith and practice, he remains a Jew. But by no stretch of reason can the Jew who has renounced those aspects of Judaism that, from a religious point of view are most central and sacred, be the touchstone of a new definition of Jewish community. The matter has been well stated by Robert Gordis:

> The right of all Jews to partial acceptance of Jewish values having been granted, inference has then been drawn that every pattern of acceptance or rejection is equally valid, with the unwarranted and all but fatal conclusion that Jewish group life must be geared to a level capable of including all who do not deny that they are Jews and no more than that . . .
> The fundamental error lies in assuming that if a group of Jews, each of whom espouses some partial aspect of Jewish life, or none at all, meet together, they constitute a community in any except the purey physical sense . . . that some Jews are interested in the synagogue, others in Zionism, others in relief, or local philanthropy, still others in anti-defamation or in good will, does not create a community but a chaos.[22]

The conclusion to be drawn from these remarks is not that secular Jewish organizations do not occupy a legitimate place in Jewish life. It does not even follow that the secular Jew may not define Jewish peoplehood in his own way and seek to orginize the Jewish community on the basis of his definition.* All of this is obviously quite proper in a voluntary, democratic society. What does follow, however, is that the rabbi and the Synagogue have at least as much a right to do the same, and that accusations of "clericalism" and "un-Jewishness" which greet such efforts are not only graceless, but betray an appalling ignorance of Jewish history and tradition.

The religious aspects of Judaism have always been, and clearly remain, the chief commitment of the American Jewish community, as has been the case throughout Jewish history. The Synagogue, for all of its shortcomings—and they are, regrettably, legion—continues to serve as the central focus of meaningful Jewish existence and as the mainstay of all organized Jewish life. It is, therefore, incumbent on our religious leadership, be it lay or rabbinic, to exercise a communal role that gives this religious element its fullest expression. It is a responsibility which Jewish religious leadership must finally assume if it is not to betray the Jewish past and forfeit the future.

---

22. Robert Gordis, "Toward a Creative Jewish Community in America," *Proceedings of the Rabbinical Assembly*, Vol. XIII (1949), pp. 321-22.

* I fail to see, however, how a secular definition of Jewish peoplehood can give the concept a content which distinguishes it from Italian, Irish or Polish peoplehood. The term, when used to describe the mystery of Israel which transcends sociological categories, is, necessarily, a theological statement.

Marshall SKLARE

The Sociology of
the American Synagogue (*)

Aux Etats-Unis la synagogue joue un rôle central dans la vie de la communauté juive. De nombreuses synagogues ont été construites depuis la fin de la guerre, et pas seulement dans les quartiers de pratique religieuse intense. Le taux d'affiliation, bien que variant selon l'importance de la ville, le statut économique et familial, est cependant très élevé.

La raison en est liée à la situation des Juifs dans la société américaine et à la nécessité d'un point de regroupement pour la survivance du groupe. Selon les orientations et les communautés locales, les exigences de conformisme religieux sont plus ou moins accentuées.

Le prototype de la synagogue américaine est le « centre synagogal », exerçant des fonctions qui dépassent le religieux : scolaires, de loisir, de rencontres diverses sous forme de clubs, etc. ; le bulletin synagogal annonce les événements familiaux. En Israël, par contre, la synagogue n'exerce pas les mêmes fonctions : l'étude et la prière sont les activités centrales et la survivance du groupe est assurée par la nation juive ; dans ce cas la synagogue a peu de signification symbolique : elle existe comme un but en elle-même.

La synagogue n'en reste pas moins une institution religieuse et certains voudraient la voir se définir plus clairement et plus strictement en ces termes. En fait, la diversité des formules est très grande : l'auteur en cite quelques types. Il n'empêche que le centre synagogal reste l'innovation institutionnelle de base du Judaïsme américain.

From all that we know about the low level of attendance at religious services among American Jews we might expect that the synagogue is a struggling institution which is banished to the periphery of Jewish life and located largely in neighborhoods where the foreign-born reside. Nothing could be further from the truth. The American synagogue is by far the strongest agency in the entire Jewish community. Many hundreds of new synagogues — Reform, Conservative, and Orthodox — were built as a consequence of population movement after World War II. The process continues. As new Jewish neighborhoods and suburbs develop, new synagogues come to be established or old synagogues

(*) Copyright © by Marshall SKLARE. From *America's Jews* to be published by Random House, Inc. (New York City).

are transferred to new locations. Not only have synagogues been built in areas where Jewish life is intensive but sooner or later they are organized even in neighborhoods which attract the more marginal Jewish families. The number of synagogues, the value of their buildings, and their location in all areas where the Jewish population totals more than a handful of families attests to the predominance of this institution in American Jewish life.[1]

There are no reliable nation-wide statistics on the rate of affiliation with synagogues. The most notable fact about synagogue affiliation is that it varies greatly with the size of the Jewish population. In small communities affiliation commonly reaches well over 80 per cent, and this despite the high intermarriage rates characteristic of such communities. In Flint, Michigan, for example, where the Jewish population is under 3,000, a total of 87 per cent of the Jews in the community are affiliated with a synagogue.[2] In communities of intermediate-size (10,000-25,000 Jewish population), the level of affiliation is lower — commonly over 70 per cent are synagogue-members. Thus in Providence, Rhode Island the figure is 77 per cent, in Springfield, Mass. it is 76 per cent, in Rochester, N.Y. 71 per cent and in Camden, N.J. it reaches the exceptionally high figure of 82 per cent.[3] In large Jewish communities the rate of affiliation is very much lower; it is commonly at about the 50 per cent mark. Thus in Detroit, Mich., 49 per cent are affiliated while in Boston, Mass. the figure is 53 per cent.[4] New York City is *sui generis* — while no study is available observation suggests that the affiliation rate is measurably lower than it is in any other large city.

Irrespective of community size membership is common in all segments of the population, with the following exceptions: it is somewhat more concentrated among the prosperous as well as among those with children between the ages of 5-15. Significantly, the rate of affiliation among the foreign-born is no higher than among the native-born. There is the further fact that even in the large cities where the rate of affiliation is low, most non-members joined a synagogue at one time or another. Former members include, for example, the widow who resigned after her husband's death and who now lives in reduced circumstances, or the prosperous family which dropped out after their children had a *Bar Mitzvah* or Confirmation. Furthermore, some of those who have never been affiliated will do so in the future. This is the case with many

---

[1] So great is the stress on the building of synagogues that it has drawn the attention of students of art and architecture. See, for example, Avram KAMPF, *Contemporary Synagogue Art: Developments in the United States 1945-1965* (New York: Union of American Hebrew Congregations, 1966).

[2] Albert J. MAYER, *Flint Jewish Population Study: 1967* (Flint, Mich., Flint Jewish Community Council, 1969), p. 45.

[3] See Sidney GOLDSTEIN, *A Population Survey of the Greater Springfield Jewish Community* (Springfield, Mass.: Springfield Jewish Community Council, 1968), p. 93.

[4] See Albert J. MAYER, *Jewish Population Study - Series II* (Detroit: Jewish Welfare Federation of Detroit, 1964-66), p. 24. For Boston see Morris AXELROD, Floyd J. FOWLER, and Arnold GURIN, *A Community Survey for Long Range Planning — A Study of the Jewish Population of Greater Boston* (Boston: Combined Jewish Philanthropies of Greater Boston, 1967), p. 136.

376

young marrieds who will join when they move from city apartments to suburban homes, and when they have children old enough to enroll in a Sunday or Hebrew School.

Whatever criticisms former members may have, and whatever the situation of those who have never affiliated, it is hard to find a principled opponent of the American synagogue.[5] Those who are outside of the synagogue are not firm opponents of the institution; absence from the membership rolls does not generally represent a clear commitment to any rival institution. It does mean of course that the individual has been strongly influenced by the secularization process. But many synagogue members have been vitally affected by the same process.

The lack of principled objection to the synagogue and the affiliation of diverse segments of the population must be added to our previous findings about wide differences in affiliation rate as between smaller and larger communities. There is little to suggest that Jews in smaller communities are more sacred in their orientation than their metropolitan cousins. In fact a case can be made out for precisely the opposite conclusion: that they are more secular in orientation, and much less traditional in their thinking. Why then do those who reside in smaller communities affiliate with greater frequency?

The smaller the community the clearer is the threat of assimilation and the clearer it is that the future of Jewish life rests upon the personal decision of each individual Jew. The decision to affiliate with a synagogue, then, means to vote « yes » to Jewish survival. And the smaller the community the more literal the voting metaphor: since every individual in the small community is asked to join, he is forced into casting his ballot. A refusal to join means placing himself in the assimilationist camp unless of course he has provided clear-cut evidence to the contrary by becoming heavily involved in some different aspect of Jewish life. The larger the community the less the chance of solicitation by significant others, the less the pressure to make a decision for survival, and above all, the more remote the threat of assimilation.

It is clear that in the largest communities, and especially in New York, synagogue membership does not have high symbolic significance. Accordingly, since many people lack the feeling that Jewish identity requires synagogue membership, non-affiliation does not mean a vote for assimilation. Conversely, one's resignation from a synagogue is not interpreted as meaning disloyalty to the group. In the metropolis, then, the synagogue must appeal on the basis of its instrumental as well as symbolic functions. Under such conditions a substantial proportion of the population find that they do not require a synagogue. They have little interest in the classical functions of the synagogue: religious services and study by adult males of Jewish texts. Non-classical functions which the synagogue has added also do not attract. Their children may be too young or too old for Hebrew School or Sunday School. Further-

---

[5] In Springfield, where inquiry was made into reasons for non-affiliation, the most frequent response was the cost of synagogue membership. Only about one out of ten went so far as to say their reason for non-affiliation was a lack of interest.

more they are not interested in the social activities provided by the synagogue, for they already are a part of a satisfying clique. Generally their group is entirely Jewish and dates back to friendships which were cemented in adolescence or early adulthood. Others are not attracted to the synagogue's social activities because they have a rich social life within their family circle. Finally in the largest communities a host of organizations and causes of a specifically Jewish nature are available outside of the orbit of the synagogue.

Whether situated in a larger or smaller community the synagogue works toward Jewish survival. It need not have been so — conceivably the synagogue in America could have followed a different course and insisted that as a religious institution it was an end in itself rather than a means to the end of Jewish survival. Such a synagogue would bar those who were strongly secular in orientation, or at least require that they accept a subordinate position. But there is religious justification for the synagogue moving in the direction it has: in Judaism the preservation of the Jewish people is an act of religious significance.

The American synagogue has accepted the secular Jew on his own terms; the institution has been more concerned with transforming him than with erecting barriers to his admission. In most congregations membership is open to all, there being no test of the applicant's religious attitudes or his observance of the *mitzvot* (the system of religious commandments). While in many Reform or Conservative congregations an applicant for membership is generally sponsored by a member of the synagogue or by one of its officials, this is only for the purpose of screening those who have an abhorrent moral reputation. The exception to the rule are certain Orthodox congregations which are interested in an applicant's observance of *mitzvot*. Such institutions prefer to restrict their roster to those whose behavior is in conformity with certain selected religious norms.

Since the typical American Jewish congregation is formed as a result of local initiative rather than under the authority of a central body, every synagogue is free to determine its own program and ritual.[6] Furthermore, since the polity among American Jews is congregational rather than episcopal, each synagogue is the equal of all others. Residents join together to hold religious services and to establish a school for their children. They raise the funds necessary to build an edifice and to hire a professional staff. The synagogue is organized in the form of a corporate body which holds periodic membership meetings at which

---

[6] In recent years the congregational unions such as the Union of American Hebrew Congregations (Reform), the United Synagogue (Conservative) and the Union of Orthodox Jewish Congregations of America (Orthodox) have taken greater initiative in forming new congregations.

The most notable exception to the freedom of the local congregation to determine its own affairs are synagogues affiliated with Young Israel (Orthodox). Title to the property of a Young Israel synagogue is vested in the national movement. The purpose of the arrangement is to prevent a congregation from instituting religious practices which are in violation of Orthodox norms.

378

the affairs of the institution are discussed and officers and board members elected. The board is responsible for determining the policies of the institution, although on strictly religious questions, as well as in certain other areas, the advice and consent of the rabbi of the congregation is commonly solicited.

The prototype of the contemporary American synagogue is the « synagogue center. » This is the synagogue which compromises with the culture and which serves the need for Jewish identification. Recognizing the impact of acculturation this type of synagogue expands its program far beyond the traditional activities of prayer and study. It seeks encounter with the Jew on his own secular level and it strives to reculturate him. The content and procedures of religious services are adapted in order to give them greater appeal, with Reform synagogues, Conservative synagogues, and Orthodox synagogues each handling the problem of cultural adaptation in characteristic fashion. Although traditionally there is no sermon during the weekly Sabbath service, part of the process of adaptation involves the introduction of this feature. Thus the sermon has become a standard feature of the weekly service in Reform, Conservative, as well as in some Orthodox congregations. The sermon is employed as an instructional as well as a hortatory device.

All synagogues sponsor some kind of program of adult Jewish study, although its character, and the importance attached to it, varies greatly from congregation to congregation. With the exception of some Orthodox synagogues women are free to participate in the program. In many places the traditional textual approach to study has been modified or supplemented. New kinds of courses have been introduced. But Jewish learning for children rather than for adults constitutes the real focus of the congregation's educational efforts. With the exception of certain Orthodox synagogues all congregations sponsor a Jewish school. While the majority of those who attend are of elementary school age, most schools aim to retain their youngsters after the high point of the educational experience: *Bar Mitzvah, Bat Mitzvah,* or Confirmation.

For the less-committed the fact that the congregation offers Jewish education is a strong inducement to affiliate. In most newer neighborhoods of the city, and in the suburbs, the only available Jewish religious schools are those conducted under congregational auspices. Some congregations make membership mandatory for enrollment, while others adjust their tuition fees to provide a financial incentive for membership.

Another important motivation for affiliation is the desire of secular-minded Jews to attend religious services on the High Holidays. While daily services, Sabbath services, and festival services are open to all the demand for seats on the High Holidays is so large that admission is commonly restricted to ticket holders. In some congregations tickets are distributed only to members while in other synagogues they are sold to the public, but at a higher price than the charge made to members. Since most High Holiday services today are conducted under the auspices of a synagogue, the institution is in a position to attract individuals who might not ordinarily be interested in an affiliation. The phenomenon of « mushroom synagogues » — opened during the High Holidays by private entrepreneurs — is on the wane and the phenomenon is rarely encountered in more prestigious neighborhoods. It has been replaced by the practice of established congregations which hold overflow services for the High Holidays or conduct services on a double shift.

Most congregations sponsor a variety of clubs for high school youth, young adults, young marrieds, adult women, adult men, and the elderly. These organizations serve to give the synagogue member another tie to the congregation. They are particularly crucial for individuals who are not strongly involved in the classical functions of prayer and study. Generally the organization composed of adult women (the « sisterhood ») is the most vital of these clubs. Membership in the clubs is so widespread that in the intermediate-size Jewish community they enroll far more members than any other Jewish organization. This is the case in Providence, for example, where 53.2 per cent of all men age 50-59 are members of a synagogue-affiliated club, as are 55 per cent of the women.[7] Recreational and associational opportunities are not limited to the synagogue affiliates, however. There are congregational socials and parties, dinner dances, specialized activity groups and fund-raising drives. All serve to increase the interaction of members. In the New York area in particular many synagogues provide a variety of athletic facilities.[8]

The contemporary synagogue is a large institution by traditional standards. While older Jewish neighborhoods in the largest cities may contain a dozen or more small congregations in addition to two or three large ones, an average synagogue in a newer neighborhood of a metropolis, or in a suburb, will generally enroll over 500 families. Congregations of this size have many members who confine their participation to specialized activities, or who participate very irregularly. Given large size and specialized or irregular participation, or even no participation at all, the printed word becomes a vital part of congregational life. Thus most congregations publish a bulletin at regular intervals. The bulletin contains the time of services and the topic of the weekly sermon, the schedules of the clubs, information about adult education lectures and courses, and news of the school. Of equal if not greater significance is the personals columns of the bulletin. Births and deaths are announced, donors are listed, the names of active workers are publicized, and significant milestones in life of members and their families are featured including birthdays, wedding anniversaries, and graduations.

---

[7] Sidney GOLDSTEIN, *The Greater Providence Jewish Community: A Population Survey* (Providence: General Jewish Committee of Providence, 1964), p. 141.

[8] One important aspect of the synagogue center (very much emphasized in the writings of Mordecai M. KAPLAN, for example) is the conception that nothing Jewish should be alien to the synagogue — that the synagogue should offer its facilities to all Jewish organizations which make a contribution to Jewish survival and that it should seek to facilitate the work of such organizations. But inasmuch as there are inherent strains in the relationship of congregation to community, this is more easily said than done.

While synagogues of the more traditional variety kind contrast sharply with the synagogue-center type of institution, it is the synagogue characteristic of modern Israel which places the contemporary American synagogue in boldest relief. The core of the program of the Israeli synagogue is the traditional activities of prayer and study. The core of the worship activities are the three daily services and the Sabbath service. Some men remain after the daily services, or come earlier, for the purpose of studying various sacred texts. They do this either by themselves, in pairs, or in groups. Most synagogues are small. Each has its officials, its leaders, and its congregants. However, individuals think of themselves as praying at a particular synagogue rather than being affiliated in any formal sense. Most synagogues do not have a professional staff — rabbis are employed by a central authority rather than by a particular congregation. While attendance and participation at services and in the study circles ebbs and flows, and although at certain holidays worshippers appear who are absent at other occasions, the interaction of the group of men who pray and study together constitutes the foundation of the institution.

Unlike the United States, then, the synagogue in Israel offers little outside of the classical functions of prayer and study of the sacred system by adult males. Unlike the United States, its existence and prosperity is not interpreted as a promise of Jewish survival at a time when the acculturation process is so advanced as to make it difficult to take such survival for granted. And unlike the United States, the Israeli synagogue is not perceived as a badge of Jewish identity or as the guarantor of the Jewish future. Rather, it is the fact of Jewish nationhood which is viewed as assuring Jewish survival. In essence, then, the synagogue in Israel has little symbolic significance; it exists as an end in itself rather than a means. And since it lacks the reinforcement and the unique role which it occupies in the United States, the Israeli synagogue is a much weaker institution and reaches a much smaller proportion of the population than its American counterpart.

Even if the American synagogue is generally a means to an end rather than ultimate value, it is still a religious institution. As such it is subject to evaluation by a unique yardstick — the yardstick of spirituality. Thus critics of the synagogue, while conceding that it makes a valuable contribution to Jewish life, are prepared to argue that it is nonetheless more of a liability than an asset. Some maintain that the American synagogue protects the individual from the demands of the Jewish religion as much as it exposes him to them. In a scathing indictment of the American synagogue Rabbi Eugene Borrowitz, a leading Reform thinker, has commented: « ...the average synagogue member ... comes ... to join the synagogue because there are few if any socially acceptable alternatives to synagogue affiliation for one who wants to maintain his Jewish identity and wants his children to be Jewish, in some sense, after him. Though this is not the only motive or level of concern to be found within the synagogue today, the Jew who does not rise about such folk-

381

feeling unquestionably and increasingly represents the synagogue's majority mood. More than that, however, it must be said that he also represents the synagogue's greatest threat... His newfound affluence and his need for status within the community have made the big building with the small sanctuary, the lavish wedding with the short ceremony, and the fabulous *Bar Mitzvah* celebration with the minimal religious significance well-established patterns among American Jewish folkways... What does it say of Jewish life in America when Reform Judaism appeals because it demands so little but confers so much status ? when people blandly proclaim that they are nonobservant Orthodox Jews ; when Conservative Judaism makes a virtue of not defining the center so that it may avoid alienating those disaffected on either side.[9]

Borowitz believes that the synagogue should become a more sectarian institution, that it should be transformed into an end rather than a means, and that it should relinquish its function of providing identity for the secular-minded, ethnically-oriented Jew. It is conceded that this policy will mean that many who presently belong will feel compelled to sever their affiliation (or, if not, have it severed for them). It is hoped that the loss of the masses will be compensated, at least in part, by the affiliation of those who — it is said — have remained outside or at the margins of congregational life because of an understandable distaste for the synagogue. As Borowitz sees it : « Clarifying Jewish faith might bring many to the conclusion that they cannot honestly participate in Judaism and the synagogue... No one wishes to lose Jews for Judaism, but the time has come when the synagogue must be saved for the religious Jews, when it must be prepared to let some Jews opt out so that those who remain in, or who come in, will not be diverted from their duty to God. As the religion of a perpetual minority, Judaism must always first be concerned with the saving remnant, and so long as the synagogue is overwhelmed by the indifferent and the apathetic who control it for their own nonreligious purposes, that remnant will continue to be deprived of its proper communal home. »[10]

More ethnically oriented religionists have proposed less drastic remedies. One such idea is the *havurah* (fellowship) a local group composed of individuals who belong to congregations but find such institutions to be so flabby and undemanding that they need other avenues to express their Jewishness. It is claimed that banding together and forming a *havurah* will protect and advance the spiritual life of those individuals who are ready for a richer religious diet than the synagogue makes available : « The *havurah* is certainly *not* intended either to supplant the congregation or even to downgrade it. There is no doubt that the congregation serves many vital functions... (but its) insufficiency inheres... in the heterogeneous character of the constituency. And the main aspect of that insufficiency lies in the fact that belonging to congregations is often no more than an innocuous gesture... Rabbis assume

---

[9] Eugene B. BOROWITZ, *A New Jewish Theology in the Making* (Philadelphia : The Westminster Press, 1968), pp. 45-46.
[10] *Ibid.*, pp. 53-54.

that the vast majority will attend only three times a year. Little — often nothing — is actually required besides the payment of dues. No commitment is asked ; none is generally given.

Now, while this may appeal to the escapists and the irresponsible, it does not appeal to those who are looking for a place in which they can take their Judaism seriously in the company of likeminded Jews. Thus, *commitment* is the key to one of the essentials of *havurah* ».[11]

The American synagogue is considerably more differentiated than its critics assume. Population size and density permitting, a variety of congregations are commonly established. Even when such congregations are similar in ideological preference they cater to different segments of the community. Such population segments are generally distinguishable by secular differences such as class position and level of general education but frequently they are also separated by differences relating to Jewishness : level of acculturation, differing conceptions of spirituality, and contrasting levels of observance of the *mitzvot*.

Lakeville, for example, is served by four Reform synagogues. All of the congregations are distinctive. One of them — the Samuel Hirsch Temple — is highly individual in its approach. It has been said that it is a synagogue for people who do not like to join synagogues. It has made a conscious effort to break with the synagogue-center concept. For a long time the congregation resisted putting up a synagogue building, for its leadership did not want to become involved in the type of activity which a building would entail. Furthermore, the Samuel Hirsch Temple in Lakeville has banned all clubs, and thus does not have a sisterhood or men's club. The congregation has sought to confine its program to the traditional activities of worship and study, though these activities are of course conducted in a style which differs markedly from the traditional approach.[12]

Differences in the Reform group are paralleled and even accentuated among traditionalists. Far Rockaway, New York, for example, is a community which is as Orthodox in reputation as Lakeville is Reform. Beneath its seeming uniformity there is great diversity among the many small synagogues which are in the area, and considerable difference between the two largest institutions — the White Shool and Congregation Shaaray Tefila : « The White Shool has developed primarily as a synagogue for the young layman who was once a *yeshiva bochur* (student in a school for advanced Talmudical learning)... It is unique as an American synagogue in that it numbers among its congregants about thirty-five ordained, non-practicing rabbis. The congregation has no *chazan* (cantor) but instead uses a battery of its own unusually gifted *baaley-tefilah* (prayer-leaders) who « work » in rotation... (the rabbi) not only gives more classes... than the average rabbi, but he offers them

---

[11] Jacob NEUSNER and Ira EISENSTEIN, *The Havurah Idea* (New York : The Reconstructionist Press, n.d.).
[12] See Marshall SKLARE and Joseph GREENBLUM, *Jewish Identity on the Suburban Frontier : A Study of Group Survival in the Open Society* (New York, Basic Books, 1967), pp. 97-178.

on a generally much higher level. In some areas — such as Gemorah (Talmud) — he may give *shiurim* (classes) on the same subject to different groups at different levels... like the European Rav, the largest part of the rabbi's time is given over to learning *Torah* and preparing *shiurim,* while a relatively small portion is devoted to the social duties and obligations which take up ninety per cent of the average American rabbi's time.

Shaaray Tefilah is tailored... to serve the total Jewish community rather than being primarily geared to the intensively *Torah*-educated Jew. Shaaray Tefilah's decorous, dignified service, led by a capable *chazan,* gives the synagogue and its divine worship an air of sacred reverence and respect for the Almighty. Many White Shool'ers, however, whose own synagogue breathes an atmosphere of an informal camaraderie prevalent in a « second home, » feel uncomfortable in the dignified atmosphere of Shaaray... On the other hand, most Shaaray'ites would feel ill at ease in the White Shool, where a considerable amount of conversation goes on during the service. The White Shool, to them, is an « overgrown *shtibel* » (an intimate setting for prayer and religious study) and far too undecorous. » [13]

Those who wish to change the American synagogue are tempted to do so by either going outside of the synagogue or by somehow convincing established institutions of the error of their ways and seeing to it that they implement higher standards of spirituality. But another option is open to the spiritual elite : they are free to establish their own synagogues. This option is afforded by the congregational structure of American Judaism, guaranteeing as it does the independence of the local synagogue. If this option is exercised the burden will then be on those new congregations which espouse elitist conceptions, for they will have to demonstrate their superiority over what has become the standard American synagogue center. Since the individual Jew is able to exercise freedom of choice such new congregations will have to compete with the standard synagogue center.

In summary, the American Jewish community has been able to establish a new kind of synagogue — the synagogue center. This development represents an institutional innovation designed to increase the chances of survival in an open society where the continuity of the ethnic group cannot be taken for granted. However critical of the synagogue center those who espouse elitist conceptions of spirituality are, their very attack is a kind of affirmation of the appeal which the synagogue center has had for American Jewry.

---

[13] Michael KAUFMAN, « Far Rockaway — Torah-Suburb By-the-Sea, » *Jewish Life,* Vol. XXVII, No. 6 (August, 1960), pp. 25-28.

Sacred Survival: American Jewry's Civil Religion

JONATHAN S. WOOCHER

SINCE THE PUBLICATION OF ROBERT BELLAH'S seminal essay in 1967, the concept of "civil religion" has become a widely-used rubric for exploring the religious dimensions of public (i.e., political) life. Bellah portrayed an American polity which understands, celebrates, and at times judges itself in terms of a distinctive religious vision of its own destiny and meaning on the stage of history.[1] But America has hardly been unique in this respect, and the notion of civil religion has proven a fertile one in settings far removed from Bellah's original focus of concern.

American Jews are not a sovereign political entity, but they do constitute a special type of collectivity, one which is appropriately defined as both a voluntary polity and a moral community. As a moral community America's Jews form a group which perceives itself as united for moral purposes beyond the satisfaction of material needs. They view themselves (as America views itself) through a religious prism, as the bearers of a special mission and place in history. To effect and express this unique communal self-understanding, American Jewry has organized itself as a voluntary polity, a matrix of institutions and agencies which carry out a public agenda of activities analogous to those of a national government.[2] Serving today as the "framing institutions" of this polity are the Jewish Federations found in almost every locality with a population of more than a few hundred Jews. As their generic name implies, these Federations began as leagues of charitable organizations, coming together for combined fund-raising and limited coordination of services. Over the course of the last half-century, both the power and the functional responsbilities of these Federations have grown enormously. Today, they plan and coordinate organized Jewish activity in virtually every sphere of communal

---

1. Robert Bellah, "Civil Religion in America," DAEDALUS, 96, No. 1 (Winter 1967): 1-21.
2. The concept of the American Jewish community as a "voluntary polity" has been developed and elaborated by Daniel J. Elazar in his book, *Community and Polity: The Organizational Dynamics of American Jewry* (Philadelphia: The Jewish Publication Society of America, 1976). On the emergence of Federations as the polity's "framing institutions" see Elazar's *Participation and Accountability in the Jewish Community* (New York: Council of Jewish Federations and Association of Jewish Community Organization Personnel, 1982).

JONATHAN S. WOOCHER *is assistant professor of Jewish Communal Service, Brandeis University.*

concern: health and social welfare, community relations, support for Israel and Jewish communities abroad, Jewish education and cultural development. The Federations are charged with the responsibility of raising the hundreds of millions of dollars which fuel the Jewish communal enterprise, and a host of Jewish agencies, operating on both the local and national levels, are linked to the Federation system financially, programmatically, and through overlapping leadership. The local Federations are themselves confederated nationally to form a country-wide institutional complex.

The American Jewish civil religion is, first and foremost, the operative religion of this polity — legitimating its activities, expressing and preserving its understanding of the meaning and mandates of the Jewish tradition. However, just as American civil religion is not the province of political leaders alone, what we will describe is far more than simply an institutional ideology. The American Jewish civil religion serves also as the faith which binds American Jewry as a whole together in a moral community, and which enables that community to locate itself in relationship to the Jewish past, present, and future.

The Evolution of the American Jewish Civil Religion

The current American Jewish civil religion is the product of an evolutionary process which has woven together strands from what has been called American Jewish folk religion and from elite ideologies which have been affirmed by important segments of American Jewry's institutional leadership.[3] These "elite" components represent the latest version of a philanthropic approach which has evolved considerably during the course of the twentieth century. American Jewish communal leaders (and American Jews in general) have always prided themselves on "taking care of their own" and on more than pulling their own weight in American society, and one of American "civil Judaism's" enduring myths is the story of the pledge ostensibly made by the first Jewish settlers in New Amsterdam in 1654 that they would not permit any one of their brethren to become a public charge. Coupled with this has been a sense of responsibility assumed by relatively fortunate American Jews for the security and welfare of co-religionists in other lands, manifested as early as the mid-nineteenth century.

These responsibilities were accepted by the American Jewish communal elite because they were consistent with their own conceptions of Judaism, presented a positive image of Jews, and could be exercised in the best spirit of Americanness. This desire to affirm the Jew's place qua

---

3. For a discussion of American Jewish folk religion and its relationship to elite formulations of Judaism, see Charles Liebman, *The Ambivalent American Jew: Politics, Religion, and Family in American Jewish Life* (Philadelphia: The Jewish Publication Society of America, 1973).

Jew in the American enterprise has been the civil religion's most enduring theme. In the early years of the twentieth century it sustained a three-element program of leadership activity, best exemplified, perhaps, in the lives of men like Louis Marshall and Jacob Schiff. For these men and their like — the founders of the American Jewish Committee and major donors to the early federation campaigns — the obligations of Jewishness included support of the needy, protection of Jewish rights (in America and abroad), and assistance to new immigrants in the process of "Americanization," of becoming educated, successful, contributing citizens like themselves. Although their "civil Judaism" was respectful of Jewish tradition, it placed little emphasis on extensive knowledge or observance of that tradition. It was concerned primarily with insuring the adjustment of Jews to the American environment and demonstrating the compatibility of Jewishness with American cultural norms. Hence, Jewish traditions and rituals which were incompatible with American cultural norms — observance of the Sabbath and dietary laws, for example — were deemed unnecessary, if not barriers, to integration.

The folk religion which the masses of Jewish immigrants brought with them from Eastern Europe was quite different in character from this civil religious ideology. It was grounded in a powerful sense of what we would today call Jewish ethnicity, even nationality, a framework for group self-definition and a sense of shared destiny with which the established communal leadership was uncomfortable. Only a minority of immigrant Jews were observant by Orthodox standards, but they shared a richer awareness and deeper ties to traditional Jewish culture and its values and folkways than did the already highly Americanized native communal leadership.

Yet the immigrants and, especially, their children also shared the basic goal of their "uptown" counterparts: to succeed as Americans. Slowly, but quite surely, a process of synthesis began to take hold. Even before World War I, Louis Brandeis had been able to present Zionism — which had broad appeal among the Eastern European immigrants but was ideologically anathema to many of the leadership establishment — as compatible with good Americanness. A Jew who supported Zionism, he argued, was demonstrating his commitment to the values that were central to the American dream, the same values which were being applied to the upbuilding of Palestine. Naturally, it was not expected that American Jews would emigrate to Palestine, but, as Americans, they must assume a responsibility for insuring the success of the Zionist endeavor. In general, during this period, there was a blurring of the lines between aiding "co-religionists" and affirming a sense of peoplehood through assuming responsibility for the welfare of fellow Jews. Philanthropy and the fight against anti-Semitism gradually brought American Jews together across most boundaries of background, religious denomination and ideology. The folk religion embraced Americanization and the elite civil religion made its peace with the concept of peoplehood. The community, as a whole, dedicated iself to the ideal of full participation in American life, and defined and shaped the Jewish tradition in such a way as to provide maximal support for this venture.

The most recent phase in the evolution of American Jewish civil religion has by no means abandoned this legacy. But it has amplified what was, perhaps, an undertone and made it a dominant note in its embrace of Jewish survival as the organized community's overriding goal. Two events — the murder of six million European Jews and the creation of the State of Israel — coupled with an urge to maintain a recognizable Jewish presence on the American canvas have propelled a collective redefinition of the communal mission. The tenets of the polity's civil religion are today largely built around what the theologian, Emil Fackenheim, calls contemporary Judaism's "614th commandment": Thou shalt not give Hitler a posthumous victory by permitting Jewish survival to be endangered again.[4] Yet, true to its origins and the deepest feelings of its adherents, civil Judaism remains very much an American, and an America-affirming, faith.

The Tenets of the American Jewish Civil Religion

The articles of faith of the civil religion are linked to the philanthropic and political ethos of the communal institutional system, thereby legitimating the activist program of the polity and its leaders. Many of the tenets of the American Jewish civil religion represent easily recognizable restatements of classical Jewish religious values. American Jewish civil religion has selected and adapted these for use in contexts heavily affected by the process of secularization and fashioned them into a coherent modern faith, one rooted in popular Jewish sentiment, resonating with the Jewish tradition, and sufficiently flexible to embrace diverse private Jewish convictions and commitments which lie beyond its own scope. There are seven such tenets:

1. The Unity and Distinctiveness of the Jewish People

The Jews constitute a single, unique people. The category of "peoplehood" is one which satisfies the desire of American Jews to assert a common Jewish identity which is rooted in something more than, or an alternative to, shared religious conviction. (Indeed, conventional theistic faith is not even regarded as a requisite for membership in the Jewish collectivity.) At the same time, it permits these Jews to continue to assert their nationality (not to mention citizenship) as Americans. The Jewish people is one, and it has a homeland — Israel. But Jews may live anywhere and be part of that people.

---

4. Emil Fackenheim, *God's Presence in History* (New York: Harper and Row, 1970).

The American Jewish civil religion strongly affirms what Simon Herman calls alignment over space and time on the basis of "interdependence of fate."[5] As a people, Jews share not only a common history, but a common destiny. This is the foundation for the civil Jewish emphasis on identification wtih all of world Jewry, regardless of differences in circumstances or lifestyle. *K'lal Yisrael* — the communality of all Jews — is a primary value in this religious system. Undoubtedly, some elements of *noblesse oblige* remain in the extraordinary efforts which the organized community mounts to help Jews in need throughout the world, yet, what is stressed is not merely their need, but that they are fellow Jews and, therefore, entitled to the support of their brethren.

For American Jewish civil religion, Jews constitute not only one people, but a unique people. The sense of Jewish distinctiveness is compounded out of several elements: the particularity of Jewish history, the condition of isolation which the State of Israel suffers in the world community, and the commitment to extraordinary achievement in the intellectual and moral realms which, many Jews feel, is shared by their fellows. In effect, this sense of distinctiveness represents a secularization of the traditional Jewish conviction of "chosenness." Like the latter, it is subject to chauvinistic reduction to a feeling of innate superiority, but, in its orthodox civil Jewish articulation, it, too, constitutes primarily an assertion of responsibility and aspiration, an ethical injunction, rather than simply an expression of accomplished fact.

2. Mutual Responsibility

This concept of responsibility is itself one of the hallmarks of the American Jewish civil religion. The Talmudic statement "*Kol Yisrael areivin zeh ba-zeh*" — all Jews are responsible for one another — serves as a central dogma of the civil Jewish faith. "Responsibility," in this context, has at least three connotations. First is responsibility for the physical security and well-being of other Jews — protection of their rights and provision for their human needs. This, as we have seen, is an idea which has been part of American Jewish civil religion from its inception. Today, the concept of responsibility extends into a second domain as well: responsibility for insuring that Jews have the opportunity to acquire, express, and transmit a Jewish identity. The notion that Jews are responsible for maintaining what is often referred to as "the quality of Jewish life," has found expression in an expanded assumption of communal responsibility for Jewish educational services — both locally and worldwide.

The third sense in which Jewish "mutual responsibility" is affirmed in the American Jewish civil religion is a good deal more subtle, but is tied even more closely to folk sensibilities. Just as American Jews continue to

---

5. Simon Herman, *Jewish Identity* (Berkeley: Sage Publications, 1977), p. 43.

feel pride in the achievements of other Jews — achievements which they had no hand in — so, too, they feel, in some way, responsible for the standards of behavior which other Jews maintain. This is more than a matter of shame or fear of opprobium spilling over onto themselves (though both of these are part of that feeling). It reflects, as well, a larger sense of what it means to be Jewish. Just as the tradition could raise suspicion about the ancestry of a Jew lacking in compassion, American Jews continue to feel that certain patterns of behavior are "unJewish." Whether it be the readiness to invoke the concept of collective responsibility in the wake of the 1982 massacres in the Palestinian refugee camps in Lebanon (while, at the same time, rejecting the right of non-Jews to render judgment!), or the unusually strong communal anguish felt as cases of wife-beating and child-abuse are discovered among Jews, the signals of this sentiment remain strong. For the civil religion, to be a Jew is to be responsible for, and to, other Jews. This entails a number of specific obligations.

3. Jewish Survival is Endangered

The first and foremost of these obligations is active concern for Jewish survival. One of the assumptions of the civil religion of American Jews, like that of Israel, is that the world is often indifferent, and sometimes hostile, to Jewish survival. The Jewish people dwells not only alone, but under constant threat. The preoccupation of organized American Jewry with anti-Semitism — in the Soviet Union, in Europe, in Argentina, in the Arab world, even in the United States— reflects this underlying world-view.

American Jewish civil religion has absorbed the syndrome which the Jewish philosopher, Simon Rawidowicz, identified in his classic essay "Israel: the Ever-Dying People"[6] — a conviction that Jewish survival is perpetually threatened and, therefore, must be defended with enormous vigor. The source of the threat, however, is not always external hostility. American Jewry, in particular, is seen as threatened precisely because the environment in which it lives is so hospitable. Here, Jewish identity is under siege from within, rather than from without. America is, indeed, different, but its difference, civil Judaism asserts, is not without a price. This focus on assimilation as a threat to Jewish survival is a relatively recent addition to the American Jewish civil religion. It does not contradict the older fundamental civil Jewish affirmation of America as a *goldene medine* for Jews, and it is consistent with rejection of the Zionist premise that Jewish life cannot survive outside of a Jewish State. What it has done, however, is, in effect, to round out the circle: the specific environment in which Jews live is not determinative of their fate. Jewish survival

---

6. Simon Rawidowicz, "Israel: The Ever-Dying People," *Studies in Jewish Thought* (Philadelphia: The Jewish Publication Society of America, 1974), pp. 210-14.

is *always* endangered, if not from one source, then from another. Thus, the life of the Jewish people is a perpetual quest to take control of its own destiny, to insure its own survival by its own strength, and the mission of the American Jewish community must be to carry on that struggle on every front.

4. Support For Israel

Nevertheless, the primary front in that battle for Jewish survival is, in the eyes of most American Jews, the State of Israel. It has been said that American Judaism recognizes only one heresy which subjects the perpetrator to immediate excommunication: denial of support for that State. The role which Israel plays in the civil religion is, indeed, central, though complex. It is, first and foremost, the homeland of the Jewish people. To that extent, those American Jews who proclaim that "we are all Zionists" are speaking truthfully. Support for Israel is predicated, therefore, not simply on its being a land of refuge for persecuted Jews, but on its symbolic significance as the center of the Jewish world. Even more, Israel is the testimony to Jewish vitality, to the people's capacity to triumph over its enemies, to meet and to beat the non-Jewish world on its own terms. For American Jewish civil religion, as much as for the Israeli, the State of Israel is the Jewish people's answer to Hitler, the renewal which makes the tragedy of the Holocaust bearable.

The civil religion of American Jews demands militant and unequivocal support for Israel — financially and politically. And, yet, the vast majority of American Jews, including most of the civil religion's strongest proponents, have no intention of settling in Israel and do not believe that such a decision is necessary in order to be a good Jew.

From the perspective of classical Zionism or Israel's own civil religion,[7] such a disjunction is virtually unintelligible. But, from the perspective of the civil religion of American Jews, it is quite consistent. Support for Israel testifies to one's loyalty to the Jewish people, to the depth of one's sense of responsibility. But, since the Jewish people is one, that testimony can be offered wherever one lives. Critics have, at times, castigated American Jews for their "checkbook" Judaism, for "Israelolatry," or for placing on Israel the burden of vicariously living out their own Jewishness. All of these charges have a measure of truth. But the dynamic behind them is not selfishness or indolence. Israel is a sacred symbol in the American Jewish civil religion, subject to all of the abuse and misuse which sacred symbols must bear. Precisely because American Jews, unlike Israelis, do not have to deal with the every-day reality of Israel, they often have difficulty in coming to grips with Israel's flaws and shortcomings. Their reluctance to envision settling in Israel may, therefore, be an

---

7. On Israel's civil religion, see Charles S. Liebman and Eliezer Don-Yehiya, *Civil Religion in Israel* (Berkeley: University of California Press, 1983).

unconscious way of protecting the religious system that they have constructed from the disconcerting and disconfirming impingement of reality.

In prescribing support for Israel, the American Jewish civil religion is trying to insure American Jews a meaningful role in the unfolding of Jewish destiny. But it does not regard Israel's fate as the sum total of that destiny; neither does it view support of Israel as the only religiously significant way of sharing in that destiny. In this respect, the civil religion remains firmly in keeping with its diasporist origins and functional for American Jews. The current rhetoric of community leaders, which emphasizes the concept of "partnership" between Israel and diaspora Jewry, reveals the true world-view and ethos of American civil Judaism. Thus, those who have described Israel as American Judaism's religion are simply mistaking the part for the whole, the single symbol for the system. As important as are Israel and support for it within American Jewish civil religion, they are not its entire substance.

5. Affirmation of Jewish Tradition

American Jewish civil religion has always maintained a respectful, if selective, attitude toward the contents of the classical Judaic tradition. For many years, to be sure, the posture of the organized (non-synagogue) American Jewish community was "secular," at least in its own self-understanding. But, in the American context, secular meant primarily non-denominational rather than anti-religious. Ideological secularists — those with a specific program of transvaluation comparable to that of the socialists or the Zionist pioneers who rebelled against traditional Judaism — never dominated the community or contributed substantially to its civil religion. For many years, American civil Judaism maintained an attitude of what might be termed "benevolent neutrality" toward traditional religious institutions, beliefs, and practices. It related itself primarily to a public agenda which was philanthropic and social in character. While it acknowledged that religious convictions might well undergird the values that it promoted, it neither insisted on the religious character of those values nor did it seek to incorporate traditional religious practices in its set of behavioral norms. American Jewish civil religion always regarded positive Jewish identification as a virtue, but it did not prescribe the form that such identification should take and it viewed the inculcation of such an identification as essentially a private responsibility.

In recent years, this tenet of the civil Jewish faith has undergone substantial modification. Today, American Jewish civil religion has moved from an attitude of benevolent neutrality to one of generalized respect for, and affirmation of, the Jewish tradition. Traditional practices are more extensively incorporated within its own ritual system and, perhaps most important, transmission of the substance of the tradition is regarded as an essential part of the overall effort to insure Jewish continuity.

The "tradition" which civil Judaism affirms is, of course, a modernized and pluralistic one. It still shies away from attempting to dictate (or even suggest) norms for personal Jewish observance, but it does regard some such observance as valuable, even important. And, in the public domain, its own arena, the civil religion has become noticeably more traditional in character. The governing principle of communal organizational life is to try to avoid activities which would be offensive to observant Jews, such as overt violations of the Sabbath or dietary laws. Even more, opportunities are now provided for the expression of traditional religious values and concerns within what were formerly regarded as "secular" contexts. Thus, Jewish worship and study have made their way into the civil religious behavioral repertoire.

The American Jewish civil religion has redefined its role as a sponsor of Jewish tradition as well. Since it regards the survival of the Jewish people as intimately bound up with (indeed, even dependent upon) the survival of the Jewish religious tradition, it has made the transmission of that tradition a communal responsibility. Because it does not explicitly endorse any specific version of that tradition (in practice, it is probably closest to moderate Conservative), what the civil religion itself transmits as the content of Jewish tradition is "homogenized" and tends to focus on the ethical dimension. But adherents of civil Judaism are now, by and large, prepared to throw the weight of communal endorsement behind a broad range of Jewish educational endeavors — from Reform to Hasidic. Since the civil religion continues to remain largely indifferent to matters of theology, and since it also continues to affirm the legitimacy of religious pluralism and individual choice, it has no real incentive to try to develop an elaborate or formally articulated religious idelogy of its own. Instead, it is satisfied to fasten on those elements of traditional Jewish values and practice which all positive Jews seem prepared to endorse. These it incorporates into its own ethos, while remaining open, if institutionally non-committed, to more ideologically focused expressions of Jewish behavior and belief.

6. *Zedakah:* Philanthropy and Social Concern

Of all the values which Jewish tradition embraces, the one which has been most prominent in the civil religion has surely been *zedakah*. As we noted above, the institutional focal point for American Jewish civil religion has been the organizational matrix framed by the local community Federations. In the light of their origins as philanthropic enterprises — and the importance which fund-raising continues to play in their operation — it is not surprising that Federations, and the evolving American Jewish civil religion, have always given *zedakah* a place of prominence in their value system. The significance of *zedakah* is heightened by the fact that the root meaning of the term is more akin to the concept of "social justice" than of "charity." Thus, as the primary institutions of the organized community — the Federations and the so-called defense (later community relations) agencies — broadened their program to include participation in the larger struggles for civil and human rights and social justice in American society, *zedakah* remained at the heart of their ideological and Jewish self-understanding.

Today, the civil religion continues to regard *zedakah* as the primary mandate of Jewish tradition and to legitimate much of the activity of the American Jewish polity in terms of it. *Zedakah* is a *mizvah*, a commandment, not an option. Hence, it is the duty of each Jew to participate in the community's philanthropic work, if only by contributing to the local Federation campaign. For the community as a whole, the work of *zedakah* — "meeting human needs," as it is often put — is the prime requisite alongside the insurance of Jewish survival itself. Indeed, what prevents the civil religion from becoming pure survivalism is the ethical impulse provided by the commitment to *zedakah*.

The underlying ethos of civil Judaism can be described as one of exemplary ethical responsibility. Because of their history and their values, Jews are expected to be more vigorous in the pursuit of social justice, as well as more generous in their support of those in need, than others. With the recent trend in American Jewish life toward a "turning inward," a preoccupation with survival and the quality of Jewish life, and a disillusionment with social activism, this component of the civil religion has been weakened. But it has by no means disappeared, just as American Jews continue to be, as a group, far more liberal politically than their socio-economic status would suggest. The easy transference which the civil religion once made between *zedakah* and left-leaning politics has been called into question. Yet, the strong underlying commitment to social justice, and the conviction that it represents a fundamental Jewish value, endure among the leaders of the communal system. At the same time, there has been no diminution in the importance placed on the expression of *zedakah* through help to Jews in need — wherever and however they may live.

Thus, *zedakah* remains the cardinal ethical value of American Jewish civil religion. Both the individual Jew and the community are judged in accordance with their readiness to live up to its standards. One may quarrel with the weight given to this single value as a criterion of Jewishness (especially when it serves to elevate the status of wealthy philanthropists at the expense of others with deeper and fuller Jewish commitments). Still, the prominence of *zedakah* as a value and the belief that Jews should be exemplary in their embodiment of it, have helped to link the civil religion to the traditional Judaic value system and to provide American Jews with a sense of mission and duty which transcends self-perpetuation.

Civil Judaism thereby responds to both the self-interested and the altruistic instincts of a population that is still concerned about its "place" in the world and is still seeking moral self-justification. Jewish survival is not a chauvinistic conceit, but a requisite for the continued fulfillment of the Jewish role as an exemplar of ethical values.

7. Americanness as a Virtue

The tenets of the American Jewish civil religion serve, as we have seen, to define the conditions of Jewish existence in the modern world and the primary mandates for behavior flowing from that world-view. Civil Judaism sees Jewish life as precious, but tenuous. Both the people and its tradition must be preserved and nurtured in the face of threats from without and within. At the same time, Jews must continue to make their survival meaningful by exemplifying the high ethical values of Jewish tradition.

Nothing in all of this is seen as, in any way, calling into question either the possibility or the desirability of full participation by Jews in American society and culture. The civil religion reserves a special place for America amidst the nations of the world. Yes, Jews have known anti-Semitism and discrimination in this country. Yes, assimilation through inter-marriage and the loss of Jewish identity are dangers which must be fought. But, fundamentally, America *is* different. For all of their anxiety, American Jews believe that this is, in Jewish terms, indeed, a "golden land." If it is not *the* homeland and *the* promised land of the Jewish people, it is still their homeland and promised land in a more immediate sense. And, as we have seen, they are not prepared to leave it.

This is not to say that the relationship of American Jews to America is entirely without ambivalence. For the civil religion, however, the emphasis is not on the doubts, but on the affirmation. American Jews can, and should, fulfill their Jewish destiny and commitments within a mostly benevolent American embrace. America has welcomed the Jews and Judaism. Jews have done well, and they have done good. Like the folk religion, the civil religion proclaims that, by being better Jews, Jews will also be better Americans, and vice versa.

The terms of the "bargain" between America and its Jews are beneficial to both. The civil religion expects Jews to take advantage of the opportunities which America provides, and to use them to help fulfill their Jewish responsibilities. Jews have earned the right to expect America to honor their concerns. In turn, American Jews are more than willing to shoulder their share of the responsibilities of American citizenship and active participation in the life of the nation. Since civil Judaism is modernistic in its approach to Jewish practice and belief, it does not perceive American social and cultural norms as constituting substantial barriers to the expression of Jewishness. If some Jews assimilate to the point of abandoning their Jewishness all together, that is a problem for Jews to deal with, but it is not a rationale for withdrawing from the larger society. By continuing to play an active role in every phase of American life, Jews will continue to serve their own interests and those of the larger society as well.

This faith in the long-term prospects for Jewish life in America stands behind the civil religion's rejection of the classical Zionist analysis of diaspora Jewish life. In America, it simply does not apply, and American Jews make their best contribution to the Jewish future by remaining where they are, strengthening their community and their position in American society and, with it, their capacity to help other Jewries in need.

Conclusion

American Jewish civil religion is a complex system of ideas and sentiments which helps American Jews define and sustain themselves as a distinctive subcommunity in both American and Jewish life. By providing Jews with a self-understanding which validates their often prodigious organizational endeavors in the sacral vocabulary of mission and destiny, it enables them to mediate between a traditional religious group identity and a secularized life-style. American Jews who accept the tenets of this civil Judaism have confronted the classic modern dilemma of integration vs. group survival and have found a vision of themselves and an ethos of responsible ethical action which purport to resolve that dilemma by embracing both of its poles.

Critics of American civil religion have noted the shallowness of its theology and the danger of its degeneration into mere national self-celebration. American civil Judaism, too, may be a flawed attempt to translate traditional religious conviction and discipline into an acceptable and politically functional idiom for an ethnic community. But, regardless of how it is ultimately judged, American Jewish civil religion has become a major force in shaping the commitments and behavior of American Jews. As the religious ideology of a community which has done both well and good — for itself, its adopted homeland, and its fellow Jews throughout the world — American civil Judaism, its evolution and its fate must be seen as an important chapter in the religious history of both America and the Jewish people in our time.

My "Commentary" Problem—and Ours

MICHAEL WYSCHOGROD

"TO THE EXTENT THAT THIS BOOK IS A CONFESsional work," writes Norman Podhoretz, the editor of *Commentary*, in the preface to *Making It*,* "to the extent that it deliberately exposes an order of feeling in myself, and by implication in others, that most of us usually do our best to keep hidden, from ourselves as well as others, it obviously constitutes the betrayal of a dirty little secret and thereby a violation of certain current standards of tastefulness." The "secret" that is betrayed concerns Mr. Podhoretz: he confesses that from the beginning he had a powerful longing for success, attention and power. To what extent this escaped the notice of those acquainted with Mr. Podhoretz (what is a secret must be unknown to someone) we are not told. In any event, we have here a work of autobiographical confession which invites equal autobiographical honesty on the part of the reviewer. It is for this reason that I, too, permit myself a degree of relevant reminiscing.

The path that led me to *Commentary* started with Morton Wishengrad, remembered for his fine scripts on the *Eternal Light*, the Jewish Theological Seminary's dramatic program on NBC radio, as well as his successful Broadway play, *The Rope Dancers*. I had met him during World War II—I was seventeen at the time and not long arrived in this country from Germany—through his brother, Michael Wishengrad, whose name in the paper had caught my eye because of its similarity to mine.

From our first meeting Morton undertook to save me—to liberate me from what he saw as the dark world of the Brooklyn Yeshiva where I was then studying and to introduce me to the world of art and literature which to him meant life. In this respect Morton's role was rather similar to that played by Mrs. K. in Podhoretz's career. She was a Gentile teacher who attempted to civilize him, to transform him from a "slum child, filthy little slum child" into an Ivy League college type. While I am quite sure Morton never saw me in quite that light, he did want me to meet the *real* America. To that end, he prescribed a diet of American

---

* *Making It.* By Norman Podhoretz. Random House. $6.95.

MICHAEL WYSCHOGROD *is an associate professor of philosophy at the City University of New York. This past year he participated in a course on Jewish theology at the Jewish Theological Seminary of America taught jointly by a Reform, Conservative and Orthodox representative. He is a member of the editorial board of* Tradition: A Journal of Orthodox Jewish Thought *and of the advisory committee of* JUDAISM.

literature starting with Thomas Wolfe's *You Can't Go Home Again*. Wolfe proved ultimately not to my taste, but be that as it may, the Wishengrads' was the first cultivated American home to which I had gained access, and this had an important effect on my development.

In 1949 I started graduate work in philosophy at Columbia University, determined to complete my Ph.D. in the minimum time possible—three years. I chose for my dissertation two rather difficult figures, Kierkegaard and Heidegger, and worked hard, first at mastering them and the related secondary literature and then, after the fall of 1952, at writing. Columbia required that properly typed copies of dissertations be submitted before April 1 for degrees to be awarded in June. I finished a hand-written copy of my dissertation in March and should have handed it to a professional typist who undoubtedly would have completed the job by the required date. But I had no money to pay a typist and so had to type it myself with two fingers on an old Remington portable that my uncle had given me. The result was that I missed the deadline by about two weeks and could not make the June degree. The summer of 1952 was therefore my first free summer; I had completed my dissertation and was ready for something a bit less strenuous than Kierkegaard and Heidegger. At this point Morton suggested that I go and see Daniel Bell who, he told me, was labor editor of *Fortune* and interested in Judaism. Bell and, I think, Irving Kristol had been attending a seminar on Judaism given by Jacob Taubes and Morton felt that Bell and I would enjoy meeting each other. Morton wrote to Bell, I telephoned, and a meeting was arranged for lunch.

BELL TURNED OUT TO BE a very pleasant and intelligent person. It now seems quite clear to me that by the time I met Bell his interest in Judaism had begun to decline. He was impressed by my Jewish background, particularly when I told him that during the six years I had been studying at City College and Columbia I had also been a student of Rabbi Joseph B. Soloveitchik, one of the great Talmudists of our time. It was clear to both of us that *Fortune* had no use for either a Talmudist or a philosopher, but, said Bell, *Commentary* was just the right place. He said he would call Nathan Glazer at *Commentary*, which he did, and, when I called Glazer a few days later, he seemed genuinely interested in my coming to see him.

Very quickly, a number of things became clear to me: first, that Glazer was an unusually sweet and bright person; second, that neither he nor anybody else around *Commentary* knew very much about Judaism; third, that Judaism was quite a charged topic in the editorial office of this distinguished magazine; and fourth, that anyone with a Ph.D. or close to getting a Ph.D. was under a cloud of suspicion as far as *Commentary* was concerned.

The *Commentary* people had a profoundly ambivalent relationship towards academia. Most of the editors were graduate-school drop-outs. They seemed to hold the conviction that the universities were populated by dull pedants whose obsession with footnotes served as a permanent barrier against good writing. Not without some justification, they believed that one of their articles had, on the average, more thought in it than a truckload of Ph.D. dissertations. Even though existentialism was the rage in those days, and even though very few persons at the time had actually read carefully the heavyweights such as Heidegger and Sartre, my offer to write about these people was met with a curious lack of interest. It became evident that, as far as they were concerned, I knew too much about the subject. By this time I had come to read the magazine with greater interest, and it became increasingly clear to me that *Commentary* was interested in "high-level" journalism. This kind of writing requires a degree of knowledge that is not so great as to prevent the making of unfounded comparisons and critical judgments whose tone of authority takes the place of solid scholarship. This is not to deny, of course, that there are indeed many among the academics who know more than they can put to significant use. But this does not by itself confer authority on the half-informed.

The story was quite different in regard to my Jewish interests. Here Glazer poured out a tale of woe. *Commentary*, he told me, had the greatest difficulty getting good contributions in the Jewish field. As they were sponsored by the American Jewish Committee, they had to run a considerable number of Jewish articles, but whereas non-Jewish material of high quality was never lacking, Jewish material of the proper grade was all but impossible to obtain. The official Jewish types—rabbis, professors at seminaries, etc.—were pompous, illiterate and vulgar. In addition, none could write proper English, and when a contribution from such a person did come in, it had to be rewritten from scratch to meet the stylistic demands of the magazine. One of their greatest headaches was the "Cedars of Lebanon" department. This feature appeared in every issue and was devoted to a translated excerpt from some more or less classical Jewish text together with an introduction in which the significance of the excerpt and its historic setting were explained. They were constantly short of material properly chosen, translated and introduced, and Glazer all but begged me to help with this task.

WHILE I DID CONTRIBUTE TO SEVERAL COLUMNS over the next several years and also reviewed a number of books in the field of Talmud and rabbinics, from the very beginning the whole situation puzzled me. Why should I, of all people, suddenly become *Commentary's* expert on Judaism? There were, after all, any number of established scholars of Judaism in this country who had much better claim to that honor than

MY "COMMENTARY" PROBLEM — AND OURS : 151

I did. While compared to Glazer and Clement Greenberg I was indeed a giant of Jewish knowledge, this was certainly not the case when my knowledge was measured by a more reasonable standard. It is only later that I came to understand the real reasons that made the people at *Commentary* look to someone like me for their Jewish contributions.

The people around *Commentary* (this was less true of Glazer than the others) were rather hostile to Judaism. Most of them were members of what Podhoretz calls the "family," the group of persons clustered mainly around *Partisan Review* and *Commentary* who shared certain crucial assumptions and experiences which made them what they were. Many of them had been Communists, had become disillusioned with Stalin but still remained Trotskyists or at least Marxists. They were profoundly alienated from both their American and Jewish identities. The break with Stalinism was the central trauma of their lives. For some, this break was accompanied by a simultaneous disillusionment with the socio-economic view of art and literature and a resultant movement toward the more purely aesthetic, religious and classical sensibilities. In their own ways, Malraux and Simone Weil are European examples of this syndrome.

The members of the family did, however, retain much of the Marxist bias even when they broke with Stalinism. Judaism to them meant either nationalism or religion, and they detested both. Podhoretz, for whom admittance to the family remains life's peak experience, writes: "So little point did the family see in Jewish survival that the threat being posed even at that moment by Hitler to the actual physical survival of Jewish men, women, and children did not, to judge by the files of *Partisan Review*, seem a matter of urgent concern. Clement Greenberg showed himself superlatively well qualified for the article on Jewish self-hatred he was to write a decade later in *Commentary* by arguing now, in 1940 (echoing Trotsky, also a Jew), that World War II—the war against Hitler—did not merit 'our' support." And yet these people were editing a Jewish magazine which, whether they liked it or not, had to have considerable Jewish content. How could the family accept such a task?

By producing a magazine that did nothing to advance the careers of Jewish Jews. This requires explanation. In *Making It*, Podhoretz exposes not only himself but the family as well: their "dirty little secret" is that they lust madly for attention. The greatest calamity that can befall the members of this family is to be ignored. There is no price too high to pay for attention, and there is no compensation sufficient for obscurity. But notice does not just happen; it requires organization, and for this the family is superlatively equipped. They can take people of pedestrian sensibilities and make something of them by means of an interlocking system of influence and reviews, in which one is either "in" or "out"; if one is in, one can do no wrong, and if one is out, no right. Podhoretz documents this in the case of an unfavorable review he wrote about Saul Bellow's *Augie March*, a review which almost cost him his membership in the family because it broke the group's cardinal rule: even when criticizing a member of the family, you must do it so as to advance his career. The building of careers is thus the preoccupation of the family, and if the family had been favorably disposed toward Jewishness or Judaism, it would have helped to establish in the realm of letters under their control the reputation of some Jewish figures. This could have been one or another of the younger Jewish religious intelligentsia who made their appearance after the war and who could have been put on the map by the family via *Commentary*. But this is precisely what the family wished not to do.

That is why I was useful to them in the Jewish realm. I was unknown and at the time apparently not out to make a name for myself in the Jewish field. Furthermore, I had no Jewish institutional affiliation, so that no Jewish institution could possibly benefit from the publicity. At the same time I was an Orthodox Jew and, therefore, could not possibly be admitted to the family. Consequently, the two book reviews on non-Jewish topics I had written (both of them dealing with the connection between psychoanalysis and philosophy) were paid for but not published. In the midst of all this, Routledge and Kegan Paul —one of Britain's leading philosophical publishers—accepted my manuscript on Kierkegaard and Heidegger, and the book appeared in 1954. It was widely reviewed, with the London *Times Literary Supplement* giving it a half page. *Commentary* did not mention it at all, though books of contributors were almost always reviewed. To have taken the contribution of an Orthodox Jew to contemporary philosophy seriously would have violated one of *Commentary's* most firmly held convictions: that Western culture is accessible only to those who have extricated themselves from the repulsive Brownsville ghetto.

BY THE FALL OF 1955 I HAD LOST INTEREST in *Commentary* rather completely. I was busy teaching philosophy at City College and writing for various publications. I had no desire to become *Commentary's* tolerated Jew, tolerated only as long as I knew my place and renounced ambitions of a general intellectual sort. In recent years, something of this role has been played by Milton Himmelfarb, a writer on the staff of the American Jewish Committee and *Commentary*'s current "Jewish" voice. Curiously enough, Himmelfarb's leanings might even be said to be traditional, though he obviously works very had at achieving just the right tone of detachment and condescension that seems to be a prerequisite for writing about Judaism for *Commentary*. In the case of

Himmelfarb, this tone does not come naturally; it is the price he pays, not for membership, but for toleration by the family.

My family and I spent the academic year 1957-58 in Israel, where I helped Bar-Ilan University set up its philosophy department. One day in December of 1958, after my return to New York, I found the following note in my mail:

> Dear Michael Wyschogrod:
>
> I have been wanting to talk with you about various matters and I wonder whether we couldn't get together sometime. I would appreciate it if you would call me.
>
> Sincerely yours,
> s/ Elliot E. Cohen
> Editor

This was an interesting development, and within a few days I found myself being ushered into Cohen's dingy office in a loft building across the street from the Empire State Building. It turned out to be a memorable visit.

Though I had been to this office many times in the past, I had never met Cohen. But something of the legend that was Cohen had reached me. I knew that Cohen himself never wrote anything but that he developed mysterious relations with writers whom he then manipulated until they wrote exactly what he wanted them to write. I had heard that Cohen was *Commentary* more than anybody else and that he had been mentally ill of late and had just recently left the Payne Whitney Clinic where he had been an in-patient for some time. In his absence, the magazine had been run by Martin Greenberg, with whom I had always had very friendly relations. He had spoken to me rather vaguely of the possibility of some fundamental changes at *Commentary*, but it was understood that in the final analysis this would be up to Cohen when he returned from the hospital. I had the feeling that Cohen's illness was a catharsis of some sort that had its effect on all the people around the magazine. I knew little else beyond this.

Cohen started by asking me about Rabbi Soloveitchik. What kind of person was he, why was he so hard to pin down on anything, and why didn't he do any writing? As Cohen talked, I was struck by the profoundly depressed and yet extremely intelligent air about him. He seemed the opposite of domineering. There was a deep gentleness about him and a total grasp of reality. He began to talk about his family. He was of Lithuanian origin. His grandfather, he told me, had been a fine Talmudist, and while I am no longer certain about this, ten years having elapsed since the meeting, I have the impression that he claimed to be related to the Soloveitchiks and the "dynasty of Brisk," the expression he applied to them. He spoke with great tenderness of his childhood memories, of the Talmudic sing-song that he heard then and that had remained with him over the years. He said that in the Thirties it was thought inconceivable that this kind of thing could take roots in America, but it had happened, and he was amazed and moved. But his life, he said, had reached a crisis. And it was to talk about this that he had written to me.

He explained that *Commentary* had been created by the American Jewish Committee to prove to the world that there were anti-Communist Jewish intellectuals. In fact, the magazine had been instrumental in weaning a whole generation of Jewish intellectuals away from worship at the altar of Lenin and Stalin. In this respect, the magazine had been a huge success. Marxism, to all intents and purposes, was dead; there no longer was any need to belabor an issue that had been settled. (Little could anyone in 1958 have predicted the New Left with its hang-ups.) But at the same time, Cohen continued, he was presiding over a group of self-hating Jews who were only too eager to bury their Judaism if this meant admission to the literary salons of Manhattan. He had brought into being a magazine, and thereby an atmosphere and a tone, that was totally devoid of the slightest love for the Jewish people. The magazine's tone was neurotic because it was self-hating, never missing an opportunity to expose the vulgarity of the Jewish community, which undoubtedly existed but which could be handled with love as well as with cold contempt. He spoke of the deep unhappiness that was his as a result of the key role that he had played in the creation of this temper and of his determination, once and for all, to swing the magazine over to the cause of Jewish self-respect and self-acceptance. This is where he wanted me to cooperate. Would I consider accepting an associate editorship on the magazine to work with him so as to undo the damage that had been done? From time to time during the conversation we would sit in silence, looking at each other and saying nothing.

I was very moved by all this. Before me was one of the unhappiest human beings I had ever met, who was struggling to re-establish his Jewish roots and, indeed, his faith. I am not, of course, privy to the direction that his psychotherapy had taken during the preceding months nor indeed to exactly what happened between the time of my meeting with him in late December of 1958 and his tragic suicide in May of 1959. But it is difficult for me to believe that the psychiatrists who worked with him could understand the depth of this man's Jewish problem. I have often speculated that the professionals translated everything he said into their own relatively primitive psychoanalytic categories, a vulgarization that would be obvious to a man of Cohen's intelligence and acumen. For my own part, I cannot say that I helped him very much. Being young, I suppose I was more than a little frightened by the depth of his depression, and the prospect, therefore, of working with Cohen, exciting as the idea he proposed inherently was, left me less than enthusiastic. In addition, by this time I was embarked on a university career, and I was still European enough to prefer the image of the professor to that of a magazine editor. The university involved, among other things, the likelihood of tenure and the economic securiy that goes with it, while the kind of job Cohen spoke of was by its nature insecure. In any case, I told him that I could not commit myself, that there were many angles to be considered, and that I would think the matter over.

In the light of Cohen's subsequent suicide, which occurred approximately five months after I saw him, I have often asked myself whether one could not simply dismiss his conversation with me as symptomatic of his illness and nothing more. I am certain that this would be a grave injustice to Cohen. There is no doubt that he was ill. But his was an illness in which a man comes to see himself and his life with utter clarity. This is the very opposite of the kind of illness where the patient loses contact with reality. The Cohen I met was a man of dignity and weight who felt that he had trespassed against his most significant self. His deep Jewish loyalties came to the fore, and, whether as a result of his contact with psychiatry or for other reasons, he had become convinced that his career had in fact been an act of aggression against the identity from which he had been fleeing and to which he was now attempting to return. The news of his suicide came to me as a very great shock. I could not free myself from the speculation that my coolness to his proposal had something to do with his death. I was, of course, also aware that such magnification of my importance in the life of a man whom I had met for two hours was a not very subtle form of self-flattery and therefore to be dismissed as quickly as possible. Nevertheless, the lingering feeling of guilt that remained does perhaps explain my reaction when I received Norman Podhoretz's first letter to me after his succession to the editorship.

BETWEEN THE TIME THAT COHEN DIED in May of 1959 and February of 1960, when Podhoretz took over, I assumed that the *Commentary* publication committee of the American Jewish Committee was looking for a new editor. I had no way of knowing whether the gentlemen charged with this responsibility had any knowledge of Cohen's agonies with the anti-Jewish tone of the magazine. But I somehow assumed that they did, and it therefore distressed me no end when it soon became clear that they had appointed as editor a person who not only would do nothing to move the magazine in the direction that Cohen had envisaged, but who would move it noticeably in the opposite direction.

That this is exactly what the new editor was doing could be discovered very easily. The first issue that appeared under the new administration saw the permanent disappearance of the "Cedars of Lebanon" department, the single most positively Jewish feature of the old *Commentary*. In its place (or at least that is how I saw it) appeared a column called "The Issue," in which the new editor delivered his evaluation of the material appearing in the magazine. This column lasted only for eight months; after that, one can assume, Mr. Podhoretz must have decided that the magazine must be permitted to speak for itself without the benefit of his clarifications. But, while it lasted, Norman Podhoretz put himself on the record as he has perhaps never done since. To take but one example: In the issue of March 1960, he proclaimed the likelihood of the appearance of a new religion which will gradually take over the world and displace those currently in existence. While he did not positively claim that this new religion would be born in the pages of the new *Commentary*, he did reassure his Jewish readers "that one ought to feel a sense of 'historic reverence' to Jewish tradition, even, or perhaps especially, if one is convinced that the curtain is about to drop on the last act of a very long play." This then was the new *Commentary*: the magazine that had come into being to report the dropping of the curtain on the last act of the play that was Jewish existence.

In April of 1960 Podhoretz wrote to ask me to review a new edition of Buber's *The Origin and Meaning of Hasidism* together with Malcolm L. Diamond's *Martin Buber: Jewish Existentialist*. He added: "I suspect that you are as fed up with the cult of Buber as I am, and I was hoping that you might write a piece that would subject him both to a rigorous philosophical analysis and an equally rigorous 'Jewish' examination." I almost blew my stack. There was the obvious illegitimacy of an editor sending books out for review with what amounted to instructions on how to review them. And why was Podhoretz out to get Buber? Because Buber was a committed Jewish voice who had made it with the avant-garde. Years ago, Podhoretz's mentor Lionel Trilling had proclaimed with little regret that in this age no Jewish voice spoke with authority. But Buber was the obvious exception to this. By highbrows all over the world he was taken at least as seriously as Niebuhr and Tillich. This could not be permitted to continue. And what would be better than having Buber's Jewishness questioned by an Orthodox writer? This, in fact, is an established technique of the magazine: anything written from the Reform or Conservative point of view would be torn to pieces by an Orthodox critic, while the Orthodox would be demolished by the others, and all along the enlightened scoffers of the family would sit back in wry amusement, muttering a disgusted "plague on both your houses." To this I would not be a party, and, being young and impetuous and not yet privy to the maxim that a writer does not antagonize the editor of an influential magazine, I replied with a blistering letter. "My first impulse," I wrote, "is to tell you that, since the conclusions of the review seem already well formulated in your mind, why not write the rest of it yourself as well?" I spoke of my respect for Buber, in spite of disagreements on some specific points, and said that I would not lend myself to the kind of assassination Podhoretz had in mind. In reply I received a long letter denying all charges. There the matter rested for some time.

Up to this point I had never met Norman Podhoretz. I was to have that pleasure in 1965 when I received a printed invitation to attend one of the symposia *Commentary* was then running. These were meetings with several speakers and an invited audience. The papers and the lectures were taped, and the proceedings published in the magazine. The session to which I was invited had something to do with U.S. aid to underdeveloped countries, a topic which would not have been of sufficient interest to me to warrant attending. In this case, however, knowing that these invitations are rather carefully considered, I took this as a gesture of reconciliation, and I attended. I even asked a question which was duly recorded and appeared in the published transcript.

It was over coffee after the meeting that I met Podhoretz. We exchanged a few innocuous words, sufficient to make it clear to me that he knew who I was. On the basis of this I concluded that time had done its work, that grievances do not last forever, and that as we grow older we mellow and mature. On the basis of this, I sent Podhoretz a note some months later asking him whether he would be interested in an article discussing the Jewish reaction to the Vatican Council's draft statement on Jews which had not yet been adopted at the time. The issue that agitated some Jewish circles was the possibility of a conversionist appeal being included in the document. In my article I argued that Jews did not have the right to demand of the Church that it refrain from appeals to conversion, because in a free world any organization has the right to express its point of view and to attempt to persuade others of its truth, provided no illegitimate means of persuasion or the threat of such illegitimate means are used. I maintained that the Church, for its part, might very well wish to reconsider its stance towards Judaism and the Jews, but that this would be quite different from the Jewish community demanding, as a matter of right, that it refrain from calling all men, including Jews, to Christ. I realized, of course, that this was not the point of view of a great many American Jews nor, in all probability, of the American Jewish Committee. Perhaps foolishly, I took seriously the statement of aims which appears in every issue of the magazine that *Commentary* "will be hospitable to diverse points of view. ... The opinions and views expressed by *Commentary*'s contributors and editors are their own; and do not necessarily express the Committee's viewpoint or position."

Podhoretz refused to print the article. He concluded his letter of rejection as follows: "In short, the main reason I am returning the piece to you is that we do not wish to publish an article whose effect is to encourage the view that the Church is justified in inserting a conversionist appeal into the Jewish document." He added: "In this case... I feel very strongly that *Commentary* has a special responsibility —a special *Jewish* responsibility, in fact, to which I would be disloyal if I published your article."

"*Oib men lebt lang genug,*" my grandmother used to say, "*vet men alles derleben*" ("If you live long enough, you'll live to see everything"). Norman Podhoretz was the defender of the Jewish interest, and I its detractor. This was the same Podhoretz who printed a glowing letter to the editor from Ned Polsky in the issue of April 1961, in which Polsky submits the following, presumably unsolicited, testimonial: "Though I read many periodicals regularly, *Commentary* became one of them only a few months ago, for the magazine interests me precisely to the extent that the new editorial regime has de-Judaized its contents." This was the same man who in March of 1961 published an article by Paul Goodman, one of Podhoretz's very favorite contributors, who argues that the problem of pornography be solved by permitting everything without exception in print and on the screen, including the televising of sexual intercourse. Here there is no Jewish responsibility to decency but only to freedom of expression, to good standing in hippiedom. But when Michael Wyschogrod suggests that the Church is entitled to invite all men into its ranks, then Jewish responsibility enters the picture and the Jewish community can sleep securely, knowing that men such as Norman Podhoretz are on faithful vigil.

Some years elapsed after this exchange, and one day I was lecturing about Martin Buber's philosophy of dialogue. As I was talking, it occurred to me that I had never sat down with Mr. Podhoretz, looked him in the eye and told him what I thought of him. I had never even told him of my talk with Elliot Cohen. So, as soon as class was out, I called the office of the magazine, got Podhoretz's secretary and identified myself. She asked me to hold on for a moment and then came on again to tell me that Mr. Podhoretz would call me back. He did not. I called twice more, each time was told by the secretary that Mr. Podhoretz would call back, and he never did. That is where the matter stands.

AND NOW, INSTEAD OF MR. PODHORETZ, I have before me *Making It*, a book explicitly designed to call attention to its author. Mr. Podhoretz is fully aware that he will be accused of tastelessness for admitting publicly a lust for fame, for being talked about. There was a time, he reminds us, when it was considered tasteless to talk candidly about sex. The result was hypocrisy and cant; today there is more honesty, because we dare to admit our sexuality, and thus it has ceased to be the "dirty little secret" it once was. But the spirit of honesty has not yet penetrated to the realm of success. There we are still supposed to pretend nonchalance about our careers and sport a becoming modesty, when in reality we are all burning for success, craving to be noticed and talked about. Where the rest of us are dishonest, Mr. Podhoretz is honest, because he admits to the lust we all possess but deny. What is more, Podhoretz diagnoses a cult of failure in our society: on the one hand we are urged to succeed, and on the other we are given to understand that if we succeed we will fall victim to the corruptions of the system. Thus we can keep our purity only by not succeeding. All this Podhoretz denies. He proclaims fame unqualifiedly delicious and that it is better to give orders than to take them, to be recognized than to be anonymous.

Jean-Paul Sartre maintains, in *Being and Nothingness*, that man's freedom consists in his being able to make a judgment about himself. Take the lazy man who announces that he is lazy. The moment he makes this judgment, he has transcended his laziness because he has demonstrated that he does not coincide with his laziness, that his real self is that part of him which makes the judgment, and that this real self is beyond the laziness. That is why confession is such a disarming strategy: the accused dissociates himself from his guilty self and takes his stand beyond it. Every public speaker knows that the best way to handle an embarrassing situation is to join the laughter. When the speaker laughs with the audience, the audience senses that the person they are laughing at is not the person who is laughing with them. By distancing himself from the ridiculed self, the real self escapes the scorn. This is exactly the effect Podhoretz has in mind. By being able to speak objectively about his lust for fame, he ceases to equal his lust for fame and is therefore not really the person he describes. A person who really lusted for fame could not step out of himself to obscure himself and to make the determination. The kind of self-consciousness practiced in the Podhoretz technique presupposes an honesty that is disingenuous because, while pretending to admit some weakness or lust, it imagines itself to have conquered the weakness by the very act of confession. Sartre calls this "bad faith." It applies with special force to the admission of a lust for fame: Podhoretz's book distances him from his lust while allowing him to indulge once again in his desperate search for notice.

TO A VERY LARGE EXTENT, the medium through which Podhoretz's hunger for attention came to be satisfied was *Commentary*. It is to be expected that, in view of the events recounted earlier in this article, I read the portions of the book dealing with *Commentary* rather attentively. Podhoretz was first offered a job on the magazine by Cohen, but he could not acccept it because he was drafted into the army. Cohen, according to Podhoretz, offered to keep the job open until his release from service, but by the time he got out, Cohen was in the hospital. Then starts an account of a sordid struggle with the person (or persons) who was (were) in effect running the magazine in Cohen's absence: "The Boss." But who is this boss? We are not told. Speaking of Cohen's absence, Podhoretz explains it thus:

> Until my appearance on the scene, this left only two editors to carry on alone: one a veteran member of the staff and the other a fairly recent arrival. These two men happened to be so closely related that they were able to act as one man after Cohen's departure, when they assumed de facto control of the magazine. Since they also behaved as one man toward me, and because of the form this behavior took, I will be doing no violence to the truth if I refer to them from now on in the singular, and as The Boss.

The persons being referred to here are Clement and Martin Greenberg. They were brothers ("happened to be so closely related"!), and they ran the magazine until Podhoretz was appointed editor. They, along with Elliot Cohen after he got out of the hospital, did not like Norman Podhoretz at all. Earlier in the book Podhoretz speaks rather favorably of Clement Greenberg. But later, when it comes to the real in-fighting, he cannot bring himself to mention their names; the name of Martin Greenberg never occurs in the book. In a book that purports to be an exercise in candor, to read page after page about The Boss and what he did and said while the persons' names are avoided in the spirit of Victorian circumlocution is, to say the least, disconcerting.

When we lay aside such stylistic aberrations, we are left with two outstanding impressions. The first is that Podhoretz, as eager as he is to think of himself as an intellectual, is really not a highbrow. He does not know enough for that; there is no body of intellectually challenging material that he controls. When he describes his years at the Seminary College of the Jewish Theological Seminary and the generally negative impression that its "strident note of apologetics and defensiveness" made on him, I cannot help but laugh. During those years I was studying Talmud with Rabbi Soloveitchik at Yeshiva University. There was nothing apologetic and defensive about the intellectual demands made on us by Rabbi Soloveitchik. The Seminary College was for the intellectual lightweights. Podhoretz was simply not qualified to study with someone like Professor Saul Lieberman at the Seminary, who would have shown him what it meant to control an area of scholarship. And the same is true of the rest of Podhoretz's education. His notion of literature is Disraeli and Bellow, not Joyce and Thomas Mann. Podhoretz has no access to the really serious literary and philosophical writing of our day—to Heidegger and T. S. Eliot, to phenomenology and Bertrand Russell. He knows nothing of avant-garde theology nor of Rilke. He can only deal with art that is sociological criticism and which is never the most serious art of any age. In fact, he cannot deal with art at all. One of the first things Podhoretz did when he assumed the editorship of *Commentary* was to drop poetry. He knows that he cannot cope with literature which is more than comment on the passing socio-economic scene, and since poetry can almost never be dealt with in those terms, he shuns it. Around Columbia, such political critics of literature were ranked distinctly below the aesthetic critics and these, in turn, below the philosophical interpreters who dealt with Heidegger's interpretation of Hoelderlin or with Hegel on tragedy. The interesting part of this is that Podhoretz undoubtedly knows all this better than anyone else; he just doesn't talk of it.

The second impression that we take away with us is one that in me aroused some compassion. Podhoretz has never been able to forget the shame of his Browsville origins. He sees himself as Mrs. K., the sympathetic Gentile teacher, saw him: *Slum child, filthy little slum child.* These words, which Podhoretz italicizes, are burned into his consciousness. He knows that he is not class, that life is a fight in which only a few get to the top. The desperate search for recognition, for being in the limelight and talked about, is the search for a salve that will numb the pain of a desperately ugly self-image, which, of course, is totally unnecessary. But necessary or not, it is there, and it is controlling. It robs the man of the slightest modicum of serenity and, therefore, of affection for his origins. Writers such as Sholem Aleichem could look at the Jewish proletariat with humor and at the same time with the deepest love because they felt themselves rooted in its spirit. But for Podhoretz, his proletarian origins gnaw at his innards as he passes through Columbia and Cambridge, and thus, though this is what he wishes least, a lower-class identity becomes fixed which he cannot erase. In a strange way, the American experience is thus turned upside down. While it remains true that in America origins count less than anywhere else, it is apparently also true that for some children of immigrant parents, the price paid for making it, or for that illusion, is not small.

However much compassion Norman Podhoretz's psychic suffering deserves, it is also true that he is not the man the American Jewish community deserves as editor of one of its influential journals. I bring myself to say this with some hesitation, and only because I have the feeling that it is something Elliot Cohen would have wanted me to say.

Acknowledgements

Berkovits, Eliezer. "Judaism in the Post-Christian Era." *JUDAISM* 15 (1966): 74–84. Reprinted with the permission of *JUDAISM*. Courtesy of Yale University Sterling Memorial Library.

Etzioni, Amitai. "The National Religious Institutions of American Jewry." *JUDAISM* 11 (1962): 112–22. Reprinted with the permission of *JUDAISM*. Courtesy of Yale University Sterling Memorial Library.

Feldman, Abraham J. "The Role of the Synagogue in the American Jewish Community." *Proceedings of the Rabbinical Assembly* 21 (1957): 190–98. Reprinted with the permission of the Rabbinical Assembly. Courtesy of the Rabbinical Assembly.

Frimer, Norman E. "The A-Theological Judaism of the American Community." *JUDAISM* 11 (1962): 144–54. Reprinted with the permission of *JUDAISM*. Courtesy of Yale University Sterling Memorial Library.

Gordis, Robert. "The Ordination of Women." *Midstream* 26 (1980): 25–31. Reprinted with the permission of the Theodor Herzl Foundation, Inc. Courtesy of Yale University Sterling Memorial Library.

Halpern, Ben. "Those Entitled to Be Jews." *JUDAISM* 34 (1985): 41–45. Reprinted with the permission of *JUDAISM*. Courtesy of *Judaism*.

Herberg, Will. "Religious Trends in American Jewry." *JUDAISM* 3 (1954): 229–40. Reprinted with the permission of *JUDAISM*. Courtesy of Yale University Sterling Memorial Library.

Herberg, Will. "The Integration of the Jew in Contemporary America." *Conservative Judaism* 15 (1961): 1–9. Reprinted with the permission of the Rabbinical Assembly. Courtesy of Yale University Divinity Library.

Hertzberg, Arthur. "The American Jew and His Religion." In Oscar I. Janowsky, ed., *The American Jew: A Reappraisal* (Philadelphia: The Jewish Publication

Society of America, 1964): 101–19, 414–17. Reprinted with the permission of The Jewish Publication Society of America. Courtesy of Yale University Sterling Memorial Library.

Heschel, Abraham Joshua. "The Nation and the Individual." *Conservative Judaism* 15 (1961): 10–26. Reprinted with the permission of the Rabbinical Assembly. Courtesy of Yale University Divinity Library.

Laderman, Manuel. "A Love-Letter to My Congregation." *JUDAISM* 20 (1971): 306–12. Reprinted with the permission of *JUDAISM*. Courtesy of Yale University Sterling Memorial Library.

Lerner, Anne Lapidus. " 'Who Hast Not Made Me a Man': The Movement for Equal Rights for Women in American Jewry." In Morris Fine, et al., eds., *American Jewish Year Book* 77 (New York: The American Jewish Committee and Philadelphia: The Jewish Publication Society of America, 1977): 3–38. Reprinted with the permission of The American Jewish Committee. Courtesy of Yale University Sterling Memorial Library.

Mayer, Egon. "Jews By Choice: Their Impact on the Contemporary American Jewish Community." *Proceedings of the Rabbinical Assembly* 45 (1983): 57–70. Reprinted with the permission of the Rabbinical Assembly. Courtesy of the Rabbinical Assembly.

Neusner, Jacob. "An Experience of Prayer." *Conservative Judaism* 15 (1961): 30–31. Reprinted with the permission of the Rabbinical Assembly. Courtesy of Yale University Divinity Library.

Neusner, Jacob. "Judaism in the Secular Age." *Journal of Ecumenical Studies* 3 (1966): 519–41. Reprinted with the permission of Temple University. Courtesy of Jacob Neusner.

Neusner, Jacob. "Synagogue and Center: The Symposium in Retrospect." *Conservative Judaism* 17 (1962–3): 2–19. Reprinted with the permission of the Rabbinical Assembly. Courtesy of Yale University Divinity Library.

Parzen, Herbert. "The Passing of Jewish Secularism in the United States." *JUDAISM* 8 (1959): 195–205. Reprinted with the permission of *JUDAISM*. Courtesy of Yale University Sterling Memorial Library.

Roseman, Kenneth D. "Power in a Midwestern Jewish Community." *American Jewish Archives* 21 (1969): 57–83. Reprinted with the permission of the *American Jewish Archives*. Courtesy of the *American Jewish Archives*.

Rubenstein, Richard L. "The Intellectual and Contemporary Jewish Life." *Conservative Judaism* 14 (1960): 40–46. Reprinted with the permission of the Rabbinical Assembly. Courtesy of Yale University Divinity Library.

Siegman, Henry. "Is the Synagogue Becoming a Church, the Rabbi a Priest? Religious and Secular Aspects of Jewish Community." JUDAISM 21 (1972): 67–78. Reprinted with the permission of *JUDAISM*. Courtesy of Yale University Sterling Memorial Library.

Sklare, Marshall. "The Sociology of the American Synagogue." *Social Compass* 18 (1971): 375–84. Reprinted with the permission of *Social Compass*. Courtesy of Yale University Seeley G. Mudd Library.

Woocher, Jonathan S. "Sacred Survival: American Jewry's Civil Religion." *JUDAISM* 34 (1985): 151–62. Reprinted with the permission of *JUDAISM*. Courtesy of Yale University Sterling Memorial Library.

Wyschogrod, Michael. "My 'Commentary' Problem—and Ours." *JUDAISM* 17 (1968): 148–61. Reprinted with the permission of *JUDAISM*. Courtesy of Yale University Sterling Memorial Library.